Teacher's Manual for

Light to the Nations II:
The Making of the Modern World

General Editor: Christopher Zehnder

Catholic Textbook Project

Catholic Textbook Project

April 2018

Dear Catholic Educator,

Thank you for undertaking the education of the next generation of American Catholics in a century filled with both perils and promise. Christ offers our youth a challenge and a hope no other religion or philosophy permits. We, their teachers and parents, cannot allow our children to be ignorant of the origins of the Faith or of the beliefs of other cultures in an increasingly challenging world. We must know our history and teach it to our children. They must know why we are different from our neighbors in the world, and why our neighbors have developed as they have. Teaching history is teaching God's providential care for his people and his promise to the rest of the world. We must teach our children hope!

But as teachers of long experience, our editors have learned that in the matter of teaching history, there is a clear paradox: *Less is more.* Students learn better and learn more when they are taught the facts of history through the stories of the past, the legends of heroes, the tales of noble causes, and the lives of saints and holy men and women. Long lists of facts—names, dates, products, and causes—fade in the memory, but the stories remain and form the character and the understanding of a child. We encourage teachers to tell the stories, to expect the questions, and to offer a skeleton of key dates. What came before what, or after what, is more important to the learning mind than memory of the exact dates involved. All history is really a true and interesting story.

May our books bring both story and facts to life for our students, and for their teachers.

Michael Van Hecke, President
Catholic Textbook Project
P.O. Box 4638
Ventura, California 93007

Introduction

How to Use This Manual and How to Use This Book

In *Light to the Nations II*, the authors have adopted a pedagogy different from that assumed by most modern textbooks. The conviction underlying this book is that history is, first and foremost, a story—an enjoyable story, a story filled with drama. We have written this book, therefore, as if we were writing a story—in this case, a continuation of the story of *Christendom* begun in *Light to the Nations I*. Our hope is that students, approaching history as a story, will learn to love history and will, thus, retain more historical knowledge than is normally the case with the more customary textbook style.

The difficulty is that the story approach to history often includes more information than what a teacher would expect most students to retain. To insist that students retain every detail, every date, would be to undermine a chief purpose of the book—to make the reading of history a matter of joy. We want students to approach history in a leisurely fashion, to read it as they would read a story, not a record of dry facts. Of course, one hopes that students will leave each chapter with more than the required knowledge, but this is best left to the capabilities of each student. Those historical facts every student should know are listed in the section, "What Students Should Know," in this teacher's manual. Beyond these basic facts, teachers should merely see that their students retain the chief outlines of the stories they will study in the book. (A teacher, however, should encourage students to stretch themselves beyond what they assume to be their own capabilities.)

How to Use *Light to the Nations* in the Classroom

We propose that the chief occupation of classroom sessions on the book be spent in having students recite, in their own words, what they remember from their assigned reading in the book and to discuss the ideas presented in the text among themselves and with the teacher. The teacher may call on different students to recount what they have read in the text or to tell what they know about the various characters or concepts they have encountered in their reading. This will help students to solidify what they have learned and give them the opportunity to practice their language skills. The teacher may, then, patiently correct any false impressions the students may have or any inaccuracies in their presentations. Such exercises should be seen as merely educational exercises without the threat of grading.

The teacher should help students grasp the major themes of each chapter. To help with this task, we have provided in the teacher's manual a "Chapter Goals" section that details the major themes of each chapter. Each chapter in the book has, as well, an activities section to help students deepen their knowledge of the time period each chapter covers.

We also recommend that teachers use the timeline provided in the teacher's manual as a reference to help students make their own timelines for each chapter. After students have completed their own timelines, the teacher may use the timeline we have provided to help students correct and fill out the timelines they have drawn up.

Light to the Nations II provides a number of maps and illustrations to enhance a student's reading of history. A teacher may continue where the book leaves off, bringing into the classroom pictures illustrative of the time period being studied or by showing educational videos. The assignment of fictional works of historical events will also help students get a feel for the time period they are studying. Recordings of period music—such as traditional folk and popular music from the regions and time periods studied in this book or the compositions of the masters of Classical, Romantic, Post-Romantic, and Modern periods—help create for students the "mood" of historical epochs. Learning to sing simple folk or popular songs from these time periods will, perhaps, be even more effective. This teacher's manual provides a list of suggested works of historical fiction as well as period music.

Another Way to Use *Light to the Nations* in the Classroom

Some teachers may find it helpful to supplement the above method of using *Light to the Nations* with readings of the text in the classroom. Hearing the text read aloud can be helpful to students who are more auditory than visual in the way they take in information.

Teachers could assign readings of portions of the text to various students, or read them aloud themselves. After such a reading, the teacher could engage the students in conversation about the information found in the text or discuss with students the meaning of the ideas presented in the text. Such classroom readings should be seen as a reinforcement, not a replacement, of the reading each student does on his or her own. By reading the text aloud, students, too, can learn to pronounce unfamiliar words and, especially, foreign names and words correctly. (This teacher's manual provides a pronunciation key for foreign names and places.)

Light to the Nations and Common Core Standards

The unique pedagogical style of *Light to the Nations* makes it a very effective tool to help teachers help students master the goals of the Common Core Standards Initiative in English language arts and social studies. In particular, the Initiative calls on history/social studies teachers to use "their content area expertise to help students meet the particular challenges of reading, writing, speaking, listening, and language." *Light to the Nations* is especially suited to these challenges.

In its literary and story approach to the narration of history, *Light to the Nations* helps students exercise themselves in the interpretation of narrative texts that rely more on description, literary coloring, analogy, and particular example than on a simple listing of facts. Students achieve the subtlety of mind necessary to understanding and interpreting complex texts and ideas. The wealth of detail used in the story mode of exposition gives students the opportunity to sift central ideas from more incidental facts.

Morever, since *Light to the Nations* does not rely solely on story, it gives students the experience of other literary styles that figure in the varied disciplines of knowledge. The text offers exercises that stimulate the critical sense in students. The short answer and essay form sought in student responses helps students develop the ability to express ideas in a complete and coherent fashion. Further, the story mode inspires a student's interest in the text. This interest, in turn, encourages the student to comprehend writing that may be somewhat more challenging than what he or she may be used to.

The Common Core Standards Initiative says its recommendations "are not meant to replace content standards … but rather to supplement them." The Common Core Standards, thus, have not dictated the *subject matter* of, or the events covered in, *Light to the Nations*. It is a text, however, well suited to the spirit and goals of the standards.

(The Catholic Textbook Project is developing supplemental material to facilitate the impletation of the Common Core Standards criteria for grades 5-8. Please check the page "Teachers' Corner" at http://catholictextbookproject.com, for upcoming announcements on when these materials will be available.)

Contents of This Teacher's Manual

Scope and Sequence
Provides a general outline of the text and the contents of each chapter.

Chapter Goals
Develops the major themes for each chapter.

Period Music
Offers suggestions of period music and composers

Some Key Terms at a Glance
Puts in one place the various historical terms, persons, events, and vocabulary highlighted in each chapter, with their definitions.

What Students Should Know
Presents the minimal knowledge of persons, places, events, and dates students should retain. We have provided, for the teacher's convenience, a brief review for each important fact.

Questions for Review
Provides, for the teacher's convenience, the answers for each question presented in the "Chapter Checkpoint" section at the end of each chapter.

Ideas in Action
Gives suggestions for doing each activity, where necessary, plus explanations and reference material, where applicable.

Chapter Quizzes and Tests
Suggests questions for quizzes for different sections of each chapter, as well as a chapter test. Since our approach in *Light to the Nations* is literary, our quizzes and tests ask mostly short answer or short essay questions. We think it is important that students develop the ability to express their thoughts in complete sentences.

Teachers, however, should not feel obligated to use these quizzes and tests either whole or in part or in the manner we have presented them. Teachers should feel free to mix questions from the tests or compose examinations of their own.

Essays
Offers essay topics to help students more deeply understand the time period they are studying. Teachers may wish to offer these essays as assignments in conjunction with the quizzes and tests, or use them in lieu of a more formal examination.

Resources for Further Reading or Investigation
This section gives suggestions for further student reading on each period covered in the text.

Timeline
The timeline presents in a linear manner the historical events recounted in this volume. The timeline is meant to aid teachers in helping students make their own timelines either individually or as a class.

Pronunciation Guide
The guide helps teachers to pronounce the foreign words and names found in the text. The teacher should help students pronounce such words correctly.

Scope and Sequence

For a free electronic file of all tests and quizzes included in the teacher manual, please contact sales@CatholicTextbookProject.com.

The National Assembly approves the
Constitution of 1791; the king signs it

The Last Days of the Monarchy
Divisions in the Legislative Assembly
The allies declare war on France
Danton and the revolutionary commune seize
control of Paris
A mob attacks the Tuileries; the king and his
family flee
The Legislative Assembly deposes the king

The Republic
The establishment of the First Republic
September Massacres
The Battle of Valmy

Chapter 5: Many Revolutions

New Party Divisions in France

The Course of the War against the Republic

The Trial and Execution of King Louis XVI

Great Britain Goes to War with France

The Government of Great Britain
King and Parliament
The development of the British government in
the 17th and 18th centuries
The character of the British Constitution
The British oligarchy

The Industrial Revolution
British colonial trade and the growth of the
middle class
The development of capitalism
The steam engine revolutionizes manufacturing
The rise of the factory system; the destruction of
the guilds and small manufacturers
Factory labor and the plight of the working class
in the cities

The Agricultural Revolution
The development of "scientific" agriculture
The development of new agricultural machinery

Enclosures and their effects on the rural population of Britain

King George III
The king and his Whig opponents; Charles
James Fox
Edmund Burke
The king's prime minister, William Pitt

Chapter 6: The Rise and Fall of Jacobin France

Factions in the National Convention
Danton's attempts to unify the factions
The Girondins vs. the Mountain
The *Enragés* and the *sans-culottes*
The treason of Dumouriez
The creation of the Committee of Public Safety

Revolt in the Vendée
The conscription law
The revolt breaks out
The capture of Fontenay

The Triumph of the Jacobins
Girondin opposition to price controls
The trial and acquittal of Jean-Paul Marat
Girondin missteps—the creation of the
Committee of Twelve
The National Convention orders the arrests of
the Girondin leaders

The Jacobin Revolution
The Constitution of 1793 approved and
suspended
Allied victories against the republic
Girondin revolts in the departments
The murder of Marat
The reform of the Committee of Public Safety
Robespierre becomes master of the Committee
France, a nation in arms

The Reign of Terror
Royalist revolts—Toulon
The Law of Suspects

INTRODUCTION: The Scientific Revolution

Chapter Overview

- The period called the Renaissance began in the 14th century and brought with it a new interest in classical culture.

- The Protestant Reformation ended the Renaissance. The end of the Renaissance marked the beginning of the "scientific revolution."

- The scientific method differs from the older method of philosophy. The scientific method is based on *induction*, while the older way of philosophy is based on *deduction.*

- Copernicus's heliocentric theory was the beginning of the scientific revolution. Because many Christians of the time thought the theory contradicted Sacred Scripture, they either rejected the theory or thought it could be used as an hypothesis, not a true account of reality.

- Galileo Galilei is remembered for his contributions to the sciences of physics and astronomy. A promoter of Copernicus's theory, he was tried and found guilty by the Holy Office for writing about the theory as fact.

- Francis Bacon rejected deduction as a way to knowledge. Induction, he said, is the only true foundation of knowledge. Bacon held the purpose of science is to subjugate and control the world.

- Newton's *Principia Mathematica* inspired philosophers in every discipline to search for laws to explain everything, from the growth of plants to chemical reactions to human morality and religion.

Chapter Goals

This chapter describes the progress of scientific thought from the 16th to the 18th centuries (the period of the "scientific revolution") and the rise of what has been described as the conflict between the Catholic/religious and scientific worldviews. Among other items, the chapter points out that the conflict has not been between scientific discovery and religion but between certain philosophical ideas and the ethos of Christendom. The purpose, therefore, of this introductory chapter is threefold:

1. To aid the teachers and students in understanding the division between the history that has preceded the 16th century and the events from that time to our own

2. To impart an understanding of some of the conflicts, issues, and events that shaped the modern world and to make judgments about such things in the light of Christian moral teaching and right reason

3. To introduce the students to the ideas and individuals that contributed to the rise of the scientific revolution and their relation to the

culture of Christendom as it had developed to that time.

The chapter opens by reviewing the culture of medieval society, which had been centered on the Christian Faith. For medieval people, the Church and the Faith were at the center of human life. Medieval people sought to create societies based on law and justice; they developed the practical arts as well as the "fine" arts; and they sought to understand the world around them through the study of philosophy. But in the Catholic society of the Middle Ages, all these earthly goods were seen to have one great purpose—they were to help lead men and women to God.

It is important for students to understand how the Renaissance and the scientific revolution changed this society. It is equally important to keep in mind that the medieval world was not a nasty and barbaric era that ended when a more advanced civilization replaced it. Like our own era, periods of history like the Middle Ages were manifestations in time of human creativity and conduct, some good and some bad. Students should understand that much of what arose in the Renaissance and the period called the scientific revolution was the continuation of trends that had begun in the Middle Ages. Furthermore, students should come away from this chapter with the foundational realization that, throughout these historical epochs, Jesus Christ has been present in the world, in the Church, and in the lives of believers.

Period Music

Any music by the following Baroque era composers:

- Matthias Weckmann (1616–1674)
- Henry Purcell (1659–1695)
- Claudio Monteverdi (1567–1643)
- Heinrich Schütz (1585–1672)
- Antonio Vivaldi (1678–1741

- Arcangelo Corelli (1653–1713)
- Tomaso Albinoni (1671–1751)
- Jean Philippe Rameau (1683–1764)
- Johann Sebastian Bach (1685–1750)
- Georg Friedrich Handel (1685–1759)
- Giuseppe Tartini (1692–1770)
- François Couperin (1668–1733)
- Jean-Philippe Rameau (1683–1764)

What Students Should Know

1. **What the scientific revolution was**

   The scientific revolution was a historical movement that began in the 16th century with the publication of Nicolaus Copernicus's heliocentric theory of the universe. The heliocentric theory says that Earth and all the planets revolve around the sun. This was a radical idea for the 16th century, for men of thought had for centuries accepted the geocentric theory of Ptolemy—that the earth, not the sun, is the center of the universe. What's more, Copernicus's theory seemed to contradict Scripture, which presents the earth as standing at the center of the universe. The heliocentric theory was but the first of many discoveries that caused people to think about the universe in new ways. It led many to think that they had to cast away the philosophy and even the religious thought that had come to characterize Christendom. It is, thus, that it was a revolution.

2. **What the method of the new science was**

   The new science focused exclusively on the natural world insofar as it can be measured and tested by experiment. Experiment is a kind of experience, but a carefully controlled experience. It tests how something acts under very controlled circumstances. It requires painstak-

Key Terms at a Glance

principles: the first ideas in thinking, from which one draws conclusions

deduction: a method of reasoning where one begins with principles and, by asking questions, draws conclusions from those principles

heliocentric: sun-centered (from the Greek word, *helios*, meaning "sun")

geocentric: Earth-centered (from the Greek word *Ge* or *Gaia*, signifying the earth goddess)

epitome: a summary or embodiment

parabolic: having the shape or form of a curve called a parabola

optics: the study of light, the changes it undergoes and produces, and what is related to it

physics: the experimental science that studies and measures the motion of bodies

mechanics: a branch of physical science that deals with physical forces and their effect on bodies

recantation: a formal rejection of a statement or idea

rationalism: the theory that truth can be known and problems solved only by the use of human reason and by experience. Rationalism denies inspiration or faith as a path to truth

empiricism: the theory that truth can come only through experience and experiment

ing observation of what one can sense and measure. No conclusions of any one experiment or set of experiments can be accepted as true; rather, they must be tested by other scientists performing other experiments. Only after many experiments give the same results do scientists decide that their conclusions are really true.

3. **Examples of medieval scholars who carried on experimental scientific studies**

Two examples of medieval scholars who carried on experimental scientific studies are St. Albertus Magnus and Bishop Robert Grosseteste.

4. **How the new science differs from the "old way" of philosophy**

One way the new science and the older philosophy do *not* differ is in the fact that both are based ultimately on experience. The old way of

philosophy, however, works off general experience, not always experiment. From thinking about his experience and that of others, the philosopher derives principles from which he reasons to conclusions—that is, he proceeds by *deduction*.

5. **What the Holy Office demanded of Galileo; how he responded, and why he was told to recant**

Galileo Galilei was a mathematician, physicist, and astronomer who held very dogmatically to Copernicus's heliocentric theory of the universe. Other scholars of the time, however, thought the Copernican theory was merely a hypothesis, not an account of the universe as it actually is. In 1616, the Holy Office condemned the Copernican view as heretical, though it allowed it to continue to be presented as a hypothesis. The Holy Office, too, ordered Galileo to reject the heliocentric theory and teach it no longer. For seven years, he abided by this order; but in 1623, he received permission from the pope to publish a dialogue on the heliocentric theory—as long as he presented it only as a hypothesis. Galileo's dialogue, however, presented the theory as true, and in 1633, the Holy Office declared that Galileo was guilty of heresy and disobedience. In obedience, he recanted the heliocentric theory.

6. The significance of the Galileo case

Since the 17th century, many have used the trial of Galileo to attack the Catholic Church, particularly her teaching on papal infallibility. More seriously, however, critics have charged that the Galileo case shows that the Church is opposed to science and progress—even though in the 16th and 17th centuries the Church actively supported scientific research. Nevertheless, the Galileo case has been seen as an example of how the Church opposes knowledge and human freedom. It has been used to drive a wedge between the Church and the modern world. Many Catholic thinkers, it is true, had said that Copernicus's theory could only be accepted as a hypothesis, not a true account of the universe, because it seemed to contradict Scripture. Yet, there were other, scientific grounds for rejecting the Copernican theory, not the least of which is the fact that it had not yet been proven to be true.

7. What Sir Francis Bacon's "Great Restoration" of philosophy entailed

Bacon thought the old way of philosophy had to be swept away and an entirely new system of philosophy put in its place. His Great Restoration was to be "a total reconstruction of sciences, [practical] arts, and all human knowledge." In his work, *Novum Organum*, he proposed induction, a form of experiment in which a scientist begins with a hypothesis and then performs experiments to prove it,

as the only basis for knowledge. Moreover, he proposed a new purpose for science or philosophy—the use of knowledge to subjugate and control the world. The purpose of knowledge, he said, is power. This idea of knowledge differs from what medieval thinkers said the goal of philosophy is. To the medieval mind, the purpose of learning is simply to know, for knowledge they saw as good in itself. Finally, said the medievals, learning and study are to help us attain the highest goal of life, which, itself, is knowledge—the knowledge of God as he is in himself.

8. The effect of Isaac Newton on philosophy and science

In his *Principia Mathematica*, Sir Isaac Newton was able to account for motion on the earth and in the heavens by reducing all motion to three principles or natural laws of motion. This inspired philosophers in every discipline to search for laws to explain everything from the growth of plants to chemical reactions to human morality and religion. And, though Newton himself asserted the necessity of God for the running of the universe, his presentation of the universe as operating like a great machine that, once set in motion, continues in motion and operates according to fixed laws, led many to question the importance of God in the universe.

9. What rationalism is

Rationalism is the theory that truth can be known and problems solved only by the use of human reason and by experience. Rationalism denies inspiration or faith as a path to truth.

10. What empiricism is

Empiricism is the theory that truth can come only through reason, experience, and experiment.

11. Identify the following:

Tycho Brahe: a Danish astronomer who rejected the Copernican theory

Johannes Kepler: A German astronomer who said that heavenly bodies move in certain patterns, which he called laws. He discovered that planets do not move in perfect circular but rather elliptical paths.

Sir William Harvey: an English scientist who discovered how blood circulates in the human body

Questions for Review

1. **Did people in the 16th and 17th centuries see any difference between science and philosophy? Why or why not?**

People in the 16th and 17th centuries made no clear distinction between science and philosophy. The words, *science* and *philosophy*, were used interchangeably in the 16th and 17th centuries. *Science* (from the Latin word, *scientia*) means simply "knowledge," which was the object of all philosophy.

2. **What is meant by "scientific method"?**

The scientific method is based on inductive reasoning. It begins with a hypothesis and then, by experiment, seeks to prove the hypothesis.

3. **What led to the split between science and faith? How could this have been prevented?**

The split between science and faith arose because some among both scientific thinkers and religious people thought the Copernican heliocentric theory contradicted the clear teaching of Scripture. The Holy Office's trial and condemnation of Galileo led many to think that the Church was opposed to science. Finally, Francis Bacon's notion that the purpose of knowledge is purely practical led people to demean any other kind of knowledge that was not inductive—including knowledge about God. This split could have been prevented by a better understanding of the nature of divine revelation and by the acknowledgement that natural science cannot account for all of reality.

4. **What was the Gregorian Calendar? Is it still being used today?**

The Gregorian Calendar was a calendar that replaced the longstanding Julian Calendar. It was introduced by Pope Gregory XIII in Rome in 1582 and adopted by the rest of Europe at different times over the following centuries. Yes, the Gregorian Calendar is still in use today.

6. **If Isaac Newton believed in God, why did his *Principia Mathematica* lead others to reject the idea of God?**

Newton presented a purely mechanical universe that did not seem to need God to keep it in operation. The idea of God, they said, was thus not necessary to explain the workings of the world.

Ideas in Action

1. **Using the *Catechism of the Catholic Church*, research what the Catholic Church teaches about human nature. Does the idea that human beings are rational animals contradict the Church's teaching that they are made in the "image and likeness of God"? Why or why not?**

The teacher can find many helpful passages from the *Catechism of the Catholic Church* to discuss as foundations for thinking about this question. A good way to get the discussion going might be to select several short passages from the *CCC*, cut these out, and hand them to the students, who should read each passage aloud. A power-point projector is also helpful in putting passages before the whole class. Some suggestions for discussion are *CCC* 1700 (the dignity of the human person), *CCC* 1701–1706 (man: the image of God), and *CCC* 2284–2300 (respect for the dignity of persons). (Students love this kind of discussion, usually, but need to have the corrective of a third party, such as the *Catechism*—a very valuable resource for any such discussion.)

2. **Begin a class scrapbook to be built throughout the year and based on the study of this textbook. Encourage students to collect (real and *faux*) pictures, postcards, artifacts, and souvenirs of each historical period to be studied.**

Beginning with this introductory chapter, ask the students to make contributions to each section's scrapbook. The contributions can be real or, more likely, fake artifacts, items of clothing, scraps of letters, pictures, scientific drawings, "lost" sketches of Copernicus, menus, instructions for drawing. Anything will do! This is the kind of activity that will pick up interest and creativity as the year goes by and the study of history continues. Some time every two weeks should be given to discussing the contributions in the scrapbook and their historical significance.

3. **Have the students make a timeline that includes the dates of major events of the period of history studied in the chapters of this volume.**

Instead of, or in addition to, a class scrapbook, begin a timeline that teacher and students will add to throughout the year.

4. **Discuss the difference between a hypothesis and a theory. Find examples of each.**

Have individual members of the class defend a hypothesis, perhaps a silly hypothesis, or set forth a theory. The teacher may get this started by writing several subjects on pieces of paper, which will then be distributed by random drawing or by assignment. Some suggestions for silly theories/hypotheses are: "The moon is made of green cheese," or "a dragon creates volcanic fire," or "all boys like to play in the mud." Some more serious topics might be taken from familiar quotations and maxims: "Man does not live by bread alone," or "a penny saved is a penny earned," or "an apple a day keeps the doctor away," or "early to bed and early to rise makes a man healthy, wealthy, and wise." Discuss the difference between an hypothesis and a theory; consider how both can serve what we call "an educated guess."

Sample Quiz I (pages 1–6)

Please answer the following in complete sentences.

1. What do we call the "revolution" that in Europe followed the Renaissance?

2. With what does all knowledge begin, according to both medieval philosophers and 17th century scientists?

3. What is deduction? Who favored deduction, medieval philosophers or 17th century "natural philosophers"?

4. Name at least one medieval scholar who carried out scientific studies.

5. Why did some Catholics and Protestants reject Copernicus's theory of the universe?

6. What do we call the theory of the universe introduced by Nicolaus Copernicus? Why is it given this name?

7. What theory about the universe did Copernicus's theory reject?

Answers to Sample Quiz I

Students' answers should approximate the following:

For a free electronic file of all tests and quizzes included in the teacher manual, please contact sales@CatholicTextbookProject.com.

1. The *scientific revolution* followed the Renaissance in Europe.

2. All knowledge begins with experience, according to both medieval philosophers and 17th century scientists.

3. Deduction is a method of reasoning where one begins with principles and, by asking questions, draws conclusions from those principles. Medieval philosophers favored deduction.

4. Possible answers:

   a) St. Albert the Great

   b) Bishop Robert Grosseteste

6. Some Catholics and Protestants rejected Copernicus's theory of the universe because they thought it contradicted Scripture, which speaks of the earth as if it were at the center of the universe.

7. Nicolaus Copernicus's theory of the universe is called the *heliocentric theory* because it says the sun is the center of the universe.

8. Copernicus's theory rejected the *geocentric theory* of the universe.

Sample Quiz II (pages 7–18)

Please answer the following in complete sentences.

1. What do we call a scientific idea that is something like an educated guess, a way of explaining what one experiences?

2. Who was the English philosopher who said that the purpose of knowledge is to gain power over nature?

3. What do we call the scientific method by which a scientist begins with a hypothesis and then tests by experiment whether the hypothesis is true?

4. Name the theory that says truth can be known and problems solved only by the use of human reason and by experiment.

5. Who was the English scientist who was able to explain all motion on the earth and in the heavens through three natural laws of motion?

6. Why did this scientist's ideas lead some people to reject the need for God to explain the universe?

7. Who was the English scientist who discovered how blood moves in the body?

Answers to Sample Quiz II

Students' answers should approximate the following:

1. A scientific idea that is something like an educated guess, a way of explaining what one experiences, is a *hypothesis.*

2. *Francis Bacon* was the English philosopher who said that the purpose of knowledge is to gain power over nature.

3. *Induction* is the scientific method by which a scientist begins with a hypothesis and then tests it by experiment whether the hypothesis is true?

4. *Empiricism* is the theory that says truth can be known and problems solved only by the use of human reason and by experiment.

For a free electronic file of all tests and quizzes included in the teacher manual, please contact sales@CatholicTextbookProject.com.

5. *Sir Isaac Newton* was the English scientist who was able to explain motion on the earth and in the heavens through three natural laws of motion.

6. Newton's ideas seem to say that the universe is like a great machine that keeps itself in motion and so does not need God to keep it in motion.

7. *William Harvey* was the English scientist who discovered how blood moves in the body.

Essays (200–250 words each)

Instructions to be given to the students: Write in complete sentences. Underline your thesis. Give three supports or examples that explain why you think what you do and that support your thesis.

1. Write an essay that describes how the cultural Renaissance and the scientific revolution changed the culture of Christendom.

2. Write an essay that spotlights one figure from this chapter that you particularly appreciate, admire, or applaud. You may describe his or her life or ideas.

Chapter Test

Please answer the following in complete sentences.

I. **Short Essay—Answer two of the following:**

1. **What was Copernicus's theory about the universe? Why do we say that his theory was the beginning of a revolution—the "Copernican Revolution"?**

2. **How did Holy Office's condemnation of Galileo and Copernicus help worsen the split between the Catholic Church and the modern world? Were the Church's critics right?**

3. **What is the purpose of science and philosophy, according to Francis Bacon? How did his ideas about knowledge differ from those of medieval thinkers?**

4. **Why did Isaac Newton's *Principia Mathematica* lead many people to think that God is not important to the universe?**

II. **Short Answer**

1. **What do we call the theory that truth can be known and problems solved only by the use of human reason and by experience?**

2. **What do we call the theory that truth can only come through experience and experiment?**

3. **Please identify:**

   a) **The medieval scholar who did experiments to gain knowledge. He was the teacher of St. Thomas Aquinas.**

   b) **The English scientist who discovered how blood circulates in the body**

   c) **The astronomer who discovered that planets move in elliptical instead of circular paths**

Answer Key to the Chapter Test

For a free electronic file of all tests and quizzes included in the teacher manual, please contact sales@CatholicTextbookProject.com.

I.

1. Nicolaus Copernicus's theory of the universe is called the *heliocentric theory*. The heliocentric theory says that the earth and all the planets revolve around the sun, and that the sun is the center of the universe. This was a radical idea for the 16th century, for men of thought had for centuries accepted the geocentric theory of Ptolemy—that the earth, not the sun, is the center of the universe. What's more, Copernicus's theory seemed to contradict Scripture, which presents the earth as standing at the center of the universe. The heliocentric theory was but the first of many discoveries that caused people to think about the universe in new ways. Because it led many to question what they had taken for granted as true, it inspired them to cast away the philosophy and even the religious thought that had come to characterize Christendom. It is, thus, that it was a revolution.

2. The Holy Office's condemnation of Galileo was used by the Church's critics as evidence that the Church is opposed to science and progress. This charge was convincing to many because the Holy Office said the Copernican system was contrary to Holy Scripture. The charge, however, was unjust, because, throughout the 16th and 17th centuries, the Church had actively supported scientific research. Many Catholic thinkers, it is true, had said that Copernicus's theory could only be accepted as a hypothesis, not a true account of the universe, because it seemed to contradict Scripture. Yet, there were other, scientific grounds for rejecting the Copernican theory, not the least of which is the fact that it had not yet been proven to be true.

3. Bacon thought the old way of philosophy had to be swept away and an entirely new system of philosophy put in its place. This system of philosophy, he said, was to have one purpose—to subjugate and control the world. The purpose of knowledge, he said, is power. It was to be used for practical purposes. This idea of knowledge differs from what medieval thinkers said the goal of philosophy is. To the medieval mind, the purpose of learning is simply to know, for knowledge, they said, is good in itself. Finally, said the medievals, learning and study are to help us attain the highest goal of life, which, itself, is knowledge—the knowledge of God as he is in himself.

4. Newton's *Principia Mathematica* showed how we can explain all motions on the earth and in the heavens by three principles or natural laws of motion. His picture of the universe made it appear as if it were a great machine—and this led many people of his time to think the universe could keep running without help from anything outside the universe. They said that everything in the universe could be explained through the laws of motion, and so God was not necessary.

II.

1. *Rationalism* is the theory that truth can be known and problems solved only by the use of human reason and by experience.

2. The theory that truth can only come through experience and experiment is called *empiricism*.

3. a) *St. Albertus Magnus* was the medieval scholar who did experiments to gain knowledge.

   b) *William Harvey* was the English scientist who discovered how blood circulates in the body.

   c) *Johannes Kepler* was the astronomer who discovered that planets move in elliptical instead of circular paths.

CHAPTER 1: The Age of Enlightenment

Chapter Overview

- In his *Discourse on Method,* Descartes claimed he had discovered a new basis for philosophy. Man could be certain of the existence of God and of the universe, he said, because he is first certain of his own existence. Though he thought he was defending the Catholic Faith, Descartes's work helped pave the way for rationalism and skepticism.

- Descartes's idea that the universe operates like a machine gave support to Deism, the belief that God set the machine of the universe in motion and left it alone to operate by the laws of nature.

- Baruch Spinoza was influenced by Descartes and Deist ideas. Spinoza taught that the universe is God, and the laws by which the universe runs are the will of God.

- The Frenchman Pierre Bayle promoted religious skepticism through his work, *The Historical and Critical Dictionary.*

- In his famous work, *Leviathian,* Thomas Hobbes said that mankind once lived in a "state of nature" in which people had no "notions of right or wrong, justice or injustice" and life was "a war of every man against every man." To escape this state of nature, people made a "social contract" with a sovereign, to whom they gave up their liberties.

- In his *Two Treatises on Government,* John Locke laid the foundation for Liberalism: the social philosophy that emphasizes freedom of the individual. Locke accepted the idea of a state of nature but thought the social contract did not remove all freedoms from people.

- Irreligion (without religion) and Liberalism spread throughout the French middle class. One of the most influential popularizers of skepticism, irreligion, and Liberalism was the French playwright, Voltaire.

- Denis Diderot's *Encyclopedia* attacked the Christian Faith and helped spread Liberal ideas throughout Europe.

- In his various works, Jean-Jacques Rousseau argued that the authority of the state comes from the combined will of the citizens. Rousseau thus inspired the movement toward democracy.

Chapter Goals

This chapter may require extra time, as it contains some hard and contradictory philosophies. Yet, it is very important to understand this era of history, as its ideas have become foundational for the modern world. Close attention must be paid to all parts of this chapter. As these philosophies of the Enlightenment continue to influence our present culture and education, it is important for students to achieve the following goals in this chapter:

- To recognize the names of the major figures of the Enlightenment

- To understand the influence of these historical figures on one another and on the culture of their time

- To appreciate the intellectual exhilaration, rise of culture, and religious challenges that affected people in the early 17th century

The student should come away from this chapter with an appreciation of the many developments of this era.

Period Music

Any music of the following Baroque-Classical Transition and Early Classical era composers:

- Domenico Scarlatti (1685–1757)

- Wilhelm Friedemann Bach (1710–1784)

- William Boyce (1711–1779)

- Carl Philipp Emanuel Bach (1714–1788)

- Christoph Willibald Gluck (1714–1787)

- Giuseppe Scarlatti (1718/1723–1777)

- Leopold Mozart (1719–1787)

What Students Should Know

1. **How Descartes's philosophical method helped bring about a revolution in European thought**

Descartes's description of the material world as a vast machine that was set in motion by God but which did not need God to continue in motion undermined the Catholic belief in Divine Providence. It did not offer any place for miracles.

Descartes's method opened the way for rationalism and skepticism. His method encouraged skepticism, since it begins by doubting everything. Those who did not think his conclusions were convincing, remained skeptics. Descartes's method also encourages rationalism. Because the universe works like a machine without God's continuing help, people came to the conclusion that only reason is needed

Key Terms at a Glance

mechanistic: working like a machine

skeptic: one who advocates *skepticism*, the doubt that anything can be known for certain to be true

libertine: a freethinker or one who acts without regard to a moral law

salon: a gathering of fashionable notables (such as artists, writers, thinkers, government leaders, and others) in the home of an important person

Huguenot: a French Protestant who accepted Calvinist beliefs

divine right of kings: the doctrine held by some Christians that God places kings on their thrones and gives them absolute power in their kingdoms

lampoon: a harsh, bitter literary piece that uses ridicule

chevalier: a title for a French nobleman; it means "knight."

satire: a literary work that uses ridicule and scorn to attack human vices to understand the universe. A machine can be understood by reason alone.

2. **What skeptiscm, libertinism, and rationalism are**

Skepticism is the conviction of those, called skeptics, who think no one can come to a certain knowledge of truth. Skeptics believe one must doubt everything because no one can be certain that what he thinks is true.

Libertinism was embraced by skeptics called libertines or "freethinkers," who called for thought and expression free from any regulation by Church or state. Some libertines called also for freedom from the moral law.

Rationalism is the conviction that human reason alone is the judge of what is true, both in science and religion.

3. **What Deism was**

Deism was the religious side of rationalism. It was developed first by English thinkers who wanted a new religion to replace the Christian Faith. It admitted the existence of God and said the universe came from him but said that God did not intervene by his providence in the workings of the universe. It accepted the mechanistic view of the universe espoused by Descartes.

4. **The central ideas of Benedict Spinoza**

Like Descartes, Spinoza said the universe operates like a machine according to unchanging laws. Unlike Descartes, however, Spinoza said the human mind is material and so not free. Spinoza said the universe is God and the natural laws of the universe are God's will.

5. **What Pierre Bayle's *Historical and Critical Dictionary* was and its importance**

Bayle's *Dictionary* was like an encyclopedia, offering a collection of articles on a variety of subjects. Though it was not overtly against religion, it gave arguments that could move readers to doubt the truth of Scripture or question religious authorities. The *Dictionary* was a powerful tool in spreading skeptical doubt. It influenced the thinkers of the Enlightenment.

6. **Who Thomas Hobbes was, what the *Leviathan* was, and what ideas it expressed**

Thomas Hobbes was a 17th century English philosopher who, in his book, the *Leviathan*, presented a very pessimistic view of human nature. Hobbes thought a human being is a kind of machine, lacking both an immaterial soul and a free will. Left to themselves, people will do only what pleases them, without thinking about morality. Hobbes said mankind originally lived in a "state of nature," where people knew nothing of morality or justice and where they constantly warred on each other. To escape from this dangerous situation, people made a "social contract" with a sovereign ruler. They abandoned all their freedoms to him in return for peace and security. The social contract gave the ruler absolute power over all aspects of his subjects' lives.

7. **How the thought of John Locke was like and unlike the thought of Hobbes**

Like Hobbes, Locke thought people originally lived in a state of nature and they formed governments through a social contract to escape the lawlessness of absolute freedom. But in his book, *Two Treatises on Government*, Locke said people followed a moral law (the natural law) in the state of nature and did not give up all of their rights when they formed a social contract. He said there were three rights that no one could justly take away from people: the rights to *life, liberty* (one's ability to do what seems good to him), and *property* (land or other material goods needed for maintaining life and exercising liberty). In forming a commonwealth, said Locke, people only gave up some of their liberties, but not liberty itself; they did not give up the inalienable rights of life, liberty, and property. People formed commonwealths, he said, to preserve their liberty; and they could overthrow governments when they violated the rights of individuals.

8. The importance of Locke's political ideas

John Locke provided a theory of government that has become the basis of most political thinking from his time to our own. It is the basis of Liberalism.

9. What Liberalism is and how it differs from medieval ideas of government and society

Liberalism refers to a system of thought that sees human beings as by nature individuals who live unconnected to anyone and have no obligation to obey any person or body of persons. It sees government as formed by a social contract in which people give up some of their liberties in order to secure their most important liberties, such as life, liberty, and property. The role of government is to make sure everyone may work for himself and his interests without hindering other individuals from working for themselves and their interests.

10. Liberalism differs from a medieval idea of human society and the role of the government in these ways:

a) Liberalism holds that human beings by nature live without connection to one another. The medievals saw that society is natural to man.

b) Because Liberalism sees government as unnatural to man; it sees it as a necessary evil. The medievals saw government as natural to man and a positive good.

c) Liberals think government exists to protect the rights of individuals to achieve their personal goals and desires. Medievals saw

the role of government as helping people attain the common good—the good of all, not just what each individual wants.

d) Medievals thought government has the duty to protect and promote the one, true religion. Liberals think no religion is true and is merely a matter of private opinion; thus, governments should protect freedom of thought and expression and not promote any particular religious group.

11. What the Enlightenment was

The Enlightenment was a movement that began in Europe in the mid-18th century. It insisted that reason and science alone should reform and guide all aspects of life. It was rationalistic in its view of the world and Liberal in its view of government. It held that governments should allow for complete freedom of expression and religion and should not protect or promote any religion in particular. Governments should allow religion to wither and die. Enlightenment thinkers tended to be Deists, though some were agnostics and even atheists.

12. Who the major French Enlightenment thinkers were

The most famous and influential of the Enlightenment thinkers (called *philosophes*) was *Voltaire,* who, through his plays, stories, and philosophical works, spread Enlightenment ideas throughout all of France and Europe. Voltaire was a rationalist and a Deist. He promoted free thought and moral libertinism and opposed what he called the "infamous one"— religion, especially the Catholic Church. A Liberal who embraced Locke's ideas, Voltaire also favored abolishing torture and the death penalty. He opposed democracy and favored a government run by an "enlightened" monarch.

Denis Diderot was the creator of one of the most important works of the Enlightenment—the *Encyclopedia*, which carried articles by Deists, atheists, and rationalists. The *Encyclopedia* spread the antireligious ideas of the Enlightenment more widely among the upper and middle classes throughout Europe.

Jean-Jacques Rousseau was a *philosophe* who lived a troubled life and held various conflicting ideas in the course of his career as a writer. At one point, he praised the life of savages and said that government, laws, religious institutions, and even the arts and sciences corrupt people. Later, he argued that mankind was happiest when people lived in small, family-centered tribal groups and did not possess private property, which, said Rousseau, corrupts society. In his most important work, *The Social Contract*, Rousseau said the power of the government comes from the people, who form a social contract in which they agree to abandon all their liberties and be ruled by the "general will" of all. Rousseau's ideal form of government is a very small republic, where people can gather in an assembly to make the laws. Because of such ideas, Rousseau has been seen as a promoter of democracy.

Questions for Review

1. **Why did Descartes's view of the mechanical universe undermine the Catholic Faith?**

Descartes held that God brought the universe into existence but he created it as a great machine that, once set in motion, continues in motion without God's help or intervention. This undermined the Catholic belief in Divine Providence.

2. **How did Hobbes's and Locke's philosophies differ?**

Hobbes held that, in the state of nature, mankind followed no moral law. Locke held that the moral law existed in the state of nature. Hobbes held that people who enter into a social contract abandon all their liberties to a ruler, who rules absolutely. Locke held that people do not give up their basic liberties when they enter a social contract, and the government does not gain absolute power. The government's function, in fact, is to protect individual liberties.

3. **What is the function of government, according to Liberalism? Whose theory of government inspired Liberalism?**

According to Liberalism, the function of government is to protect individual rights by making sure that some citizens do not violate the rights of others. Locke's theory of government inspired Liberalism.

4. **In what ways does Rousseau's "natural society" differ from modern American society?**

In *The Social Contract,* Rousseau said the ideal form of government is a small republic where citizens gather in an assembly to make the laws. This is quite different from modern American society, where large, central governments make the most important laws for society and where representatives vote for laws in the name of the citizens.

5. **Why were people in France so divided in world-view and politics?**

Much of France in the 18th century held to ideas of government developed during the Middle Ages and under the influence of the Catholic Church. Many, but far fewer of the French, held to Liberal, Enlightenment ideas of government that were in many respects the contrary of the older ideas. Their rejection of religion, too, set them apart from their fellow countrymen.

Ideas in Action

1. **Look at the portraits of the people who lived at the time of the Enlightenment. Discuss what work would have been required to wear a wig, heavy makeup, dresses for women and costumes for men, shoes, hat, and accessories.**

   Students could be assigned the task of discovering when such dress went out of style and whether what came after was very different. What are some reasons 18th century dress went out of style? Why would people ever have wished to dress that way in the first place?

2. **Research and discuss what a school of the Enlightenment period would have looked like in structure, size of classroom, and subjects studied.**

   Among the questions to consider might be: What sorts of people would have attended schools during this period? Would they have been members of the upper classes? Or were there schools for poorer folks? Would the schools have been influenced by Enlightenment thought? Would they have religious influences or be more secular? Were schools then more demanding academically then schools are today?

3. **Listen to 18th-century music from Europe and England. Does any of it have the "Enlightenment spirit"?**

   To discern this quality in the music of what is called the Classical period, students should listen to recordings of music from the Baroque as a contrast. (We list Baroque composers in the teacher's manual chapter covering "Introduction: The Scientific Revolution"; we list Classical composers in this chapter and the next of the teacher's manual.)

Sample Quiz I (pages 21–29)

Please answer the following in complete sentences.

1. Who was the French philosopher who said, "I think, therefore I am"? He thought the universe is a machine made by God.

2. What is Divine Providence?

3. What is the name for the 18th-century religion that admitted the existence of God but denied his providence?

4. Who was the Dutch philosopher who abandoned his Jewish faith and in its place held to scientific philosophy and said the universe is God?

5. What is the term for those who held the belief that no one can have certain knowledge of truth and that there should be no restrictions on freedom of speech and thought.

6. Who was the "Father of the Enlightenment" and the author of *The Historical and Critical Dictionary*?

7. What were people like in the "state of nature," according to Thomas Hobbes? How did people escape from the state of nature?

8. John Locke said when people left the state of nature, they did not give up all of their freedoms and rights. What three rights, especially, are inalienable, according to Locke?

9. What is the best form of government, according to John Locke?

Answers to Sample Quiz I

Students' answers should approximate the following.

1. *René Descartes* is the philosopher who said, "I think, therefore I am," and who thought the universe is a machine made by God.

2. Divine Providence is the idea that God not only created the world but continually keeps it in existence and cares for human beings and all creation.

3. *Deism* is the 18th-century religion that admitted the existence of God but denied his providence.

4. *Baruch (Benedict) Spinoza* is the philosopher who held that the universe is God.

5. *Skeptics* (or *libertines*) believed that no one can have certain knowledge of truth and that there should be no restrictions on freedom of speech and thought.

For a free electronic file of all tests and quizzes included in the teacher manual, please contact sales@CatholicTextbookProject.com.

6. *Pierre Bayle* was the "Father of the Enlightenment" and the author of the *Dictionary*.

7. According to Hobbes, the state of nature was where people were absolutely free and knew nothing of morality or justice and where they constantly warred on each other. To escape from this dangerous situation, people made a "social contract" with a sovereign ruler to whom they gave up all their freedoms in exchange for safety.

8. The three inalienable rights, according to Locke, are *life*, *liberty*, and *property*.

9. According to Locke, the best form of government is one controlled by the majority of the citizens who rule through a representative form of government, like Parliament.

Sample Quiz II (pages 29–38)

Please answer the following in complete sentences.

1. **What do we call the political philosophy that said governments exist only to protect the rights of individuals to do as they see fit, as long as they do not hurt one another?**

2. **The political philosophy mentioned in question 1 said that all men originally lived in a state of nature, in which they were completely free. Did Catholic political thinkers of the Middle Ages believe in a state of nature? Why or why not?**

3. **What do we call the 18th-century movement that insisted that reason and science alone should reform and guide all aspects of life? This movement was rationalistic and said governments should not promote any religion in particular.**

4. **Who or what was *l'infame*, the "infamous one," according to Voltaire?**

5. **What form of government did Voltaire favor?**

6. **Who was the *philosophe* who came up with the *Encyclopedia*?**

7. **Which *philosophe* said the best form of government is a republic small enough to allow the citizens to gather in an assembly to make laws?**

8. **What is the name of the book (written by the *philosophe* referred to in question 7) that said the power of the government comes from the people, who form a social contract in which they agree to abandon all their liberties to be ruled by the "general will" of the citizens?**

Answer Key to Sample Quiz II

Students' answers should approximate the following.

1. *Liberalism* is the name for the political philosophy that said governments exist only to protect the rights of individuals to do as they see fit, as long as they do not hurt one another.

2. No, medieval Catholic thinkers did not think men lived originally in a state of nature like that described by Liberals. In the state of nature, people live as individuals, unconnected with each other. Medieval people thought God made human beings to live in society, under government. Only in society can people achieve the common good—the best good for man.

3. The *Enlightenment* is what we call the 18th-century movement that insisted that reason and science alone should reform and guide all aspects of life.

For a free electronic file of all tests and quizzes included in the teacher manual, please contact sales@CatholicTextbookProject.com.

4. For Voltaire, *l'infame* was *religion*, especially the *Catholic Church*.

5. Voltaire favored an *absolute monarchy*.

6. The *philosophe* who came up with the *Encyclopedia* was *Denis Diderot*.

7. *Jean-Jacques Rousseau* was the *philosophe* who said the best form of government is a republic small enough to allow the citizens to gather in an assembly to make laws.

8. *The Social Contract* is the name of the book that said the power of the government comes from the people.

Essays (200–500 words each)

Instructions to be given to the students: Write in complete sentences. Underline your thesis. Give three supports or examples that explain why you think what you do and that support your thesis.

1. Choose one of the 18th-century French intellectuals and write an essay that states his ideas and the consequences of those ideas.

2. Write an essay that summarizes the philosophies of Thomas Hobbes and John Locke. How are they alike? How do they differ?

Chapter Test

Please answer the following in complete sentences.

I. Short Essay—Answer one of the following:

1. What is skepticism? What is rationalism? How did Descartes's method of doing philosophy encourage both skepticism and rationalism?

2. Both Thomas Hobbes and John Locke thought that mankind lived in a "state of nature." What is a social contract? How did Hobbes's and Locke's ideas about the state of nature and the social contract differ? (Your answer should include Locke's idea of the three inalienable rights.)

You must answer the following:

3. List three ways in which Liberalism differs from a medieval idea of human society and the role of the government.

II. Short answer:

1. How does the Deist idea of God differ from the Christian idea of God?

2. Why was Pierre Bayle's *Dictionary* important in the history of the Enlightenment?

3. What things should be the guides of life in society, according to Enlightenment thinkers?

4   Which Enlightenment thinker said the best form of government is a very small republic, where people could gather in an assembly to make laws?

5. What is Denis Diderot famous for?

6. What Enlightenment writer, through his plays, stories, and philosophical works, spread Enlightenment ideas throughout France and Europe?

Answer Key to the Chapter Test

Students' answers should approximate the following.

For a free electronic file of all tests and quizzes included in the teacher manual, please contact sales@CatholicTextbookProject.com.

I.

1. Skepticism is the belief that no one can come to a certain knowledge of the truth. Rationalism is the conviction that only human reason can judge what is true in science and religion. Since Descartes began his method of doing philosophy by doubting everything, he encouraged skepticism, which doubts everything. Descartes's method encouraged people to think skeptically—and those who did not think his conclusions were convincing, remained skeptics. Through his method, Descartes came to the conclusion that the universe works like a machine. God does not intervene in the universe, he said; there are no miracles. This encouraged the idea that only reason is needed to understand the universe, since a machine can be understood by reason.

2. Both Thomas Hobbes and John Locke thought that mankind once lived in a "state of nature"—that is, a condition where there was no government or law and every person did what he wanted to do. To escape from this state of nature, people formed a social contract—that is, they agreed to give up their liberty to a government in return for safety. Hobbes thought

that men in the state of nature knew nothing about morality and justice. Locke, however, thought people followed a natural moral law in the state of nature. Hobbes thought that men gave up all of their liberty when they made a social contract. Locke, however, thought people gave up only some of their rights. They did not, and could not, give up the three inalienable rights of life, liberty, and property.

3. Liberalism differed from the medieval idea of human society and the role of the government in these ways (*possible answers*):

   a) Liberalism sees that human beings by nature live without connection with one another. The medievals saw that society is natural to man.

   b) Because Liberalism sees government as unnatural to man, it sees it as a necessary evil. The medievals saw government as natural to man and a positive good.

   c) Liberals think government exists to protect the rights of individuals to achieve their personal goals and desires. Medievals saw the role of government is to help people attain the common good—the good of all, not just what each individual wants.

   d) Medievals thought government has the duty to protect and promote the one, true religion. Liberals think no religion is true and is merely a matter of private opinion; thus, governments should protect freedom of thought and expression and not promote any particular religious group.

II.

1. Christians think of God not only as the creator of the universe but as the one who guides the universe by his providence. Deism, however, says that God does not intervene by his providence in the workings of the universe. It accepts the mechanistic view of the universe espoused by Descartes.

2. Pierre Bayle's *Dictionary* gave arguments that could move readers to doubt the truth of Scripture or question religious authorities. The *Dictionary* was a powerful tool in spreading skeptical doubt and influenced the thinkers of the Enlightenment.

3. Enlightenment thinkers thought *only reason and science* should guide life in society.

4. *Jean-Jacques Rousseau* said the best form of government is a very small republic, where people could gather in an assembly to make laws.

5. Denis Diderot is famous for creating the *Encyclopedia*.

6. *Volatire* is the Enlightenment writer who, through his plays, stories, and philosophical works, spread Enlightenment ideas throughout France and Europe.

CHAPTER 2: The Age of Enlightened Despots

Chapter Overview

- Tsar Pyotr the Great worked to modernize Russia by imitating the culture of western Europe. To accomplish this, Pyotr put all aspects of Russian life under his control, including the Russian Orthodox Church. Pyotr opened trade routes and created a standing army like other European nations had.

- Tsarina Katerina the Great continued Pyotr the Great's work, to make Russia a great power. By the end of Katerina's reign, Russia had become a powerful, modern European state.

- The electors of Brandenburg worked to make their realm, Brandenburg-Prussia, a European power. During the reign of Elector Friedrich III (King Friedrich I), Brandenburg-Prussia became the kingdom of Prussia. King Friedrich Wilhelm I built up Prussia's army, making it the best-trained army in Europe.

- King Friedrich II, the "Great," wanted to rule Prussia as a "philosopher king." But like other European monarchs, he expanded his empire by conquest. In the War of the Austrian Succession, he broke his father's agreement to recognize Maria Theresa as the Austrian ruler and seized Silesia from Austria. By this war and the Seven Years' War, Friedrich made Prussia a great world power.

- Maria Theresia was able to keep her throne through the War of the Austrian Succession. She worked to improve the economy of her lands as well as the lives of her people. She strengthened the military by increasing its numbers and improving its discipline. Though a pious ruler, Maria Theresia increased state control over the Church. Though she deplored the first Partition of Poland, she allowed her son, Emperor Josef II, to divide Polish lands with Friedrich II of Prussia and Tsarina Katerina the Great of Russia.

- After his mother's death, Emperor Josef II of Austria tried to reform the empire according to the ideals of the Enlightenment. His policy of bringing the Austrian Church more firmly under his control brought him into conflict with the pope and his own subjects.

Chapter Goals

This chapter has fewer concepts and philosophies to grasp than the preceding chapter. The actions of men and nations dominate this chapter, with a particular spotlight on Russia, Prussia, and Austria. The chapter covers events that immediately precede the French Revolution.

- Students should understand what the life and politics of Russia were at the time Peter the Great (Pyotr the Great) became tsar. They should also be able to describe what Pyotr did to bring Russia to the cultural level of the rest of Europe and why he chose to imitate the customs of western Europe.

- The students should comprehend that Germany was divided in religion and culture at the end of the Thirty Years' War. They should understand the implications of this division for the future of the people of Germany.

- The students should know the important dates, concepts, events and figures that are discussed in this chapter.

As the characters and events of this chapter unfold, the students should have a clear understanding that there are very different types of rulers and leaders. There should be a moral understanding of the good or evil implications for justice that various types of rulers have on their subjects and society. They should gain an understanding of the different ways Enlightenment ideas affected Europe.

Period Music

Russian music is very different from the classical music that arose in western Europe. Russian music may sound unfamiliar to many of us, but it is very beautiful music. The deep voices and slow chant of the Russian Divine Liturgy are profoundly moving and should be experienced.

One composer students should experience is Dmitri Bortnyansky (1751–1825). He was a Ukrainian composer who travelled to Italy to learn Western music technique before returning to Russia. Bortnyansky has been called the "Russian Mozart." He wrote many hymns and was primarily known for his sacred choral concertos. He helped westernize the Eastern Slavonic tradition.

Two recordings that feature Russian music are:

- *Ancient Echoes*, performed by the Academy Chorus (directed by Alexander Sedov). The recording features the music of Bortnyansky and others. (Audio CD—1995)

- *Sacred Treasures: Choral Masterworks from Russia*, a collection of ancient music of the Russian Orthodox Church. Choirs Conducted by Georgi Robev, Valery Polyansky, Nikolai Matveyev. (Audio CD—1998)

As mentioned in the text, Austria, and, particularly, Vienna, was a center of music in the 18th century. Two of the most famous composers in history, Josef Haydn and Wolfgang Amadeus Mozart, flourished during the reigns of Maria Theresia and Josef II. Both are representatives of the Classical style in music. We suggest the following works by these composers:

- Haydn:

  Mass No. 12 in B flat major, *Theresienmesse* (named in honor of Maria Theresa of the Two Sicilies)

  Mass No. 10 in C Major, *Missa in tempore belli* (Mass in time of war)

  Symphony No. 94 in G Major, "Surprise"

  Die Schöpfung ("The Creation"), an oratorio

  Die Jahrszeiten ("The Seasons"), an oratorio

  Gott Erhalten Franz den Kaiser ("God save Franz, the Emperor"), an anthem written in honor of Emperor Franz II. It became the anthem for the Holy Roman and Austrian emperors from the 18th century to 1917.

- Mozart:

  Symphony No. 41 in C major (KV 551), "Jupiter"

  Motet, Ave Verum Corpus, in D major (KV 618)

  String Quintet No. 4 in G minor, (KV 516)

  Le Nozze di Figaro ("Marriage of Figaro"), opera

Don Giovanni, opera

Die Zauberflöte ("The Magic Flute"), opera

Requiem *Mass* in D minor (KV 626)

- Other Composers:

François Joseph Gossec (1734–1829)—French

Antonio Salieri (1750–1825)—Italian

Antonio Soler (1729–1783)—Spanish

William Boyce (1711–1779)—English

Samuel Wesley (1766–1837)—English

What Students Should Know

1. **What Tsar Pyotr the Great's vision for Russia was and how he realized it**

Pyotr I dreamed of modernizing Russia, enriching it with the arts and science of western Europe and turning it into a great power that would awe even the greatest nations of the West. To accomplish his goals, he crushed the power of the boyars and abolished their old ruling assembly, the *duma*. In this way, he gained absolute power over Russia. He brought the Russian Orthodox Church under his sway by abolishing the patriarchate. Pyotr sought to westernize Russia by bringing western European workers and artisans to Russia to teach their arts and skills to the Russians. He forced the Russian people to adopt Western customs and dress and established elementary schools, a museum, and the Imperial Academy of Science. To build up his army, he established conscription. He used his army in wars against the Turks and the Swedes and in this way gained important outlets to the Baltic and Black seas. On the Baltic coast, he built a new capital for Russia—a thoroughly western city named St. Petersburg.

2. **Who Katerina the Great was and what she accomplished**

Katerina the Great was a German princess who became tsarina and empress of Russia in 1762. As tsarina, she ruled as autocratically as Pyotr the Great had and used her power to further modernize Russia. She was very influenced by French Enlightenment ideas and instituted

---

Key Terms at a Glance

Muscovy: the realm or principality of Moscow; the region directly ruled by Moscow

standing army: a permanent army; an army kept in both peace and wartime

secularize: to move from church to state authority or ownership

diet: an assembly of princes gathered to make laws or decide on measures a government should take

Magyar: referring to the Hungarian people and their language

despot: a ruler exercising absolute power. A government ruled by a despot is a *despotism* and is called *despotic*.

chancellor: a state official; a monarch's chief minister of state affairs

bull: a papal statement sealed with the official seal, called *bulla* in Latin.

partition: the act of dividing into parts or shares

reforms based on these ideas in Russia. Yet, despite her "enlightened" ideas and policies, Katerina's measures benefited the rich and powerful. The conditions for the poor worsened; serfdom increased and grew harsher. Militarily, Katerina forced the Turks to restore lands they had taken since the days of Pyotr the Great, and she joined with Prussia and Austria in the First Partition of Poland.

3. **What the Holy Roman Empire was like after the Peace of Westphalia**

The treaty, signed in 1648, which ended the Thirty Years' War brought about a new political order in the Holy Roman Empire. It allowed every German prince to choose the religion he wanted his people to follow, and so the empire was divided into Catholic and Protestant states. Both before and after the treaty, the empire was divided politically into about 300 states. The two most powerful states to emerge from this confusion were Austria, whose Habsburg ruler generally held the title of emperor, and Prussia. The empire was highly decentralized; the emperor had little power over the princes over whom he nominally ruled.

4. **How Prussia became a kingdom and what King Friedrich Wilhelm I did to make it powerful**

What became the kingdom of Prussia included the duchy of Brandenburg, ruled by a duke of the Hohenzollern family, who was also an elector of the Holy Roman Empire. The Hohenzollern duke also ruled East Prussia, which was not part of the empire. By 1700, the Hohenzollern duke held other lands as well. In 1701, the Holy Roman emperor allowed the Elector Friedrich III to hold the title of king. Friedrich named his kingdom after Prussia.

To secure the power of Prussia, King Friedrich Wilhelm I lived frugally and used the money he saved to build up his army. Under

very able officers, he forced his troops to undergo ruthless discipline until they became one of the most effective fighting forces in Europe. He encouraged agriculture and industry and worked to weaken the power of his nobles.

5. **What an enlightened despot was**

An enlightened despot was a ruler who used absolute royal power to establish laws and policies based on Enlightenment philosophy in his country.

6. **Describe what King Friedrich II, the Great, did in Prussia**

As king of Prussia, Friedrich II tried to rule as an enlightened despot. Without religious beliefs of his own, he allowed his subjects complete religious freedom. He demanded that his nobles serve the kingdom and not just themselves by developing their agricultural lands. He planned the economic life of his kingdom, encouraging manufacturing and commerce. Like his father, he established schools for everyone in his kingdom and improved the Berlin Academy of Sciences. Though he did not abolish serfdom, he worked to lower the taxes peasants had to pay to their lords and the government.

7. **Who Maria Theresia was and how she ruled her realms**

Maria Theresia was archduchess of Austria and queen of Hungary. Her husband was Franz II, who became Holy Roman emperor. A devout Catholic, Maria Theresia saw it as her religious duty to improve her subjects' lives. Though she did not abolish serfdom, she worked to make the serfs' lot in life more bearable and to protect the poor from oppression. She improved education in Austria at the university level and established middle and high schools throughout her realm. She worked to preserve and promote the Catholic Faith in her dominions and forbade free religious expression as well as the publication and sale of immoral and heretical books. When her son, Josef II, became co-ruler with her in 1765, she approved measures to increase the control of the state over the Catholic Church in Austria. With Josef, she established compulsory education of children and abolished the torture of criminals.

8. What were the cause and results of the War of the Austrian Succession

The cause of the war was the refusal on the part of Friedrich the Great of Prussia, France, and Bavaria to honor the Pragmatic Sanction—the decree by which Emperor Karl VI assured that his daughter, Maria Theresia, could inherit his realms. The war began in 1740 when Friedrich the Great conquered the Austrian region of Silesia. It pitted Austria and Great Britain against Prussia, France, and Spain. To concentrate solely on France, Great Britain made peace with Prussia in 1745, which forced Maria Theresia and Franz II to do the same a few months later. At war's end, Prussia held on to Silesia, and Franz II secured the title of Holy Roman Emperor.

9. What were the cause and results of the Seven Years' War

The cause of the Seven Years' War was Maria Theresia's build up of an alliance of nations to help her against Friedrich the Great of Prussia and recover Silesia from him. In this war, France, Russia, and Saxony sided with Austria, while Great Britain joined Prussia. The war began in 1756 when Friedrich the Great invaded Saxony and then Austrian-held Bohemia, laying siege to Prague. Though Friedrich won a great battle at Leuthen in 1757, for several years his enemies prevailed against him. In the end, though, Friedrich was

victorious. The war formally ended in 1763 with the signing of two treaties: the Treaty of Hubertusburg, in which Maria Theresia formally gave Silesia over to Prussia, and the Treaty of Paris, in which France surrendered nearly all her North American colonies to Great Britain and Louisiana to Spain.

10. The importance of the Seven Years' War

The Seven Years' War was the first world war, for it was fought in North America, India, and Africa, as well as Europe. The war established Great Britain as the world's foremost naval and colonial power and marked the beginning of Prussia as a great European power.

11. What Josephism was

Josephism refers to Emperor Josef II's attempts to model the government and laws of the Habsburg domains on Enlightenment principles. Josef attempted to establish an enlightened despotism over his domains by abolishing all local customs and governments (including the Hungarian diet), centralizing all lawmaking in his hands, and taking absolute control over the Catholic Church in Austria, Hungary, and the Austrian Netherlands. Josef did not only seek to control the Church's government, but to abolish monasteries and to regulate the worship and devotions of the Church in his domains. He granted complete religious freedom and freedom of expression, though he censored religious books he thought too superstitious. Through his abolition of serfdom and his lowering of taxes on peasants at first brought him the support of the poor, they turned against him when he forced their sons to serve in the military. In the end, his reforms turned all segments of society against him and, shortly before his death in 1790, he rescinded most of his reforms.

Questions for Review

1. How was Russia modernized during Pyotr the Great's reign?

Pyotr the Great modernized Russia by bringing the arts and sciences of western Europe to Russia. He ordered his people to adopt western ways and customs. He built up a large army, like the armies of the western European rulers. He broke the power of the boyars and the Orthodox Church.

2. Why did Voltaire call Emperor Friedrich II a "Philosopher-King"?

Voltaire called Friedrich this on account of a book he wrote before becoming king. In the book, called *The Anti-Machiavelli*, Friedrich rejected the idea that a ruler should do everything possible, even immoral deeds, to obtain and keep power. The ruler, said Friedrich, should think of himself not as the master, but as the first servant of those he rules, acting towards them with kindness and mercy.

3. Why was Maria Theresia called "a true mother of her people"?

Maria Theresia was given this title by her people because she worked hard to bring justice and prosperity to all her subjects, both rich and poor.

4. What is an enlightened despot? Why is Emperor Josef II a good example of an enlightened despot?

An enlightened despot is a term referring to a ruler who used absolute royal power to establish laws and policies based on Enlightenment philosophy in his country. Josef II is a good example of an enlightened despot because he sought to use absolute royal power to regulate all of life in his domains according to the political and social ideals of the Enlightenment. Though he ultimately failed to achieve his goals, he represented the most thorough attempt in the 18th century to establish such a despotism.

Ideas in Action

1. Imagine that you are a steward in the house of Pyotr the Great. Write an inventory account of what goods (food, furnishings, etc.) you might need to purchase to Europeanize the tsar's household. Explain what goods they would replace.

Different groups of students could research what food and other goods were common in western Europe, on the one hand, and in Russia, on the other, during the 18th century. How did people in, say, France dress at this time? How did Russians dress? Since Pyotr the Great's westernizing policies in regards to such matters chiefly affected the upper classes, students should focus their research on the aristocracy of both Russia and western Europe.

2. Research the effects of cold and snow on Russian cities and life at the time of Pyotr.

3. What sort of new foods might have been created by cultural exchange between Russia, Germany, France, and England at this time? Prepare an ethnic dish or dessert of this period and share it with the class.

Sample Quiz I (pages 41–48)

Please answer the following in complete sentences.

1. What were Tsar Pyotr the Great's two goals for Russia?

2. List three things Pyotr the Great did to accomplish his goals.

3. What was the name of the new capital city Pyotr the Great built? Where did he build it?

4. Who was the Russian ruler that brought Pyotr the Great's dreams to fulfillment?

5. Did the ruler referred to in question 4 better the lives of the poor in Russia? Please explain.

Answers to Sample Quiz I

Students' answers should approximate the following.

1. Tsar Pyotr the Great's goals for Russia were:

   a) to modernize Russia

   b) to turn Russia into a great power that would awe even the greatest nations of the West

2. Pyotr the Great's accomplishments were (possible answers):

   a) He crushed the power of the boyars and abolished their old ruling assembly, the *duma*.

   b) He brought the Russian Orthodox Church under his sway by abolishing the patriarchate.

   c) He brought western European workers and artisans to Russia to teach their arts and skills to the Russians.

For a free electronic file of all tests and quizzes included in the teacher manual, please contact sales@CatholicTextbookProject.com.

   d) He forced the Russian people to adopt Western customs and dress.

   e) He established elementary schools, a museum, and the Imperial Academy of Science.

   f) He established conscription.

   g) He gained important outlets to the Baltic and Black seas.

3. Pyotr the Great's new capital was St. Petersburg, which he built on the coast of the Baltic Sea.

4. Katerina the Great was the Russian ruler that brought Pyotr the Great's dreams to fulfillment.

5. No, she did not better the lives of the poor. Under her rule, conditions for the poor worsened. Serfdom increased and grew harsher.

Sample Quiz II (pages 48–57)

Please answer the following in complete sentences.

1. What was the peace treaty that ended the Thirty Years' War in 1648? Name one effect of this treaty.

2. What is the name of the royal family that ruled Prussia?

   a) Wittelsbach   c) Hohenzollern

   b) Habsburg   d) Hohenstaufen

3. What was the capital city of Prussia?

4. Who was the king of Prussia who built up the Prussian army and hated all things French? Who was his son who loved all things French?

5. What was the name of the family that ruled Austria?

   a) Wittelsbach   c) Hohenzollern

   b) Habsburg   d) Hohenstaufen

6. Maria Theresia was the archduchess of Austria and queen of Hungary. Her father was archduke of Austria and king of Hungary, but he held another office over all of Germany, including Prussia and Austria. What was this office?

7. In 1740, the king of Prussia ignored the Pragmatic Sanction and invaded Silesia. This was the beginning of what war?

Answers to Sample Quiz II

Students' answers should approximate the following.

1. The peace treaty that ended the Thirty Years' War in 1648 was the *Peace of Westphalia.*

2. *Hohenzollern* (c) is the name of the royal family that ruled Prussia.

3. *Berlin* was the capital city of Prussia.

4. *Friedrich Wilhelm I* was the king of Prussia who built up the Prussian army and hated all things French. His son was *King Friedrich II* (or *Fritz*).

For a free electronic file of all tests and quizzes included in the teacher manual, please contact sales@CatholicTextbookProject.com.

5. *Habsburg* (b) was the name of the family that ruled Austria.

6. Maria Theresia's father was *Holy Roman emperor.*

7. The king of Prussia's invasion of Silesia was the beginning of the *War of the Austrian Succession.*

Sample Quiz III (pages 57–66)

Please answer the following in complete sentences.

1. **What German state became a great European power because of the Seven Years' War? What nation became the foremost naval power in the world because of the war?**

2. **The Seven Years' War has been called the first world war because it was fought not only in Europe but throughout the world. Name one other place the war was fought.**

3. **Name one thing Maria Theresia did as archduchess of Austria and queen of Hungary.**

4. **Name one thing Friedrich the Great did as king of Prussia.**

5. **What do we call a ruler who used absolute power to force his country's laws and customs to follow Enlightenment philosophy?**

6. **What is the name given to Emperor Josef II's efforts to "enlighten" his realms and to control every aspect of the Catholic Church in Austria?**

Answers to Sample Quiz III

Students' answers should approximate the following.

1. *Prussia* was the German state that became a great European power because of the Seven Years' War. *Great Britain* (or *England*) became the foremost naval power in the world because of the war.

2. The Seven Years' War was fought in (possible answers):

    a) North America   c) India

    b) Africa

3. Maria Theresia's accomplishments (possible answers):

    a) She improved the lives of the serfs.

    b) She protected the poor from oppression.

    c) She improved education in Austria.

    d) She worked to preserve and promote the Catholic Faith.

    e) She approved measures to increase state control over the Church.

    f) She established compulsory education of children.

    g) She abolished the torture of criminals.

For a free electronic file of all tests and quizzes included in the teacher manual, please contact sales@CatholicTextbookProject.com.

4. Friedrich the Great's accomplishments (possible answers):

    a) He allowed complete religious freedom.

    b) He demanded that his nobles develop their agricultural lands.

    c) He encouraged manufacturing and commerce.

    d) He established schools for everyone in his kingdom.

    e) He improved the Berlin Academy of Sciences.

    f) He worked to lower the taxes peasants had to pay to their lords and the government.

5. A ruler who used absolute power to force his country's laws and customs to follow Enlightenment philosophy is called an *enlightened despot*.

6. *Josephism* is the name given to Emperor Josef II's efforts to "enlighten" his realms and to control every aspect of the Catholic Church in Austria.

Essays (200–500 words each)

Instructions to be given to the students: Write in complete sentences. Underline your thesis. Give three supports or examples that explain why you think what you do and that support your thesis.

1. Describe the changes in Russia as it became Europeanized.

2. Explain what it was that "Young Fritz" loved about French culture instead of his Prussian heritage and why this made his father so angry.

3. Compare and contrast King Friedrich the Great and Maria Theresia of Austria. How were they alike as rulers? How did they differ?

Chapter Test

Please answer the following in complete sentences.

I. Short Essay—Answer two of the following:

1. **What is an "enlightened despot"? Why would an enlightened despot favor complete freedom of religion in his realm?**

2. **What were Pyotr the Great's two great goals for Russia? List three things he did to accomplish these goals.**

3. **List three things Maria Theresia did as archduchess of Austria and queen of Hungary.**

4. **List three things Friedrich the Great did as king of Prussia.**

II. Short Answer:

1. **Who was the Russian ruler who brought Pyotr the Great's dreams to fulfillment?**

2. **What was the Pragmatic Sanction?**

3. **What caused the War of the Austrian Succession? What did Friedrich the Great gain in this war?**

4. **Why is the Seven Years' War called the first world war in history?**

5. **Why was the Seven Years' War important to Prussia? Why was it important to Great Britain?**

6. **Why did Pope Pius VI object to Josephism?**

Answer Key to the Chapter Test

Students' answers should approximate the following.

I.

1. An "enlightened despot" was, first and foremost, a despot; that is, he was a ruler who exercised absolute power. He was an *enlightened* despot because his goal was to impose reforms based on ideas of government favored by such Enlightenment thinkers as Voltaire. Enlightened despots thought what the human mind discovers by reason and science should be the basis of all laws and arrangements in society. Because Enlightenment thinkers thought religion was basically irrational and unscientific, they did not think it should influence society but should be only something that concerned individuals. Because they thought religion is private, they thought the government should not promote or protect any one religion but should allow everyone to practice the religion he wished to follow. Thus, an enlightened despot favored complete religious freedom in his realm.

2. Pyotr the Great's two great goals were *to modernize Russia* and *to turn it into a great power* that would awe even the greatest nations of the West. To accomplish his goals, he did the following (possible answers):

    a) He crushed the power of the boyars and abolished their old ruling assembly, the *duma*.

    b) He brought the Russian Orthodox Church under his sway by abolishing the patriarchate.

    c) He brought western European workers and artisans to Russia to teach their arts and skills to the Russians.

    d) He forced the Russian people to adopt Western customs and dress.

For a free electronic file of all tests and quizzes included in the teacher manual, please contact sales@CatholicTextbookProject.com.

    e) He established elementary schools, a museum, and the Imperial Academy of Science.

    f) To build up his army, he established conscription.

    g) He waged wars and gained important outlets to the Baltic and Black seas.

    h) On the Baltic coast, he built a new capital for Russia: St. Petersburg.

3. Maria Theresia's accomplishments (possible answers):

    a) She improved the lives of the serfs.

    b) She protected the poor from oppression.

    c) She improved education in Austria.

    d) She worked to preserve and promote the Catholic Faith.

    e) She approved measures to increase state control over the Church.

    f) She established compulsory education of children.

    g) She abolished the torture of criminals.

4. Friedrich the Great's accomplishments (possible answers):

    a) He allowed complete religious freedom.

    b) He demanded that his nobles develop their agricultural lands.

    c) He encouraged manufacturing and commerce.

    d) He established schools for everyone in his kingdom.

    e) He improved the Berlin Academy of Sciences.

    f) He worked to lower the taxes peasants had to pay to their lords and the government.

II.

1. The Russian ruler who brought Pyotr the Great's dreams to fulfillment was Tsarina *Katerina the Great*.

2. The Pragmatic Sanction was the decree by which Emperor Karl VI sought to assure that his daughter, Maria Theresia, could inherit his realms.

3. The War of the Austrian Succession came about because King Friedrich the Great ignored the Pragmatic Sanction and, with his armies, invaded Austrian-held Silesia. At war's end, Friedrich and Prussia held possession of Silesia.

4. The Seven Years' War is called the first world war in history because it was fought not only in Europe, but in America, Africa, and Asia.

5. The Seven Years' War was important to Prussia because it made Prussia a great European power. It was important to Great Britain because it established Great Britain as the world's foremost naval and colonial power.

6. Pope Pius VI objected to Josephism because it sought to bring the Church in Austria under the control of the government.

CHAPTER 3: The Church before the Revolution

Chapter Overview

- In the 18th century, the Catholic Church lost much of her power and influence in Europe.

- Gallicanism was an influential movement in France during the 17th and 18th centuries. Gallicans held that the king, not the pope, was in most matters the supreme head of the French Church.

- Another influential movement was Jansenism, a heresy that taught that human nature was entirely corrupted by the Fall and that only those with perfect contrition should take Communion. Jansenists, like Gallicans, said the Church is subject to the king or government.

- The movement called Freemasonry attracted many *philosophes* in the 18th century. It encouraged Deism and so undermined the Catholic Faith.

- Pope Benedict XIV was a unique pope in the 18th century. Firm in fighting false teaching, he was respected even by *philosophes* for his intelligence and his wit.

- *Philosophes* and enlightened monarchs throughout Europe wanted to destroy the Society of Jesus. Pressured by monarchs, Pope Clement XIV suppressed the Society in 1773.

- Though the 18th-century Church had good clergy, many bishops and priests were weak and even corrupt. The Faith, however, remained the center of life for most of the common people.

- The 18th century saw the formation of new religious orders, such as the Passionists and the Redemptorists.

Chapter Goals

This chapter tells the story of the Church in the 18th century, before the French Revolution. It describes the challenges the Church faced, the ills from which she suffered, and the signs of life and hope found in her. In general, the student should understand the following general points:

- That the division of Christendom into Protestant and Catholic blocs meant that much of Europe paid little or no attention to what the popes said or commanded. Even Catholic monarchs ignored papal authority or tried to weaken it, both in the universal Church and in their domains. This was because monarchs and, especially, their ministers had been deeply influenced by Enlightenment ideals and by such heretical and schismatic movements as Jansenism, Gallicanism, Josephism, and Febronianism.

- That the Church, though a divine institution, is also human, and the human beings who direct the Church's life often make mistakes or, even, actively oppose the mission of the Church and the ideals of the Gospel of Christ. Even well-intentioned persons, through ignorance or weakness, can make mistakes. The fact that both bishops and the pope can make errors in judgment in prudential decisions, however, does not affect such charisms as the Church's infallibility in the teaching of doctrine or her indefectibility; for it is finally, not men, but the Holy Spirit who guides the Church. Indeed, the story of failures on the part of churchmen underlines most vividly the miracle of the Church and wonder of God's Providence.

- That even in the darkest moments of her history, God provides the Church witnesses of the true, integral Gospel. These witnesses can be popes, bishops, and clergy; they can be men and women who seek a more intense union with God in the religious life; or they can be the common faithful, striving in their daily lives to follow Christ. The 18th century provides us with examples of such witnesses.

- That, in whatever age we live, we must actively understand what the Second Vatican Council called the "signs of the times," while remaining faithful to the teachings and the traditions of the Church. Failure to understand the times in which we live could render us unable to respond properly to the challenges the Church faces and make us less capable of bringing the Gospel of Christ to the world.

Period Music

Consult the list of composers in Chapter 2 of this teacher's manual.

What Students Should Know

1. **What Gallicanism, Febronianism, and Jansenism were**

   Gallicanism was an idea prevalent in France from the 16th–18th centuries that held that the king, not the pope, was in most matters the supreme head of the French Church. Gallicanists rejected such teachings as *papal supremacy* (that the pope is the supreme head of the Church and so no other power can exercise authority over the pope) and *papal infallibility* (the teaching, not defined in the 18th century but widely held, that the pope, when exercising the supreme authority in teaching on faith and morals, can make no error). Gallicanists held that the king not only had authority over the Church's secular possessions but, to some degree, over her spiritual authority.

   Febronianism was an attempt to apply the political ideas of Locke and Rousseau to the Church. It held that, just as governments receive their authority from the people, so bishops receive their right to rule from the Christian faithful. The pope, thus, has no real authority over other bishops.

   Jansenism was a heresy that taught that human nature had been so corrupted by the Fall that, without grace, even our most virtuous actions are sins. Jansenists held that only those with perfect contrition should take Communion. Like Gallicans, Jansenists held that the Church is subject to the king or government.

2. **Why Catholic governments ignored the Church and the popes in the 18th century**

   One reason Catholic monarchs in Europe ignored the Church was because of the influence of Enlightenment ideas, as well as such doctrines as Gallicanism. The ruling powers

Key Terms at a Glance

Gallicanism: The idea that the king or secular head of government is in most matters the supreme head of the Church. This doctrine is called *Gallican* since it arose in France (in Latin, *Gallia*).

Febronianism: the ideas of Johann Nikolaus von Hontheim (Febronius), who said that the pope has no authority over other bishops because local bishops receive the right to rule from the Christian faithful

Jansenism: the belief that human nature was completely corrupted by the Fall and that only those with perfect contrition should receive Holy Communion

papal supremacy: the doctrine that the pope is the supreme or sovereign head of the Church; that no person or body (such as an ecumenical council) can exercise any power over the pope

papal infallibility: the doctrine that, when exercising his supreme authority in teaching on faith and morals, the pope can make no error

parlement: a French court of law; the *Parlement* of Paris was the supreme court of France.

conclave: a gathering of cardinals that meets to elect a pope

pluralism: the holding by one man of more than one Church benefice or office at once

Freemasonry: a secret society for freethinkers, philosophers, and enlightenment statesmen that practiced mystical rites. Freemasons encouraged Deism. They saw God as the "Great Architect" and rejected Jesus Christ as savior, thus undermining the Catholic Faith.

Pietism: a movement begun among German Lutherans that stressed piety, mysticism, and living a Christ-like life.

Ultramontane: the name given to those who favored strong papal control over national churches (from *ultra,* meaning "beyond" or "on the other side," and *mons, montis,* meaning "mountain"—"on the other side of the mountains" or the Alps)

minor orders: in the Latin church before the Second Vatican Council, a term referring to orders or offices of the clergy below the order of deacon. The minor orders were acolyte, exorcist, lector, porter, and subdeacon.

subdeacon: the last minor order before one is ordained deacon. In the Extraordinary Rite (Tridentine) Mass, the subdeacon may carry the chalice with wine to the altar for the Offertory, prepare the gifts for the Eucharist, and read the Epistle lesson to the people.

third orders: a term that refers to lay members of religious orders who do not necessarily live in a religious community but participate in some degree in its prayer life and charitable works

viceroy: a governor who rules in the name of a king

secular priest: a priest who is not part of a religious order; a diocesan priest. A secular priest pledges obedience to his bishop and takes a vow of celibacy, but he does not take a vow of poverty. He thus can own property.

were increasingly influenced by ministers who saw religion as superstition and insisted that the spiritual power be subject to the secular power. Rulers ignored the popes because most of those who held the See of Peter, though good men, did not have the intellectual ability, imagination, and firmness of character to understand the times they lived in. The kings of France and Spain, as well as the Holy Roman emperor, could influence the election of popes and so prevent the choice of men who would strongly oppose their power and interests.

3. **Who Pope Benedict XIV was and why he was such a unique 18th-century pope**

Prospero Lorenzo Lambertini, who became Pope Benedict XIV, was not only pious and graced with a strong faith (traits he shared with other 18th century popes), but he was one of the greatest scholars ever to sit on the throne of Peter. He was known for his love of art, literature, and music. He had a sharp wit that rivaled the wit of Voltaire. He not only condemned falsehoods but sought to answer them with understanding and intelligence. He thus insisted that Catholics be as well educated as their opponents were. He was the first pope to communicate with the universal Church by encyclical letters.

4. **What Freemasonry was and its relationship to the Church**

Freemasonry was (and is) a secret society that confessed a Deist view of God and was a center for the promotion of Enlightenment ideas. For Freemasons, God is merely the "Great Architect" of the universe, not the Christian God. Freemasonry divided into two major groups or "rites"—the English and Scottish rites. Local groupings of Freemasons were called lodges. In the early 18th century, Freemasonry was not clearly anti-Christian or anti-Catholic; indeed, even churchmen joined lodges. After a time, however, first the Jesuits, then some local bishops, forbade membership in Freemasonic lodges. Pope Clement XII condemned Freemasonry in 1738, and Pope Benedict XIV repeated the condemnation in 1751.

5. **Why did European rulers call for the suppression of the Jesuit order? Who suppressed the order? What were the effects of the suppression?**

Since the 16th century, the Jesuits had been the pope's chief support in the Church's struggle against Protestantism. They had provided the Church with brilliant scholars and theologians as well as missionaries who spread the Faith throughout the world. In the 18th century, the Jesuits had become champions in the battle against rationalism and irreligion and so were hated by *philosophes* and Enlightenment politicians. These especially reckoned the Jesuits as dangerous because they staffed colleges and universities, educated the sons of nobles and the middle class, served as confessors to Catholic rulers throughout Europe, and often played an important role in the appointment of bishops and abbots. Because of the Jesuits' power and influence, the Catholic proponents of enlightened despotism wanted them suppressed.

The Bourbon rulers of France, Spain, and Naples pressured Pope Clement XIII to suppress the Jesuits, but he refused to accede to their demands. The next pope, Clement XIV, fearing the monarchs would take their national churches into schism, gave in to their demand. He suppressed the Society of Jesus on July 21, 1773. Only in Prussia and Russia did branches of it continue to exist. The suppression had devastating effects. Jesuit schools and college were left without teachers. Many apostolates in Europe, as well as missions in foreign lands, were abandoned. The pope lost one of his most important supports in the fight against secularization and rationalism. The suppression encouraged the *philosophes,* for they thought it spelled the impending destruction of the Catholic Church.

6. How Protestants responded to the Enlightenment

Though some Protestant ministers and thinkers engaged in literary controversy with libertines and *philosophes*, other Protestants chose simply to withdraw from the intellectual struggle and seek a more personal relationship with God. The German Pietists, for instance, tended to think dogma was not important; instead, they stressed pious feelings, mysticism, and the reform of one's life to become more Christ-like. The Society of Friends, the "Quakers," rejected clergy and all external religious observances in search of the "inner light." In response to Europe's many wars, they became pacifists. An Anglican clergyman, John Wesley (1703–1791), countered the lack of fervor in the Church of England by working out a method of achieving sanctity by cultivating religious fervor, piety, and charity, as well as emphasizing personal conversion. He was known as the founder of what has become known as the Methodist Church.

7. Who Pius VI was

Pius VI was Clement XIV's successor as pope. Despite the crises facing the Church of his day, he imitated the Renaissance popes by patronizing art and carrying on civic works in Rome. He was a lover of pageantry. The clergy surrounding him were more interested in gaining new offices for themselves and their favorites than they were in serving the Church. The pope himself practiced nepotism. Pius VI, however, did stand up at times for the rights of the Church—as when he opposed the establishment of a Jansenist-inspired independent church in Tuscany.

8. The evils afflicting the Church in the 18th century

Many were the evils afflicting the Church in the 18th century. Catholic monarchs, influenced by such doctrines as Gallicanism, were seeking to establish national churches almost entirely under their control. These same monarchs had a good deal of influence over papal elections. Too many clergy (bishops, priests, and lower clergy) were more interested in attaining wealth, power, and influence than in carrying out their spiritual duties. Courtier *abbés* fawned on monarchs, and many of them lived openly immoral lives and espoused anti-Christian Enlightenment ideas. Pluralism was again a problem, and bishops were often absent from their dioceses. Worldliness affected even religious orders and monasteries. One of the Church's biggest weaknesses during this period was the fact that churchmen were too identified with the state.

9. The signs of the Church's health in the 18th century

Despite all the forces arrayed against her, the Church in the 18th century remained the center of life for most of the common people of Catholic Europe. All aspects of life continued to be influenced by the Catholic Faith. Religious orders directed numerous hospitals, hospices, and orphanages, and laity were actively involved in corporal deeds of mercy. The Church provided both university and secondary education as well as elementary schools. Despite the bad or weak bishops and clergy, Catholic Europe could boast of many worthy pastors of souls, some of whom performed heroic acts of charity for the poor and needy. Furthermore, the 18th century produced some remarkable saints, some of whom founded new religious orders.

Questions for Review

1. **Give two reasons why many people in the 18th century thought the Christian Faith was doomed.**

   Possible Answers:

   a) the loss of faith among increasing numbers of people

   b) the challenges to papal authority, such as Gallicanism, Febronianism, Josephism, and Jansenism

   c) the loyalty shown by bishops first to their secular rulers rather than the pope

   d) the inability of most of the popes of the period to address adequately the challenges the Church faced

   e) the suppression of the Jesuits

2. **Who were the Freemasons, and how did their society begin?**

   Freemasons was the name given to those who belonged to a secret society that confessed a Deist view of God and was a center for the promotion of Enlightenment ideas. Their society had its roots in a medieval guild that, in the latter part of the 17th century, became a center of resistance to the Stuart kings of England. By the beginning of the 18th century, Freemason lodges became centers for introducing men to Enlightenment thought.

3. **Why did Pombal want to destroy the Jesuits?**

   Pombal wanted to destroy the Jesuits because he was a disciple of Enlightenment philosophy, against which the Jesuits were some of the most effective opponents. Pombal, too, saw the Church as the chief obstacle to kingly power; he thought by destroying the Jesuits, he could undermine the Church's influence. Pombal came into conflict with the Jesuits over the Reductions in Paraguay, which had recently come under the government of Pombal's king, José I.

4. **What evils afflicted the Church in the 18th century?**

   a) attempts by Catholic monarchs to establish national churches nearly free of papal power

   b) the influence these same monarchs had over papal elections

   c) too great an interest in wealth-making and luxury among the clergy

   d) courtier *abbés*

   e) clergy who lived openly immoral lives and espoused anti-Christian Enlightenment ideas

   f) pluralism and the absence of bishops from their dioceses

   g) churchmen too identified with the state

5. **What were the signs of health in the 18th-century Church?**

   a) The Church in the 18th century remained the center of life for most of the common people of Catholic Europe.

   b) All aspects of life continued to be influenced by the Catholic Faith.

   c) Religious orders directed numerous hospitals, hospices, and orphanages, and laity were actively involved in corporal deeds of mercy.

   d) The Church provided both university and secondary education as well as elementary schools.

   e) the many worthy pastors of souls, some of whom performed heroic acts of charity for the poor and needy

   f) remarkable saints, some of whom founded new religious orders.

6. **Why was Spain less affected by the Enlightenment than France and other European countries?**

   Spain was not as affected as other European countries by the Enlightenment because the Church was stronger in Spain than elsewhere. Spain's population had more clergy per capita. Many of the Spanish bishops were taken from the lower classes. Spain had experienced a Church reform movement, in which bishops founded seminaries and priests conducted missions to deepen the faith of the people.

Ideas in Action

1. Research the religious orders begun in the 18th century. Divide the research on the orders among the students, and give verbal reports on the religious orders. Describe what they did and, if they are still are in existence today, what they do now.

2. Discuss the current political and social situation that exists in our present world, and consider what sort of new religious orders might best serve the mission of the Church today.

3. Research the hymns written by John Wesley, including both their words and melodies.

4. Listen to the music of some of the composers (Catholic and others) of this period. (Examples: Johann Sebastian Bach, Josef Haydn, Wolfgang Amadeus Mozart, Giuseppe Tartini, and Georg Friedrich Handel.) What similarities and differences can you find between the music of these composers?

   Consult the lists of composers in the previous chapters of this teacher's manual for more composers.

6. Make illustrated drawings of the various religious habits worn by different orders of this period. Give details explaining why each particular of the habit may have been chosen.

7. Write a fictional story of a character—man, woman or child—either Catholic or Protestant, who lived in 18th-century France or England and was preparing to emigrate to the New World to escape religious persecution.

Sample Quiz I (pages 69–79)

Please answer the following in complete sentences.

1. What was the name for the powerful group of Catholic clergy and laymen who taught that, because of the Fall, human nature became so corrupt that, without grace, our virtuous acts are sins. They said that only believers with perfect contrition should receive absolution in the Sacrament of Penance and take Communion.

2. Who was the 18th-century pope known as one of the greatest scholars ever to sit on the throne of St. Peter? He was the first pope to issue encyclical letters.

3. Why did Pope Clement XIV say, "I have cut off my right hand," after he suppressed Jesuits?

4. According to the Gallicanists, who was the head of the Church in France?

5. What is the name given to those who favored strong papal control over national churches?

6. What was the secret society of freethinkers, philosophers, and enlightened statesmen who practiced mystical rites, which all members pledged to keep secret. What did this society call God?

7. Why, according to Febronius, did the pope have no real authority over the Catholic faithful?

Answers to Sample Quiz I

Students' answers should approximate the following.

1. *Jansenist* was the name for the Catholic clergy and laymen who taught that, because of the Fall, human nature became so corrupt that, without grace, our virtuous acts are sins.

2. *Benedict XIV* was the 18th century pope known as one of the greatest scholars ever to sit on the throne of St. Peter.

3. Pope Clement XIV said, "I have cut off my right hand," after he suppressed Jesuits because he lost one of the most powerful supports he had against secularism and rationalism.

4. According to Gallicanists, *the king* was the head of the Church in France.

For a free electronic file of all tests and quizzes included in the teacher manual, please contact sales@CatholicTextbookProject.com.

5. *Ultramontane* is the name given to those who favored strong papal control over national churches.

6. The *Freemasons* was the secret society of freethinkers, philosophers, and enlightened statesmen. They called God the *Great Architect*.

7. Febronius said the pope has no real authority over the Catholic faithful because he and all the bishops received their authority from the Catholic people.

Sample Quiz II (pages 79–88)

Please answer the following in complete sentences.

1. Who was the pope who focused his attention on building projects and building up the Vatican's art collection? Like many of the Renaissance popes before him, he practiced nepotism.

2. Who were the German Protestants who stressed piety, mysticism, and a Christ-like life rather than doctrine?

3. Who is the founder of what is today called the Methodist Church? What Christian group did he belong to until his death?

4. List two evils that afflicted the Catholic Church in the 18th century.

5. Give two signs of the spiritual health of the Catholic Church in the 18th century.

Answers to Sample Quiz II

Students' answers should approximate the following

1. *Pius VI* was the pope who focused his attention on building projects and building up the Vatican's art collection and who, like the Renaissance popes before him, practiced nepotism.

2. The *Pietists* were German Protestants who stressed piety, mysticism, and a Christ-like life rather than doctrine?

3. *John Wesley* is the founder of what is today called the Methodist Church? He belonged to the *Church of England* (or the *Anglican Church*) until his death.

4. Evils that afflicted the Catholic Church in the 18th century (possible answers):

   a) attempts by Catholic monarchs to establish national churches nearly free of papal power

   b) the influence these same monarchs had over papal elections

   c) too great an interest in wealth-making and luxury among the clergy

   d) courtier *abbés*

   e) clergy who lived openly immoral lives and espoused anti-Christian Enlightenment ideas

For a free electronic file of all tests and quizzes included in the teacher manual, please contact sales@CatholicTextbookProject.com.

   f) pluralism and the absence of bishops from their dioceses

   g) churchmen who identified themselves too much with the state

5. Signs of the spiritual health of the Catholic Church in the 18th century (possible answers):

   a) The Church in the 18th century remained the center of life for most of the common people of Catholic Europe.

   b) All aspects of life continued to be influenced by the Catholic Faith.

   c) Religious orders directed numerous hospitals, hospices, and orphanages, and laity were actively involved in corporal deeds of mercy.

   d) The Church provided both university and secondary education as well as elementary schools.

   e) the many worthy pastors of souls, some of whom performed heroic acts of charity for the poor and needy

   f) remarkable saints, some of whom founded new religious orders.

Essays (200–500 words each)

Instructions to be given to the students: Write in complete sentences. Underline your thesis. Give three supports or examples that explain why you think what you do and that support your thesis.

1. Describe an idea that you think most threatened the Catholic Church in the 18th century. Why do you think this idea was so dangerous to the Church?

2. Explain why people like Voltaire thought the Catholic Church was coming to an end in the 18th century.

Chapter Test

Please answer the following in complete sentences.

I. **Short Essay—Answer two of the following:**

1. **Describe the beliefs of Freemasonry. What was the Catholic Church's response to Freemasonry?**

2. **Why did European Catholic monarchs ignore the popes in the 18th century? How did they try to make sure that only men who would give them no trouble were elected pope?**

3. **Why did European rulers want the pope to suppress the Society of Jesus? Give two effects of the suppression of the Jesuits.**

4. **Give three examples of the evils afflicting the Church in the 18th century.**

5. **Give three signs of the Church's health in the 18th century.**

II. **Short Answer:**

1. **What is the name of the group that said the king had authority not only over the Church's secular possessions but, to some degree, over his spiritual authority as as well?**

2. **What is the name of the heresy that said that human nature had been so corrupted by the Fall that, without grace, even our most virtuous actions are sins?**

3. **Who was the first pope to write encyclicals to the entire Church?**

4. **What was the German Protestant group that stressed pious feelings, mysticism, and reforming one's life, rather than dogma?**

5. **Who was the pope who wanted to restore the Renaissance in Rome?**

6. **What Protestant group rejected clergy and all external religious observances in order to search for the "inner light"? Its members were also pacifists.**

Answer Key to Chapter Test

Students' answers should approximate the following.

I.

1. Freemasonry was a secret society that confessed a Deist view of God and was a center for the promotion of Enlightenment ideas. For Freemasons, God is merely the "Great Architect" of the universe, not the Christian God. The Catholic Church condemned Freemasonry and forbade Catholics to join Freemasonic lodges.

2. One reason Catholic monarchs in Europe ignored the Church was because of the influence of Enlightenment ideas, as well as such doctrines as Gallicanism. The ruling powers were increasingly influenced by ministers who saw religion as superstition and insisted that the spiritual power be subject to the secular power. Rulers ignored the popes because most of those who held the See of Peter, though good men, did not have the intellectual ability, imagination, and firmness of character to understand the times in which they lived. The kings of France and Spain, as well as the Holy Roman emperor, could influence the election of popes and so prevent the choice of men who would strongly oppose their power and interests.

3. European rulers wanted the pope to suppress the Society of Jesus because of the Jesuits' power and influence. The Jesuits had become the Church's great champions against rationalism and the Enlightenment—and Europe's rulers were influenced by Enlightenment ideas.

   The effects of the suppression of the Jesuits (possible answers):

   a) Jesuit schools and colleges were left without teachers.

For a free electronic file of all tests and quizzes included in the teacher manual, please contact sales@CatholicTextbookProject.com.

   b) Many apostolates in Europe, as well as missions in foreign lands, were abandoned.

   c) The pope lost one of his most important supports in the fight against secularization and rationalism.

   d) The *philosophes* were encouraged, for they thought the suppression spelled the impending destruction of the Catholic Church.

4. Examples of the evils afflicting the Church in the 18th century (possible answers):

   a) attempts by Catholic monarchs to establish national churches nearly free of papal power

   b) the influence these same monarchs had over papal elections

   c) too great an interest in wealth-making and luxury among the clergy

   d) courtier *abbés*

   e) clergy who lived openly immoral lives and espoused anti-Christian Enlightenment ideas

   f) pluralism and the absence of bishops from their dioceses

   g) churchmen who identified themselves too much with the state

5. Signs of the spiritual health of the Catholic Church in the 18th century (possible answers):

   a) The Church in the 18th century remained the center of life for most of the common people of Catholic Europe.

   b) All aspects of life continued to be influenced by the Catholic Faith.

c) Religious orders directed numerous hospitals, hospices, and orphanages, and laity were actively involved in corporal deeds of mercy.

d) The Church provided both university and secondary education as well as elementary schools.

e) the many worthy pastors of souls, some of whom performed heroic acts of charity for the poor and needy

f) remarkable saints, some of whom founded new religious orders

II.

1. The *Gallicans* said the king had authority not only over the Church's secular possessions but, to some degree, over his spiritual authority as well.

2. *Jansenism* is the name of the heresy that said that human nature had been so corrupted by the Fall that, without grace, even our most virtuous actions are sins.

3. *Benedict XIV* was the first pope to write encyclicals to the entire Church.

4. The *Pietists* stressed pious feelings, mysticism, and reforming one's life, rather than dogma.

5. *Pius VI* was the pope who wanted to restore the Renaissance in Rome.

6. The *Quakers* (or *Society of Friends*) rejected clergy and all external religious observances in order to search for the "inner light"?

CHAPTER 4: Revolution in France

Chapter Overview

- By the mid 18th century, France was near bankruptcy. Social injustice, heavy taxation of the lower classes, special privileges given to the aristocracy, the ambitions of the middle class—these and other ills made France ripe for a revolution.

- King Louis XVI called an Estates-General to solve the problem of France's looming bankruptcy. When the estates met, the Third Estate seized power and formed itself into the National Assembly, claiming to be the sovereign authority of France.

- The storming of the Bastille on July 14, 1789, marked the first great triumph of the revolution over the ancient regime.

- The National Assembly and then the National Convention worked to create a new constitution for France—a constitutional monarchy. The fruit of these labors was the Constitution of 1791. The National Assembly drew up as well a statement of human rights, called the *Declaration of the Rights of Man and of the Citizen.*

- The National Convention passed its first anti-Catholic measure, the *Civil Constitution of the Clergy,* to bring the Catholic Church fully under the control of the government and to give the government the ability to seize Church property. The *Civil Constitution* alienated Catholics and clergy from the revolution and led to outbreaks of revolt against the government.

- King Louis XVI deeply opposed the revolution, because it undermined what he thought was his God-given authority as king and attacked the Church. Hoping to lead a resistance against the revolutionary government, he attempted to flee to Germany. But before he could reach safety, he was captured by French authorities and forced to return to Paris.

- Because of the king's attempted flight to Germany, extremists at a rally held on Paris's *Champ de Mars* demanded that he be tried for treason. The National Guard fired upon the crowd. This came to be known as the Massacre of the *Champ de Mars.*

- War was declared between the Holy Roman Empire and Prussia on one side and France on the other. Thinking King Louis XVI had betrayed his people, a mob forced the royal family to flee from the Tuileries Palace. The French Legislative Assembly then abolished the monarchy, replacing the king with an executive council of deputies.

- The French victory at the Battle of Valmy ended the allies' war against France.

Chapter Goals

This chapter tells the story of one of the pivotal events in history—the French Revolution. Like other revolutions, the French Revolution was inspired by deep societal problems. It was a purging of pent-up grievances. The French Revolution, thus, is an important case study in revolution itself—what causes revolution and what its results tend to be. We will see the results of the French Revolution in subsequent chapters, while this chapter focuses more on the causes.

- Students should be shown how the problems of France in the 18th century coalesced with the ideas of the Enlightenment to bring about the revolution and, thus, how ideas, not just material events, have consequences. It is not just material causes that make society what it is, but ideas. Indeed, the same problems addressed under the inspiration of different ideas than those that actually inspired the French Revolution could have led to very different results

- Students should see the centrality of human personalities as the cause of events. For instance, how would have events played out differently if France had had a more decisive king than Louis XVI?

- Students should understand how the ideals of the French Revolution—especially as enshrined in the *Declaration of the Rights of Man and of the Citizen*—are the ideals that inspire Western Civilization in our time.

- Students should understand how the French revolutionary government's treatment of the Church was rooted both in Enlightenment ideas as well as longstanding Church and state relations.

Period Music

Please consult the list of composers in Chapter 2 of this teacher's manual.

What Students Should Know

1. **What were the problems in France that led to the French Revolution**

   - The government was too centralized under the king.

   - The king's government had broken the political power of the nobles without removing their privileges.

   - Though they had hardly any function in society, nobles still demanded dues and services from the peasants and restricted their liberty to hunt and fish.

   - Local and royal taxes, tithes, as well as service burdens, fell almost entirely on the peasants. Royal services, such as the *corvée*, made peasants neglect their own farms and practice poor cultivation. Nobles paid few taxes, and the Church only what it decided to contribute.

   - The cities, especially Paris, swelled with poor who were full of bitterness against the aristocracy and the government.

   - The government in France was spending more money than it was taking in in taxes and faced bankruptcy.

2. **Who the bourgeoisie were and why they were ready for revolution**

   The bourgeoisie were the middle class—merchants, bankers, shopkeepers, and professional men, such as lawyers and doctors. Some were immensely rich, while others had more moderate wealth, while still others had very modest incomes. The French bourgeoisie wanted

Key Terms at a Glance

regalia: the emblems and symbols of royal authority (crown, scepter, robes, etc.)

tithe: small tax or contribution—originally, the tenth part of something, paid as a tax or contribution

bourgeoisie: (boor-zhwa-ZEE) the middle class or a social order dominated by the middle class. A person of the middle class is *bourgeois* (boor-ZHWA).

electoral college: a group or body of electors who cast votes for elected officials

commune: a corporation or body of officials that governs a town or city

ancient regime: the political and social system of Europe before the French Revolution

suspensive veto: by giving a *veto* (Latin, meaning "I refuse") to a bill, a king or head of government refuses to sign it into law. A *suspensive veto* is the power only to delay the process of a bill becoming a law. If, after a certain number of times, a head of government refuses to sign a bill, it becomes law anyhow.

department: a political region (like a county or state) instituted by the French revolutionary government

nonjuror: a clergyman who refused to take an oath to support the *Civil Constitution of the Clergy*

execute: (in law) to sign bills so that they become laws. Someone who executes laws is called the *executive*. In the British government, the executive was the king; in the United States government, the executive is the president.

suffrage: the right to vote in political elections

indirect vote: a vote cast not for a candidate for a public office but for an elector, who in turn votes for the candidate favored by the voters

proletariat: the poorest class; the working class, especially of the cities

counterrevolutionary: someone who leads or participates in a counterrevolution—a revolution directed to overthrowing a government or system set up by a previous revolution

governmental reforms. They wanted a greater share in the government of the kingdom. They looked to Great Britain as their ideal of freedom until the founding of the United States, a republic based on the ideals of Liberal thinkers such as John Locke, Voltaire, and Rousseau. The bourgeoisie was, thus, greatly affected by Liberalism.

3. **What events led to the French Revolution**

- To solve the French government's bankruptcy crisis, King Louis XVI called a

meeting of the Estates-General at Versailles for May 1789.

- Under the influence of its Liberal leaders, the Third Estate (commons) insisted that the First Estate (the clergy) and the Second Estate (nobility) form one assembly with it. When the king refused to allow this, the Third Estate established itself as the National Assembly—the sole representative of the French people. When, at last, the king saw the National Assembly was gaining influence and power, he recognized it on June 27, 1789.

- King Louis XVI was determined to end the revolution and called in his German mercenary regiments to Paris. This, and the dismissal of the finance minister, Jacques Necker, inspired an uprising among the poor of Paris. On July 14, 1789, about 1,000 armed men and women assaulted and captured a fortress, the Bastille. The next day, the king again gave in to revolutionary demands.

4. What the *Declaration of the Rights of Man and of the Citizen* was and said

The *Declaration* was a decree issued by the French National Assembly on August 26, 1789. Drawing on the ideas of Rousseau, it made Enlightenment Liberalism the philosophy of the state. It made the following declarations:

- The law expresses the general will of the people; the people are sovereign and all political power comes from them.

- All citizens are equal. "Men are born and remain free and equal in rights," it said.

- The purpose of government is to preserve "the natural and imprescriptible rights of man . . . life, liberty, property, security, and resistance to oppression."

- Citizens have the right speak their ideas and opinions and the right to religious freedom.

5. Why the National Assembly decided to confiscate Church property; what other measures it undertook against the Church; what effects these measures had

The National Assembly confiscated the Church's property in France because it had not solved the financial crisis. The Assembly thought the Church's wealth could save the government from bankruptcy. Among other measures the National Assembly undertook against the Church are the following:

- It suppressed religious houses and monasteries throughout France.

- On July 12, 1790, it issued the *Civil Constitution of the Clergy,* in which it removed (except in matters of doctrine) the French Church entirely out from under the authority of the pope.

The *Civil Constitution* and other anticlerical measures had the effect of turning many of the French, who had formerly supported it against the revolution. It caused divisions within the French Church, for most of the bishops and over half of the priests refused to swear an oath to the *Civil Constitution.* The official state Church, thus, went into schism.

6. What the Constitution of 1791 was

The Constitution of 1791 was the first written constitution of the French revolutionary government. As a constitutional monarchy, it kept the king as head of state, or the executive, but gave him scarcely any power. Instead, the one-house legislature, the Legislative Assembly, held the supreme lawmaking power in the government. The constitution was not democratic, for it gave the suffrage only to taxpaying and property-owning citizens—and then, they only had an indirect vote: a vote cast not for a candidate but for an elector who, in turn, voted for a candidate.

7. Who the opponents of the Constitution of 1791 were

The opponents of the Constitution of 1791 were those, such as the royalists, who wanted to return to the ancient regime, the political and social system of Europe before the French Revolution. They included members of the nobility and of the clergy, but also peasants who were angry about the government's attacks on religion. Other opponents thought the constitution was not revolutionary enough; they wanted a democratic republic without any state church. These included the Cordeliers, led by Georges Danton, and the Jacobins, led by Maximilien Robespierre.

8. Why King Louis XVI conspired against the French revolutionary government

King Louis XVI thought the French revolutionary government had unjustly seized power from him. He saw that, as the king, he had received his authority from God and thus thought that no one could justly take it from him. A devout Catholic, he objected to the anticlerical legislation of both the National Assembly and the Legislative Assembly.

9. How the republic was founded

In the war the allied powers of the European monarchies were waging against France, the French armies were suffering many defeats. The extremist revolutionaries were certain the king was conspiring against them and was in contact with the enemy. On August 9, 1792, Danton and other extremist leaders seized control of Paris's city government, the commune, and on the following day led thousands of Parisians in an assault on the Tuileries palace. The king, the queen, and the dauphin fled to the chambers of the Legislative Assembly, where the delegates voted to depose Louis. Thus ended the government under the Constitution of 1791. It was replaced by a republican government, with a legislative assembly and an executive council.

10. The importance of the Battle of Valmy

At the battle of Valmy, fought on September 20, 1792, the Prussians failed to drive the French from the hill of Valmy. Over the next week, Danton's agents negotiated for the withdrawal of the Allied troops from France. On September 30, the Allies agreed to withdrawal. The republic was saved.

Questions for Review

1. **How did medieval French government differ from the French government under Louis XVI?**

The government of France under Louis XVI was highly centralized. The king was the absolute authority in France. The nobles were reduced to powerless ornaments of the royal court. In the Middle Ages, however, the king was nowhere as powerful as he was under Louis XVI. Nobles were quite powerful and, sometimes, more powerful than the king himself. The government was decentralized; the king shared power with the nobles and the Church. The Estates-General represented the three estates of France—the clergy, the aristocracy, and the commoners. It advised the king and could influence the king's decisions. Each province in France had its local assembly of the Estates that had local administrative authority. *Parlements*, or regional courts, too, had local administrative duties.

2. **Why would French peasants have been discontent in the years before the French Revolution?**

French peasants were discontent in the years before the French Revolution because they bore heavy burdens and had little freedom to better their lot. Though they themselves had hardly any function in society, nobles still demanded dues and service from the peasants and restricted their liberty to hunt and fish. Local and royal taxes, Church tithes, as well as service burdens fell almost entirely on the peasants. Royal services, such as the *corvée*, forced peasants to neglect their own farms and so practice poor cultivation.

Why was the *bourgeoisie* discontent?

The *bourgeoisie* were a dynamic class of society that was looking forward to changes in society that would benefit their class. They wanted a greater share in the government of the kingdom. They were deeply influenced by Liberalism and favored reforms that would introduce a kind of parliamentary system into France, the removal of restrictions on business, and freedom of thought and religion.

3. **What changes in government did the Third Estate want the Estates-General of 1789 to make?**

In their *cahiers* sent to the king, the Third Estate called for Liberal reforms to the government. They wanted freedom for the press, taxes that were more just, and equality for all classes in France. They wanted a part in directing the future of France.

4. **Why did the *Declaration of the Rights of Man and of the Citizen* not mention the Catholic Church?**

The *Declaration* did not mention the Catholic Church because the document's authors were Liberals who wanted to diminish and even erase the role of the Church in French society. A very large number of the members of the National Assembly, which drew up and approved the Declaration, were not Catholics but Deists or Freemasons.

5. **What measures did the National Assembly take against the Church?**

The National Assembly took the following measures against the Church:

a) It confiscated and brought under state control all the lands belonging to the Church.

b) It suppressed religious orders and monasteries and forbade anyone to take religious vows.

c) In the *Civil Constitution of the Clergy,* it removed papal authority in the choice of bishops, who were henceforth to be elected; it abolished dioceses. Thus, the Assembly brought the French Catholic Church into schism.

d) It demanded that all priests and bishops take an oath of loyalty to the *Civil Constitution* and forbade those who refused to take the oath to function as priests. Bishops who refused were to be deposed.

6. **How did the Girondins and the Feuillants differ?**

The Feuillants favored a constitutional monarchy like the one established by the Constitution of 1791; indeed, they supported this constitution. They supported the Constitutional Church. They were thus the "conservatives" and sat on the right side of the Assembly hall.

The Girondins favored the overthrow of the monarchy and an end to all state religion. They sat on the left side of the Assembly Hall and opposed the Constitution of 1791.

7. **What were the reasons King Louis XVI, the Girondins, and the Feuillants each had for going to war?**

King Louis XVI wanted to go to war because he hoped that allied monarchies would overthrow the revolutionary government and restore his absolute rule over France.

The Feuillants wanted to go to war because they thought it would unite France like nothing else could.

The Girondins wanted war because they saw it as an opportunity to spread the revolution to all the oppressed peoples of Europe.

Ideas in Action

1. Research the life of Marie Antoinette. Was she as frivolous as has been claimed? What other qualities, both good and bad, did she have?

   This chapter and the next, as well as Chapter 2, contain information on Marie Antoinette that could help guide students in this activity. However, students should still consult outside sources.

2. Imagine that you are a French priest who has learned about the *Civil Constitution of the Clergy* but wants to remain faithful to the Church. Write a diary of your struggles to remain faithful to God, the Church, your parish, and your country.

3. Imagine that you are a French peasant or a member of the middle class at the time of the French Revolution. Write an account of why you would support the revolution, or why you would not.

4. Make a detailed map of the city of Paris at the time of the French Revolution. Show these key locations: the Bastille, Notre Dame cathedral, government buildings, and royal houses.

   Since Paris was the vibrant center of the revolution, this activity could help students deepen their understanding of the events in this and subsequent chapters. Geography is the handmaiden of history.

Sample Quiz I (pages 91–101)

Please answer the following in complete sentences.

1. List three of the problems in France that led to the French Revolution.

2. Who were the bourgeoisie?

3. Give one reason the French bourgeoisie were ready for revolution.

4. What group in France belonged to the First Estate? Who belonged to the Second Estate? Who belonged to the Third Estate?

5. Why did King Louis XVI call a meeting of the Estates-General?

6. By calling itself the National Assembly, what was the Third Estate claiming to be?

7. On what date did the storming of the Bastille take place?

Answers to Sample Quiz I

Students' answers should approximate the following.

1. The problems leading to the French Revolution (possible answers):

   a) The government was too centralized under the king.

   b) The king's government had broken the political power of the nobles without removing their privileges.

   c) Though they had hardly any function in society, nobles still demanded dues and service from the peasants and restricted their liberty to hunt and fish.

   d) Local and royal taxes, tithes, as well as service burdens fell almost entirely on the peasants.

   e) Royal services, such as the *corvée,* made peasants neglect their own farms and practice poor cultivation.

   f) Nobles paid few taxes, and the Church only what it decided to contribute.

   g) The cities, especially Paris, swelled with poor, who were full of bitterness against the aristocracy and the government.

   h) The government in France was spending more money than it was taking in in taxes and faced bankruptcy.

2. The bourgeoisie were the middle class—merchants, bankers, shopkeepers, and professional men, such as lawyers and doctors. Some were immensely rich, while others had more moderate wealth while still others had very modest incomes.

3. Reasons why the French bourgeoisie were ready for revolution (possible answers):

   a) They wanted a greater share in the government of the kingdom.

   b) They admired the governments of Great Britain and the United States and wanted the French government to emulate them.

   c) The bourgeoisie were greatly affected by Liberalism.

4. The *clergy* belonged to the First Estate. The *nobility* belonged to the Second Estate. The *commoners* belonged to Third Estate.

5. King Louis XVI called a meeting of the Estates-General to solve the problem of bankruptcy that France had fallen into.

6. By calling itself the National Assembly, the Third Estate was claiming to be the sovereign power in France—the representative of the French people.

7. The storming of the Bastille took place on *July 14, 1789.*

Sample Quiz II (pages 101–118)

Please answer the following in complete sentences.

1. Who is the sovereign power in France, according to the *Declaration of the Rights of Man and of the Citizen*?

2. What did the *Declaration* say about the rights of citizens?

3. Why did the French National Assembly confiscate the property of the Church in France?

4. Why did Pope Pius VI condemn the *Civil Constitution of the Clergy*?

5. Could the king stop laws passed by the Legislative Assembly under the Constitution of 1791? Please explain.

6. Please give one reason King Louis XVI wanted to overthrow the French revolutionary government.

7. Who *supported* the Constitution of 1791? (Multiple answers possible.)

   a) Girondins   f) Cordeliers

   b) Feuillants   g) Danton

   c) *émigrés*   h) Robespierre

   d) Jacobins   i) Louis XVI

   e) Jean-Paul Marat

8. Who *opposed* the Constitution of 1791? (Use the list in question 7. Multiple answers possible.)

Answers to Sample Quiz II

Students' answers should approximate the following

1. The *people of France* is the sovereign power in France, according to the *Declaration of the Rights of Man and of the Citizen*.

2. The *Declaration of the Rights of Man and of the Citizen* said all citizens have equal rights

3. The French National Assembly confiscated the property of the Church in France to save the government from bankruptcy

4. Pope Pius VI condemned the *Civil Constitution of the Clergy* because it separated the Church in France from the authority of the pope. It brought the French Church into schism.

5. The king could stop or veto laws passed by the Legislative Assembly, but only for a limited number of times. He had a suspensive veto, not an absolute veto.

6. King Louis XVI wanted to overthrow the French revolutionary government because (possible answers):

   a) He thought the French revolutionary government had unjustly seized power from him.

   b) He objected to the anticlerical legislation of the both the National Assembly and the Legislative Assembly.

7. The Feuillants (b) *supported* the Constitution of 1791.

8. The Girondins (a), the *émigrés* (c), the Jacobins (d), Marat (e), the Cordeliers (f), Danton (g), Robespierre (h), and Louis XVI (i) all *opposed* the Constitution of 1791

Essays (200–500 words each)

Instructions to be given to the students: Write in complete sentences. Underline your thesis. Give three supports or examples that explain why you think what you do and that support your thesis.

1. Imagine yourself to be a clergyman (bishop or priest) or a nobleman living before the revolution. Tell why you are either content or discontent with the way things are going for you and your society.

2. Do you think a revolution could help or hinder a society. Use the French Revolution as an example.

Chapter Test

Please answer the following in complete sentences.

I. **Short Essay—Answer two of the following:**

1. Give four problems that afflicted France before 1789 and that led to the outbreak of the French Revolution.

2. Describe the events that led to the storming of the Bastille. (Consider the following questions in your essay: Why did Louis XVI call for a meeting of the Estates-General? What did the Third Estate demand from the king and the other Estates? What did the Third Estate claim for itself? What was the king's response?)

3. What were the main ideas of the *Declaration of the Rights of Man and of the Citizen*? On whose philosophy of government and society was it based?

4. What was the *Civil Constitution of the Clergy*? What did it do? How did bishops and priests respond to it? What effects did it have on the relationship of Catholics to the revolution? What effect did it have on King Louis XVI?

II. **Short Answer:**

1. Give two reasons the bourgeoisie favored the French Revolution.

2. Why did the French National Assembly decide to confiscate Church property?

3. Was the Constitution of 1791 democratic? Please explain.

4. Why did extremist revolutionaries such as the Cordeliers and the Jacobins decide to overthrow King Louis XVI in August 1792?

5. Name the battle that saved the French Revolution. On what date was it fought?

6. What do we call the power a head of state has only to delay a bill becoming a law, not stop it altogether?

7. What was the name for the political and social system of Europe before the French Revolution?

8. What was the name given to a clergyman who refused to take an oath to support the *Civil Constitution of the Clergy*?

Answer Key to Chapter Test

Students' answers should approximate the following:

I.

1. The following are the problems that afflicted France before 1789 (possible answers):

   a) The government was too centralized under the king.

   b) The king's government had broken the political power of the nobles without removing their privileges.

   c) Though they had hardly any function in society, nobles still demanded dues and service from the peasants and restricted their liberty to hunt and fish.

   d) Local and royal taxes, tithes, as well as service burdens fell almost entirely on the peasants.

   e) Royal services, such as the *corvée,* made peasants neglect their own farms and practice poor cultivation.

   f) Nobles paid few taxes and the Church, only what it decided to contribute.

   g) The cities, especially Paris, swelled with poor who were full of bitterness against the aristocracy and the government.

   h) The government in France was spending more money than it was taking in in taxes and faced bankruptcy.

2. Among the problems afflicting France before 1789 was the fact that the French government was facing bankruptcy. To solve this problem, Louis XVI called a meeting of the Estates-General. When the Estates-General met, the Third Estate (commons), under the influence of Liberal ideas, insisted that the First Estate (the clergy) and the Second Estate (nobility) form one assembly with it. When the king refused to allow this, the Third Estate established itself as the National Assembly—the sole representative of the French people. When, at last, the king saw the National Assembly was gaining influence and power, he recognized it on June 27, 1789. Yet, despite his recognition of the new government, King Louis XVI was determined to end the revolution. He called in his German mercenary regiments to Paris and he dismissed a popular minister. These acts inspired an uprising among the poor of Paris. On July 14, 1789, about 1,000 armed men and women assaulted and captured a fortress, the Bastille. The next day, the king again gave in to revolutionary demands.

3. The main ideas of the *Declaration of the Rights of Man and of the Citizen* are as follows:

   a) The law expresses the general will of the people; the people are sovereign and all political power comes from them.

   b) All citizens are equal.

   c) The purpose of government is to preserve the natural rights of man, which are life, liberty, property, security, and resistance to oppression.

   d) Citizens have the right to speak their ideas and opinions and the right to religious freedom.

   The Declaration drew its basic ideas from the philosophy of Rousseau.

4. The *Civil Constitution of the Clergy* removed (except in matters of doctrine) the French Church entirely out from under the authority of the pope. It brought the French Church into schism. In response to the *Civil Constitution,* most bishops and priests refused to take an oath to obey it. Thus, it caused divisions in the

French Church. The *Civil Constitution* had the effect of turning many of the French, who had formerly supported the revolution, against it. It was one of the reasons King Louis XVI turned against the revolution, for he was a devout Catholic and resented the fact that he had been forced to sign the bill into law.

II.

1. The reasons the bourgeoisie favored the French Revolution (possible answers):

   a) The French bourgeoisie wanted governmental reforms.

   b) They wanted a greater share in the government of the kingdom.

   c) They were inspired by Liberal thinkers such as John Locke, Voltaire, and Rousseau.

2. The French National Assembly decide to confiscate Church property because it needed money to solve the bankruptcy crisis. The Assembly thought Church property could supply it with the wealth it needed to do so.

3. The Constitution of 1791 was not democratic because it only allowed those who paid taxes and owned property to vote. Even these had only an indirect vote, for they did not vote for the candidates themselves but for electors who, in turn, voted for candidates.

4. Extremist revolutionaries such as the Cordeliers and the Jacobins decided to overthrow King Louis XVI in August 1792 because they thought he was conspiring with France's enemies to overthrow the revolutionary government.

5. The *Battle of Valmy* saved the French Revolution. It was fought on September 20, 1792.

6. A *suspensive veto* is the power a head of state has only to delay a bill becoming a law, not stop it altogether.

7. The *ancient regime* was the name for the political and social system of Europe before the French Revolution.

8. A clergyman who refused to take an oath to support the *Civil Constitution of the Clergy* was called a *nonjuror.*

CHAPTER 5: Many Revolutions

Chapter Overview

- The French National Convention convicted Louis XVI of treason and condemned him to death. The king was beheaded on January 21, 1793.

- The execution of Louis XVI turned public opinion in England against the French republic. The British government dismissed the French ambassador from London. The French government then declared war on Great Britain.

- After the Glorious Revolution, the British government became a constitutional monarchy. Parliament became the predominant power in the British government.

- Two parties dominated the British government: the Tories (who supported royal power, but not absolute monarchy) and the Whigs (who favored the predominance of Parliament, especially the House of Commons).

- Queen Anne was the last British monarch to veto an act of Parliament. The Hanoverian kings, George I and George II, favored the Whigs and allowed Parliament to direct the affairs of the United Kingdom. The reigns of George I and George II saw the development of the office of prime minister.

- The British Constitution is not a written document, but a set of traditions and governmental

procedures that have arisen over centuries simply from the practice of governing. In the 18th century, the king of Great Britain was the chief executive, while the Parliament (made up of the House of Commons and the House of Lords) served as the legislature. The king was dependent on Parliament. In Parliament, the House of Lords represented the aristocracy. The House of Commons supposedly represented the people of Great Britain, but in reality it was an oligarchy.

- Trade with the colonies allowed middle-class people in Great Britain to become very rich. The aristocracy invested their wealth and became even wealthier. The merchant aristocracy and middle class came to wield great power in Parliament—a power they used to further their own interests.

- The increased commercial activity in Great Britain developed into capitalism, the large-scale organization of business, where those who possess a store of wealth or *capital* hire laborers to engage in activities that increase wealth. In capitalism, a few own and control wealth-producing enterprises, while the vast majority of the people engaged in those enterprises (the workingmen) control only their labor, which they sell to the capitalists for a wage.

- Capitalists invested in new machinery and developed large industries, against which smaller manufacturers and the manufacturing guilds could not compete. The development of capitalism thus led to the destruction of the guild system in Great Britain.

- Capitalism led to what is called the Industrial Revolution. Though this revolution brought about an amazing growth in the manufacture of goods, it brought misery and poverty to many laborers. Capitalists justified their treatment of workers by the Liberal economic doctrine called *laissez-faire*. Workers reacted with strikes and violence. Parliament sided with employers against the workers.

- Large landowners in Great Britain, wanting to consolidate lands to make it easier to practice "scientific" agriculture, pushed for the enclosure of agricultural lands. Parliament mandated enclosures, which led to a drastic reduction in the rural population of England and Wales and devastated rural communities.

- King George III tried to restore kingly power in Great Britain. He appointed Tories to his cabinet.

- George III's prime minister, William Pitt, at first seemed to support reform of the British government. When Britain went to war with revolutionary France, however, Pitt began to take stern measures against reform.

Chapter Goals

This chapter juxtaposes two very different revolutions: the French Revolution, which overthrew a social order by political means, and Great Britain's industrial/agricultural revolution that did the same by means of the "rule of law" and the pressure of economic change. We tend to think of revolutions as directed to the overthrow of governments; and,

indeed, this is the proper meaning of the term, revolution. Yet, a society can have a stable government, maintain all its forms of law, and still undergo profound changes that we can describe as revolutionary.

This chapter briefly covers some material dealt with in *Light to the Nations I*—the struggles between the Stuarts and Parliament, the Glorious Revolution, the establishment of parliamentary supremacy, the reigns of William and Mary, and the establishment of the Hanoverian dynasty. Teachers may thus use this chapter as a review of what the students learned the previous year. The material will not be the central focus of the "What Students Should Know" section, below.

Period Music

Please consult the list of composers in Chapter 2 of this teacher's manual.

What Students Should Know

1. **The party divisions in the National Convention of the French republic**

   The fall of the constitutional monarchy led to a new division of parties in the French revolutionary government. The Girondins replaced the Feuillants on the right side of the convention hall. Though once extremists, the Girondins were now the conservatives, since they stood for the Liberal ideals that had inspired the revolution—individual freedom, limited suffrage, and the independence of local governments outside of France. The Girondins place on the left of the convention hall, the "Mountain," had been taken by the Jacobins and Cordeliers, who favored offering the suffrage to every French male as well as a highly centralized government. The Mountain also favored carrying the revolution to all of Europe.

Key Terms at a Glance

stadtholder: head of state in the Dutch Netherlands

constitutional monarchy: a form of government where the head of government is a king or monarch whose powers are limited by a constitution

oligarchy: government by a few; particularly, by wealthy people for the benefit of their class

capitalism: the large-scale organization of business, where those who possess a store of wealth or *capital* (which includes money, raw materials, tools, land, factories, etc.) hire laborers to engage in activities that increase wealth

textile: cloth; especially a woven or knit cloth

tenement: a house used as a dwelling; an apartment or flat

pauperism: the state of being a pauper, or poor

arable: able to be plowed and planted with crops

yeoman: a small farmer who cultivates his own land; a freeholder

cereal crops: crops such as wheat, rye, barley, and corn

crop rotation: the practice of growing different crops in succession on the same piece of land in order to preserve and enhance soil fertility

subsistence farming: a kind of farming that provides all or most of what is needed by a farm family, and where much of the crop is not put up for sale on the market

poor rates: taxes raised to support the poor

workhouse: a house set up to care for the poor at public expense

Encyclopedists: Denis Diderot and the authors of his *Encyclopedia*

2. Why the Jacobins and Cordeliers (the Mountain) pushed for the execution of King Louis XVI; what reason they gave for condemning him to death

The Mountain feared that if Louis XVI remained alive, he could be the focal point about which a counterrevolution could form; thus they wanted him dead. They brought charges of treason—aiding the enemy in war—as grounds for his execution.

3. The reasons the Girondins gave for sparing the king

The Girondins questioned whether the National Convention had the authority to try a man who had formerly been head of state.

They said the people of France, not the deputies, should decide on the king's fate.

4. When Louis XVI was executed and by what means

Louis XVI was executed on Monday, January 21, 1793, by guillotine.

5. What effect the execution of Louis XVI had on the French republic's war against the coalition

The execution of the king shocked and appalled the English people. Many in Great Britain had sympathized with the revolution; but the execution turned them against it. King George III's prime minister, William Pitt, took advantage of popular outrage and dismissed the French foreign minister from London. In response to this insult, the French government declared war on Great Britain on February 1, 1793. In this way, Great Britain joined the coalition forces arrayed against the French revolutionary republic.

6. The basic structure of the government of Great Britain

By the 18th century, the British government was a constitutional monarchy. Parliament was the legislative body, while the king was the executive. Parliament was the predominant power in the British government. It was made up of the House of Commons and the House of Lords. In theory, at least, the House of Lords represented the prelates of the Church of England and the aristocratic lords, while the House of Commons represented everyone else.

Two parties dominated the British government: the Tories and the Whigs. The Tories supported royal power, but not absolute monarchy. In religious matters, they supported the Established (Protestant) Church of England (Anglican). The Whigs favored the predominance of Parliament, especially the House of Commons, and insisted on a very limited role for the king in government. They represented the more radical Protestants (such as the Puritans) and the class of those engaged in commerce.

7. The character of the British Constitution

The British Constitution is not a written document but a set of traditions and governmental procedures that have arisen over centuries simply from the practice of governing. Though some written laws, such as the *Magna Carta* and the Declaration of Rights, form part of the constitution, it is mostly unwritten.

8. How the British government was an oligarchy

Though Parliament was said to represent all the people in Great Britain, very few people had the suffrage. Local aristocrats could control elections in rural districts either by buying votes or intimidating voters. In rural districts, members of Parliament were either aristocrats or sponsored by aristocrats. Many towns had no right of representation in Parliament, while towns that no longer existed (rotten boroughs) sent members to the House of Commons. Aristocrats and the wealthy bought the right to represent the rotten boroughs. Thus, in the 18th century, Parliament was controlled by the aristocracy and wealthy merchants and was an *oligarchy*—a government by a few, particularly the wealthy, for the benefit of their class. Even the Whigs and Tories had few differences between them, and they joined forces to further the interests of the oligarchy.

9. What capitalism is and how it developed in Great Britain

Trade with the British colonies overseas allowed middle-class people in Great Britain to become very rich. The aristocracy invested their wealth and became even wealthier. The merchant aristocracy and middle class came to wield great power in Parliament—a power they used to further their own interests. The increased commercial activity in Great Britain developed into capitalism, the large-scale organization of business where those who possess a store of wealth or *capital* hire laborers to engage in activities that increase wealth. In capitalism, a few own and control wealth-producing enterprises, while the vast majority of the people engaged in those enterprises (the workingmen) control only their labor, which they sell to the capitalists for a wage.

10. How scientific discoveries led to the Industrial Revolution

Scientists in Great Britain had always had a more practical bent than their colleagues on the continent. The British scientists had made important discoveries about the use of steam and the properties of gases, which had practical uses in the manufacture of new, labor-saving machinery. The invention of the steam engine and the development of less expensive ways of smelting iron set the stage for the Industrial Revolution.

New machines, such as the Spinning Jenny and Arkwright's water frame, led to dramatic changes in the textile industry. Large factories, powered by steam engines, replaced smaller manufacturers. These factories rose in cities, which increased dramatically in population. Because these factories were so expensive to build, factory owners had to rely on loans from banks. Banks, thus, grew in power and influence in Great Britain.

11. The lot of the workers under the industrial system

The huge factories required a large number of workers. These workers labored in dismal conditions for typically 14 hours a day, 6 days a week. They earned very low wages. If they were injured, they would be fired without any means to support themselves. Factories employed women and children as well. The factory system led to a great increase in the number of poor in Great Britain.

12. How people justified the treatment of workers

Capitalists justified their treatment of workers by appealing to the Liberal economic doctrine called *laissez-faire.* Especially as developed by Adam Smith, this doctrine said the government should not try to control economic activity by regulating prices or wages or by any restriction whatsoever. Each person should be allowed to follow his own personal interest in economic activity. Only in this way would society achieve wealth and prosperity.

13. How workers reacted to the new economic system

Workers reacted to the economic system with strikes and violence, sometimes destroying the new machines. Parliament sided with employers against the workers.

14. What the Enclosures were and their effects

Large landowners in Great Britain, wanting to consolidate lands to make it easier to practice "scientific" agriculture and to use new farming machinery, pushed for the enclosure of agricultural lands. The enclosures entailed the conversion of strip fields into compact fields enclosed by fences and the abolition of common lands. The enclosures had the effect of depriving many peasant farmers of land or the use of land. Parliament mandated enclosures, which led to a drastic reduction in the rural population of England and Wales and devastated rural communities. Those who lived on the land were in many cases reduced to poverty. Those who left the land for the cities to work in the new factories also suffered from poverty.

15. Identify the following:

George III: the Hanoverian king of Great Britain, the first of his line to think of himself as an Englishman, not a German. Known as the patriot king, George III was admired for his high personal morals. He sought to rule as a king, and he challenged Parliament by appointing Tory ministers when the Whigs were in the majority.

Charles James Fox: an English Whig statesman and one of the king's Whig opponents. Though addicted to gambling and drinking, Fox had a genuine concern for the poor and oppressed and called for justice, religious tolerance, and the abolition of England's slave trade. He favored democratic reforms to the government and had a high regard for the French Revolution.

Edmund Burke: a Whig member of Parliament who wrote that the French revolutionaries' attack on the traditional order of France would end in disaster. Burke rejected the notion of natural human rights, saying the only rights men have come through the religious and cultural traditions of the society in which they live. It is thus important, Burke said, for men to conserve the religious and political society they live in and put down revolution.

Questions for Review

1. **Why did the radical French republicans want to eliminate all kings not only in France, but everywhere in Europe?**

   The radical French revolutionaries thought the revolution should include more than just France. They believed it was a kind of crusade—a war of ideals—against all kings. Only republican government was fully just in their eyes.

2. **Why did Georges Danton want France to keep peace with Great Britain?**

   Danton feared that if Great Britain joined its forces to those of France's enemies, the cause of the revolution would fail. Thus, he wanted Great Britain to remain at peace with France.

3. **What was the guillotine? Why was it invented? After whom was it named?**

   The guillotine was an instrument of execution that used a blade that, descending down a wooden scaffold, quickly and painlessly severed the neck of the person being executed. It was invented to make execution as painless as possible. It was named after its inventor, Joseph-Ignace Guillotin.

4. **Why did the execution of Louis XVI prompt England to make war on France?**

   The execution of Louis XVI shocked the sensibilities of the English people. They called on their government to go to war with France. William Pitt responded by dismissing the French minister from London—an act the French government took as an insult. Because of it, the National Convention declared war on Great Britain.

5. **What are the names of the two houses of Parliament in the English government? What groups in British society did each house represent?**

   The two houses of Parliament are the House of Lords and the House of Commons. The Lords represented the nobility and the prelates of the Church of England. The Commons represented everyone else in society.

6. **What is a constitutional monarchy?**

   A constitutional monarchy is a form of government where the head of government is a king or monarch whose powers are limited by a constitution.

7. **What was the king's role in the British government in the 18th century?**

   The king was the head of the government in 18th-century Great Britain. He was supreme commander of the armed forces of the realm, and he could veto acts of Parliament. Yet, he could make no laws or raise taxes on his own but had to rely on Parliament for funds, even to wage war.

8. **Why did the Industrial Revolution cause such social upheaval in England?**

   The Industrial Revolution introduced labor-saving machines into the production of products, particularly textiles. This made large-scale production possible and changed the nature of manufacturing. Since the factories required much financing, the need for them led to the growth of banks. The large factories drove smaller competitors out of business, and this brought about more widespread poverty. Small craftsmen rebelled against the new state of things, and workers joined together to strike for higher wages. But, since Parliament and local government sided with the wealthy factory owners, these uprisings came to naught.

9. **What is meant by the agricultural revolution? What were enclosures?**

The agricultural revolution refers to the introduction of machines and more "scientific" methods of cultivation into farming, thus increasing the yield of crops. To accommodate the new farm machinery, Parliament ordered the enclosure of farm lands. Enclosure entailed reconfiguring strip fields into compact fields and enclosing them with a fence.

10. **What caused the English to turn against the ideals of the French Revolution?**

Atrocities, such as the September Massacres, as well as the execution of Louis XVI, caused the English to turn against French revolutionary ideals.

Ideas in Action

1. **Imagine you are living in late 18th-century France, in Paris or in one of the departments. Write a fictional letter to a relative living in the newly formed United States, summing up the events of the year 1792. When the year began, France was functioning as a constitutional monarchy; but by the end of the year, King Louis XVI had been condemned as a traitor by the National Convention. You still do not know whether or not he will be condemned to death. Write your letter either as a royalist, a Girondin, or a Jacobin.**

2. **Read the last will and testament written by King Louis XVI on Christmas Day 1792. (The document can be found on the Internet.) Discuss the character of the man who would have written such a statement.**

3. **Research the workhouses of England and discuss the pros and cons of such public housing for the poor.**

4. **List the good effects of work. Explain what keeps people from getting work.**

5. **Have students bring in poems or songs written in the 18th century about the conditions of the Industrial Revolution and the desire for a pristine natural world. Read the poems aloud and discuss them.**

Sample Quiz I (pages 123–134)

Please answer the following in complete sentences.

1. Which of the French political parties stood for individual freedom, limited suffrage, and the independence of local governments outside of Paris? (More than one answer possible.)

    a) Feuillants   c) Girondins

    b) Cordeliers   d) Jacobins

2. Which of the French political parties listed in question 1 stood for a highly centralized government and for offering the suffrage to every French male? (More than one answer possible.)

3. Which of the French political parties listed in question 1 called for the execution of King Louis XVI? (More than one answer possible.) Why did they want to have him executed?

4. When was Louis XVI executed? How was he executed?

5. What were the two houses of the British parliament called?

6. What was the English political party that favored the power of Parliament over the king and a very limited role for the king in the government?

7. What do we call a government by the few, particularly the wealthy, for the benefit of their class?

Answers to Sample Quiz I

Students' answers should approximate the following.

1. The Girondins (c) stood for individual freedom, limited suffrage, and the independence of local governments outside of Paris.

2. The Cordeliers (b) and Jacobins (d) stood for a highly centralized government and for offering the suffrage to every French male.

3. The Cordeliers (b) and Jacobins (d) called for the execution of King Louis XVI? They wanted the king executed because they thought he could be the focal point about which a counter-revolution could form; and, they said, he had committed treason.

4. Louis XVI was executed on *January 21, 1793,* by *guillotine.*

5. The two houses of the British parliament were called the *House of Commons* and the *House of Lords.*

6. The *Whigs* favored the power of Parliament over the king and a very limited role for the king in the government.

7. An *oligarchy* is a government by the few, particularly the wealthy, for the benefit of their class.

Sample Quiz II (pages 134–143)

Please answer the following in complete sentences.

1. **Please describe capitalism. In this system, do a few or many own wealth-controlling enterprises? Do a few or many control only their own labor?**

2. **What invention made it possible for people to build large factories in cities, away from waterways?**

3. **Give one example of the working conditions of laborers in 18th-century factories.**

4. **What do we call the Liberal economic idea that says the government should not try to control economic activity by regulating prices or wages or by any restriction whatsoever; each person should be allowed to follow his own personal interest in economic activity?**

5. **What do we call the conversion of strip fields into compact fields enclosed by fences that occurred in the 18th century?**

6. **Please identify the following:**

   a) **the "patriot king" of Great Britain**

   b) **an English Whig and member of Parliament who stood for the poor and oppressed and called for justice, religious tolerance, and the abolition of England's slave trade**

Answers to Sample Quiz II

Students' answers should approximate the following

1. Capitalism is an economic system in which *a few* own wealth-controlling enterprises, while *the many* control only their own labor.

2. The invention of the *steam engine* made it possible for people to build large factories in cities, away from waterways.

3. Possible answers:

   a) The workers labored in dismal conditions.

   b) They labored for typically 14 hours a day, 6 days a week.

   c) They earned very low wages.

   d) If they were injured, they would be fired without any means to support themselves.

   e) Factories employed women and children

4. *Laissez-faire* is the name for the Liberal economic idea that says the government should not try to control economic activity by regulating prices or wages or by any restriction whatsoever and each person should be allowed to follow his own personal interest in economic activity.

5. *Enclosure* is the name for the conversion of strip fields into compact fields enclosed by fences.

6. Please identify the following:

   a) *George III* was the "patriot king" of Great Britain.

   b) *Charles James Fox* was the English Whig and member of Parliament who stood for the poor and oppressed and called for justice, religious tolerance, and the abolition of England's slave trade

Essays (200–500 words each)

Instructions to be given to the students: Write in complete sentences. Underline your thesis. Give three supports or examples that explain why you think what you do and that support your thesis.

1. Describe how the economic revolutions affected English society. In particular, what effects did they have on the lives of the common people?

2. Give an account of the life of one political leader from this chapter that you think had the most effect on England.

Chapter Test

Please answer the following in complete sentences.

I. **Short Essay—Answer two of the following:**

1. **What were the differences between the Girondins and the Mountain? Which group favored the execution of Louis XVI, and why? Which group opposed the execution of Louis XVI, and why?**

2. **What is an oligarchy? Was the British government in the 18th century an oligarchy? Please explain.**

3. **Describe three ways the Industrial Revolution changed life in Great Britain in the 18th century.**

4. **What were enclosures? Why did the wealthy in England call for enclosures in the 18th century? What effect did enclosures have on rural people?**

II. **Short Answer:**

1. **When was Louis XVI executed? How was he executed?**

2. **Which house of Parliament, in theory at least, represented most people in Great Britain. Which house represented the aristocracy and the bishops of the Anglican Church?**

3. **Which party in the British government supported royal power, but not absolute monarchy, as well as the Established (Anglican) Church of England?**

4. **How does the British Constitution differ from such constitutions as the Constitution of 1791 and the United States Constitution?**

5. **What is a constitutional monarchy?**

6. **What is capitalism?**

7. **Please identify the following:**

   a) **The king of Great Britain who wanted to rule as a true king and so challenged Parliament by appointing Tory ministers when the Whigs were in the majority.**

   b) **The English Whig member of Parliament who hated the French Revolution and objected to the idea that people have natural rights. He said true rights come only through the religious and cultural traditions of the society in which one lives.**

   c) **The prime minister who led Great Britain into the war with France.**

Answer Key to Chapter Test

Students' answers should approximate the following:

I.

1. The Girondins stood for the Liberal ideals that had inspired the revolution—individual freedom, limited suffrage, and the independence of local governments outside of Paris. They thought liberty could be preserved only if the government was not highly centralized. The Mountain did not object to individual liberty, but they wanted a more democratic government, with the suffrage offered to every French male. They also favored a highly centralized government. The two groups also differed as to where they sat in the chambers of the National Convention. The Mountain sat on the left side of the chambers, while the Girondins sat on the right.

2. An oligarchy is a government by a few, particularly the wealthy, for the benefit of their class. The British government in the 18th century was just such a government because both houses of Parliament served the interests of the aristocracy and the wealthy middle class. The House of Lords most clearly did so. Though the House of Commons supposedly stood for the vast majority of British subjects, in reality it was controlled by the wealthy. Most British subjects did not have the right to vote, and those that did were easily influenced by the wealthy. In rural districts, local aristocrats could control elections either by buying votes or intimidating voters. They could also buy the right to represent towns that no longer existed (rotten boroughs). In these ways, aristocrats and the wealthy middle class came to control the House of Commons.

3. The Industrial Revolution led to great changes in how certain industries (such as textiles) operated. Possible answers:

   a) Large factories, powered by steam engines, replaced smaller manufacturers.

   b) These factories rose in cities, which increased dramatically in population.

   c) Because these factories were so expensive to build, factory owners had to rely on loans from banks. Banks, thus, grew in power and influence in Great Britain.

   d) The lot of workers worsened. They worked very long hours, six days a week, for very little pay.

   e) The factory system led to a great increase in the number of poor in Great Britain.

4. *Enclosures* were the conversion of strip fields into compact fields enclosed by fences. They also entailed the abolition of common lands. The wealthy in England called for enclosures because, in the 18th century, new techniques in cultivating crops ("scientific" agriculture) as well as the invention of new farm machines required, it was said, a different kind of farm field than the strip fields that were then in use. These developments of the "agricultural revolution" required more compact fields, protected by fences. The enclosures had devastating effects on the rural populations of Britain. Those who had no legal claim to lands—such as those who had only customary rights to use land—were turned off the land. They had either to work for often very low wages or move to the cities. Enclosures greatly decreased the number of people who lived in rural areas, and they destroyed rural communities.

II.

1. Louis XVI was executed on *January 21, 1793,* by the *guillotine.*

2. The *House of Commons* in Parliament, in theory at least, represented most people in Great Britain. The *House of Lords* represented

the aristocracy and the bishops of the Anglican Church?

3. The *Tories* supported royal power, but not absolute monarchy, as well as the Established (Anglican) Church of England.

4. The British Constitution differs from such constitutions as the Constitution of 1791 and the United States Constitution because it is *mostly unwritten*.

5. A constitutional monarchy is a form of government where the head of government is a king or monarch whose powers are limited by a constitution.

6. Capitalism is the large-scale organization of business where those who possess a store of wealth or *capital* hire laborers to engage in activities that increase wealth. In capitalism, a few own and control wealth-producing enterprises, while the vast majority of the people engaged in those enterprises (the workingmen) control only their labor, which they sell to the capitalists for a wage.

7. Please identify the following:

    a) *George III* was the king of Great Britain who wanted to rule as a true king and so challenged Parliament by appointing Tory ministers when the Whigs were in the majority.

    b) *Edmund Burke* was the English Whig member of Parliament who hated the French Revolution and objected to the idea that people have natural rights.

    c) William Pitt was the prime minister who led Great Britain into the war with France.

CHAPTER 6

The Rise and Fall of Jacobin France

Chapter Overview

- The French National Convention was divided between the party of the right, the Girondins, and the party of the left, the Jacobins. The Girondins had their base of power in the provinces, while the Jacobins had the support of radicals in Paris. Rivalry between the parties brought unrest to Paris.

- Faced with foreign invasion, counterrevolutionary rebellion in France, and the struggle between the Girondins and the Jacobins in Paris, the French Revolution seemed doomed to defeat. To save the revolution, Georges Danton convinced the Convention to establish a Revolutionary Tribunal with the authority to try and convict anyone suspected of conspiring against the revolution, as well as a Committee of Public Safety, which would have the power of a dictator over France.

- Angry over attacks against the Catholic Church and the French government's conscription law, the peasants of La Vendée in western France rose up against the revolutionary regime. At first, the Vendeans won several victories over republican forces.

- Girondin attacks on the radicals in Paris led finally to their downfall. On June 2, 1793, Jacobins forced the National Convention to arrest Girondin leaders. The Jacobins thus came to control the Convention.

- Under Jacobin control, the National Convention approved the democratic Constitution of 1793. The Convention, however, voted to suspend it for the time being. The constitution never went into effect.

- During the summer of 1793, the Convention voted more powers to the Committee of Public Safety, which had fallen under the influence of Maximilien Robespierre. The Committee commenced the Reign of Terror, which claimed Queen Marie Antoinette and the Girondin leaders as victims. The Terror spread from Paris to all of France.

- Following a plan suggested by Napoleone Buonaparte, revolutionary troops took the royalist stronghold of Toulon on December 19, 1793.

- By December 1793, revolutionary forces had destroyed Vendean insurgent forces. The revolutionary tribunal in the Vendée executed thousands.

- Under the Jacobins, the French government's persecution of the Catholic Church intensified. The persecution included both nonjuror and constitutional clergy. In November 1793, the Paris commune turned Paris's Notre Dame Cathedral into the Temple of Reason and placed a shrine to the Goddess of Reason in the sanctuary.

- Beginning in November 1793, Danton worked to end the extreme measures of the Reign of Terror. Robespierre, however, turned against Danton as well as the atheist extremists. Under Robespierre's leadership, the Committee of Public Safety ordered the arrest and execution of Danton and his allies, as well as the leaders of the atheists.

- Under the generalship of Lazare Carnot, French revolutionary armies began to score victories against the forces of the coalition of Great Britain, Austria, Spain, and Piedmont-Sardinia. In July, French revolutionary armies began their invasion of Holland.

- Under Robespierre's dictatorship, the Reign of Terror grew more violent, claiming thousands of victims. The Festival of the Supreme Being on June 8, 1794, marked the pinnacle of Robespierre's power.

- Tired of the Terror, the National Convention on July 27, 1794, condemned Robespierre and his allies on the Committee of Public Safety to death. The more conservative Thermidorians then seized control of the Convention.

- Two uprisings in the spring of 1795 threatened the Thermidorian-controlled Convention, but both were put down. The Convention's approval of the Constitution of the Year III stirred up a new insurrection, which was put down by government forces under Napoleone Buonaparte on October 5, 1795.

Chapter Goals

This chapter continues the story of the French Revolution. It tells how the revolution developed from its more moderately Liberal beginnings to become a virulently radical movement that used the totalitarian tools of violence and terror to achieve its ends. It shows how the wrong means (such as Danton's institution of the Committee of Public Safety), even if undertaken for what their authors think the most noble reasons, can easily escape from their control and become monstrous instruments of injustice. A movement inspired by false principles in its beginnings can easily fall into the most egregious evils in its consummation.

The chapter illustrates how even men with whom we might disagree can display a nobility of spirit. This is true of Danton, the Girondins, and even Robespierre. Such object lessons can help students learn that human beings are complex and that false ideas do not entirely destroy human dignity—and that noble traits of character do not necessarily indicate the truth of one's ideals.

Students can learn, furthermore, how our Catholic forebears bravely stood up for the Church and the Faith in times of great duress. Though the acts of individual Catholics cannot always escape censure, their willingness to fight and die for Christ should inspire us with the desire to do the same in our own time and context.

Finally, the chapter demonstrates a common characteristic of revolution—how it can shift from the moderate, to the radical, and then to reaction. The next chapter will show how a movement for freedom and democracy easily fell at last into dictatorship.

Period Music

Please consult the list of composers in Chapter 2 of this teacher's manual.

Key Terms at a Glance

sans-culottes: members of Paris's poor working class. The word literally means "those without knee breeches," because their trousers legs were long, not cut off at the knee like those worn by the bourgeoisie.

pantheist: one who believes the universe and all of nature is God (from the Greek words *pan*, meaning "all," and *theos*, meaning "God")

Committee of Public Safety: a committee established by the French National Convention in April 1793. The Committee had nine members (later 12) who could meet in secret and had complete control over the armies and the courts. What the Committee decided was final, and no one (not even the Convention) could question it or overturn its decisions.

Revolutionary Tribunal: a court established by the French National Convention. The Revolutionary Tribunal tried and convicted anyone suspected of conspiring against the revolution. The tribunal's decisions were final.

Constitution of 1793: a constitution approved by the French National Convention in 1793 but never put into effect. The Constitution of 1793 may be the most democratic constitution ever written. It allowed the majority of citizens to vote. It gave the departments of France the power to accept or reject measures proposed by the one-house National Assembly.

Reign of Terror: a great purge of anyone who was accused of being an enemy of the French Revolution. The Reign of Terror began with the formation of the Committee of Public Safety and increased its violence until the execution of Maximilien Robespierre in the summer of 1794.

The Directory: the government of France formed by the Constitution of the Year III (1795). The government was called the Directory because its executive authority was held by five men, called directors. The directors were chosen by the legislature, which was composed of two houses: the Council of 500 and the Council of Ancients.

What Students Should Know

1. **Why the Jacobins and other radical revolutionary groups objected to the Girondins**

   As we saw in the last chapter, the Jacobins and Girondins had very different goals for the revolution. Other extremists, such as the *Enragés* and the *sans-culottes*, were growing more and more restless because the government's money was becoming increasingly worthless, and the price of food, fuel, and clothing was increasing. These extremists denounced the bourgeois merchants for growing rich off the sufferings of the people and called on the Convention to force merchants to sell their hoarded goods at prices the common workman could afford. The Girondins, however, opposed such measures because they violated *laissez-faire* theories of economics.

2. **Who instituted the Revolutionary Tribunal and the Committee of Public Safety and why. The character of the Revolutionary Tribunal and the Committee of Public Safety**

   Georges Danton called on the National Convention to institute the Revolutionary Tribunal and the Committee of Public Safety because he thought the government had to have a way to exercise dictatorial power over all of France. Faced with the threat of invasion by the European powers, by traitors such as Dumouriez, and by opposition to the revolution within France herself, Danton thought such a power was necessary if the revolution were not to fail. The Revolutionary Tribunal was a court with the authority to try and convict anyone suspected of conspiring against the revolution. The Committee, established on April 4, 1793, had nine members (later 12) who could meet in secret and would have complete control over the armies and the courts. What the Committee decided would be final, and no one (not even the Convention) could question its decisions.

3. **Where the Vendée is; why the peasants there revolted against the revolutionary government, for whom and what they fought**

The Vendée is a region and department in western France, just south of the Loire River. It was a region that had not benefited much from the revolution; it was strongly Catholic and had a culture reminiscent of the Middle Ages. The Vendean peasants objected strongly to the government's policies toward the Catholic Church; but it was the government's conscription law that lit the spark that set off the rebellion in March 1793. The army formed from the peasant insurgents, the Royal and Catholic Army (first called the Grand Catholic Army), fought for the restoration of the throne of France; yet, even so, it was not for the Bourbon king it primarily fought but for religion. Though they wore the white cockade (the symbol of the *Bourbons*) into battle, the insurgents' bore another insignia—the Sacred Heart of Jesus, surmounted by a cross.

4. **How the Jacobins came to control the National Convention**

To overcome their extremist opponents, the Girondins in the Convention carried out arrests of extremist leaders and established a Committee of Twelve to investigate conspiracy against the government. Such measures led to their downfall. With the Paris mobs supporting them, the Jacobins forced the National Convention to arrest Girondin leaders on June 2, 1793. In this way the Jacobins came to dominate the government.

5. **How France and the revolution changed under Jacobin rule**

Under Jacobin control, the National Convention approved the democratic Constitution of 1793. The Convention, however, voted to suspend it for the time being, and it never went into effect. During the summer of 1793, the Convention voted more powers to the Committee of Public Safety, which had fallen under the influence of Maximilien Robespierre and his close associate, Antoine de Saint-Just. A Committee member, Lazare Carnot, organized the revolutionary armed forces and materiél so that it could more effectively meet the threat of foreign invasion and Girondin and royalist uprisings in France. The Convention instituted a draft and organized all of French society to support the war effort, making France a nation in arms.

6. **What the Terror was, who was behind it, and who its victims were**

The Terror refers to the measures taken by the Committee of Public Safety to stamp out all opposition to the revolution in France. It was instituted by the Law of Suspects, which gave the Committee the authority to arrest anyone suspected of being a counterrevolutionary. No evidence was needed to prove a person's guilt; a simple accusation would be enough to imprison someone. The Revolutionary Tribunal then tried the accused and engineered their condemnation and execution. The accused could not defend themselves.

Prisons filled with those suspected of treason. By August 1793, thousands would be executed.

Danton, among others, wanted the Terror used only against those who threatened France with invasion or civil war. Yet, under the control of Robespierre, the Committee used the Terror to bring about Robespierre's dream of a republic of liberty, equality, fraternity, and perfect virtue. Robespierre was profoundly inspired by Rousseau's ideas of liberty and the state. It was because Robespierre could not tolerate anyone who disagreed with his goals for France that the Terror became ever harsher and more bloody.

7. How the Jacobin government attacked religion

Because, for the revolutionaries, the state was the highest authority in the land and the source of all good things to its citizens, the revolutionary government took over functions that had belonged to the Church. These included giving aid to the poor, running schools, and registering marriages. Finally, the government permitted divorce.

Though, at first, the government's anti-Catholic laws were against nonjuror priests, it began to take measures against the Constitutional Church, forcing its priests to bless marriages of couples, one of whose members was divorced or unbaptized. Priests who refused could be banished. In Paris, the commune, under the influence of atheists and pantheists, made Notre Dame cathedral into a "Temple of Reason" and placed a shrine to the Goddess of Reason in the sanctuary. On November 10, 1793, a popular singer was enthroned as the goddess in the cathedral sanctuary. Later in the month, the commune seized all churches in Paris and forbade all Catholic worship in them.

8. What Maximilien Robespierre thought about religion

Though he was not a Christian, Robespierre was a strong believer in God—the Deist God. He thought it was necessary for people to believe in an afterlife where the virtuous would be rewarded and the bad punished. He thought the idea of a Being that watches over the innocent and punishes crime is wholly democratic. It was for this that he opposed the atheists and pantheists and, together with Danton, rose up against those who were seeking to destroy religion. It was Robespierre's devotion to religion that led to the Festival of the Supreme Being on June 8, 1794—a religious rite to express France's belief in the God of Nature and the immortality of the soul.

9. How Robespierre gained supreme power and how he fell

At first, Robespierre and Danton were allies in their struggle against the atheists and pantheists; but then it became clear to Robespierre that Danton was seeking to end the extreme measures of the Committee of Public Safety. Robespierre thus had Danton and his supporters executed, along with other political enemies. In the weeks following the Festival of the Supreme Being, it was Robespierre's increasingly bloody policies—his attempts to purify the republic—that finally turned even the Mountain against him. Tired of the Terror, the National Convention on July 17, 1794 condemned Robespierre and his allies to death. Thus ended the period of Jacobin ascendancy in France.

10. What followed the fall of Robespierre and the Jacobins

The Thermidoreans, who came to power after Robespierre's death, set about dismantling the Terror, though they used its methods against their enemies. The men who took power, however, were not extremists like Robespierre (who supported the interests of the poor) but those who favored the bourgeoisie. They removed laws forcing merchants to sell their goods at set prices. Hunger and poverty inspired the *sans-culottes* to rise against the new government, but they were put down. It was the Thermidoreans who established the Constitution of the Year III, the Directory, made up of executives called directors and a two-house National Assembly. A rebellion by the sections of Paris on 13th Vendémiaire (October 5) 1795 would have toppled the government had not Napoleone Buonaparte placed artillery around the Tuileries to protect the Assembly.

11. **How royalists (legitimists) differ from supporters of constitutional monarchy**

Both royalist and constitutional monarchists are supporters of government by a king. Royalists, however, think the monarch should be the supreme lawmaker and executive authority and think he has to come from a traditional kingly line, such as the Bourbons. Constitutional monarchists do not necessarily insist on this. They favor a king as the executive authority in government but want a parliament to make the laws.

12. **Identify the following:**

Jacques Cathelineau: a leader of the Vendean "Royal and Catholic Army"; called the Saint of Anjou

Jacques Hébert: a Jacobin and leader of the *Enragés*. A radical atheist, Hébert stirred up the *sans-culottes* against the National Convention.

Jean-Paul Marat: a Jacobin who called for the destruction of the Girondins. He was stabbed to death in his bathtub by the Girondin, Charlotte Corday.

Lazare Carnot: the organizer of the French revolutionary army that achieved multiple military victories against the allies in the spring of 1794

Napoleone Buonaparte: a Corsican who became an officer of artillery in the French army and later a general. A brilliant military tactician, Buonaparte came up with the strategy that forced the British fleet to evacuate Toulon harbor. He led the forces that saved the National Convention from being overthrown by the National Guard and the Paris sections.

Questions for Review

1. **Who were the *sans-culottes*? What does their name mean?**

The *sans-culottes* were those who belonged to Paris's working class. The name means "those without knee breeches."

2. **What were the *Enragés*? Were they the allies of the Jacobins? Please explain.**

The *Enragés* were extremist enemies of the Girondins, who provoked riots in Paris.

3. **What three words expressed the ideals of the French Revolution?**

The three words that express the ideals of the French Revolution were *liberty, equality,* and *fraternity.*

4. **Why did Danton want the National Convention to establish the Committee of Public Safety? What kind of powers did it have?**

Danton called on the National Convention to institute the Committee of Public Safety because he thought the government had to have an arm that could exercise dictatorial power over all of France. Faced with the threat of invasion by the European powers, by traitors such as Dumouriez, and by opposition to the revolution with France herself, Danton thought such a power was necessary if the revolution were not to fail. The Committee could meet in secret and would have complete control over the armies and the courts. Whatever the Committee decided would be final, and no one (not even the Convention) could question its decisions.

5. **Why did the peasants of the Vendée rise up against the French Revolution?**

The Vendean peasants objected to the revolutionary government's acts against the Catholic Church in France. The spark that set off their rebellion, though, was the conscription law passed by the National Convention.

6. **What did Robespierre want to accomplish by using terror?**

Using terror, Robespierre thought he could rid France of those who would stand in the way of his attempts to establish a republic of liberty, equality, fraternity, and perfect virtue.

7. **What was the Festival of the Supreme Being?**

The Festival of the Supreme Being was a religious festival Robespierre instituted to express France's belief in the God of Nature and the immortality of the soul.

8. **What part did Napoleone Buonaparte play in the military events of the French Revolution?**

Napoleon came up with the plan by which revolutionary troops were able to take the royalist stronghold of Toulon by driving out the British fleet on December 19, 1793. On October 5, 1795, he saved the revolutionary government from insurrection and saved the Constitution of the Year III.

Ideas in Action

1. Read one or more of the volumes of the *Horatio Hornblower* series by C. S. Forester. The books are set at the time of the French Revolution and the war with England.

2. Learn to sing the anthem of the Vendean Royal and Catholic Army, "La Marseillaise Blanc," either in French or English. (The words in both English and French are in "Highways and Byways" section of *Light to the Nations II.* The anthem has the same melody as "La Marseillaise," which can be found on the Internet.) Based on "La Marseillaise Blanc," discuss what kind of society the Vendean counterrevolutionaries were fighting for.

The following verses give some idea for what the Vendeans were fighting:

> *Who come . . . /To take our daughters and our wives.*—the safety and protection of their families

> *. . .Who would make the law in our homes*—the integrity of the family home, free from government intrusion

> *. . .Who would settle in the house/Of our adorable Jesus*—the freedom and honor of the Church and of the Sacraments

3. Define the ideals of the French Revolution, and discuss the kind of society that the revolutionaries desired. Did they end up achieving such a society?

4. Write a fictional diary of a person, any person, living in Paris at the time of Jacobin control.

5. Read Charles Dickens's *A Tale of Two Cities,* and discuss the choices of the characters portrayed in that novel.

6. Build ship models of the warships of this period. (Kits are available in hobby and craft stores.)

Sample Quiz I (pages 147–160)

Please answer the following in complete sentences.

1. Who convinced the National Convention to establish a court with the authority to try and convict anyone suspected of conspiring against the revolution? What was the name of this court?

2. Why were the peasants of the Vendée angry with the French revolutionary government?

3. Name another group in France that was trying to overthrow the Jacobin revolutionary government.

4. How were the Jacobins able to seize control of the National Assembly?

5. Who was the man who wanted to use the Terror to establish a republic of liberty, equality, fraternity, and perfect virtue in France?

6. What did atheistic and pantheistic revolutionaries set up in Notre Dame cathedral in Paris?

7. Which of the following had the task of organizing the republic's armed forces materiél?

   a) Antoine
   de Saint-Just

   b) Jacques Hébert

   c) Jacques
   Cathelineau

   d) Lazare Carnot

Answers to Sample Quiz I

Students' answers should approximate the following.

1. *Georges Danton* convinced the National Convention to establish a court with the authority to try and convict anyone suspected of conspiring against the revolution. The name of this court was the *Revolutionary Tribunal*.

2. The peasants of the Vendée were angry with the French revolutionary government because (one of the following):

   a) the government was attacking their religion

   b) the government was forcing them to join the military

3. Groups trying to overthrow the Jacobin revolutionary government were *royalists* (a) and the *Girondins* (b).

4. The Jacobins were able to seize control of the National Assembly by forcing it to arrest Girondin leaders.

5. *Maximilien Robespierre* was the man who wanted to use the Terror to establish a republic of liberty, equality, fraternity, and perfect virtue in France?

6. Atheistic and pantheistic revolutionaries set up a *Temple of Reason* in Notre Dame cathedral in Paris.

7. *Lazare Carnot* (d) had the task of organizing the republic's armed forces materiél?

Sample Quiz II (pages 160–171)

Please answer the following in complete sentences.

1. What two religious ideas did Robespierre think it was necessary for people believe?

2. Why did Robespierre finally turn against Danton? What happened to Danton?

3. What is the name of the event Robespierre held on June 8, 1794 to express France's belief in the God of Nature and the immortality of the soul?

4. What is the name for the government set up by the Constitution of the Year III?

5. Who saved the French revolutionary government on 13th *Vendemiare* with a "whiff of grapeshot"?

6. What do we call those who think the head of government, or the executive, should come from a traditional kingly line, such as the Bourbons?

Answers to Sample Quiz II

Students' answers should approximate the following

1. Robespierre thought it was necessary people believe in *God's existence* and the *immortality of the soul.*

2. Robespierre turned against Danton because he was trying to stop the extreme measures of the Terror. Danton was executed by the guillotine.

3. The *Festival of the Supreme Being* was the event Robespierre held on June 8, 1794, to express France's belief in the God of Nature and the immortality of the soul.

4. The name for the government set up by the Constitution of the Year III is the *Directory*

5. *Napoleone Buonaparte* saved the French revolutionary government on *13th Vendémiare* with a "whiff of grapeshot."

6. *Royalists* is the name for those who think the head of government, or the executive, should come from a traditional kingly line, such as the Bourbons.

Essays (200–500 words each)

Instructions to be given to the students: Write in complete sentences. Underline your thesis. Give three supports or examples that explain why you think what you do and that support your thesis.

1. Compare the ideas of the Jacobins and the Girondins. How did they think alike? How did they differ? Which party best represented the French revolutionary ideas of liberty, equality, and fraternity?

2. Why do you think Deism was a more attractive religious idea for the French revolutionaries than the Catholic Faith? Is the Catholic Faith necessarily opposed to the ideas of liberty, equality, and fraternity?

Chapter Test

Please answer the following in complete sentences.

I. **Short Essay—Answer one of the following:**

1. Why did the peasants of the Vendée revolt against the French revolutionary government? What cause or causes did the Vendeans fight for? What was the most important cause for them?

2. Why did Danton call for the establishment of the Committee of Public Safety? What powers did it have? How did Danton's ideas about how to use the Committee and the Terror differ from Robespierre's? Why did Robespierre use the Committee and carry on the Terror as he did?

II. **Short Answer:**

1. Which French revolutionary group or groups thought merchants in Paris should be allowed to charge whatever price they wanted on their goods, even if they were selling food to hungry people? (More than one answer possible.)

   a) Feuillants   d) Girondins

   b) Cordeliers   e) Jacobins

   c) *Enragés*   f) *sans-culottes*

2. Which French revolutionary group or groups listed in question 1 were growing increasingly restless because the price of food, fuel, and clothing was increasing? (More than one answer possible.)

3. Why did Robespierre want to destroy atheists and pantheists?

4. Why did Robespierre turn against Danton and bring about his death?

5. How did Napoleone Buonaparte help the revolution?

6. Please identify

   a) Charlotte Corday

   b) Jacques Cathelineau

   c) The organizer of the French revolutionary army that achieved multiple military victories against the allies in the spring of 1794

   d) Robespierre's close associate on the Committee of Public Safety; a radical who wanted to establish a republic based on the ideas of Rousseau

Answer Key to the Chapter Test

Students' answers should approximate the following:

I.

1. The peasants of the Vendée revolted against the French revolutionary government for two reasons. Firstly, because of the government's attacks on the Catholic Church. The Vendeans were devout Catholics who opposed the Constitutional Church and supported the nonjuror priests. The second reason the Vendeans revolted against the government was on account of its conscription law; for, compulsory military service was against peasant traditions.

   The Vendeans fought for the restoration of the king and his government over France; but, more importantly, they fought for their religion. This seemed the most important cause for them; for though they wore the white cockade, their most important symbols were religious; and they marched into battle singing a religious hymn rather than an anthem in honor of the king. Too, when the French revolutionary government at last gave into their religious demands and granted them immunity from conscription, the Vendeans laid down their arms—despite the fact that the king's government had not been restored.

2. Danton called for the establishment of the Committee of Public Safety as a means to protect France from the threat of invasion from without and anti-government intrigues and rebellions from within. The Committee had the powers of a dictator. It could meet in secret and had complete control over the armies and the courts. What the Committee decided would be final, and no one (not even the Convention) could question its decisions.

   While Danton saw the Committee and the Terror as instruments to be used only against anyone who opposed the revolution, Robespierre saw it as means to rid France of anyone who opposed his ideal of the perfect republic—a republic based on the ideals of liberty, equality, fraternity, and perfect virtue. He thus did not use the Terror only against those who directly threatened the republic, but against anyone who disagreed with him.

II.

1. The Girondins (d) thought merchants in Paris should be allowed to charge whatever price they wanted for their goods, even if they were selling food to hungry people.

2. The *Enragés* (c) and the *sans-culottes* (f) were growing increasingly restless because the price of food, fuel, and clothing was increasing.

3. Robespierre wanted to destroy atheists and pantheists because he thought a belief in God and in an afterlife where the good are rewarded and the evil punished was a necessity for people in a republic.

4. Robespierre turned against Danton because Danton was seeking to end the extreme measures of the Committee of Public Safety, which Robespierre promoted

5. Buonaparte helped the revolution by coming up with the strategy that forced the British fleet to evacuate Toulon harbor. He led the forces that saved the National Convention from being overthrown by the National Guard and the Paris sections.

6. Please identify

   a) Charlotte Corday was the Girondin woman who assassinated Marat.

   b) Jacques Cathelineau was the leader of the Vendean army. He was known as the Saint of Anjou.

   c) *Lazare Carnot* was the organizer of the French revolutionary army that achieved multiple military victories against the allies in the spring of 1794.

   d) Antoine de Saint-Just was Robespierre's close associate on the Committee of Public Safety and a radical who wanted to establish a republic based on the ideas of Rousseau.

CHAPTER 7: The Triumph of the Little Corporal

Chapter Overview

- In the spring of 1796, Napoleon Bonaparte led the Army of Italy into northern Italy. By the end of April, Bonaparte had conquered Piedmont. In May, he forced the Austrians to flee and then captured Milan. On June 19, Napoleon signed an armistice with Pope Pius VI.

- From July 1796 to February 1797, Napoleon's armies defeated the Austrians in several battles. On February 2, 1797, the Austrian army surrendered to Napoleon. On February 19, Napoleon signed a treaty with Pius VI, forcing the pope to give up the Romagna to France. A year later, French General Louis-Alexandre Berthier, under orders from the French Directory, conquered Rome and forced the pope to go into exile.

- In April 1798, the Austrians signed a peace treaty with France. Napoleon returned to Paris, where he decided to lead an invasion of Egypt. In Egypt, Napoleon defeated the Egyptian army, seized Cairo, and invaded Palestine. Unable to conquer Palestine, Napoleon withdrew into Egypt, where he abandoned his men and secretly returned to France.

- While Napoleon was in Egypt, a new coalition of nations declared war on France and retook much of what Napoleon had conquered in Italy. These defeats were among the reasons the French became dissatisfied with the Directory. Joining in a plot against the government, Napoleon overthrew the Directory on November 10, 1799, and established a new government called the Consulate—basically the dictatorship of Napoleon Bonaparte.

- On March 14, 1800, the College of Cardinals elected Pope Pius VII in Venice. On July 3, 1800, Pius entered Rome and took up the government of the Papal States.

- As First Consul, Napoleon brought peace to the Vendée. In June 1800, he defeated the Austrians at Marengo in Piedmont, recapturing all of Lombardy for France. In February 1801, the Austrians signed the Treaty of Luneville with France, ending the war on the continent. Only Great Britain now was at war with France.

- Following the end of the continental war, Napoleon made legal and economic reforms in France.

- In 1802, France and Great Britain made peace in the Treaty of Amiens. Peace between the nations, however, ended in May 1803. Even before that date, Napoleon was planning an invasion of England.

- Seeking peace with the Catholic Church, Napoleon signed a concordat with Pope Pius VII in the summer of 1801.

- Hoping to make his reforms in France permanent, Napoleon convinced the French Senate to proclaim him First Consul for Life in August 1802.

- In May 1804, the Senate of France proclaimed Napoleon emperor of France. Fearing that this alone would not give him legitimacy, Napoleon asked the pope to come to Paris to crown him emperor. Pius VII hesitated, but in the end he agreed. On December 2, 1804, Pius VII was present at Napoleon's imperial coronation in Notre Dame cathedral in Paris. After Pius anointed Napoleon, Napoleon took the imperial crown and placed it on his own head.

Chapter Goals

The character of Napoleon Bonaparte perhaps does not play as prominent a role as it should in our understanding of the development of the modern world. This is, in part, because the 20th century presented us with examples of tyrants against whose deeds the "tyrannies" of Napoleon pale by comparison. Yet, Napoleon loomed large in the imagination of the 19th century. For some he was a tyrant, the "Corsican gravedigger"; for others, he was a savior, a champion of justice. But whatever they thought of him, no one in the 19th century thought Napoleon insignificant. And Napoleon was not insignificant, for it was he who took the French Revolution and stabilized it. It was Napoleon who imbedded the revolutionary ideals in the laws and hearts of Europe. His empire might have been short-lived, but its effects have been far reaching. They influence our world today.

Thus, we present the story of Napoleon in the detail we do here, not because it makes a good tale—or, *not just* because it makes a good tale—but because his career is one of the great turning points in the history of Christendom, Europe, and, indeed, the world.

Period Music

- Ludwig van Beethoven, Symphony No. 3 in B Flat Major, *Eroica* (Op. 55). Beethoven, who wrote this symphony in 1804, originally dedicated it to Napoleon. The title, *Eroica*, is Italian for "heroic."

- *Coronation Music for Napoleon I.* Performed by the soloists, chorus, and orchestra of the Capella, Saint Petersbourg (CD).

- *La Harpe au Temps de l'Impératrice Joséphine.* Catherine Michel, harp. Produced by the Fondation Napoléon, Malmaison, and La Maison de Chateaubriand.

What Students Should Know

1. **Where Napoleon came from and how he came to France**

   Napoleon was born on the island of Corsica on August 15, 1769. Though Corsica was basically Italian, it had become a French territory. At age 10, Napoleon's father sent him to a military academy in France. Napoleon first served in the royal army as an artillery officer and then in the revolutionary army.

2. **How Napoleon Bonaparte became the hero of France and the French republic**

   Napoleon became the hero of France and the French republic by his invasion of Italy in 1796 and his victories over the Piedmontese and Austrians. The victory that especially gave him the reputation of a hero was the Battle of Lodi on May 7, 1796.

3. **The differences between how the French government and Napoleon treated Pope Pius VI**

   The French Directory was intent on destroying the Catholic Church. It wanted not only to overthrow the Church's temporal power (the Papal States) but the institution of the Church

Key Terms at a Glance

Piedmont: a region of northwestern Italy. In the late 18th century, it formed part of the combined Kingdom of Sardinia-Piedmont under King Vittorio Amedeo III.

civil ceremony: in the case of marriage, the contracting of a marriage before an officer of the civil government, such as a justice of the peace; a non-sacramental marriage

armistice: a temporary ceasing of hostilities on the agreement of both sides in a conflict

cede: to yield or grant something, such as land, usually by treaty; to transfer

coup d'état: a sudden, violent overthrow of a government

Constitution of the Year VIII: the French republican government, also called the Consulate, formed on December 15, 1799. The Constitution of the Year VIII established a government of three executives, each having the title of consul

and together holding all power in France. Along with the consuls, the constitution established a three-house legislature—an 80-member Senate, a 100-member Tribunate, and a 300-member Legislative Body.

Code Napoléon: Napoleon's reform of the law of France that became law on March 5, 1803

concordat: a treaty or agreement between two powers about how they should deal with each other politically. In August 1801, Napoleon, the First Consul of France, signed a concordat with Pope Pius VII's secretary of state. It was issued in April 1802.

tribunate: the office of a tribune, originally an official of the ancient Roman Republic whose task was to stand for the common people against the power of the patricians (aristocracy)

plebiscite: a vote by which the people of a country voice their approval of or opposition to a measure carried out by the government

---

itself. In France, the directors had been persecuting nonjuror priests and had worked to weaken the Constitutional Church.

Napoleon, however, would not carry out the Directory's plans against the Church. In an armistice and, later, in the Treaty of Tolentino (February 19, 1797), the pope had to abandon rich lands belonging to the Papal States to France and pay a large sum of money to the Directory government. Napoleon, however, allowed the pope to keep his temporal power.

4. What happened to Pope Pius VI

Elections in the spring of 1797 seemed to guarantee a new French government that would be more friendly to the Church; but in September 1797, a *coup d'état* established revolutionary control over the government. This new government struck out against the Church in France. In late 1797, it used the killing of a French general in Rome (though he had joined a riot against governmental troops) as a pretext to march on Rome. On February 13, 1798, the French general Louis-Alexandre Berthier entered Rome and took Pius VI prisoner. When the pope refused to give up his temporal power (because, he said, it had come from God), Berthier declared the pope deposed, proclaimed Rome a republic, and banished Pius. Over the next year and a half, Pope Pius was taken to various cities. He died in exile in Valence on August 29, 1799.

5. **The course of events that led to Napoleon's dictatorship**

   a) Napoleon continued the war against Austria in northeastern Italy. He compelled Austria to sign the Peace of Leoben on April 18, 1797.

   b) Napoleon returned to Paris.

   c) Napoleon set out for the conquest of Egypt, May 1798, in order to conquer it and cut off Great Britain's communications with India.

   d) After a little over a year in Egypt, Napoleon returned secretly to France.

   e) Under the Directory, France had been losing everything she had won in previous years, especially by Napoleon. Many thought the government was leading France into ruin.

   f) Napoleon returned to France. He conspired with others to overthrow the government.

   g) With his co-conspirators, Napoleon forced the French National Assembly to disband on the "19th Brumaire" (November 10, 1799).

   h) Napoleon and his co-conspirators established the Consulate with Napoleon as First Consul—effectively the dictator of France.

6. **Who became pope after Pius VI**

   Pius VII was elected pope and crowned on March 21, 1800, in Venice.

7. **What reforms Napoleon brought to France**

   a) He solved the bankruptcy crisis that had brought on the French Revolution in 1789.

   b) He changed the way taxes were collected; common people paid fewer taxes than ever before.

   c) He rewrote the laws that governed France. His collection of laws was called the *Code Napoléon.*

   d) He tried to make France more self-sufficient in food.

   e) He instituted public works—new canals, new roads, new markets.

8. **Napoleon's relations with the Church**

   Napoleon in many ways favored the Catholic Church. He did so to reconcile believers with his government—and he saw that the Directory's religious policies had led in part to its downfall. Seeking to end the schism between the Constitutional Church and Rome, Napoleon signed a concordat with Pope Pius VII in the summer of 1801. The concordat did not restore the Catholic Church as the sole religion of France, and it gave the government some control over the Church; but otherwise, it reestablished papal authority over the French Church. Napoleon showed great friendliness toward the Church for a time. Though he suppressed some religious congregations, he permitted the restoration of several female religious associations that worked in schools and hospitals. He placed government schools under the direction of Catholic clergy.

9. **Why Napoleon wanted to become, first, First Consul for life and, then, emperor**

   Napoleon's term as First Consul was limited and, thus, he was worried that if he did not remain in power, all his reforms in France would come to nothing. He later came to the conclusion that the title of First Consul, even for life, would not give him legitimacy. Thus, he won from the Senate the title of emperor; and to make this title look legitimate, he asked the pope to crown him emperor. The Senate gave Napoleon the imperial title, not that of king, for the latter was distasteful to many in France because of its association with the ancient regime.

10. **How the imperial coronation of Napoleon did not go according to the pope's wishes**

Pius VII was hesitant to crown Napoleon but agreed only if he himself would perform the crowning as well as the anointing. (The crowning signified the superiority of the spiritual over the temporal power.) But at Napoleon's coronation on December 2, 1804, Napoleon took the crown and placed it on his own head.

11. **What the imperial coronation signified for Napoleon**

The title of emperor evoked memories of the ancient Roman Empire which, for centuries, had been the political ideal for all Europe. As emperor, Napoleon began to see himself as the new Charlemagne; and like Charlemagne, he was determined to restore the might and glory of the ancient Roman Empire.

12. **Identify the following:**

Josephine Beauharnais: Napoleon's wife and the first empress of France

Cardinal Ercole Consalvi: president of the conclave that elected Pope Pius VII and that pope's first secretary of state

Questions for Review

1. **What is the importance of the Battle of Lodi?**

It was at Lodi that Napoleon first understood his own military genius. He gained the full confidence of his men. Lodi gave birth to the legend of the invincible Napoleon.

2. **Why did Napoleon not destroy and suppress the Catholic Church when he had control of northern Italy?**

Though he objected to the Church's power in society, he thought she would make a good tool for the government. Thus, he did not destroy the Church.

3. **Who signed the peace treaty at Tolentino? What did the treaty do?**

The treaty was signed by Pope Pius VI and Napoleon Bonaparte. In the treaty, the pope had to give up the rich Romagna to France, disband his army, and pay France a vast sum of money. The treaty, however, did not demand that the pope take back his condemnation of the French republic's measures against religion, nor was he forced to abandon his temporal power.

4. **How did the Directory treat the Catholic Church in France? How did their treatment of the Church differ from Napoleon's, when he took control of the government?**

The Directory intensified the persecution of nonjuror priests and tried to weaken the Constitutional Church. The directors forbade public religious gatherings and even the ringing of bells for religious services. They wanted to destroy the Catholic Church. Napoleon, on the other hand, tried to court the favor of the Church and gave it many benefits. Instead of persecuting nonjuror priests, he restored the Constitutional Church to the bosom of the Catholic Church by signing a concordat with the pope.

5. **Why did Napoleon seem invincible after the Battle of Marengo?**

Napoleon seemed invincible after Marengo because it looked as if he were heading for certain defeat. Then, at the last minute, reinforcements arrived, allowing the army to turn the tide of battle.

6. Why did Napoleon plan to invade England?

Napoleon planned to invade England because he said the British government had reneged on what it had agreed to in the Treaty of Amiens. He complained that the government of George III allowed the Bourbon princes to live in England and even supported them with money. English ridicule angered him.

7. When the Senate voted on May 18, 1804 to crown Napoleon, what title did it give to him? Why did they give him this title?

The Senate gave Napoleon the title of emperor. It gave him this title because only a royal title could make Napoleon seem legitimate. The title, king, however, was distasteful to many in France because it was associated with the ancient regime. Too, the title emperor invoked the memories of the Roman Empire; by taking it, Napoleon was proclaiming himself the new Caesar.

8. How did the concordat signed by Pope Pius VII and Napoleon both help and hinder the Church in France?

The concordat helped the Church in France because it reestablished its unity with Rome. The Church could act with more liberty than before. Yet, it still had to suffer some control by the state. Too, the Church became beholden to Napoleon and had to be careful not to anger him, lest he repudiate the concordat or enforce the Organic Articles. The concordat put the Church at Napoleon's mercy.

9. Compare and contrast the characters of Pius VI and Pius VII. Who do you think was the better pope? Please explain.

Students here should make two lists, one each showing the character traits of each pope. For Pius VI, students can consult not only this chapter, but chapters 3, 4, and 6.

Ideas in Action

1. Research folk songs about Napoleon Bonaparte that were written in the early 1800s and later.

2. Research, list, and discuss the laws that were enacted under the *Code Napoléon*.

3. Make a chronological chart listing the events that led to Napoleon's coming to power in France.

4. Research some of the political cartoons that were published at the time of Napoleon's rule. Discuss the role of such cartoons in politics.

Sample Quiz I (pages 177–191)

Please answer the following in complete sentences.

1. Where was Napoleon Bonaparte born? Was he French? Please explain.

2. At what battle did Napoleon become the hero of the French Republic?

3. What did the French Directory want Napoleon to do with the pope? What did Napoleon do instead? What did he demand from the pope?

4. Napoleon returned to Paris after he completed his conquests in Italy. Where did he go after he returned to Paris? What did he want to accomplish?

5. What did Napoleon and his companions do on the 19th Brumaire 1799?

6. Who was the pope after Pius VI's death? In what year did he become pope?

Answers to Sample Quiz I

Students' answers should approximate the following.

1. Napoleon Bonaparte was born on the island of *Corsica.* He was not French but *Italian.*

2. Napoleon became the hero of the French Republic at the *Battle of Lodi.*

3. The French Directory wanted Napoleon to overthrow the pope's government and the institution of the Church itself. Napoleon did not do this. But he did force the pope to give up territory and pay a large sum of money to the French government.

4. After Napoleon returned to Paris, he led an invasion of Egypt. His goal was to conquer Egypt for France and cut off Great Britain's communications with India.

5. Napoleon and his companions overthrew the French government, the Directory, on the 19th Brumaire 1799. They established a new government that was really Napoleon's dictatorship.

6. Pius VII was the pope after Pius VI's death. He became pope in 1800.

Sample Quiz II (pages 191–202)

Please answer the following in complete sentences.

1. Please give one reform Napoleon made in France as First Consul.

2. What is the name for the agreement that Napoleon came to with the Catholic Church in 1801?

3. Napoleon was worried that his reforms in France would come to nothing after he stepped down as First Consul. What did he have the French Senate do in order to assure that his reforms would continue?

4. What title did Napoleon receive on December 2, 1804?

5. Who was Pope Pius VII's secretary of state?

   a) Ercole Consalvi

   b) Cardinal Jean-Siffrein Maury

   c) Barnaba Chiaramonti

   d) Joachim Murat

6. Who was Napoleon's wife?

Answers to Sample Quiz II

Students' answers should approximate the following

1. Possible answers:

   a) He solved the bankruptcy crisis that had brought on the French Revolution in 1789.

   b) He changed the way taxes were collected; common people paid fewer taxes than ever before.

   c) He rewrote the laws that governed France. His collection of laws was called the *Code Napoléon.*

   d) He tried to make France more self-sufficient in food.

   e) He instituted public works—new canals, new roads, new markets

2. The *concordat* is the name for the agreement that Napoleon came to with the Catholic Church in 1801.

3. The French Senate made Napoleon First Consul for Life to insure that his reforms would continue.

4. Napoleon was crowned *emperor* of France on December 2, 1804?

5. *Ercole Consalvi* (a) was Pope Pius VII's secretary of state.

6. Napoleon's wife was *Josephine.*

Essays (200–500 words each)

Instructions to be given to the students: Write in complete sentences. Underline your thesis. Give three supports or examples that explain why you think what you do and that support your thesis.

1. Describe Napoleon's conquests. What was he trying to accomplish? Did he succeed?

2. Do you think Napoleon was just greedy for power? Did he carry on his conquests and pursue political power for purely selfish motives? Please explain.

Chapter Test

Please answer the following in complete sentences.

I. Short Essay—Answer two of the following:

1. Briefly describe the events in Napoleon's life between his return from Italy in 1797 (following the Peace of Tolentino) and the 19th Brumaire, when he became First Consul of France.

2. How did Napoleon treat the Church? (Give a couple of examples how Napoleon behaved toward the Church.) How did his treatment of the Church differ from that of the French Directory? Why did Napoleon treat the Church like he did?

3. Why did Napoleon want the title of "emperor" instead of king? What did the title signify for him? Why did he want Pope Pius VII to perform the coronation ceremony?

II. Short Answer:

1. From where did Napoleon come? Why did he come to France?

2. List two reforms Napoleon brought to France as First Consul.

3. What happened on 19th Brumaire 1799?

4. What did the concordat Napoleon signed with Pope Pius VII in 1801 bring an end to?

5. What two tasks was Pope Pius VII to perform at Napoleon's coronation on December 2, 1804? Did the pope perform these tasks? Please explain.

Answer Key to the Chapter Test

Students' answers should approximate the following:

I.

1. The events in Napoleon's life between his return from Italy in 1797 to the 19th Brumaire:

   a) Napoleon returned to Paris.

   b) Napoleon set out for the conquest of Egypt, May 1798.

   c) After a little over a year in Egypt, Napoleon returned secretly to France.

   d) Under the Directory, France had been losing everything she had won in previous years, especially by Napoleon. Many thought the government was leading France into ruin.

   e) Napoleon returned to France. He conspired with others to overthrow the government.

   f) With his co-conspirators, Napoleon forced the French National Assembly to disband on the "19th Brumaire" (November 10) 1799.

   g) Napoleon and his co-conspirators established the Consulate with Napoleon as First Consul—effectively the dictator of France.

2. Examples of how Napoleon treated the Church (possible answers):

   a) He forced Pope Pius VI to abandon some of the best lands of the Papal States and pay a large sum of money. Yet, he did not force the pope to abandon his temporal authority.

   b) Seeking to end the schism between the Constitutional Church and Rome, Napoleon signed a concordat with Pope Pius VII in the summer of 1801. The concordat did not restore the Catholic Church as the sole religion of France and it gave the government some control over the Church; but otherwise, it reestablished papal authority over the French Church.

   c) Napoleon showed great friendliness toward the Church for a time. Though he suppressed some religious congregations, he permitted the restoration of several female religious associations that worked in schools and hospitals.

   d) Napoleon placed government schools under the direction of Catholic clergy.

   Napoleon's policies toward the Church differed markedly from how the French Directory had treated the Church. The Directory sought to overthrow the temporal power of the pope and to destroy the Church as an institution. Napoleon, however, tried to act in a friendly manner toward the Church in order to reconcile Catholics with his government.

3. Napoleon wanted the title of "emperor" instead of king because many people in France associated the title of king with the ancient regime, the enemies of the revolution. For Napoleon, too, the title of emperor brought up memories of the ancient Roman Empire, which for centuries had been the political ideal for all Europe. As emperor, Napoleon began to see himself as the new Charlemagne; and like Charlemagne, he was determined to restore the might and glory of the ancient Roman Empire. He wanted Pope Pius VII to perform the coronation ceremony because it would make the imperial title look more legitimate than if it had come just from the French Senate. Since Napoleon wanted to be like Charlemagne, he thought he had to have a papal coronation—for the pope had crowned Charlemagne emperor.

II.

1. Napoleon came from the island of Corsica? His father sent him to France to attend a military academy so he could become an officer in the French military.

2. Possible answers:

   a) He solved the bankruptcy crisis that had brought on the French Revolution in 1789.

   b) He changed the way taxes were collected; common people paid fewer taxes than ever before.

   c) He rewrote the laws that governed France. His collection of laws was called the *Code Napoléon.*

   d) He tried to make France more self-sufficient in food.

   e) He instituted public works—new canals, new roads, new markets

3. Napoleon and his co-conspirators overthrew the French government on on 19th Brumaire 1799, and Napoleon became First Consul of France.

4. The concordat between Napoleon and Pope Pius VII ended the schism between the French Church and the pope.

5. Pope Pius VII was both to consecrate Napoleon and crown him during the coronation ceremony on December 2, 1804. The pope performed the consecration, but Napoleon seized the crown before the pope could get it and placed it on his own head.

CHAPTER 8: The Wars of Napoleon

Chapter Overview

- Aleksandr I became tsar and emperor of Russia following the murder of his father, Tsar Pavel I, on the night of March 23–24, 1801.

- In 1805, Russia and Austria joined Great Britain in an alliance against France. Learning of the alliance, Napoleon redirected his *Grande Armée* from his planned invasion of England and led it into Germany. He defeated the Austrians under Mack at Ulm, forced the Russians beyond Vienna, and then decisively defeated the Austrians and Russians at Austerlitz on December 2, 1805. Following this battle, Emperor Franz II signed a peace treaty with Napoleon and withdrew from the war. The British under Lord Horatio Nelson, however, defeated the French fleet at the Battle of Trafalgar on October 21, 1805.

- Napoleon was able to draw several German states of the Holy Roman Empire into an alliance with himself; it was called the Confederation of the Rhine. Franz II, fearing that Napoleon would seize the title of Holy Roman emperor for himself, formally dissolved the empire on August 6, 1806.

- In October 1806, Prussia, Russia, and Great Britain formed the Fourth Coalition against Napoleon. After defeating the Prussians at Jena and Auerstädt on October 14, 1806, Napoleon entered Berlin. There he issued his Berlin Decrees, establishing the Continental System.

- Though Napoleon's army suffered heavy losses against the Russians in a battle at the village of Preussisches Eylau in February 1807, he triumphed over the Russians at Friedland in June. The Treaty of Tilsit (July 7, 1807) ended the war. Though Prussia had to surrender territories to Napoleon, the French emperor was able to make an alliance with Tsar Aleksandr.

- Taking advantage of troubles in Spain, Napoleon forced King Fernando VII of Spain to abdicate. In his place, Napoleon made his own brother, Joseph Bonaparte, king of Spain. Receiving support from the British, the Spanish people rose in revolt against Joseph Bonaparte and Napoleon. The Spaniards were fighting both for their Bourbon king and to preserve their Catholic Faith against Napoleon.

- On April 9, 1809, Austria and Great Britain formed the Fifth Coalition against Napoleon. Moving into Bavaria, Napoleon defeated the Austrians and took Vienna in May. Though he suffered a defeat at Aspern and Essling in May 1809, Napoleon was able to defeat the Austrians at Wagram in July. In October 1809, Austria signed a treaty with France, thus bringing an end to the Fifth Coalition.

- Since the signing of the concordat, Napoleon had experienced problems with Pope Pius VII.

Pius would not ally himself with Napoleon against Great Britain, nor would he go along with Napoleon's plans to make the papacy the servant of the French empire. At last, in May 1809, when Napoleon issued a declaration abolishing the pope's temporal rule, Pius excommunicated the emperor. Napoleon responded by capturing the pope and forcing him to go into exile in France.

- Napoleon divorced his wife Josephine because she could not give him an heir. In April 1810, he married Archduchess Maria Louisa, the daughter of Emperor Franz I of Austria. On March 20, Maria Louisa gave birth to a son, to whom his father gave the title, King of Rome.

- Since the Treaty of Tilsit, the friendship between Napoleon and Tsar Aleksandr I cooled. When Aleksandr issued a decree that violated Napoleon's Berlin Decrees and broke the Treaty of Tilsit, Napoleon decided to lead the *Grande Armée* in an invasion of Russia.

- Napoleon's *Grande Armée* crossed into Russia in June 1812. He captured the important city of Smolensk and then defeated the Russian army at Borodino on September 7. Upon entering Moscow, however, Napoleon discovered that most of its inhabitants had fled. Fire broke out, destroying most of the city. Seeing he could not winter in Moscow, Napoleon began his retreat on October 19, 1812. By the time the French reached the western border of Russia, the *Grande Armée* was no more.

Chapter Goals

The career of Tsar Aleksandr I illustrates the power Liberalism had over minds in the early 19th century. Here was the tsar and autocrat of Russia meditating fondly on the doctrines of Rousseau! Did he stop to consider what he stood to lose should Liberalism catch on in Russia? Did he contemplate the example of King Louis VI or that of the king of Great Britain? Did he really want to lose much of his power to elected representatives who might not rest content with the power granted them but seek for more? Even if Aleksandr was inspired by generous ideals, did he fully understand what those ideals entailed?

The teacher should introduce such questions to students. How often do we fail to see the disconnection between our ideals and our actions? Even the actions we undertake for the sake of our ideals may be at odds with those very ideals. Perhaps even the ideals we hold contradict one another. Napoleon, for instance, was furthering the spread of Liberal republican ideology at the same time as he was seeking to reestablish the Roman Empire. Not only did his deeds seem to belie his ideals, but even his ideals were at odds with one another.

This chapter, too, gives us a glimpse into the understanding the Church has had of herself in relation to the civil order. Napoleon wanted a Church subject to the chief power in the state, but the Church could not submit herself to such a condition without abandoning her character and divine constitution in the process. The Church has never seen herself as subject to the state nor even as a coequal to the state. As this understanding has been expressed, the state looks to the temporal good of men while the Church looks to their eternal benefit. Since the temporal order serves the eternal order, so the goals of the state serve the goals of the Church. This is not to say that the Church interferes in the proper activities of the state, but that even these have to be guided by what the Church reveals of truth and goodness. As Pius VII told Napoleon, "it would be absurd to say that the spirit must obey the flesh, the heavenly obey the earthly."

Finally, the career of Napoleon as it is presented in this chapter offers an object lesson in *hubris*— the Greek word for overweening pride. Napoleon did not know his limits, and this brought about his downfall.

Period Music

Consult the list of composers in Chapter 7 of this teacher's manual.

What Students Should Know

1. What goals Tsar Aleksandr I had for Russia

Influenced by Liberal Enlightenment ideas, Aleksandr wanted Russia to adopt the political ways of "enlightened" western Europe. He looked to establish a constitution; he encouraged trade and manufacturing. He founded new schools, military academies, and universities. He sought to ease the condition of the serfs. At the same time, Aleksandr built up the Russian army and established a system of conscription.

2. The importance of the war of the Third Coalition

Since becoming First Consul in 1799, Napoleon had focused on reforming the French government. His thoughts began to turn toward conquest because he perceived that Great Britain threatened him. He was proposing an invasion of England when he heard of the new alliance formed against him—the alliance of Great Britain, Austria, and Russia. Napoleon turned aside from the invasion of England and began the campaign that ended at Austerlitz, the Battle of the Three Emperors, on December 2, 1805. This was Napoleon's greatest victory and it ended the war against the Third Coalition. The war itself, however, led to others, for it was the beginning of Napoleon's career of conquest

Key Terms at a Glance

deposition: the forceful removal of a ruler from office

sovereignty: supreme power, especially over a nation or other political group

vex: to irritate, annoy

blockade: a wartime action by which one warring power uses troops or warships to block the entrance of food, war supplies, or other goods into its enemy's ports, cities, or other possessions

Berlin Decrees: decrees issued by Emperor Napoleon I of France establishing what became known as the Continental System

Continental System: the system established by the Berlin Decrees through which the Emperor Napoleon attempted to force European countries to close their ports to British merchant ships or other ships carrying British goods

guerilla warfare: irregular warfare, especially by small groups carrying out sudden attacks

octave: the eighth day after a major Church feast day; also, the eight-day period after the feast day. For instance, the first Sunday (traditionally called Low Sunday) after Easter Sunday is the octave of Easter; the period between the Easter and Low Sunday is also referred to as being "within the octave of Easter."

Kaiser: German word meaning "emperor" (like *tsar*, *Kaiser* is from the Latin, *Caesar*)

prelate: a high ranking churchman, such as an abbot, bishop, archbishop, cardinal, or patriarch

consort: a spouse, either husband or wife

cupola: in architecture a usually dome-like structure on the top of a building or tower that turned him from more peaceful pursuits into an empire builder.

3. What the Battle of Trafalgar was and its significance

The Battle of Trafalgar was the sea battle fought on October 21, 1805, in which the British fleet under Lord Horatio Nelson defeated the French and Spanish fleet. The battle established Great Britain as the foremost sea power in the world.

4. What happened to the Holy Roman Empire

Since his rise to power, Napoleon had seized several German imperial lands. In 1806, he convinced 16 German states to withdraw formally from the Holy Roman Empire. These states formed the Confederation of the Rhine and proclaimed Napoleon Bonaparte as their protector. Emperor Franz II saw this violation of his rights as emperor as the harbinger of further power grabs. To keep Napoleon from seizing the title of Holy Roman emperor, Franz II, formally dissolved the empire on August 6, 1806.

5. Why Napoleon and the pope had a falling out. What its results were

Important differences arose between Napoleon and Pius VII. Napoleon violated the concordat in Italy. Pius VII would not annul Jerome Bonaparte's marriage to an American Protestant. Napoleon did not respect the pope's feudal rights in Naples. The pope would not acknowledge Napoleon Bonaparte as Roman emperor. Napoleon seized papal territories. The pope would not go to war with Great Britain, and he refused to load the curia with candidates acceptable to Napoleon. This was the last straw for Napoleon. In February 1808, French troops occupied Rome. Then, in June, 1809, Napoleon abolished the Papal States. The pope responded by excommunicating

Napoleon. Finally, in July 1809, Napoleon Bonaparte's general in Rome forced the pope to go into exile.

6. How Napoleon seized power in Spain and what the results were

In March 1808, the Bourbon king of Spain, Carlos IV, was driven from power by his son, who proclaimed himself King Fernando VII. Carlos's government allowed France to send an army through Spain to Portugal, which it had conquered. To remove this inconvenience of having to pass through a land he did not control, Napoleon took it upon himself to adjudicate the controversy between Carlos and Fernando. After he "convinced" them to give him the Spanish throne, Napoleon made his brother, Joseph Bonaparte, king of Spain. The new government began to restrict the freedom of the Catholic Church. The Spanish, however, who were devoted to the House of Bourbon and their Catholic religion, rose up against Joseph Bonaparte. This was basically a peasant rebellion which Napoleon could not crush.

7. What Napoleon's Grand Dream for Europe was

As First Consul of France, Napoleon's goal had been to save the political and social reforms of the French Revolution. When he became emperor, he did not abandon this dream but added another to it. He saw himself as the one who would bring back Europe's unity under a restored "Roman Empire." European nations would no longer war on one another. Justice and peace would flourish. The Church would serve the empire, teaching respect and obedience toward the emperor. The chief obstacle to this dream, he saw, was Great Britain with its banks and oligarchy. Pope Pius VII, too, did not agree to the role Napoleon laid out for the Church, for, he said, the Church of Christ, whose purpose was to bring men to heaven, was not to serve an earthly power.

8. **Why Napoleon Bonaparte invaded Russia. What his fatal mistake was. What the results were.**

Napoleon and Tsar Aleksandr I had had friendly relations, but their friendship eventually cooled. Aleksandr had goals for Russia that did not necessarily accord with Napoleon's policies. The final break between the powers came in 1810 when Aleksandr violated the Berlin Decrees, which he had previously agreed to uphold. To punish this betrayal, Napoleon gathered an enormous army and invaded Russia in late June 1812. In August, he captured Smolensk; but, instead of stopping there, he moved against Moscow, despite the near approach of the bitterly cold Russian winter. After defeating the Russians at Borodino in early September, Napoleon entered Moscow only to find that most of its inhabitants had fled. Fire broke out, destroying most of the city. Seeing he could not winter in Moscow, Napoleon began his retreat in mid-October— but by then it was too late. The bitter cold and the assaults of the Russians devastated Napoleon's forces. By the time it had reached Russia's western border, the *Grande Armée* was all but destroyed.

9. **What Andreas Hofer accomplished**

Andreas Hofer was an innkeeper in the Austrian Tyrol who led a rebellion against Bavaria, which had taken control of the Tyrol, violated peasant traditions, and tried to suppress Catholic worship and practice. Fighting for the Church and Emperor Franz, Hofer and his fellow insurgents were able to drive the Bavarian and French forces from the Tyrol for a time. But, in the end, the French and Bavarians were victorious; Hofer was captured

and taken to Mantua, where he was executed in 1810.

10. **Identify the following:**

Berlin Decrees: decrees issued by Emperor Napoleon I of France establishing what became known as the Continental System

Kremlin: the ancient palace of the tsars of Russia, in Moscow

Berlin Decrees: decrees issued by Emperor Napoleon I of France establishing what became known as the Continental System

Continental System: the system established by the Berlin Decrees through which the Emperor Napoleon attempted to force European countries to close their ports to British merchant ships or other ships carrying British goods

Joachim Murat: one of Napoleon's most trusted soldiers since 13th Vendemiare 1795. Murat married Napoleon's sister. After he sent Joseph Bonaparte to Spain, Napoleon made Murat king of Naples.

Jerome Bonaparte: the youngest Bonaparte brother, whom Napoleon appointed king of Westphalia

Joseph Bonaparte: king of Naples; later appointed king of Spain by his brother, Napoleon

Empress Maria Louisa: the daughter of Emperor Franz I of Austria; Napoleon's second wife and the mother of his son, Napoleon II

Napoleon François Joseph Charles Bonaparte: son of Napoleon Bonaparte and his second wife, Maria Louisa; Napoleon II, the King of Rome

Questions for Review

1. **How did Tsar Aleksandr I show himself to be an enlightened autocrat?**

   Tsar Aleksandr looked to establish a constitution; he encouraged trade and manufacturing. He founded new schools, military academies, and universities. He sought to ease the condition of the serfs. At the same time, Aleksandr built up the Russian army and established a system of conscription.

2. **What was the name of the great British sea victory over the French and Spanish fleet? When did it occur? Who commanded the British fleet?**

   The Battle of Trafalgar was the name of the great British sea victory over the French and Spanish fleet. It was fought on October 21, 1805. Lord Horatio Nelson commanded the British fleet.

3. **What battle has been called Napoleon's greatest military victory? When did it occur? Against whom did he fight?**

   The Battle of Austerlitz (or, the Battle of the Three Emperors) has been called Napoleon's greatest military victory. It was fought on December 2, 1805. Napoleon fought against the Austrians (Emperor Franz I) and the Russians (Tsar Aleksandr I).

4. **Why did Napoleon want to invade and conquer England?**

   Napoleon wanted to invade and conquer England because he saw Great Britain, with its banks and oligarchy, as his chief foe and the source of all the opposition against him.

5. **What was Napoleon's great dream for himself and Europe?**

   Napoleon's great dream was to save and expand the political and social reforms of the French Revolution. He saw himself as the one who would bring back Europe's unity under a restored "Roman Empire." European nations would no longer war on one another. Justice and peace would flourish. The Church would serve the empire, teaching respect and obedience toward the emperor.

6. **What role did Napoleon think the pope and the Church should play in his grand dream?**

   Napoleon saw the Church as a tool of the government. In his mind, the Church would serve his empire, teaching respect and obedience toward the emperor. That would be the Church's function.

7. **When did Emperor Franz II dissolve the Holy Roman Empire? Why did he dissolve it?**

   Emperor Franz II dissolved the Holy Roman Empire on August 6, 1806. He dissolved the empire to keep Napoleon from taking the title of Holy Roman emperor for himself.

8. **What Catholic feast day did St. Napoleon's Day take the place of in France? Why did the French Catholic bishops approve this feast day change?**

   St. Napoleon's Day took the place of the Feast of the Assumption of Mary. The French bishops approved the change because, since the signing of the concordat, they had come out publicly in support of Napoleon and did what he demanded. Priests who displeased Napoleon could find themselves imprisoned.

9. **What did Napoleon find when he arrived in Moscow?**

   When he arrived in Moscow, Napoleon found a nearly abandoned city. The Russian people, rich and poor, had abandoned the capital and fled.

10. **What happened to Napoleon's army in its long retreat from Moscow to France?**

Two things—the bitter cold of the Russian winter and continual assaults by Russian army and guerilla forces—devastated Napoleon's army. By the time it had reached Russia's western border, the army was all but destroyed.

Ideas in Action

1. As a class, make a topographical map of Europe including mountains, rivers, and forests. Show the routes of Napoleon's campaigns, the places where the major battles were fought, and which countries were involved. Indicate the dates upon which Napoleon achieved his goals.

2. Imagine you are a person who lived at the time of the Napoleonic Wars. Write a letter to a relative and recount an event of this time period that affected you and your family.

3. Learn the formal dances of the late 18th century. Have a "Jane Austen party" and, wearing costumes of the era, dance the patterns that were popular at balls in this period.

4. Locate the words (in German and English) of the Tyrolese hymn, *Zu Mantua in Banden* ("At Mantua in Bonds"), by Julius Mosen. The hymn tells of the heroic death of Andreas Hofer. Words and music can be found on the Internet. See if you can sing the hymn.

5. Research the weapons of the period of the Napoleonic Wars—swords, bayonets, artillery, muskets, and pistols.

6. Research the average temperature, snowfall, and conditions of Russia's winter weather to get an idea of how severe the winter of 1812 might have been.

Sample Quiz I (pages 205–216)

Please answer the following in complete sentences.

1. Name one thing Tsar Aleksandr I did that shows that he was an "enlightened" ruler.

2. What three nations were allied against Napoleon in the war of the Third Coalition?

3. At what battle did Napoleon defeat the Third Coalition? (The battle was Napoleon's greatest victory.)

4. What was the sea battle where the British fleet defeated the French fleet? Who commanded the British fleet during this battle? (This battle established Great Britain as the world's greatest sea power.)

5. What was the name of the decrees by which Napoleon established the Continental System?

6. What was the Continental System?

Answers to Sample Quiz I

Students' answers should approximate the following.

1. *Possible Answers:*

   a) He looked to establish a constitution.

   b) He encouraged trade and manufacturing.

   c) He founded new schools, military academies, and universities.

   d) He sought to ease the condition of the serfs.

   e) He built up the Russian army and established a system of conscription.

2. *Great Britain, Austria,* and *Russia* were the three nations allied against Napoleon in the war of the Third Coalition.

3. Napoleon defeated the Third Coalition at the *Battle of Austerlitz* (or, the *Battle of the Three Emperors*).

4. The British defeated the French at the *Battle of Trafalgar. Lord Horatio Nelson* commanded the British fleet during this battle.

5. The *Berlin Decrees* established the Continental System.

6. The Continental System was the system by which Napoleon attempted to force European nations to close their ports to British merchant ships or other ships carrying British goods

Sample Quiz II (pages 216–233)

Please answer the following in complete sentences.

1. **How did Pope Pius VII respond when, in June 1809, Napoleon abolished the Papal States?**

2. **Why did the Spanish people revolt against Joseph Bonaparte and Napoleon?**

3. **Describe one of Napoleon's goals as emperor.**

4. **What happened to Napoleon's army after it left Moscow in 1812?**

5. **Who was the Tyrolese patriot who led an armed resistance against the Bavarian government and the French?**

Answers to Sample Quiz II

Students' answers should approximate the following

1. Pope Pius VII excommunicated Napoleon after he abolished the Papal States in 1809.

2. The Spanish people revolted against Napoleon and Joseph Bonaparte because Napoleon had overthrown the House of Bourbon (to which the Spanish were devoted) and because the new government had been restricting the freedom of the Catholic Church.

3. Napoleon's goals as emperor (possible answers):

   a) to save and expand the political and social reforms of the French Revolution

   b) to bring unity and peace to Europe under a restored Roman Empire

4. After it left Moscow in 1812, Napoleon's army was destroyed by the winter cold and the attacks of the Russian army and guerilla forces.

5. *Andreas Hofer* was the Tyrolese patriot who led an armed resistance against the Bavarian government and the French.

Essays (200–500 words each)

Instructions to be given to the students: Write in complete sentences. Underline your thesis. Give three supports or examples that explain why you think what you do and that support your thesis.

1. Describe the character and deeds of a character that you admire in this chapter.

2. Describe one of Napoleon's battles and show why it was important.

Chapter Test

Please answer the following in complete sentences.

I. **Short Essay**

1. **Napoleon thought of himself as more than the emperor of France—he considered himself the Roman emperor. What were Napoleon's two goals for his new Roman Empire? What role did he think the Catholic Church should play in his empire? Did the pope accept the new role Napoleon had for him? Please explain.**

II. **Short Answer:**

1. **List two things Tsar Aleksandr I did that showed that he was an "enlightened" ruler.**

2. **In 1806, Napoleon convinced 16 German states to withdraw from the Holy Roman Empire and form a new alliance among themselves and with himself. What was the name of this new alliance?**

3. **Why did Emperor Franz II dissolve the Holy Roman Empire? On what date did he dissolve it?**

4. **Why did Napoleon decide to invade Russia in 1812?**

5. **What was the name of the system established by the Berlin Decrees by which Napoleon attempted to force the European nations to close their ports to British merchant ships carrying British goods?**

6. **Who was the patriot who led the Tyrolese peasants in a rebellion against the Bavarians and French? He was executed at Mantua in 1810.**

7. **How did the Spanish react to Napoleon when he replaced their king with Joseph Bonaparte?**

Answer Key to the Chapter Test

Students' answers should approximate the following:

I.

1. Napoleon's first goal for his new Roman Empire was to save the political and social reforms of the French Revolution and to extend them to all the nations of Europe. Another of Napoleon's goals was to restore Europe's unity under a restored "Roman Empire." European nations would no longer war on one another. Justice and peace would flourish. The Church would serve the empire, teaching respect and obedience toward the emperor. Pope Pius VII, however, did not agree to this new role for the Church, for, he said, the Church of Christ, whose purpose is to bring men to heaven, is not to serve an earthly power and so be subject to earthly not spiritual goals.

II.

1. *Possible Answers:*

   a) He looked to establish a constitution.

   b) He encouraged trade and manufacturing.

   c) He founded new schools, military academies, and universities.

   d) He sought to ease the condition of the serfs.

   e) He built up the Russian army and established a system of conscription.

2. The new alliance formed by Napoleon and the German states was called the *Confederation of the Rhine.*

3. Emperor Franz II dissolved the Holy Roman Empire to keep Napoleon from taking the title of Holy Roman emperor for himself. Franz dissolved the empire on *August 6, 1806.*

4. Aleksandr had goals for Russia that did not necessarily accord with Napoleon's policies. The final break between the powers came when Aleksandr violated the Berlin Decrees, which he had previously agreed to uphold. To punish this betrayal, Napoleon gathered an enormous army and invaded Russia in late June 1812.

5. The *Continental System* was the name for the system established by the Berlin Decrees.

6. *Andreas Hofer* was the patriot who led the Tyrolese peasants in a rebellion against the Bavarians and French.

7. The Spanish rose up in rebellion against Napoleon when he replaced their king with Joseph Bonaparte.

CHAPTER 9: Metternich's Europe

Chapter Overview

- Aleksandr I of Russia, with Great Britain, Prussia, and Sweden, formed the Sixth Coalition against Napoleon. Prince Klemens von Metternich, however, held Austria back from joining the coalition. Despite Austria's reluctance, people in the German states formed the *Tugendbund* to drive the French from Germany.

- From April to October 1813, Napoleon defeated the coalition allies in several battles. Napoleon's fortune changed, however, when he failed to keep Austria from joining the coalition. At the Battle of Leipzig (October 16–19, 1813), Napoleon suffered a great defeat. He and his remaining army were forced to return to France.

- Though all of Europe, it seemed, was united against him, Napoleon refused to give in to the allies' demands. Though outnumbered, he defeated coalition armies in several engagements and came close to driving them from France. But, finally, led by Tsar Aleksandr, the coalition army took Paris. On April 11, 1814, Napoleon surrendered to the allies. Though he had to abdicate the throne of France, he was made the emperor of the island of Elba in the Mediterranean Sea.

- With the passing of Napoleon, Prince Klemens von Metternich of Austria became the new leader of Europe. The early period of the "Age of Metternich" saw the restoration of legitimate monarchs throughout Europe. One of these monarchs was King Louis XVIII of France.

- Metternich wanted to establish a new order in Europe that would uphold the ancient regime, respect religion, and bring peace. This "Concert of Europe" would unite European monarchs in a league to prevent revolutions and stamp out Liberalism. The Concert of Europe idea was the basis of the Treaty of Paris, signed on May 30, 1814. The Congress of Vienna, which met from November 1, 1814 to June 9, 1815, sought to put the Concert of Europe into effect.

- While the Congress of Vienna met, Napoleon returned to France and reestablished himself as emperor in Paris. Napoleon's bid to restore his power ended when the British and Prussians under the Duke of Wellington defeated Napoleon's forces at Waterloo on June 18, 1815. Following this defeat, Napoleon was forced into exile on St. Helena, an island 800 miles off the western coast of Africa.

- The Holy Roman Empire was not restored after the fall of Napoleon. Instead, Germany was organized into a confederation of independent states, dominated by Austria. This was the German Confederation.

- To make sure European nations kept to their agreements at the Congress of Vienna and to keep Liberalism down, Metternich oversaw the formation of the Quadruple Alliance, a league made up of Great Britain, Prussia, Russia, and Austria (and later, France). Tsar Aleksandr formed the Holy Alliance, a league between European nations formed to make sure that the Quadruple Alliance operated according to Christian principles and ideals.

- Post-Napoleonic Europe witnessed the rise of the idea of nationalism, the devotion to a people or a nation based on shared language, history, and customs. Europe experienced a revival of religion as well, though Liberal ideals continued to inspire many.

- In Austria, Metternich curtailed the freedom of speech and of the press to suppress Liberalism. Similar measures spread to the German Confederation when the German diet approved the Karlsbad Decrees in 1819.

- To keep his throne, King Louis XVIII made no attempt to restore the ancient regime in France. France remained a constitutional monarchy, and the *Code Napoléon* remained her code of laws.

- In Spain, King Fernando VII broke the power of the Liberals and dissolved their government under the Constitution of 1812. For five years, he reigned as absolute monarch of Spain. But in 1819, a rebellion forced him to restore the Constitution of 1812. The Quadruple Alliance, however, decided to intervene to restore the absolute monarchy in Spain. In 1823, a French army restored Fernando to power. Following his return to power, the king directed a brutal purge of Spanish Liberals.

- In Italy, Liberals favored not only constitutional reforms, but the unification of the Italian peninsula under one government. A secret society, the Carbonari, formed to achieve this unification, by violence if necessary.

Chapter Goals

This chapter describes how, after Napoleon's first abdication, Europe experienced a period of reaction. The ruling classes, both lay and ecclesiastical, sought refuge from the excesses of Liberalism in the institutions of the ancient regime. They sought to act as if the French Revolution had never occurred. Of course, they did not ignore Liberalism; instead, they sought to suppress it by force.

It is important for students to understand that history often moves in patterns of action and reaction. As far as our story is concerned, the excesses of Liberalism and the Revolution (especially in regards to religion) had shocked and appalled many. The revolutionaries and Napoleon had created an atmosphere where reaction could flourish. The victims of the revolution could not calmly consider the claims of Liberalism—or anything that looked like Liberalism—for the simple reason that it was impossible for them to think with any equanimity about Liberalism. One could see this as an unhealthy reaction, but it is perfectly understandable in the context of 1789-1814. A weeding out of truth from error in regards to Liberalism was not possible for most people, for they could not separate the ideas from the excesses of those who held them.

Period Music

Consult the list of composers in Chapter 7 of this teacher's manual.

What Students Should Know

1. The significance of the Battle of Leipzig

It is a sign of the greatness (though not necessarily the goodness) of Napoleon's character and his military genius that he could continue to pull off victories against the allies, even after the disaster in Russia. The Battle of Leipzig (in Germany), however, was a fatal blow to Napoleon. He lost 73,000 men, and the remainder of his army was forced to retreat. And, though he continued to cause the allies problems, Leipzig was a blow from which Napoleon did not recover. It led to his first abdication.

2. Who Prince Klemens von Metternich was

Metternich was the son of an Austrian diplomat. From his youth, Prince Klemens had

---

Key Terms at a Glance

balance of power: an arrangement of power between nations to prevent one nation from being able to impose its will on other nations or to interfere in them.

Concert of Europe: Metternich's plan to unite European governments in a union to maintain peace and stability on the European continent.

German Confederation: a loose alliance of 38 German states formed by the Congress of Vienna to replace the union they had under the Holy Roman Empire.

indemnity: payment made as compensation for damage or hurt inflicted by one party on another

Quadruple Alliance: a league between Great Britain, Russia, Austria, and Prussia (later, France) by which the terms of the Treaty of Paris were enforced and Liberal revolutions kept down.

Holy Alliance: a league between European nations formed to make sure that the Quadruple Alliance operated according to Christian principles and ideals

secular state: a state or government that gives no special recognition, aid, or protection to a particular religion; a non-religious state

nationalism: the devotion to a people or a nation based on shared language, history, and customs. Nationalists often think that people should give their highest devotion and loyalty to their nation.

anticlerical: opposed to the power or influence of the clergy in government or society

Ultramontanism: the idea that the pope should have strong control over national churches.

Karlsbad Decrees: laws approved by the diet of the German Confederation that called for government supervision of universities and the press and forbade any member state of the confederation to adopt a non-monarchical or anti-monarchical constitution

junta: (pronounced HOON-tah) a group controlling a government, especially following a revolution

protocol: a memorandum or document written as a preliminary suggestion for a treaty

Viaticum: the Eucharist given to one in danger of dying (literally, "food for a journey" or "food for the road," from the Latin word, *via*)

learned to fear and hate revolution, for he had come in contact with some of the excesses of the French Revolution and had heard stories told by its victims who had fled from France. Metternich himself became a diplomat; and in 1809, he became the Austrian emperor's minister of foreign affairs—a very important and influential position

Metternich opposed democracy. He thought that only legitimate monarchs made governments safe and stable, while republics and democracies became despotisms. Saving princely government, thus, became the goal of Metternich's career. Legitimacy for him was the most important principle in government, even if legitimate monarchs were themselves tyrants.

Since Metternich was the chief organizer of the Congress of Vienna, his efforts molded Europe for nearly 30 years afterwards. This period is thus called the Age of Metternich.

3. What the Congress of Vienna was

The Congress of Vienna was a gathering of representatives of European nations in Vienna to decide how to govern Europe after the fall of Napoleon's empire. It restored Louis XVIII to power in France and recognized other rulers of the ancient regime. It established Metternich's Concert of Europe (a plan to unite European governments in a union to maintain peace and stability on the European continent), and the Quadruple Alliance (a league between Great Britain, Russia, Austria, and Prussia—and, later, France) by which the terms of the Treaty of Paris were enforced and Liberal revolutions kept down. The Congress did not restore the Holy Roman Empire to Franz of Austria but set up the German Confederation, a loose alliance of 38 states where Austria had a predominate number of votes. The Congress restored the Papal States to Pope Pius VII.

4. What the Holy Alliance was

The Holy Alliance was the idea of Tsar Aleksandr I, who had come under the influence of Pietists. It was a league between European nations formed to make sure that the Quadruple Alliance operated according to Christian principles and ideals. Though really only the tsar took it seriously, the Holy Alliance became one of the chief guiding forces of European life in the first half of the 19th century and gave a kind of religious character to Metternich's attempts to preserve the ancient regime and to suppress movements for democracy, nationalism, and social justice. Liberals hated the Holy Alliance because they thought it was a dishonest use of religion to cover up oppression and undermine freedom.

5. What a modern state is

In a modern state, all citizens are seen to have common rights and duties, are ruled by the same law, and enjoy common benefits. The modern state, too, demands the highest sense of loyalty from each citizen: nothing—not one's local region, his religion, or his family—must stand between the citizen and his devotion to the state. The modern state is usually secular—that is, it does not recognize any religion as true but treats religion as just a private matter.

6. How Napoleon inspired nationalism. What nationalism is

Though many Liberal Europeans had at first admired Napoleon and cheered his victories, they had come to resent his "sovereign" rule. In seeking to make France the center of Europe, Napoleon had evinced a national preference. The spirit of what we call *nationalism*—the devotion to a people or a nation based on shared language, history, and customs—was not new to Europe, but it intensified in the years after Napoleon. Though many people who rose up against Napoleon did so for love of country, many, if not most, nationalist leaders in Italy in and Eastern Europe were Liberals. Thus, for many, the struggle for national glory and independence became inseparable from the cause of constitutional government and democracy.

7. **The condition of religion after the fall of Napoleon**

   a) There appeared to be a new age of freedom for the Church.

   b) Because of the violence of the French Revolution and the Napoleonic wars, Christians saw the ancient regime as the friend of religion and republicans as its foe.

   c) European leaders showed great respect for religion, the Church, and the pope, and spoke of the union of "throne and altar." Church and state were seen as joined in a common cause, bolstering each other's authority. The ideal of throne and altar helped strengthen the conviction that resisting a legitimate ruler was the same as resisting God.

   d) Both Protestants and Catholics were undergoing a religious revival. The courage of the martyrs of the Revolution inspired people. Rebellion was discredited because of the violence of both the French Revolution and Napoleon's wars.

   e) Rulers were content to let the pope rule the Church as long as he left the task of governing Europe to them.

8. **What different opinions were to be found among Christians as to how Europe was to be restored**

   a) Some, like Metternich, simply wanted to restore the ancient regime.

   b) Some, such as Tsar Aleksandr I, wanted to institute some Liberal reforms but wanted the Christian spirit to guide the dealings nations had with one another.

   c) Some wanted to restore the Catholic Church to the place she had held in society during the Middle Ages.

   d) De Maistre hoped for the birth of a new Christian age—either with the Catholic Faith, with the pope as its head, predominating, or inspired by a new religion.

9. **What the purpose of the Concert of Europe was according to Metternich**

   Metternich hoped that under the direction of the Quadruple Alliance, the Concert of Europe would guarantee the future peace of the continent. Since he thought Liberalism was the chief source of war, Metternich thought it was the task of the Concert of Europe to eradicate it. He wanted to suppress all major changes, not only in Austria and Hungary, but in the German Confederation. The allied nations would meet in congresses to deal with threats to the Concert of Europe.

10. **Identify the following:**

    sovereignty: supreme power, especially over a nation or other political group

    balance of power: an arrangement of power between nations to prevent one nation from being able to impose its will on other nations or to interfere in them.

    indemnity: payment made as compensation for damage or hurt inflicted by one party on another

    anticlerical: opposed to the power or influence of the clergy in government or society

Louis XVIII: Louis Stanislas, the duke of Provence, who became king of France after the fall of the First Empire

Arthur Wellesley, Duke of Wellington: the English general who defeated Napoleon at Waterloo

Klemens Maria Hofbauer: a Redemptorist priest remembered as "the Apostle of Vienna"

Fernando VII: the king of Spain who opposed the Spanish Constitution of 1812 and harshly suppressed Liberalism

Constitution of 1812: the liberal constitution of Spain, similar to the French Constitution of 1791. Unlike the French constitution, the Constitution of 1812 proclaimed the Catholic Faith as the religion of the nation. The constitution however deprived the Church of political power in Spain.

Carbonari: "charcoal burners," a secret society, organized in lodges like the Freemasons, which practiced mysterious rites and worked to win freedom from "tyranny" and independence for all of Italy.

Questions for Review

1. **Why was Tsar Aleksandr I so determined to rid Europe of Napoleon?**

   Napoleon's invasion of Russia in 1812 and his subsequent retreat left Russia devastated. Tens of thousands of Russians were dead, their fields overrun, their villages destroyed. Viewing this devastation, Aleksandr thought Napoleon the enemy of man and God. He wanted to take revenge on Napoleon for what had happened to Russia.

2. **Why was the Battle of Leipzig called the Battle of the Nations?**

   The allied army that opposed Napoleon at Leipzig was made up of many nationalities. For this reason, Leipzig has been called the Battle of the Nations.

3. **Why did Pope Pius VII end up rejecting the second concordat he signed with Napoleon?**

   Pope Pius felt qualms of conscience for signing the concordat because it gave the emperor increased powers over the bishops and the Church. Pius feared he had betrayed the Church by signing the concordat. So it was that he ended up repudiating it.

4. **What were the some of the reasons Metternich became an undying foe of Liberal revolution and a staunch defender of the ancient regime?**

   Metternich was an undying foe of Liberal revolution because, as a youth, he had witnessed revolutionary violence and heard dark tales of the revolution from those who had escaped from revolutionary France. He came to think that only legitimate monarchs made governments safe and stable, while republics and democracies became despotisms. Saving the ancient regime, thus, became the goal of Metternich's career.

5. **What is the "100 Days"?**

   The 100 Days refers to the period of Napoleon's return to France after his exile to Elba and his resuming the government of France. It ended after Waterloo when Napoleon abdicated for the second time.

6. **Which general was victorious at the Battle of Waterloo? Why is this battle one of the most important battles in history?**

   The general who was victorious at Waterloo was Arthur Wellesley, the Duke of Wellington. The battle was so important because it was the decisive defeat of Napoleon, ending his power for good.

7. **What nations were the most powerful in Europe after the fall of Napoleon?**

The nations that were most powerful after Napoleon's fall were Great Britain, Russia, Austria, and Prussia.

8. **Why did Liberals hate the Holy Alliance?**

   Liberals hated the Holy Alliance because they thought it was a dishonest use of religion to cover up oppression and undermine freedom.

9. **Why was the Constitution of 1812 unpopular with many in Spain?**

   It was unpopular because Liberalism was unpopular in Spain. The Spanish were for the most part devoted to their traditional ways and the Catholic Church.

10. **What were the goals of the Carbonari for Italy?**

    The Carbonari wanted to free Italy from the rule of foreign princes and to form an independent, united Italy with Rome as her capital.

Ideas in Action

1. **"Able Was I Ere I Saw Elba" is a long palindrome used to mark the defeat of Napoleon and his exile on Elba. Look up the meaning of** *palindrome* **and see how one works. Find, or write, other palindromes.**

2. **Listen to the audiotapes or read the popular books by Patrick O'Brien, set in the Napoleonic Wars—especially** *Treason's Harbor* **and** *The Hundred Days.*

3. **Make a chart of the route Napoleon took from England to the Island of St. Helena. Research whether the route would have gone with the current toward Brazil and back to Africa, or down the western coast of Africa.**

4. **Research the history of one of the small realms of Italy restored by the Congress of Vienna.**

5. **Play the Milton Bradley board game of the Napoleonic era, "Broadsides and Boarding Parties," or the board game, "Age of Napoleon," designed by Renaud Verlaque.**

Sample Quiz I (pages 237–250)

Please answer the following in complete sentences.

1. **Who lost the Battle of Leipzig?**

2. **Why did Metternich support no other form of government except legitimate monarchy?**

3. **What was the name of the gathering of representatives of European nations in Vienna who met to decide how to govern Europe after the fall of Napoleon's empire?**

4. **What was the name for the loose alliance of 38 German states dominated by Austria that replaced the Holy Roman Empire?**

5. **What were the two purposes of the Quadruple Alliance of Austria, Great Britain, Russia, and Prussia?**

6. **Which of the following terms refers to an arrangement of power between nations to prevent one nation from being able to impose its will on other nations or to interfere in them?**

   a) indemnity   c) balance of power

   b) sovereignty   d) anticlerical

7. **Which of the terms above refers to compensation made for damage or hurt inflicted by one person or group on another?**

8. **Which of the terms listed in question 5 refers to someone or something that is opposed to the power or influence of the clergy in government or society?**

Answers to Sample Quiz I

Students' answers should approximate the following.

1. *Napoleon* lost the Battle of Leipzig.

2. Metternich only supported legitimate monarchy because he thought that only legitimate monarchs made governments safe and stable, while republics and democracies became despotisms.

3. The gathering of representatives in Vienna was called the *Congress of Vienna.*

4. The *German Confederation* was the name for the loose alliance of 38 German states.

5. The purposes of the Quadruple Alliance were:

   a) to make sure the terms of the Treaty of Paris were enforced

   b) to unite European governments in a union to maintain peace and stability on the European continent

6. *Balance of power* (c) refers to an arrangement of power between nations to prevent one nation from being able to impose its will on other nations or to interfere in them.

7. *Indemnity* (a) refers to compensation made for damage or hurt inflicted by one party on another.

8. *Anticlerical* (d) refers to someone or something that is opposed to the power or influence of the clergy in government or society.

Sample Quiz II (pages 250–262)

Please answer the following in complete sentences.

1. **Give one characteristic of a modern state.**

2. **What is nationalism?**

3. **What did Metternich think the Concert of Europe had to do in order to get rid of war and assure peace in Europe?**

4. **Who was the king of Spain who opposed the Spanish Constitution of 1812 and harshly suppressed Liberalism?**

5. **What was the name for the secret society that was organized in lodges like the Freemasons, practiced mysterious rites, and worked to win freedom from "tyranny" and independence for all of Italy?**

Answers to Sample Quiz II

Students' answers should approximate the following

1. Possible answers:

   a) In a modern state, all citizens are seen to have common rights and duties, are ruled by the same law, and enjoy common benefits.

   b) The modern state demands the highest sense of loyalty from each citizen: nothing —not a man's local region, his religion, or his family—must stand between the citizen and his devotion to the state.

   c) The modern state is usually secular—that is, it does not recognize any religion as true but treats religion as just a private matter.

2. Nationalism is the devotion to a people or a nation based on shared language, history, and customs.

3. Metternich thought that the Concert of Europe had to eradicate Liberalism to assure peace in Europe.

4. *Fernando VII* was the king of Spain who opposed the Spanish Constitution of 1812 and harshly suppressed Liberalism.

5. The name of the secret society organized in lodges that worked to win freedom from "tyranny" and independence for all of Italy was the *Carbonari*.

Essays (200–500 words each)

Instructions to be given to the students: Write in complete sentences. Underline your thesis. Give three supports or examples that explain why you think what you do and that support your thesis.

1. Why did European rulers show a greater respect for the Church after the defeat of Napoleon than they had before? Why did they give up such ideas as Gallicanism, Febronianism, and Josephism?

2. Describe the different opinions Christians had as how best to restore Europe after the fall of Napoleon.

Chapter Test

Please answer the following in complete sentences.

I. **Short Essay—Answer two of the following:**

1. Describe what a modern state is like, outlining its most important characteristics.

2. What is nationalism? How did Napoleon strengthen the spirit of nationalism in Europe? Were all nationalists also Liberals? Please explain.

3. What was the Holy Alliance? Whose idea was it? What was its purpose? Why did Liberals hate it?

II. **Short Answer:**

1. Why did Metternich support only legitimate monarchies and reject democracy and republican governments?

2. What was the Quadruple Alliance? What was its purpose? Who established it?

3. What was the name for the loose alliance of 38 German states that replaced the Holy Roman Empire and the Confederation of the Rhine? What German state was the most powerful in this alliance?

4. What is the term for supreme power, exercised especially over a nation or other political group?

5. What do we call an arrangement of power between nations in order to prevent one nation from being able to impose its will on other nations or to interfere in them.

6. Who became king of France after Napoleon?

7. Who was the Redemptorist priest who is remembered as "the Apostle of Vienna"?

Answer Key to Chapter Test

Students' answers should approximate the following:

I.

1. In a modern state, all citizens are seen to have common rights and duties, are ruled by the same law, and enjoy common benefits. The modern state, too, demands the highest sense of loyalty from each citizen: nothing—not a man's local region, his religion, or his family—must stand between the citizen and his devotion to the state. The modern state is usually secular—that is, it does not recognize any religion as true but treats religion as just a private matter.

2. Nationalism is the devotion to a people or a nation based on shared language, history, and customs. Napoleon inspired nationalism in Europe by his attempt to unite the European nations in an empire under his control. This grab for power led many Europeans who had at first admired Napoleon and cheered his victories, to resent his "sovereign" rule—especially since he wanted to make France the center of Europe, a nationalist goal. So it was that nationalism intensified in the years after Napoleon.

Not all nationalists were Liberals. Many of the people who rose up against Napoleon did so simply for love of country. Yet, in Italy and Eastern Europe, many if not most nationalist leaders were Liberals. Thus, for many, the struggle for national glory and independence became inseparable from the cause of constitutional government and democracy.

3. The Holy Alliance was a league between European nations formed to make sure that the Quadruple Alliance operated according to

Christian principles and ideals. It was created by Tsar Aleksandr I. It became one of the chief guiding forces of European life in the first half of the 19th century and gave a kind of religious character to Metternich's attempts to preserve the ancient regime and to suppress Liberal and other social movements. Liberals hated the Holy Alliance because they thought it was a dishonest use of religion to cover up oppression and undermine freedom.

II.

1. Metternich thought that only legitimate monarchs made governments safe and stable, while republics and democracies became despotisms. Thus, he made it his chief goal to preserve legitimate monarchy.

2. The Quadruple Alliance was a league between Great Britain, Russia, Austria, and Prussia (and later, France) by which the terms of the Treaty of Paris were enforced and Liberal revolutions kept down. It was established by the Congress of Vienna.

3. The *German Confederation* was the name for the loose alliance of 38 German states that replaced the Holy Roman Empire and the Confederation of the Rhine. *Austria* was the most powerful German state in this alliance.

4. *Sovereignty* is term for supreme power, exercised especially over a nation or other political group.

5. We call such an arrangement *balance of power.*

6. *Louis XVIII* became king of France after the fall of Napoleon.

7. *Klemens Maria Hofbauer* was the priest remembered as the "Apostle of Vienna."

CHAPTER 10: Romanticism and Revolt, Part I

Chapter Overview

- The dominant art style of the 18th century is called "classical." Inspired by Enlightenment rationalism, the classical style emphasized reason, proportion, brilliance, and wit. It insisted that art follow certain strict rules and rarely, if ever, deviate from them. In the late 18th century a new art movement arose—Romanticism. Romanticism rejected classical artistic ideals. Romantic artists tried to introduce mysticism into art.

- Some Romantics became Catholic. Others were attracted to the Catholic Faith, though they never entered the Church. Others, however, drifted away from religion altogether. The Romantic tendency to emphasize emotion over reason led some to adopt revolutionary political ideas and moral libertinism. Romantics tended to embrace nationalism.

- Though it began in Germany, the Romantic movement spread into England and eventually into southern Europe, France, and Russia. It affected literature and all other art forms, especially music.

- Though the Industrial Revolution and the enclosure of agricultural lands brought great changes to England, very few Englishmen were influenced by revolutionary ideals. The suffering of the rural poor, however, led the Englishman William Cobbett to fight for justice for England's small farmers and farmworkers. In his newspaper, the *Political Register*, Cobbett attacked corruption in government, as well as financiers and speculators, as the enemies of the rural poor.

- Eventually, the number of people in England calling for reform of the government increased. Reformers wanted universal manhood suffrage, voting by secret ballot, Catholic emancipation, and other measures. The first step toward reform of the government was the Catholic Relief Act of 1829, which gave Catholics the right to sit in Parliament and repealed the last anti-Catholic laws in Ireland.

- Poverty, hunger, and oppression sparked the Last Laborers' Revolt in England in 1830–1831. Bands of peasants destroyed agricultural machines and burned haystacks. The government crushed the revolt.

- Beginning in 1832 with Lord Grey's Reform, Parliament passed laws to abolish many of the abuses in the British government. These laws, however, did not seriously jeopardize the oligarchy's control of the government.

- Beginning about 1820, Tsar Aleksandr I of Russia abandoned the Liberal ideas he held when he was young and became an opponent of Liberal reforms. His brother, Nikolai I, who became tsar after Aleksandr's death in 1825, continued his brother's anti-Liberal policies and promoted autocracy, the Russian national culture, and the Orthodox Faith. He restricted Russian foreign travel, censored books and periodicals, and organized a secret police force. Nikolai imprisoned anyone who tried to lure Russians away from the Orthodox Church.

- As the Defender of Orthodoxy, Tsar Nikolai I aided the Greeks in their revolution against the Ottoman Empire. The uprising, which began in 1821, continued into 1829. In 1827, France and Great Britain joined Russia in coming to the aid of the Greek insurgents. When the war at last ended, Greece was independent, but under the sultan's overlordship. Serbia, Wallachia, and Moldavia, too, won a degree of independence. In 1832, Russia, France, Great Britain, and Bavaria recognized Greece as an independent kingdom.

- The great powers did not restore Poland to independence after the fall of Napoleon. Instead, Tsar Aleksandr I divided his Polish possessions into two parts. One of these parts was called Congress Poland—a kingdom separate from Russia but having Russia's tsar as its king. Despite its semi-independence, Congress Poland suffered from a variety of oppressions. In 1830, the Poles rose up against Russian rule. Though at first successful, the Polish revolution suffered from serious weaknesses. Russian forces finally crushed the uprising in September 1831.

- In 1832, Tsar Nikolai I abolished Congress Poland, making it just another province of the Russian Empire. He attempted to replace the Polish language with the Russian language in government. He struck out against the Catholic Church in Poland and persecuted Eastern Catholics, to force them into the Orthodox Church.

Chapter Goals

This chapter introduces an important counterpoint to Enlightenment rationalism—the movement called Romanticism. It is important that students understand what Romanticism was and how it was more than a reaction to rationalism. At the same time, students should understand that Romanticism had its weaknesses that led to certain excesses, resulting in a further cultural decline in some aspects of European life. Students should consider how and in what ways Romanticism may influence us to this day.

The story of William Cobbett illustrates how a traditional and even "backward looking" viewpoint can inspire a radical and even progressive response. Cobbett did not stand up for the farmer out of some new ideological perspective; rather, his calls for justice and societal reform were rooted in traditional European and Christian notions of the nature of the family and the role of government in the life of the nation. As we shall see in subsequent chapters, Cobbett was but one of many social reformers whose prescriptions were not so much revolution but restoration.

Russia, on the other hand, presents us with the example of a nation that was merely conservative of the *status quo*. And, as subsequent chapters will show, this unthinking conservativism would be productive of the most radical consequences, by way of reaction.

Period Music

The following composers may be described as early Romantic or Classical/Romantic transition composers:

Ludwig van Beethoven (1770–1827):

The following are but a few suggestions gleaned from Beethoven's numerous compositions:

- Symphony No. 1 in C major, Opus 21: composed 1799–1800, this is a good example of Beethoven's more classical-style compositions. It is good to contrast with his Symphony No. 3, *Eroica*.

- Symphony No. 5 in C minor, Opus 67: composed 1804–1808

- Symphony No. 6 in F major, Opus 68 ("Pastoral"): composed 1804–1808

- Symphony No. 9 in D minor, Opus 125 ("Choral"): composed 1817–1824

- Violin Concerto in D major (1806)

- Piano Concerto No. 3 in C minor: composed 1800–1801

- Piano Concerto No. 5 in E-flat major ("Emperor"): composed 1809–1810

- Violin Sonata No. 4 in A minor, Opus 23 (1801)

- Violin Sonata No. 5 in F major, Opus 24 (1801)—"Spring"

- Violin Sonata No. 9 in A major, Opus 47 (1803)—"Kreutzer"

- *Fidelio*, an opera in two acts, Opus 72 (1814)

- *Missa Solemnis* in D major (1827)

- String Quartets Nos. 12-16 (1823–1826)— many find these pieces difficult to listen to. They are highly experimental and give one a foretaste of later, 20th century styles. Despite their difficulty, however, they are worth the effort of listening, at least by the teacher.

Fernando Sor (1778–1839), a Spanish composer for the classical guitar

Niccolò Paganini (1782–1840), a famous violin virtuoso who transformed the art of violin playing

Carl Maria von Weber (1786–1826)

- *Der Freischütz* (a Romantic opera that inspired Richard Wagner)

- *Oberon, or the Elf King's Oath* (a Romantic opera)

Gioachino Rossini (1792–1868)

- *Il Barbiere di Siviglia* (the "Barber of Seville"), a comic opera in two acts

- *Guillaume Tell* ("William Tell"), an opera in four acts. This opera includes the famous "William Tell Overture" of cartoon fame.

What Students Should Know

1. **What the classical style in art was**

   The classical style was an art style that flourished in the 18th century and stressed an imitation of the classical Greek and Roman spirit in literature, plastic arts, and music. Inspired by Enlightenment rationalism, the classical style emphasized reason, proportion, brilliance, and wit.

2. **The leading characteristics of Romanticism**

   a) The word *romantic* refers to the spirit men like Friedrich von Schlegel thought was behind the fanciful literary works of the Middle Ages.

   b) Romanticism held that reason works to create works of art in order to express infinite beauty in finite forms.

   c) Romanticism rejected the idea that true knowledge comes only by experience and experiment. It upheld mysticism—the sense that the world contains mysteries that cannot be grasped by the senses or by reason alone.

   d) It was not a movement of clearly defined ideas.

Key Terms at a Glance

literary critic: one who gives his opinions on works of literature and helps others to understand them

plastic art: a visual art, such as painting or sculpture; nonplastic arts include literature and music

classical style: an art style that flourished in the 18th century and stressed an imitation of the classical Greek and Roman spirit in literature, plastic arts, and music. Inspired by Enlightenment rationalism, the classical style emphasized reason, proportion, brilliance, and wit.

mysticism: the sense or knowledge that the world contains mysteries that cannot be grasped by the senses or by reason alone

political economist: someone who studies the relationship between economics (buying, selling, trade, etc.) and the laws and customs of nations

decentralized: not centralized. In decentralized states, power and authority are shared by the central government and local governments and institutions, such as the family, the Church, and guilds. Medieval kingdoms were decentralized; Louis XIV's France was not.

habeas corpus: a right that protects citizens from illegal imprisonment

universal manhood suffrage: the right of all adult male citizens to vote

benefice: lands and the wealth they produce, given as a grant to a member of the clergy

Home Office: a department of the British government that protected peace and security within the kingdom

seditious libel: a damaging published statement that incites others to rise against lawful authority

peer: a member of one of the five ranks of the British aristocracy—dukes, marquises, earls, viscounts, and barons

primate: a bishop who has the first place in honor or authority among bishops in a given region or nation

Levant: the countries bordering the eastern Mediterranean

pasha: an official of high rank in the Ottoman Empire

suzerain: an overlord

unconditional surrender: surrender without any conditions or promises

novitiate: the state of being a new member or *novice* of a religious order; also, a house where novices are trained

Uniate: the name given to those eastern Christians and churches that came into union (the *Unia*) with the pope in Rome. Today, such churches are generally called Byzantine Catholic or Greek Catholic; the term *Uniate* is generally considered to be offensive. We use it in this chapter because, in the early 19th century, it was the term commonly used to designate the eastern Catholic churches.

3. **Why so many Romantics became Catholic**

    Since they valued highly a mystical apprehension of reality, many Romantics were drawn to the Catholic Church, which offered a mystical vision of faith.

4. **What were the good and bad effects of Romanticism**

    Romanticism had a good influence on culture in the 19th century because it opened minds and hearts again to religion and away from a narrow, rationalistic view of the world. However, it had bad effects, for it tended to make one's feelings and emotions the sole guide of right and wrong and so undermined the conviction that there is absolute truth and that humans can come to know it.

5. **What Romanticism influenced**

    Romanticism, of course, influenced the arts primarily. It was first a literary movement, but then it spread to painting and, especially, music. Indeed, most people probably associate Romanticism primarily with music—and it was to be in music that its influence would last longest. If the father of Romanticism itself was Schlegel, the father of Romantic music was Beethoven. Yet, Romanticism did not just influence art; it gave form to how people thought about the world around them. Schlegel, for instance, formed Romantic political ideals. Romanticism led people to choose religion—such as those who became Catholic or those who embraced, say, pantheism. Romanticism not only turned against Enlightenment theories of art but against the Enlightenment itself. This shows that Romanticism was a way of looking at the world as well as an art theory.

6. **Why, in spite of the enclosure of agricultural lands, the industrial revolution, and the gathering of people in industrial centers, did revolutionary ideas influence only a few in England**

    In part, this was because the English associated revolutionary ideas with Napoleon, and Napoleon was the national enemy. Since the Tory government led the resistance to Napoleon, Englishmen tended to side with the Tories against those who criticized them and called for governmental reform. Even after the fall of Napoleon, Englishmen remained committed to the ideals of national unity, the British Constitution, and individual freedom. There was little support for democracy.

7. **What happened after Waterloo that led some to question whether or not England was really the land of constitutional freedom and the "envy of surrounding nations."**

    The first years after the Battle of Waterloo were particularly hard on the English working people, both in the cities and the countryside. Periods of unprecedented economic depression (a period of low business activity and production along with high unemployment) threw workers into unemployment. Bad harvests in the countryside meant less work for farmworkers, many of whom were already living in poverty because of enclosures.

8. **Who William Cobbett was, what he thought were the ills affecting the English rural population, and what his solutions were**

    William Cobbett was an English political writer and social critic. He deeply loved England, English traditions, the English people, and the English countryside. He protested against the effects the agricultural revolution and enclosures were having on the poor; how rising prices for goods (on account of the war) were causing great sufferings. Peasants were losing their hold on the land, and landlords were demanding shorter leases and higher rents—

and when peasants couldn't afford these, they were evicted. Cobbett said that financiers (those who deal on a large scale with money for investment in businesses or banks) and speculators (those who buy property or goods hoping to sell them for a higher price than what they bought them for) were taking advantage of the farmers for quick profits.

Cobbett agreed with many of the measures the reform members suggested for the British government, but he thought the best way to help the common Englishman was to make it possible for as many people as possible to own their own property like farms and shops for manufacturing goods. He wanted England to return to the time when wealth was well distributed or divided among all social classes.

9. **What other reformers were calling for**

Among the reform measures called for by "radicals" are the following:

a) Abolishing "pocket" and "rotten" boroughs

b) Extending the right to vote to the new industrial cities and to wider groups of people

c) Giving a salary to members of Parliament so that others besides the rich could sit in Parliament

d) Yearly elections for members of Parliament

e) Universal manhood suffrage

f) Voting by secret ballot

10. **What Catholic emancipation was**

Since the 16th century, English law had forbidden Catholics to serve in Parliament or to vote for members of Parliament. Penal laws carrying punishments of fines, imprisonment, and even death (for priests) were still on the law books. In Ireland, only Protestants could serve as magistrates, and Catholics had to pay tithes to support the Protestant Church of Ireland.

Catholic emancipation referred to the attempt to overturn these disabilities against Catholics. The first step toward reform of the government was the Catholic Relief Act of 1829, which gave Catholics the right to sit in Parliament and repealed the last anti-Catholic laws in Ireland.

11. **What caused the Last Laborers' Revolt and what were its results**

Poverty and hunger in the countryside, stemming from the enclosures, inspired unrest among the peasants of the English countryside. The new agricultural machines put more men out of work. The revolt began in August 1830 when about 400 workmen destroyed threshing machines belonging to local farmers. Over the next few months, the revolt spread into nearly every county in England. It was put down by early 1831. About 450 men were exiled to British colonies overseas, either for a period of years or for life. Some were condemned to slavery. Family members were separated.

12. **What Earl Grey's reform measures of 1832 entailed**

a) Small towns, rotten boroughs, new industrial towns, and the most populous counties received representation in Parliament

b) Still, the number of new voters was not great, and it included mostly those who belonged to the prosperous urban middle class.

c) The Whigs (Liberals) became predominant in government. Under their control, Parliament abolished black slavery in the British Empire, removed cruel laws dealing with imprisonment and punishment of criminals, and established a bureau to look out for public health.

d) Still, Great Britain remained an oligarchy of industrialists, financiers, merchants, and aristocrats.

13. How Tsar Aleksandr I changed during the latter part of his reign

Aleksandr came to regret his acceptance and promotion of Liberal reforms. He turned his back entirely on Liberal reforms. His government crushed attempts made by Russians to oppose government policies. By the 1820s, he had given up any idea of freeing the serfs.

14. Who the Decembrists were and what they did

The Decembrists were prominent men who were Liberals and members of secret societies who favored a constitution for Russia. On December 26, 1825, when Tsar Nikolai I was formally to take power in St. Petersburg, the Russian soldiers who were present rioted (at the instigation of the Decembrists). The insurrection was put down, and Nikolai ordered the arrest of the Decembrist conspirators, most of whom were exiled, though a few were executed.

15. What kind of ruler Tsar Nikolai I was

Nikolai deeply loved Russia and sincerely desired to lead her to happiness and glory. He was an anti-Liberal whose guiding principles were "Autocracy, Orthodoxy, and Nationality." He would have nothing to do with constitutional government but insisted on autocratic government. Russia, he thought, was the bastion of the Orthodox faith, and so Russian culture and traditions were to be preserved from and purified of all that was not Russian and Orthodox. He wanted to preserve Russians from non-Russian ideas by such measures as restricting Russian foreign travel, censoring books and periodicals, and organizing a secret police force. Those who were found guilty of proselytizing Orthodox Christians could be imprisoned and even sent to Siberia. Special rewards were given to those who converted people of other religions to the Orthodox Church.

16. How Greek Christians suffered under the Ottoman Empire

Under the Muslim Ottomans, Orthodox Christians had suffered bitterly for centuries. Their young sons had been seized and forced to become Muslim, and they were drafted into the sultan's elite military guard, the Janissaries and forced to become Muslim. The Greek people had fallen into poverty and barbarism,

17. The course of the Greek war of independence

As the Defender of Orthodoxy, Tsar Nikolai I aided the Greeks in their revolution against the Ottoman Empire. The uprising, which began in 1821, continued into 1829. In 1827, France and Great Britain joined Russia in coming to the aid of the Greek insurgents. When the war at last ended, Greece was independent but under the sultan's overlordship. Serbia, Wallachia, and Moldavia, too, won a degree of independence. In 1832, Russia, France, Great Britain, and Bavaria recognized Greece as an independent kingdom.

18. What happened to Poland after the fall of Napoleon

The great powers did not restore Poland to independence after the fall of Napoleon. Instead, Tsar Aleksandr I divided his Polish possessions into two parts. One of these parts was called Congress Poland—a kingdom separate from Russia but having Russia's tsar as its king. The tsar ruled Congress Poland through a lieutenant governor. Its official religion was Catholic, though it tolerated other religions.

Yet, despite its semi-independence, Congress Poland suffered from a variety of oppressions under the lieutenant governor, Grand Duke Konstantin. He used secret police against Polish patriotic movements, replaced Poles with Russians in government and the military, and ignored the government's constitution. Under Tsar Nikolai I, Konstantin's rule grew even harsher. The tsar ignored the complaints of members of the Polish parliament, the *Sejm*.

19. **The course of the Uprising of 1830 and what happened afterwards**

In 1830, the Poles rose up against Russian rule. Though at first successful and receiving funds from western Europe and the United States of America, the Polish revolution suffered from serious weaknesses. Russian forces finally crushed the Uprising in September 1831.

In 1832, Tsar Nikolai I abolished Congress Poland, making it just another province of the Russian Empire. He attempted to replace the Polish language with the Russian language in government. He struck out against the Catholic Church in Poland and persecuted Eastern Catholics, to force them into the Orthodox Church.

20. **Identify the following:**

Friedrich von Schlegel: A German writer who was one of the chief founders of the Romantic movement

Ludwig van Beethoven: A German composer and founder of the Romantic movement in music

Charles, Earl Grey: prime minister of Great Britain, 1830–1834; a supporter of government reform who pushed a reform bill through Parliament in 1831–1832

universal manhood suffrage: the right of all adult male citizens to vote

habeas corpus: a right that protects citizens from illegal imprisonment

disenfranchise: to remove the right to vote from someone; *to enfranchise* means to grant someone the right to vote

peer: a member of one of the five ranks of the British aristocracy—dukes, marquises, earls, viscounts, and barons

unconditional surrender: surrender without any conditions or promises

Questions for Review

1. **Why did Friedrich von Schlegel's friends call him *Messias*?**

Schlegel's friend called him *Messias* because of the important role he played in the development of the Romantic movement in literature.

2. **How did Romantic ideas about art differ from classical ideas?**

The classical style stressed an imitation of the classical Greek and Roman spirit in literature, plastic arts, and music. Artists were to imitate the natural world but in the manner the Greeks and Romans did their art. A classical artwork had to be strictly rational; it could express emotion, but only if it observed strict rules that classicists thought were drawn from principles discoverable by reason.

Romantics, on the other hand, thought the purpose of art is to express the infinite beauty the artist perceives with his mind. Romantics did not reject reason, for they thought it disciplines how an artist works and creates art. Yet, Romantics were drawn to mysticism—the sense or knowledge that the world contains mysteries that cannot be grasped by the senses or by reason alone. Classicism emphasized that the artist imitates what he sees; Romanticism thought art expresses the unseen world.

3. **Why were so many Romantic artists and thinkers attracted to the Catholic Church?**

Romantics were attracted to the Catholic Church because they saw she had not only created the medieval culture they so admired but still preserved a mystical view of God and the universe.

4. **What did William Cobbett mean by the word *freedom*?**

By freedom, Cobbett meant the ownership of private, productive property, such as a farm or manufacturing shop.

5. **What was Catholic emancipation in British history?**

Catholic emancipation referred to the removal of laws that restricted Catholic freedom, forced Catholics to support Protestant religion, forbade them the right to vote or serve in office, and imposed similar burdens. The goal of Catholic emancipation was to realize in law the equal status of Catholic subjects.

6. **Why did English rural workers rise up in the Last Laborers' Revolt in 1830?**

Poverty and hunger in the countryside, stemming from the enclosures, inspired unrest among the peasants of the English countryside. The new agricultural machines put men out of work. These causes brought about the revolt in 1830.

7. **Why did rich industrialists support Earl Grey's reform bill? Why did William Cobbett?**

Industrialists and merchants supported the reform bill because they saw it as a way of increasing their influence in the government. Though he did not think the reform bill went far enough, Cobbett urged his followers to support it since, he said, it was the best that anyone could expect at the time.

8. **What sort of men backed the Decembrist uprising in Russia in 1825? What ideas about government and society did they support?**

The Decembrist revolutionaries were prominent men who were Liberals and men belonging to secret societies. They wanted to transform Russia from an autocracy to a constitutional monarchy.

9. **Tsar Nikolai I guided his reign by the ideals of *autocracy, orthodoxy,* and *nationality*. To what does each of these terms refer?**

By *autocracy,* Nikolai meant absolute monarchy—his own, without any constitutional checks. By *orthodoxy,* he meant the Russian Orthodox Church, which, he said, must be preserved and promoted. He saw Russia as the bastion of the Orthodox Church. By *nationality,* Nikolai meant Russian culture and identity, which he thought he had to preserve from all outside influences.

10. **Why did the Poles rebel against Russian rule in 1830?**

Under indirect Russian rule, Congress Poland suffered from a variety of oppressions. The lieutenant governor Konstantin used secret police against Polish patriotic movements, replaced Poles with Russians in government and the military, and ignored the government's constitution. Under Tsar Nikolai I, Konstantin's rule grew even harsher. The tsar ignored the complaints of members of the Polish parliament, the *Sejm*.

Ideas in Action

1. **Listen to Wolfgang Amadeus Mozart's Symphony Number 41 in C Major, K. 551 (the *Jupiter Symphony*), a classical-era composition. Then listen to Beethoven's Symphony Number 3 in E Flat Major, Op. 55 (*Eroica*), his first fully Romantic composition. Discuss how the styles of the symphonies differ. How do they demonstrate the differences between the Romantic and classical styles?**

2. **William Cobbett despised potatoes; but it has been said that this New World root vegetable had contributed to the better health of Europeans since the 16th century, when it was introduced into the European diet.**

Research the history of the potato—where it originally came from, how it was brought to Europe, and whether it has truly been beneficial to human health and well-being.

3. Research the history of one of the Byzantine Catholic Churches of Eastern Europe—the Ruthenian Byzantine Catholic Church, for example, or the Ukrainian Greek Catholic Church. When did they come into full union with the pope? What difficulties have they encountered in their history since that time? How are they alike, and how do they differ, from Orthodox Churches in Eastern Europe?

4. Dorothea Schlegel's son, Philipp Veit, himself converted to the Catholic Faith. A painter, he joined a group of artists called the Nazarenes, who rejected the classical art style of the art academies of Europe. Research the Nazarenes and their artistic ideas. Find prints of their work.

5. The English novelist Charles Dickens learned how the poor of London lived after his father, John Dickens, was imprisoned for debt. At one point, Charles had to accept employment in a warehouse, where he worked 10 hours a day for very little pay. Such experiences became the basis of many of Dickens's novels. One of these novels is *David Copperfield*, where Dickens based a character, Mr. Micawber, on his father. Read *David Copperfield* or another Dickens novel, such as *Oliver Twist, Hard Times,* or *Great Expectations.*

Sample Quiz I (pages 265–271)

Please answer the following in complete sentences.

1. Who was the man called the *Messias* of Romanticism?

2. What did classical artists try to imitate in their works of art?

3. What did Romantic artists try to express in their works of art?

4. Who was the composer who first introduced romanticism into music?

Answers to Sample Quiz I

Students' answers should approximate the following.

1. *Friedrich von Schlegel* was called the *Messias* of Romanticism.

2. Classical artists tried to imitate nature, what they saw, but in the way the ancients did art.

3. Romantic artists tried to express *infinite beauty* in their pieces of art.

4. The composer who introduced Romanticism into music was *Ludwig van Beethoven.*

Sample Quiz II (pages 271–280)

Please answer the following in complete sentences.

1. Were the English during the Napoleonic wars in favor of revolutionary ideas, like those the French revolutionaries had adopted? Please explain.

2. What is the term for those men who deal on a large scale with money for investment in businesses or banks? What is the term for those who buy property or goods hoping to sell them for a higher price than what they bought them for? Why did William Cobbett like neither of these two groups?

3. What did Cobbett think was the best way to help the common Englishman?

4. What is the name for the attempt in early 19th century Great Britain to remove laws and restrictions against Catholics?

5. What especially did the workers seek to destroy during the Last Laborers' Revolt?

6. Who was the prime minister of Great Britain who was able to get Parliament to pass a reform bill in 1832?

Answers to Sample Quiz II

Students' answers should approximate the following

1. The English were not in favor of revolutionary ideas during the Napoleonic wars because they associated such ideas with Napoleon, the enemy of England. Instead of revolutionary ideas, the English held to the ideals of national unity, the British Constitution, and individual freedom.

2. *Financiers* are men who deal on a large scale with money for investment in businesses or banks. *Speculators* are those who buy property or goods hoping to sell them for a higher price than what they bought them for. Cobbett liked neither financiers nor speculators because he thought they were taking advantage of the farmers for quick profits.

3. Cobbett thought the best way to help the common Englishman was to make it possible for as many people as possible to own their own property, like farms and shops for manufacturing goods.

4. *Catholic Emancipation* is the name for the attempt in early 19th century Great Britain to remove laws and restrictions against Catholics.

5. Workers sought to destroy *threshing machines* during the Last Laborers' Revolt.

6. *Earl Grey* was the prime minister who was able to get Parliament to pass the reform bill in 1832.

Sample Quiz III (pages 280–289)

Please answer the following in complete sentences.

1. **What was the name for the Liberals and members of secret societies who tried to overthrow Tsar Nikolai I on December 26, 1825?**

2. **What three terms express the ideals that guided Tsar Nikolai as Russia's tsar?**

3. **Why did Tsar Nikolai I decide to help the Greeks in their revolution against the Ottoman Empire?**

4. **What was the name of the Polish state formed by Tsar Aleksandr I over which he was king but which he ruled independently from Russia?**

5. **Who was victorious in the Polish Uprising of 1830? What happened to Poland?**

Answers to Sample Quiz III

Students' answers should approximate the following.

1. *Decembrists* was the name for the men who tried to overthrow Nikolai I.

2. *Autocracy, Orthodoxy,* and *Nationality* express the ideals that guided Tsar Nikolai's reign.

3. Tsar Nikolai I decided to help the Greeks in their revolution because they were Orthodox Christians and he saw himself as the Defender of Orthodoxy.

4. The Polish state formed by Tsar Aleksandr I was *Congress Poland.*

5. The Russians were victorious over the Poles in the Uprising of 1830. Tsar Nikolai abolished Congress Poland and made it just another province of Russia.

Essays (200–500 words each)

Instructions to be given to the students: Write in complete sentences. Underline your thesis. Give three supports or examples that explain why you think what you do and that support your thesis.

1. Compare Romantic with classical views of art. How are they alike? How do they differ? Which school of art do you think has a better explanation of art?

2. According to William Cobbett, what was the best way to help common Englishmen in the early 19th century? Based on what you have read in this book about the Industrial Revolution, the French Revolution, and the enclosures, do you think he was right? Why or why not?

Chapter Test

Please answer the following in complete sentences.

I. Short Essay—Answer two of the following:

1. What arts were influenced by Romanticism? Was Romanticism just a set of ideas about how to do art, or did it apply to other areas of life as well? Please explain.

2. What caused the English to rise up in the Last Laborers' Revolt? Was the revolt bloody like the French Revolution? What did the peasants mostly destroy, and why? Was the revolt successful?

3. Autocracy, Orthodoxy, and Nationality were the guiding ideas of Tsar Nikolai I's reign. What did he mean by autocracy? What did he reject because of this ideal? What did Orthodoxy refer to? Give one way he tried to preserve it. What did he mean by nationality? Describe one way he tried to preserve nationality.

II. Short Answer:

1. What good effect did Romanticism have on Europe in the 19th century? What was Romanticism's bad effect?

2. What was the name of the man his friends called the *Messias* of the Romantic movement?

3. Name two ways reformers in England wanted to reform the British government in the early 19th century.

4. Did the poor in the cities and countryside gain more power in the British government after Earl Grey's reform measures took effect? Please explain.

5. What did the Catholic Relief Act of 1829 do?

6. What eventually happened to Greece after its war of independence?

7. Who was the founder of the Romantic movement in music?

8. What is universal manhood suffrage?

Answer Key to Chapter Test

Students' answers should approximate the following:

I.

1. Romanticism was first a literary movement, but then it spread to other arts, including painting and music. Yet, Romanticism did not just influence art; it gave form to how people thought about the world around them. Schlegel, for instance, formed Romantic political ideals. Romanticism led people to choose religion—such as those who became Catholic or those who embraced, say, pantheism. Romantics saw themselves as in rebellion to 18th century rationalism. This shows that Romanticism was a way of looking at the world as well as an art theory.

2. There was much poverty and hunger in the English countryside, stemming from the enclosures. Threshing machines were putting farm laborers out of work, thus causing more poverty and hunger. Such conditions inspired the English peasants to rise in revolt. The revolt, however, was not bloody like the French Revolution had been. The chief victims of

violence were the threshing machines, which peasant mobs destroyed. The revolt, however, was not successful; it was put down by the government only a few months after it had begun.

3. By autocracy, Tsar Nikolai meant the absolute power of the tsar over all of Russia. Because of this idea, he rejected notions of Liberal government such as constitutional monarchy, or republicanism, or democracy. Orthodoxy referred to the Russian Orthodox Church. Ways Nikolai tried to preserve Orthodoxy were (possible answers):

   a) Those who were found guilty of proselytizing Orthodox Christians could be imprisoned and even sent to Siberia.

   b) Special rewards were given to those who converted people of other religions to the Orthodox Church.

   By Nationality, Nikolai I meant the Russian culture. He tried to preserve this by (possible answers):

   a) Restricting the ability of Russians to travel outside of Russia

   b) Censoring books and periodicals

   c) Organizing a secret police force

II.

1. Romanticism had a good influence on culture in the 19th century because it opened minds and hearts again to religion and away from a narrow, rationalistic view of the world. However, it tended to make one's feelings and emotions the sole guide of right and wrong and so undermined the conviction that there is absolute truth and that humans can come to know it.

2. *Friedrich von Schlegel* was called the *Messias* of the Romantic movement.

3. Possible answers:

   a) Abolishing "pocket" and "rotten" boroughs

   b) Extending the right to vote to the new industrial cities and to wider groups of people

   c) Giving a salary to members of Parliament so that others besides the rich could sit in Parliament

   d) Establishing yearly elections for members of Parliament

   e) Instituting universal manhood suffrage

   f) Mandating voting by secret ballot

4. No, the poor did not gain more power in the British government after Earl Grey's reform measures took effect. The British government remained an oligarchy.

5. The Catholic Relief Act of 1829 gave Catholics the right to sit in Parliament and repealed the last anti-Catholic laws in Ireland.

6. Greece eventually became an independent kingdom after its war of independence.

7. Ludwig van Beethoven was the founder of the Romantic movement in music.

8. Universal manhood suffrage is the right of all male citizens to vote.

CHAPTER 11: Romanticism and Revolt, Part II

Chapter Overview

- King Charles X was a very different man from his brother, King Louis XVIII. While Louis XVIII did not try to overthrow the constitutional monarchy of France, Charles X acted in ways that worried supporters of constitutional monarchy. He favored royalists in government and enacted measures that benefited the Catholic Church in France. When, at last, he enacted a new election law and suspended freedom of the press, revolution broke out in Paris. Charles X abdicated the throne on July 30, 1830.

- After Charles X's abdication, Louis Philippe, the Count of Orléans, became lieutenant governor and then, on August 7, 1830, "King of the French." Though Louis Philippe acted as a good republican and a true Liberal, favoring the interests of the bourgeoisie, he was working to build a new dynasty for himself and his family.

- France's July Revolution inspired the Belgians to revolt against King Willem I of the Netherlands. The Belgian rebellion began in late August 1830. The revolutionaries, made up of both Liberals and Catholics, established a provisional government whose laws reflected Liberal ideas. In 1831, the Belgian government asked Leopold of Saxe-Coburg Gotha to become king of Belgium. Similar Liberal uprisings in Germany, though at first successful, failed.

- In the years after the unsuccessful Carbonari rebellion in Sicily in 1821, the various states of Italy took stern measures against Liberals and members of revolutionary societies. Liberals in Italy were drawn mostly from the middle class and did not include the vast majority of the peasantry.

- The successors of Pope Pius VII were unwilling to entertain Liberal ideas or to change the traditional ways by which the Papal States had been governed. In 1831, Pope Gregory XI faced a rebellion in the Romagna that was engulfing some Habsburg-controlled states in Italy as well. Unable to put down the rebellion himself, Gregory had to rely on the Austrian army. The Austrians occupied the Romagna while French forces took the papal city of Ancona.

- After ending the rebellion, Austria, with other allied powers, demanded that Gregory institute Liberal reforms in the Papal States. Though he enacted some reforms, Gregory opposed making his government republican. In his encyclical, *Mirari Vos*, Gregory condemned Liberal errors, including indifferentism.

- Though he aspired to be a novelist and poet, Giuseppe Mazzini of Genoa dedicated himself to the political movement to drive foreign power from Italy and to unite all of the Italian peninsula and Sicily under one government. In 1831, he formed a group called Young Italy to inspire the youth of Italy to work, by violence if necessary, for the freedom and union of Italy.

- Mazzini and the Carbonari represented the radical wing of Italian Liberals because they wanted not only a united Italy, but a republican government. Other groups wanted a constitutional monarchy for Italy, while still others favored a federation of independent Italian states. One of the thorniest questions facing proponents of a new Italy was the Roman Question—what to do about the temporal authority of the pope.

- Throughout Europe, Liberalism was splitting into factions. More conservative Liberals favored *laissez-faire* in economics and republicanism in government, with a limited suffrage. Other Liberals, however, began calling for greater democracy and, in particular, a universal suffrage. More radical yet were the followers of Saint-Simon, the father of French socialism. Another important socialist of the period was Louis Blanc, who wanted the government to abolish private property and assure an equal wage to every worker. More radical yet was Pierre Joseph Proudhon, who wanted to abolish government as well as private property. Proudhon called the state of society he favored *anarchy*.

- By the 1840s, Catholic thinkers were responding to what became known as the social question. Though many Catholics still favored the ancient regime, others thought the Church had to accommodate itself to the new Liberal society. In addressing the social question, some Catholic thinkers looked to the Middle Ages as a model. One Catholic, Frédéric Ozanam (the founder of the Society of St. Vincent de Paul), rejected both capitalism and socialism and called for cooperative relationships between employers and employees as well as justice for workers.

- Pius IX received the reputation of being a Liberal soon after becoming pope in 1846. He granted amnesty to political prisoners who gave their word not to conspire against the papal government, reformed the institutions of the Papal States, and established an advisory senate for the realm. Yet, Pius was not a Liberal; indeed, he gave up nothing of what he deemed were the powers essential to the papacy both in the spiritual and temporal order.

- By 1848, it was clear to Liberals, democrats, and socialists in France that Louis Philippe was not the "citizen king" he had claimed to be. He had limited the suffrage and targeted what the French saw as their political liberties. On February 22, 1848, revolution broke out in Paris against the king; and two days later, Louis Philippe abdicated.

- Louis Philippe's reign was followed by the establishment of France's Second Republic. The new government was formed from a coalition of Liberals, Catholics, and socialists. This made the government unstable, which earned it disfavor in the departments outside of Paris. Hoping for stability, many of the French supported the candidacy of Prince Louis-Napoleon Bonaparte, who was elected president of France in December 1848.

Chapter Goals

In this chapter we see how our civilization continued to struggle with Liberalism. We see the continuing vibrancy of Liberalism; we get the sense that Metternich's attempts to stamp it out were ultimately vain and even counterproductive. The papacy's response, too, was merely reactive and largely ineffective. Pius IX's attempts to accommodate what he could of measures Liberals demanded were generous—but could they appease men who were opposed to what the Church saw as her essential constitution?

We see, too, a new question confronting our civilization—the social question, a question not directly addressed by Liberalism. Liberalism had asked a political question, having to do with the power of government and its relation to civil society and individuals and their freedom. In addressing this question, Liberalism had proposed an economic theory, *laissez-faire*. This theory had led to much suffering among the poor and thus gave rise to what we call the "social question," addressing how society can bring justice to the poor workers and assure them dignity and freedom from exploitation. Various answers were given to this question—socialism, anarchism, and the first flowering of what would become Catholic social teaching. The teacher should be careful that students understand the answers of these various groups, for, in one form or another, they will be quite significant in the remaining decades of the 19th century and into the 20th century.

Period Music

- Daniel-François-Esprit Auber, *La Muette de Portici*, Orchestre Philharmonique de Monte-Carlo, Thomas Fulton, conductor. EMI Classics (Angel Records) CD—This is the opera that inspired the Belgian revolution of 1830.

- Hector Berlioz, *Grande Symphonie Funèbre et Triomphale* (written in 1840 to commemorate the 10th anniversary of the July Revolution of 1830)

What Students Should Know

1. **Why Liberals were dissatisfied with King Charles X**

   Charles X pushed policies that worried republican Liberals and Liberal proponents of constitutional monarchy—such as appointing royalists as his chief ministers. By paying *émigrés* for their lost lands, he angered the bourgeoisie. Liberals were upset with the king because he seemed to be reestablishing the Catholic Church in France. He dissolved a Liberal legislature, annulled elections to another legislature, and then removed the right to vote from the majority of those who voted in the election.

2. **What the July Revolution was, why it occurred, and what its result was**

   The July Revolution was an uprising in Paris against King Charles X. It occurred because Liberals were dissatisfied with Charles X's attempts to restore the ancient regime and the Catholic Church in France. Riots among the poor and unemployed workers began on the evening of July 27, 1830. The next days, the riots spread. By July 29, it was clear to Charles X that he was dealing with a revolution. On July 30, he abdicated, naming as king his grandson, Henri, Count of Chambord.

3. **Who Louis Philippe was**

   Louis Philippe was descended from a younger brother of King Louis XIV. Louis Philippe's father, the Duke of Orléans, had joined the revolutionaries and voted for the execution of his cousin, Louis XVI. Louis Philippe had joined the Jacobin Club (before it was extremist), but fled with Dumoriez to the Austrians. For a time, Louis Philippe lived in America, but he returned to Europe. Louis XVIII invited Louis Philippe to return to France, where he

Key Terms at a Glance

franchise: the right to vote

tariff: a duty or tax placed on goods imported into a country

provisional: temporary. A *provisional government* is a temporary government established until a permanent government is put in place.

Patrimony of St. Peter: that portion of the Papal States which included Rome and the lands of the duchy of Rome surrounding it

liberation of Italy: the goal of those who wanted to free Italy from Austrian and Habsburg rule

pacification: noun form of the verb *pacify*, to restore to a peaceful state; to subdue

reactionary: one who reacts, who responds to an idea by taking the opposite opinion or an act by doing the opposite to that act

indifferentism: the belief that people do not have the duty to believe in God by worshiping in and practicing the one true religion

Roman Question: the problem of what to do about the pope's temporal power in a united Italy

egalitarian: one who believes in equality, in removing all social, political, and economic inequalities among men

Saint-Simonianism: the socialist ideas of Claude Henri de Rouvroy, the Count of Saint-Simon. He taught that society should own all property in common under the control of a group of industrial chiefs. A group of scientists should help these industrialists to direct society toward peace and prosperity and replace the Church as the spiritual guide of society.

socialism: the doctrine that all productive property (factories, farms, and shops) should be taken from the ownership of individuals and entrusted to the government

anarchism: the idea that individuals should be free to join organizations in society or to leave them. Such organizations would have direction and even a kind of government, but the government would not be able to use force to make anyone do anything.

throne and altar: the watchword of royalist Catholics who wanted to restore the old alliance of the Church and Catholic monarchy

social question: the problem confronting people of the mid-19th century of how to bring justice to the poor workers and assure their dignity and freedom from exploitation

joined the Liberal opposition to the king and lived like a wealthy bourgeois, not a prince.

Since Louis Philippe had sworn to support King Henri V, Charles appointed him lieutenant governor. But Louis Philippe, instead, accepted the provisional government's offer to make him King of the French.

As king, Louis Philippe abolished the white lily flag for the revolutionary tricolor. He said his authority came, not from God, but from the French people—he was a "citizen king" and the "King of the French."

Yet, though Louis Philippe acted like a Liberal, he was not a true one. His real intent was to build a new dynasty. During the years of his reign, France restricted the right to vote to mostly landowners and owners of industrial property. The French government favored the wealthy bourgeoisie over every other class.

4. What effects the July Revolution had elsewhere in France

The July Revolution inspired a similar revolution in Belgium (then the southern Netherlands) in 1830. The revolution resulted in the independence of Belgium from Holland. Though Catholics had played an important part in the revolution, the new constitution for Belgium reflected the influence of Liberalism, including provisions for freedom of religion and of the press. The July Revolution resulted in German rulers granting Liberal constitutions; but, with the support of Metternich, German rulers were able in the end to reassert their anti-Liberal regimes.

5. What was the condition of Italy in the years 1815–1830

The governments of the states into which Italy was divided took stern measures against Liberals and members of revolutionary societies, such as the Carbonari. Rulers, such as Fernando I of the Kingdom of the Two Sicilies, could be harsh and cruel. Liberals and revolutionaries were drawn mostly from the middle classes; peasants remained aloof from such movements. Liberals, however, were divided, for some favored a federation of Italian states, while others wanted a united Italian state.

6. The condition of the Papal States during this time period

Both good and bad things could be told about the Papal States in the first quarter of the 19th century. The pope's government was mild on the whole. It showed genuine concern for the good of its citizens; it provided free healthcare and its taxes were low. The government attempted to control bandits; Leo XII tried to rid the government of corrupt officials.

Still, papal officials were often incompetent, and the courts of law were not properly run. Middle and upper class laymen resented the fact that only clergymen held the top positions in the pope's government.

7. The character of Popes Leo XII and Pius VIII

Leo XII worked to improve living conditions in the Papal States, but he defended old ways and customs without questioning whether they were truly good or proper for the times. He had no patience with questions of political reform but insisted on obedience to constituted authority. His ministers used harsh measures against revolutionists. Pius VIII abolished Leo XII's secret police and recognized the government of Louis Philippe, but he died only 20 months into his reign.

8. The character of Pope Gregory XVI and his reign

During his reign of 15 years, Pope Gregory XVI faced two revolutions that sought to overthrow his temporal power. Both were put down by Austria. He worked for the health and prosperity of the people of the Papal States, founding hospitals, orphanages, and public baths. His first secretary of state, however, used harsh measures against the Carbonari, using a group called the Centurions who would at times execute anyone they suspected of being a revolutionary. In the fifth year of his reign, Gregory replaced this secretary of state with another.

In *Mirari Vos*, an important encyclical Gregory published in 1832, he condemned the doctrines of Liberalism, including indifferentism, the belief that people do not have the duty to believe in God by worshiping in and practicing the one true religion—the Catholic Faith. In this encyclical, the pope condemned *liberty of conscience*, the freedom to believe whatever one wants and to follow that belief in society, and *freedom to publish* whatever opinions one has. He said the freedom to publish falsehood was like the freedom to distribute poison—something no one could rightly tolerate.

9. What the different groups of Italian Liberals were

The Italian Liberals mirrored Liberals in other countries. There were Liberals who preferred a constitutional monarchy like that of France under Louis Philippe. There were Liberals who favored a republic. Some wanted a united Italy; others, a federation of independent states. One chief difference between the groups had to do with how they addressed the Roman Question—what to do about the pope's temporal power. Extremists wanted simply to abolish the Papal States, while others favored preserving the pope's temporal power under one form or another.

10. Who Giuseppe Mazzini was and what he accomplished

Mazzini as a Romantic Italian nationalist who saw it as his "apostolate" to free Italy from tyrants and bring all Italian states under one, republican government. He founded Young Italy, an organization to inspire Italian youth to work, by violence if necessary, for the freedom and union of Italy. Mazzini favored abolishing the pope's temporal power. He favored replacing the Catholic Church and, indeed, all the churches of Europe with a new religion of brotherhood. Under Mazzini's leadership, Young Italy became an important force in Italian politics and society.

11. What the social question was and how various thinkers responded to it

Since the 18th century, the application of the theory of *laissez-faire* in the economy had led to much suffering among the poor and thus gave rise to what we call the "social question"—how society can bring justice to the poor workers and assure them dignity and freedom from exploitation. Various answers were given to this question. One answer was *socialism*, the doctrine that all productive property (factories, farms, and shops) should be taken from the ownership of individuals and entrusted to the government. Socialists thus believed in abolishing all private property. They thought the government would direct the use of property for the good of all, especially the poor.

The anarchists agreed with the socialists that all private property should be abolished; but they disagreed with the socialist doctrine that all property should be given to the government. Anarchists believed that all government should be abolished. Instead, they wanted *anarchy*. What Pierre Joseph Proudhon, the father of anarchism, meant by anarchy was not a condition of society where everyone simply does what he wants, but a society where individuals freely join together in various organizations to achieve their goals. The government of these organizations, however, would not be able to use force to make anyone do anything. Individuals would remain free both to join and leave these organizations.

Catholic thinkers began to awaken to the social question during this period. We have seen that certain Catholic Romantics like Schlegel objected to *laissez-faire* theories. But the first "modern" attempt to address the social question was by Blessed Antoine-Frédéric Ozanam, the founder of the St. Vincent de Paul Society. Ozanam condemned both capitalism and socialism. Capitalism, he said, treated men as mere tools of production for the sake of the rich and powerful and was thus little better than slavery. Socialism enslaved men to the state. He said society needed to embrace the "spirit of sacrifice" and triumph over the "spirit of selfishness." More concretely, Ozanam said:

a) Employers should look on their workers not as tools but as "associates"—fellow workers in the business enterprise.

b) Workers should receive a "natural wage"—one large enough to support a frugal worker and his family in reasonable comfort.

c) A father should make enough money so that his wife and children need not work.

12. **When Pius IX became pope**

Pius IX became pope, following the death of Gregory XVI, in June 1846.

13. **Why Pius IX was called a Liberal Pope**

As archbishop of Spoletto, Pius had earned the reputation of being a Liberal because he spared the lives of revolutionaries when they fled to the city. As pope, he granted amnesty to all political refugees; pardoned political prisoners (if they swore not to plot against the government); reformed hospitals, prisons, and religious houses; built a railroad and erected streetlights; and allowed Jews to live outside the ghetto and receive Catholic charity services. But it was the establishment of a senate, with lay delegates popularly elected, that fixed Pius's "Liberal" reputation. However, the senate had only an advisory power in the government. Pius gave up none of his authority, for he believed that the pope could not be subject to any other power, even on the political level.

14. **How Louis Philippe fell from power**

By 1848, it was clear to Liberals, democrats, and socialists in France that Louis Philippe was not the "citizen king" he had claimed to be. He had limited the suffrage and targeted what the French saw as their political liberties. On February 22, 1848, revolution broke out in Paris against the king; and two days later, Louis Philippe abdicated.

15. **What followed Louis Philippe's abdication**

Louis Philippe's reign was followed by the establishment of France's Second Republic. The new government was formed from a coalition of Liberals, Catholics, and socialists. It dissolved the monarchy and appointed a provisional government. The revolution that established the Second Republic was not, like the French Revolution, anti-Christian or even anticlerical. The revolutionaries held religion in high respect.

The new government, however, had to include socialists; for, the revolution of 1848 was more about social justice than Liberal governmental reforms. When, however, the government abandoned some socialist-inspired measures, Paris was rocked by a workers' uprising, which was put down.

The seeming instability of the new government earned it disfavor in the departments outside of Paris. Hoping for stability, many of the French supported the candidacy of Prince Louis-Napoleon Bonaparte, Napoleon I's nephew, who was elected president of France in December 1848.

16. **Identify the following:**

Louis Blanc: a French socialist thinker and politician

egalitarian: one who believes in equality, in removing all social, political, and economic inequalities among men

reactionary: one who responds to an idea by taking the opposite opinion or an act by doing the opposite to that act

Questions for Review

1. **What did King Charles X do to anger Liberals in France?**

Charles X angered Liberals by such policies as appointing royalists as his chief ministers, paying *émigrés* for their lost lands, restoring women's monasteries, by backing the "Law of Sacrilege," allowing the Jesuits into France, and commanding the censorship of journals and periodicals. He dissolved a Liberal legislature, annulled elections to another legislature, and removed the right to vote from the majority of those who voted in the election.

2. **Why did supporters of constitutional monarchy back Louis Philippe as king of France? Did he turn out to be the sort of king they thought he would be? Please explain.**

Backers of constitutional monarchy backed Louis Philippe because he had the reputation of being a Liberal. He behaved, not as a prince, but as a bourgeois gentleman. He had also been a member of the Liberal opposition to King Louis XVIII. Louis Philippe, however, was no true Liberal. His chief interest was not in advancing liberty, equality, and fraternity but in establishing for his family a dynasty to replace that of his Bourbon cousin, Charles X. During the years of his reign, France restricted the right to vote to mostly landowners and owners of industrial property. The French government favored the wealthy bourgeoisie over every other class.

3. **What happened in Belgium and Germany because of the French revolution of 1830?**

Inspired by the French revolution of 1830, Belgians rose up against the government of King Willem I of Holland and established Belgium as an independent constitutional monarchy. In Germany, inspired by the Spirit of 1830, Liberals forced the king of Saxony and the elector of Hesse to approve Liberal constitutions. In 1837, William IV established a constitution for Hanover. None of these reforms, however, lasted in Germany

4. **What apostolate did Giuseppe Mazzini think he had? Did all Italian patriots share his ideas? Please explain.**

Mazzini saw it as his "apostolate" to free Italy from tyrants and bring all Italian states under one, republican government. Not all Italian patriots, however, shared his ideas. Some wanted Italian unity, but under a constitutional monarchy. Others did not favor a united Italian state but a sort of federation of the existing independent states.

5. **What, according to Pope Gregory XVI's encyclical *Mirari Vos*, are the errors of Liberalism?**

In *Mirari Vos*, Gregory condemned the doctrines of Liberalism, including indifferentism, the belief that people do not have the duty to believe in God by worshiping in and practicing the one true religion—the Catholic Faith. In this encyclical, the pope condemned *liberty of conscience*, the freedom to believe whatever one wants and to act according to that belief in society, and the *freedom to publish* whatever opinions one has.

6. **How were the ideas of Louis Blanc and Pierre Joseph Proudhon alike? How did they differ?**

Both Blanc and Proudhon thought that injustice in society arose from the ownership of private property. Both thus wanted to abolish private property. Blanc wanted the government to take control of all private property. Proudhon, however, did not want government ownership of property; he wanted no government at all. Instead, he favored voluntary associations.

7. **What did Frédéric Ozanam think about socialism and capitalism? How, according to Ozanam, was society to be saved from capitalism and socialism?**

Ozanam, was the founder of the St. Vincent de Paul Society. Ozanam condemned both capitalism and socialism. Capitalism, he said, treated men as mere tools of production for the sake of the rich and powerful and was thus little better than slavery. Socialism, he said, enslaved men to the state. He said society needed to embrace the "spirit of sacrifice" and triumph over the "spirit of selfishness." More concretely, Ozanam said:

a) Employers should look on their workers not as tools but as "associates," fellow workers in the business enterprise

b) Workers should receive a "natural wage"—one large enough to support a frugal worker and his family in reasonable comfort.

c) A father should make enough money so that his wife and children need not work.

8. **Why did some people think Pius IX was a Liberal pope?**

As archbishop of Spoletto, Pius had earned the reputation of being a Liberal because he spared the lives of revolutionaries when they fled to the city. As pope, he granted amnesty to all political refugees; pardoned political prisoners (if they swore not to plot against the government); reformed hospitals, prisons, and religious houses; built a railroad and erected streetlights; and allowed Jews to live outside the ghetto and receive Catholic charity services. But it was the establishment of an advisory senate, with lay delegates popularly elected, that fixed Pius's "Liberal" reputation.

However, the senate had only an advisory power in the government.

9. **Why did so many people in France support Prince Louis-Napoleon Bonaparte for president in the election of 1848?**

Because of a socialist uprising in the summer of 1848, many people in France thought the Second Republic did not provide a stable enough government. They feared further uprising and instability. They wanted a stable government, and they looked to Louis-Napoleon to provide it for them. They had little reason to expect that he could provide the desired stability; but, the fact that his name was Bonaparte was, it seems, enough. His uncle, Napoleon I, had brought stability to France during the tumultuous years following the first French Revolution; and, the people thought, another Bonaparte could do the same.

Ideas in Action

1. **In France, the tricolor flag became a symbol of the revolution. Other European nations also have tricolor flags. Identify which European countries have tricolor flags and which do not. What tricolor flags were inspired by the French Revolution? What tricolor flags does it seem were not? What tricolor flags date back to the Revolution?**

2. **The kings of England and those of France claimed to have the royal touch. Research the history of the royal touch in England and France. When did kings first use the royal touch in both countries? Who were the last English and French kings to use the royal touch? Did any other monarchs besides the French and English claim to have the royal touch?**

3. Listen to some of the music of the period. Suggestions: Hector Berlioz—*Symphonie Fantastique; Grande Symphonie Funèbre et Triomphale* (written in 1840 to commemorate the 10th anniversary of the July Revolution of 1830); Robert Schumann—Symphony No. 1 in B Flat, *Spring* (1841); any of his *Lieder* (Songs); Franz Schubert—Symphony No. 8 "Unfinished"; any of his *Lieder*, especially *Der Erlkönig* ("The Erlking"); Vincenzo Bellini—opera arias; Carl Maria von Weber—*Der Freischütz* (either the entire opera or selections from it.); Daniel Auber—*La Muette de Portici* (the opera that inspired the 1830 revolution in Belgium); Gioachino Rossini—*Guillaume Tell*.

Sample Quiz I (pages 293–304)

Please answer the following in complete sentences.

1. Name two things King Charles X did that angered French Liberals.

2. Who became king after Charles X abdicated? What title did this new ruler have?

3. What nation, inspired by the 1830 revolution in France, threw off the "foreign" king who ruled it and established itself as an independent constitutional monarchy?

4. Give one of the errors of Liberalism according to Pope Gregory XVI's *Mirari Nos*.

5. What was the name for the problem of what to do about the pope's temporal power in an independent, united Italy?

6. What was the name for the movement Giuseppe Mazzini started to inspire Italian youth to fight for the union of all Italy under a republican government?

Answers to Sample Quiz I

Students' answers should approximate the following.

1. Possible answers:

   a) Charles X appointed royalists as his chief ministers.

   b) He paid *émigrés* for their lost lands.

   c) He seemed to be taking steps to reestablish the Catholic Church in France.

   d) He dissolved a Liberal legislature.

   e) He annulled elections to another legislature.

2. Louis Philippe became king after Charles X abdicated. Louis Philippe was called King of the French (or, citizen king).

3. *Belgium* threw off the king of Holland and established an independent constitutional monarchy in 1830.

4. In *Mirari Vos*, Pope Gregory XVI condemned such Liberal errors as:

   a) *indifferentism*, the belief that people do not have the duty to believe in God by worshiping in and practicing the one true religion—the Catholic Faith.

   b) *liberty of conscience*, the freedom to believe whatever one wants and to follow that belief in society,

   c) the *freedom to publish* whatever opinions one has, even in if they are false.

5. The problem of what to do about the pope's temporal power in an independent, united Italy was the *Roman Question*.

6. *Young Italy* was the name of the movement started by Mazzini.

Sample Quiz II (pages 304–318)

Please answer the following in complete sentences.

1. **In the 19th century, people tried to give answers to what was called the social question—how society can bring justice to poor workers and assure them dignity and freedom from exploitation. Various answers were given to this question.**

   a) **What do we call the answer that said that we have to abolish all private property and all government?**

   b) **What do we call the answer that said we have to abolish all private property and give the control of all property to the government?**

2. **Blessed Antoine-Frédéric Ozanam said workers should get a "natural wage." What did he mean by a natural wage?**

3. **What organization did Ozanam found?**

4. **Give two reasons why people thought Pius IX was a "Liberal pope."**

5. **How did Louis Philippe fall from power? What is the name of the government that followed him?**

6. **Who became president of France in 1848 because the French people wanted someone who could bring stability to the government?**

Answers to Sample Quiz II

Students' answers should approximate the following

1. Answers:

   a) *Anarchism* is the answer that we have to abolish all private property and all government.

   b) *Socialism* is the answer that we have to abolish all private property and give control of all property to the government.

2. According to Ozanam, a natural wage is a wage large enough to support a frugal worker and his family in reasonable comfort.

3. Ozanam founded the *Saint Vincent de Paul Society*.

4. Possible answers:

   a) As archbishop of Spoletto, he spared the lives of revolutionaries when they fled to the city.

   b) As pope, he granted amnesty to all political refugees.

   c) As pope, he pardoned political prisoners (if they swore not to plot against the government).

   d) He reformed hospitals, prisons, and religious houses.

   e) He built a railroad and erected streetlights.

   f) He allowed Jews to live outside the ghetto and receive Catholic charity services.

   g) He established a senate, with lay delegates popularly elected, to serve him as an advisory power in the government.

5. Louis Philippe fell from power when a revolution broke out against him in Paris. He abdicated two days later. The government that followed Louis Philippe is called the *Second Republic*.

6. *Prince Louis-Napoleon Bonaparte* became president of France because the French people wanted someone who could bring stability to the government.

Essays (200–500 words each)

Instructions to be given to the students: Write in complete sentences. Underline your thesis. Give three supports or examples that explain why you think what you do and that support your thesis.

1. How were Antoine-Frédéric Ozanam and Louis Blanc alike (in their goals and ideas)? How did they differ? Do you think Ozanam would have agreed more with Blanc or with those who believed in *laissez-faire* capitalism?

2. Popes Gregory XVI and Pius IX had very different ways of reacting to Liberalism. Compare and contrast how they did so. Whose ways of acting made more sense given what the times they lived in were like? Please explain.

Chapter Test

Please answer the following in complete sentences.

I. Short Essay—Answer two of the following:

1. Describe the July Revolution of 1830? (Why did it occur? Where did it occur? How did it begin? How did it end? What ruler or rulers were overthrown? What ruler or rulers came into power? In what country did the July Revolution inspire a similar revolution?)

2. Describe what the government of the Papal States was like before Pius IX became pope. What good things could be said about it? What bad things? Show two ways Pius IX tried to improve life in the Papal States.

3. What did Blessed Antoine-Frédéric Ozanam think about capitalism? What did he think about socialism? What spirit did society have to have to really change for the better, according to Ozanam? Give two concrete proposals he made on how to solve poverty in which workers lived.

II. Short Answer:

1. Why was Louis Philippe called "King of the French" and not king of France?

2. Was Louis Philippe's chief purpose as king to spread Liberal freedom in France? Please explain.

3. What is indifferentism? What did Pope Gregory XVI say about it?

4. Identify:

   a) one who believes in equality, in removing all social, political, and economic inequalities among men

   b) one who responds to an idea by taking the opposite opinion or an act by doing the opposite to that act

   c) an organization founded by Giuseppe Mazzini to inspire Italian youth to work, by violence if necessary, for the freedom and union of Italy

Answer Key to the Chapter Test

Students' answers should approximate the following:

I.

1. The July Revolution of 1830 was an uprising in Paris against King Charles X of France. It occurred because Liberals were dissatisfied with Charles X's attempts to restore the ancient regime and the Catholic Church in France. The revolution began with riots among the poor and unemployed workers. The next day, the riots spread. After only two days, it was clear to Charles X that he was dealing with a revolution. On July 30, 1830, he abdicated, naming his grandson king. In Charles's place, the French legislature named Louis Philippe, the Duke of Orléans, king. The July Revolution inspired a similar uprising in Belgium.

2. The pope's government in the Papal States before Pius IX was mostly mild. It showed genuine concern for the good of its citizens; it provided free healthcare and its taxes were low. The government attempted to control bandits. Leo XII tried to rid the government of corrupt officials.

   Still, papal officials were often incompetent, and the courts of law were not properly run.

Middle and upper class laymen resented the fact that only clergymen held the top positions in the pope's government.

Pope Pius IX tried to improve matters in the Papal States by (possible answers):

a) granting amnesty to all political refugees

b) pardoning political prisoners (if they swore not to plot against the government)

c) reforming hospitals, prisons, and religious houses

d) building a railroad and erecting streetlights

e) allowing Jews to live outside the ghetto and receive Catholic charity services

g) establishing a senate, with lay delegates popularly elected, to serve him as an advisory power in the government.

3. Ozanam condemned capitalism because, he said, it treated men as mere tools of production for the sake of the rich and powerful and was thus little better than slavery. Socialism, said Osanam, enslaved men to the state. He said society needed to embrace the "spirit of sacrifice" and triumph over the "spirit of selfishness." More concretely, Ozanam said (possible answers):

a) Employers should look on their workers not as tools but as "associates," fellow workers in the business enterprise

b) Workers should receive a "natural wage"—one large enough to support a frugal worker and his family in reasonable comfort.

c) A father should make enough money so that his wife and children need not work.

II.

1. Louis Philippe was called King of the French to show that he received his authority to rule from the French people.

2. Louis Philippe's chief purpose as king was not to spread Liberal freedom but to establish a dynasty.

3. Indifferentism is the belief that people do not have the duty to believe in God by worshiping in and practicing the one true religion—the Catholic Faith. Pope Gregory XVI said indifferentism is wrong. He condemned it.

4. a) One who believes in equality is an *egalitarian.*

b) One who responds to an idea by taking the opposite opinion or an act by doing the opposite to that act is a *reactionary.*

c) The organization founded by Giuseppe Mazzini was *Young Italy.*

Chapter Overview

- On March 3, 1848, Lajos Kossuth delivered an address to the Hungarian diet in which he declared that not just Hungary, but the entire Austrian Empire needed constitutional reform. In a few days, Kossuth's speech reached Vienna, where it stirred Liberal students to action. An uprising in Vienna on March 13, 1848, ended in the resignation of Prince Klemens von Metternich and his flight from Vienna.

- Without Metternich, the Austrian imperial government gave in to the revolutionary students' and workers' demands. Two days after, the Austrian Council of State recognized the revolutionary Central Committee as legal and agreed to call a *Reichsrat* to draw up a constitution for Austria, Emperor Ferdinand I left Vienna. From Salzburg, he called for resistance to the revolutionaries in Vienna.

- Riots against Austrian rule broke out in Milan on March 18, 1848. Invited by Milan, King Carlo Alberto of Piedmont-Sardinia entered the city on March 24. Venice also revolted against Austrian rule on March 22. In the south, Sicily rose up against King Fernando II, while other Italian rulers, including Pope Pius IX, granted constitutions to their people. The pope's refusal to support a war against Austria turned Italian Liberals against him.

- Revolutionary feeling was strong in the cities of Germany. In Prussia, King Friedrich Wilhelm IV pledged his support for a constitution. In March, the German Confederation's *Bundestag* called for the formation of a new assembly for all of Germany. This resulted in elections of delegates for a new government, the Frankfurt Diet.

- In June and July 1848, Austrian forces in northern Italy began to score victories against revolutionary forces and those of King Carlo Alberto. By early August, the Austrians had driven the Piedmontese from Milan and entered the city.

- Magyar nationalism in Hungary and German nationalism in Austria alienated non-Germans and non-Magyars from the revolutionary cause in the summer of 1848. In Austria, too, peasants began turning against the revolution. In early October, radical students and workers seized full control of the city government in Vienna, while Emperor Ferdinand called on all his subjects to rally to him. Imperial forces lay siege to Vienna and drove back a Hungarian army that was coming to the city's aid. On November 1, imperial forces took Vienna, ending the revolution in Austria.

- Pope Pius IX's refusal to join in the war against Austria turned the Liberals in Italy against him. On November 15, revolutionaries in Rome assassinated the pope's chief minister, Count Pellegrino Rossi; the next day, a full-scale revolution broke out against the pope. At last the pope, in disguise, fled Rome to Gaeta.

- Following the end of the revolution in Vienna, Emperor Ferdinand I abdicated and Franz Josef, his nephew, became emperor in his place. When Franz Josef announced a united government for both Austria and Hungary, the Hungarian Diet, led by Lajos Kossuth, called for resistance. Successful in arms against the Austrians, the diet declared Hungary's independence of the Habsburgs and named Kossuth the first regent-president.

- The Frankfurt Diet voted to offer the crown of a united Germany to the Hohenzollerns instead of the Habsburgs. But King Friedrich Wilhelm's refusal to accept the crown and the withdrawal of both Austrian and Prussian delegates from the diet sealed its fate. The diet's demise in May 1849 marked the end of the 1848 revolution in Germany.

- The forces of independent Hungary could not withstand the alliance of Emperor Franz Josef and Tsar Nikolai I. In August 1849, Hungary surrendered and submitted once again to Habsburg rule.

- In February 1849, Tuscany declared itself a republic after Duke Leopold II fled to Gaeta. Revolutionaries in Rome declared the Republic of Rome. In March 1849, King Carlo Alberto renewed his war with Austria; but at Novara, Piedmontese forces were defeated in a battle with the Austrians. In April, Pope Pius IX asked Catholic powers to overthrow Rome's revolutionary government. The same month, the Tuscan revolution was overthrown and Duke Leopold was asked to resume his government of Tuscany. In early July, Rome's republican government surrendered to French forces.

- Acting as the champion of the French people against the antidemocratic policies of France's National Assembly, Louis-Napoleon Bonaparte won great popularity. In December 1851, Louis-Napoleon, in a *coup d'etat*, overthrew the National Assembly. In January 1852, Louis-Napoleon established a new constitution that gave the president the powers of a dictator. In December 1852, the French people voted to approve the establishment of another empire. In this way Louis-Napoleon became Emperor Napoleon III of France.

- France's Second Empire was a highly centralized government under Emperor Napoleon III, who dreamed of an industrialized France directed by a benevolent emperor and a group of scientific experts. The French people lost many of their political liberties, but France prospered for many years under the Second Empire.

- The crushing of Italy's revolutions in 1849 meant the return of monarchical government to all of Italy, including the Papal States. Only Piedmont-Sardinia kept its constitution, though it was not very democratic. King Vittorio Emanuele of Piedmont-Sardinia benefited from having a brilliant but unscrupulous prime minister, Camillo Benso, the Count of Cavour. Though at first he laughed at the idea of a united Italy, Cavour eventually adopted it as a means of increasing the power of Piedmont-Sardinia.

- Allied with Napoleon III, Piedmont-Sardinia went to war with Austria in May 1859. By July, the French and Piedmontese had driven the Austrians out of western Lombardy. Meanwhile, revolutions drove Habsburg-backed rulers from central Italy, and revolutionaries in papal-controlled Romagna declared the region's independence. Fearing how this war would reflect on his popularity in

France, Napoleon III concluded a peace with the Austrians in July. All of Lombardy went to Piedmont-Sardinia while Venezia remained an Austrian domain.

- In March 1860, Cavour (with Napoleon's blessing) held a plebiscite in which the people of Modena, Parma, Tuscany, and the Romagna voted to be annexed to Piedmont-Sardinia. In May of the same year, Giuseppe Garibaldi led an invasion of Sicily; by July, he was master of the island. In September, Garibaldi invaded Naples.

- Fearing that Garibaldi would set up his own government in Naples and Sicily, Cavour and King Vittorio Emanuele moved the Piedmontese forces south. After seizing the papal lands of Umbria and the Marches, the Piedmontese moved into the city of Naples. There, Garibaldi agreed to surrender his forces to them. In this way Vittorio Emanuele became master of most of Northern Italy and all of southern Italy and Sicily, as well as most of central Italy except the Patrimony of St. Peter. In March 1861, representatives from all these regions, gathered in Turin, proclaimed Vittorio Emanuele king of Italy.

Chapter Goals

This chapter covers one of the pivotal periods in European history—the period of the "Year of Revolutions," 1848-1849 and events subsequent to it. The period begins with the overthrow of Metternich and his Concert of Europe, which had dominated Europe for nearly 34 years. The events of this period demonstrate just how shallow and ultimately futile Metternich's system was; it was held together by force, which is ever effective only for a short time if it does not meet a corresponding acquiescence on the part of the people. Liberalism and nationalism had sunk deep into our civiliza-

tion's consciousness; they could not be eradicated by alliances and military force.

It is thus that we call this period the "Triumph of Liberalism"—even though, outwardly, it appeared that the forces of "reaction" had triumphed. It is important for students to understand the revolutionary character of this period. It is also important that they understand how both sides had gone beyond the point of mutual understanding and compromise—if there ever was a time they were capable of this. The treatment of Pope Pius IX, who tried to accommodate himself to certain aspects of Liberalism as far as he thought the constitution of the Church allowed, underlines how uncompromising Liberalism was. The inability of Europe's rulers to consider the demands of justice toward populations in their realms demonstrates the same problem.

The events in this chapter also demonstrate the exclusiveness of nationalism. This will not be the last time we see this; for nationalism, a force that was shattering the ancient unity of Christendom, would in only a few decades destroy the unity not only of Europe but the world.

Period Music

French Romantic

- Hector Berlioz (1803–1869)

- Charles Gounod (1818–1893). His most famous works are the operas *Faust*, and *Romeo and Juliette*.

- Jacques Offenbach (1819–1880). *The Tales of Hoffman* (1851)—an opera

German Romantic

- Johann Strauss I (1804–1849). A composer famous for his waltzes. His work, *Radetzky March*, was written in honor of Count Josef Radetzky von Radetz.

- Fanny Mendelssohn (1805–1847)

- Felix Mendelssohn (1809–1847)

- Robert Schumann (1810–1856)

- Clara Schumann (1819–1896)

- Franz Liszt (1811–1886)

Italian Romantic

- Giuseppe Verdi (1813–1901). A very popular Italian Romantic and nationalist opera composer. Operas composed by him in the period covered by this chapter include the following:

  Macbeth (1847)

  Luisa Miller (1849)

  Rigoletto (1851)

  Il Trovatore (1853)

  La Traviata (1853)

Polish Romantic

- Frédéric Chopin (1810–1849)

Russian Romantic

- Mikhail Glinka (1804–1857)—A nationalist composer

What Students Should Know

1. **Why the Magyars of Hungary were discontent with Austrian rule**

   Hungary (which included other races besides Magyars) had a special status in the Austrian Empire. Though it had the same monarch as Austria and other Habsburg domains, Hungary had its own constitution and its own diet. Yet, under Metternich's influence, the Hungarian diet did not meet for 13 years after the fall of Napoleon. Magyar nationalists (mostly from among the middle class, the nobility, and the intellectuals) wanted greater independence for Hungary as well as Liberal political reforms (including greater freedom for non-Catholics in Hungary to practice their religion.)

2. **Who Lajos Kossuth was**

   Kossuth was the leader of the extremist Magyar nationalists. A Lutheran Magyar, Kossuth wanted complete religious freedom for non-Catholics in Hungary, including the right for Catholics and non-Catholics to marry. Kossuth supported the Liberal Ten Points, demanding popular representation in the diet, equality for

Key Terms at a Glance

piazza: a plaza or open square in European and, especially, Italian towns

pyx: a small metal container used to hold the Eucharist

regency: government by a representative of a king, or *regent*

canaille: a worker, a member of the rabble; riffraff

demobilize: to dismiss or discharge from military service

irregular army: an armed force that is not a part of an official army

plebiscite: a vote by which all the people of an entire country or a district of that country express an opinion

Reichsrat: the National Convention of Austria, established during the revolution of 1848

risorgimento: Italian for "rebirth." It was the name for the movement for a new Liberal order in Italy.

everyone before the law, and absolute religious freedom. The Ten Points would not have passed through the diet, however, except that news of the 1848 revolution in Paris reached Pressburg. Addressing the diet on March 3, 1848, Kossuth said, not just Hungary, but the entire Austrian Empire needed reform.

3. Why Metternich fell from power

Kossuth's speech reached Vienna in only a few days. Copies, spread throughout the Austrian capital, stirred up students and Viennese townsmen. Faced with this immense uprising, Metternich saw he had no choice but to offer his resignation to Emperor Ferdinand. Resigning on March 13, 1848, Metternich fled Austria for England.

4. The course of the revolution in Vienna

The Viennese insurgents demanded one diet for the entire Austrian Empire. They wanted an end to all censorship of the press and freedom for university professors and students to express their ideas. They wanted religious freedom and little or no government interference in business. They wanted the right to bear arms. After Metternich resigned, the imperial government established a National Guard under revolutionary control. Insurgents, however, did not accept other measures suggested by the government. In May, they formed a Central Committee, which they forced the government to recognize. The imperial government agreed to a meeting of the *Reichsrat* to draw up a constitution for the empire. Delegates to the *Reichsrat* would be elected by universal manhood suffrage. Emperor Ferdinand, however, fled Vienna and from Innsbruck called on all faithful subjects to rise against the revolutionaries.

5. How the revolution in Italy began and progressed in 1848

While the rebellion was moving forward in Vienna, Austria faced riots against its rule in Milan, beginning on March 18, 1848. Milan invited King Carlo Alberto of Piedmont-Sardinia to take the lead in the rebellion of Lombardy against Austria. Carlo Alberto entered the city on March 24. Venice also revolted against Austrian rule on March 22. In the south, Sicily had risen up against King Fernando II, while other Italian rulers granted constitutions to their people. Pope Pius IX, too, granted a constitution for the Papal States, as well as a two-house legislature that had limited powers to pass laws, though the pope and the curia held the right to veto any law. Pius was careful to uphold papal authority. The pope however refused to support the war against Austria because as Vicar of Christ he could not bless a war against a Catholic nation.

However, in June and July 1848, Austrian forces in northern Italy began to score victories against revolutionary forces and those of King Carlo Alberto. By early August, the Austrians had driven the Piedmontese from Milan and entered the city and restored Austrian rule.

6. The course of the 1848 revolution in Germany

Revolutionary feeling was not strong in the cities of Germany; most Germans seemed content under the current order. Yet poor harvests in 1845 and 1846 and blight led to hardship that inspired revolutionary feeling, including support for democracy and socialism. When news reached Berlin of Metternich's fall, crowds gathered in the city, and King Friedrich Wilhelm IV of Prussia pledged his support for a constitution following a massacre of townsmen by his army. In March 1848, the German Confederation's *Bundestag* called for the formation of a new assembly for all of Germany. This resulted in elections of delegates for a new government inspired by Liberal ideals, the Frankfurt Diet.

7. **How the 1848 revolution ended in Austria**

Magyar nationalism in Hungary (which led to the oppression of minority groups such as Croats and Slavs) and German nationalism in Austria (which ignored the Slavic majority and cheered the victories of the Austrian Empire in Italy, even though won against Liberals) alienated non-Germans and non-Magyars from the revolutionary cause in the summer of 1848. In Austria, too, peasants began turning against the revolution. In early October, radical students and workers seized full control of the city government in Vienna, while Emperor Ferdinand called on all his subjects to rally to him. Imperial forces lay siege to Vienna and drove back a Hungarian army that was coming to the city's aid. On November 1, imperial forces took Vienna, ending the revolution in Austria.

8. **The course of the second wave of revolutions in Italy**

Pope Pius IX's refusal to join in the war against Austria turned the Liberals in Italy against him. On November 15, 1848, revolutionaries in Rome assassinated the pope's chief minister, Count Pellegrino Rossi; the next day, a full-scale revolution broke out against the pope. At last the pope, in disguise, fled Rome to Gaeta.

In February 1849, Tuscany declared itself a republic after Duke Leopold II fled to Gaeta. Revolutionaries in Rome declared the Republic of Rome. In March 1849, King Carlo Alberto renewed his war with Austria; but at Novara, Piedmontese forces were defeated in a battle with the Austrians. In April, Pope Pius IX asked Catholic powers to overthrow Rome's revolutionary government. The same month, the Tuscan revolution was overthrown and Duke Leopold was asked to resume his government of Tuscany. In early July, Rome's republican government surrendered to French forces

sent by the Prince-President, Louis-Napoleon Bonaparte.

9. **What happened during the Hungarian revolution**

Following the end of the revolution in Vienna, the Austrian Emperor Ferdinand I abdicated, and Franz Josef, his nephew, became emperor in his place. When Franz Josef announced a united government for both Austria and Hungary, the Hungarian Diet, led by Lajos Kossuth, called for resistance. Successful in arms against the Austrians, the diet declared Hungary's independence of the Habsburgs and named Kossuth the first regent-president. The Austrian army was at first triumphant against Hungarian forces, but then Artúr Görgei took command of the Hungarians and won several victories against the Austrians. Strife, however, arose between Kossuth and Görgei, and Franz Josef made an alliance with Tsar Nikolai I of Russia. The forces of independent Hungary could not withstand the alliance of Austria and Russia. In August 1849, Hungary surrendered and submitted once again to Habsburg rule.

10. **How the 1848 revolution ended in Germany**

Because of its war with Hungary, Austria could not control events in the Frankfurt Diet. In discussing the future constitution it had planned for Germany, members of the Frankfurt Diet wanted to cut Austria (with its large non-German populations) off from Germany. Thus, the diet voted to offer the crown of a united Germany to the Hohenzollerns instead of the Habsburgs. But King Friedrich Wilhelm's refusal to accept the crown and the withdrawal of both Austrian and Prussian delegates from the diet meant it could no longer effectively function. The diet's demise in May 1849 marked the end of the 1848 revolution in Germany.

11. How Louis-Napoleon Bonaparte founded the Second Empire

Acting as the champion of the French people against the antidemocratic policies of France's National Assembly, Louis-Napoleon Bonaparte won great popularity. In December 1851, Louis-Napoleon, in a *coup d'etat,* overthrew the National Assembly. In January 1852, Louis-Napoleon established a new constitution that gave the president the powers of a dictator. In December 1852, the French people, who wanted a stable government and peace, voted to approve the establishment of another empire. Just as Napoleon I had brought them these blessings, they thought, so could his nephew. In this way Louis-Napoleon became Emperor Napoleon III of France.

12. The character of the Second Empire

France's Second Empire was a highly centralized government under Emperor Napoleon III. Yet, though he seized absolute control over the government (while keeping a token legislature), Napoleon III had Liberal goals. He saw himself as the true representative of the French people. He wanted to guide them to justice at home and peace with other nations. A follower of the socialist Saint-Simon, Napoleon dreamed of an industrialized France directed by a benevolent emperor and a group of scientific experts. The French people lost many of their political liberties, but France prospered for many years under the Second Empire.

13. The course of events that led to the founding of the kingdom of Italy

King Vittorio Emanuele II of Piedmont-Sardinia benefited from having a brilliant but unscrupulous prime minister, Camillo Benso, the Count of Cavour. Though at first he laughed at the idea of a united Italy, Cavour eventually adopted it as a means of increasing the power of Piedmont-Sardinia.

Allied with Napoleon III, Piedmont-Sardinia went to war with Austria in May 1859. By July, the French and Piedmontese had driven the Austrians out of western Lombardy. Meanwhile, revolutions drove Habsburg-backed rulers from central Italy. Revolutionaries in Romagna, part of the Papal States, declared the region's independence. Fearing that supporting a war that harmed the pope would reflect badly on his popularity in France, Napoleon III broke his word to Cavour and concluded a peace with the Austrians in July. All of Lombardy went to Piedmont-Sardinia while Venezia remained an Austrian domain.

In March 1860, Cavour (with Napoleon's blessing) held a plebiscite in which the people of Modena, Parma, Tuscany, and the Romagna voted to be annexed to Piedmont-Sardinia. In May of the same year, Giuseppe Garibaldi led an invasion of Sicily; by July, he was master of the island. In September, Garibaldi invaded Naples.

Fearing that Garibaldi would set up his own government in Naples and Sicily, Cavour and King Vittorio Emanuele moved the Piedmontese forces south. After seizing the papal lands of Umbria and the Marches, the Piedmontese moved into the city of Naples. There, Garibaldi agreed to surrender his forces to them. In this way, Vittorio Emanuele became master of most of northern Italy and all of southern Italy and Sicily, as well as most of central Italy except the Patrimony of St. Peter. In March 1861, representatives from all these regions, gathered in Turin, proclaimed Vittorio Emanuele king of Italy.

14. **Identify the following:**

plebiscite: a vote by which all the people of an entire country or a district of that country express an opinion

Reichsrat: the National Convention of Austria, established during the revolution of 1848

risorgimento: Italian for "rebirth." It was the name for the movement for a new Liberal order in Italy.

Questions for Review

1. **How did Magyar Liberals like Lajos Kossuth treat the non-Magyar peoples of the kingdom of Hungary?**

Liberals like Kossuth wanted full citizen rights and freedoms for the Magyar people while refusing to grant the same to the Slavs, Croatians, Ruthenians, Romanians, and other peoples living within the kingdom of Hungary.

2. **Who led the 1848 revolution in Vienna? What sort of reforms did the Austrian revolutionaries want to make in government?**

University students and workers led the revolution in Vienna. The Viennese revolutionaries demanded one diet for the entire Austrian Empire. They wanted an end to all censorship of the press and freedom for university professors and students to express their ideas. They wanted religious freedom and little or no government interference in business. They wanted the right to bear arms.

3. **Why did peasants finally turn against the 1848 revolutions in Austria and northern Italy?**

In northern Italy, revolutionary leaders, fearing common folk might seize control of the revolution, told peasants who wanted to enter the revolutionary army to return home. Worse,

the government refused to remove the heaviest taxes from the peasants, which meant they had a heavier tax burden than the rich did. In Austria, Emperor Ferdinand as well as the *Reichsrat* abolished a land tax peasants had been forced to pay. With this matter taken care of, peasants lost interest in the revolution and gave their allegiance to the emperor.

4. **Why didn't Pope Pius IX establish a fully republican government in the Papal States?**

Pius IX didn't establish a fully republican government in the Papal States because such a government would be too independent of him and thus become a threat to the independence of the papacy and, thus, of the Church. Pius believed the pope could not be subject to any power, spiritual or temporal.

5. **Why did Italian Liberals finally turn against Pope Pius IX?**

Italian Liberals turned against Pope Pius IX because he refused to join or bless the war against Austria.

6. **Why did the Frankfurt Diet want to offer the crown of Germany to Prussia rather than the Austrian Habsburg emperor?**

Under the influence of nationalism, the members of the Frankfurt Diet thought that Austria, having a large number of non-German nationalities within its borders, would compromise the national purity of Germany. They thus offered the crown to Prussia, since it was the largest German state after Austria.

7. **Was the republican government of Rome, founded after Pope Pius IX was driven from the city, a good and just government? Please explain.**

The Roman government was inept and weak. It could not keep the peace or protect either the city or the countryside from robberies, murders, and other crimes committed by private gangs. Though claiming to respect the Church's authority, it publicly mocked the Catholic religion, seized Church property, turned churches into dance halls and stables, stole sacred objects, and destroyed sacred art.

8. **Why did the French people want Louis-Napoleon Bonaparte to become dictator and, finally, emperor of France?**

Louis-Napoleon had been careful to cultivate the friendship and support of the various groups in French society. The National Assembly, too, struck at the people's liberties by abolishing universal suffrage and limiting the freedom of the press. Louis-Napoleon said he supported the restoration of these rights against an assembly that not only violated the people's rights but refused to allow him to serve another term. In this way he won support for a dictatorship. The French people agreed to establish him as emperor because they thought that only as emperor could he effectively protect the peace and security of France. They were tired of social upheaval.

9. **What two men were mostly responsible for overthrowing the small kingdoms and principalities of Italy and uniting them under the government of King Vittorio Emanuele II?**

The two men mostly responsible for this were Camillo Benso, the Count of Cavour, and Giuseppe Garibaldi.

10. **Why can we say that Liberalism was triumphant after the revolutions of 1848–1849?**

We can say Liberalism was triumphant because the victory of the ancient regime could not last. In the years following the 1848 revolutions, rulers found it necessary to at least pretend they supported such Liberal reforms as equality, parliaments, constitutions, and even democracy. Some rulers granted reforms out of fear, but others eagerly supported them; for, rulers came to realize, the surest way to gain and keep power was winning the support of the masses of the people.

Ideas in Action

1. **Discuss how the 1848 revolution in Austria was like and unlike the French Revolution that began in 1789.**

2. **Research the hymn, *Jesus meine Zuversicht* ("Jesus Christ, My Sure Defense"), the hymn the crowds sang at King Friedrich Wilhelm IV's public humiliation. Learn to sing it in English or, if possible, in the original German. (Words and music may be found on the Internet.)**

3. **Though they no longer have any political power, descendants of the Habsburg and Bourbon rulers of central and southern Italy still hold on to the titles their ancestors once possessed. In other words, there are still those who are called the archduke of Tuscany, the duke of Parma, and the king of the Two Sicilies. Research one of these families and make a genealogy of those who claim such titles, beginning with the prince who last held power and continuing to today. The ruling houses are Habsburg-Lorraine (for the Grand Duchy of Tuscany), Austria-Este (for the Duchy of Modena), Bourbon-Parma (Duchy of Parma), and Bourbon–Two Sicilies (Kingdom of the Two Sicilies).**

Sample Quiz I (pages 323–333)

Please answer the following in complete sentences.

1. Name three regions of its empire besides Vienna where the Habsburg government faced rebellions in 1848?

2. Who was the Liberal Magyar leader whose speech given on March 3, 1848 inspired students in Vienna to rebel against the emperor and Metternich? In his speech, this man said the entire Austrian Empire needed reform.

3. List two reforms the Viennese revolutionaries demanded from the Austrian government.

4. Why did Pope Pius IX insist on keeping the right to veto any law approved by the legislature he had established?

5. What was the name of the new legislature established by the German Confederation in 1848?

Answers to Sample Quiz I

Students' answers should approximate the following.

1. In 1848, the Habsburg government faced rebellions in, *Hungary, Lombardy* (or Milan), *Venezia* (or Venice), and Prague (Bohemia).

2. The Liberal Magyar leader whose speech inspired Viennese students was *Lajos Kossuth.*

3. The Viennese revolutionaries demanded the following reforms from the Habsburg government (possible answers):

   a) one diet for the entire Austrian Empire

   b) an end to all censorship of the press and freedom for university professors and students to express their ideas

   c) religious freedom

   d) little or no government interference in business

   e) the right to bear arms

4. Pope Pius IX was careful to uphold papal temporal authority because he thought the pope should be subject to no earthly power. If the legislature could pass laws he was opposed to, it could gain political power over him.

5. The *Frankfurt Diet* was name of the new legislature established by the German Confederation in 1848.

Sample Quiz II (pages 333–340)

Please answer the following in complete sentences.

1. Why did Liberals in Italy turn against Pope Pius IX?

2. Who was the king who waged war against the Austrians to drive them from northern Italy? What Italian kingdom did he rule? Who was victorious?

3. What nation most helped Pope Pius IX regain Rome? Who was the head of government in that nation?

4. Who became emperor of Austria after Ferdinand I abdicated?

5. Why was Austria able finally to overcome Hungarian forces in 1849?

Answers to Sample Quiz II

Students' answers should approximate the following

1. Liberals in Italy turned against Pius IX because he refused to join them in the war against Austria.

2. The king who went to war with Austria was *Carlo Alberto*. He was king of *Piedmont-Sardinia* (or just Piedmont). The *Austrians* were victorious in the war.

3. *France* most helped Pope Pius IX regain Rome. *Prince Louis-Napoleon Bonaparte* was France's head of state.

4. *Franz Josef* became emperor after Ferdinand I abdicated.

5. Austria was able to finally overcome Hungary because of aid from Tsar Nikolai I of Russia.

Sample Quiz III (pages 343–352)

Please answer the following in complete sentences.

1. Who established the Second Empire in France?

2. Who was the prime minister who worked to unite all of Italy under King Vittorio Emanuele II of Piedmont-Sardinia?

3. Who joined Piedmont-Sardinia in its war against Austria in 1859?

4. Who conquered Sicily and southern Italy in 1860?

5. What new title did Vittorio Emanuele II receive in March 1861?

Answers to Sample Quiz III

Students' answers should approximate the following

1. *Napoleon III* (or *Louis-Napoleon Bonaparte*) established the Second Empire.

2. *Count Cavour* (or *Camillo Benso*) worked to unite Italy under King Vittorio Emanuele II.

3. *Napoleon III of France* joined Piedmont-Sardinia in its war against Austria in 1859.

4. *Giuseppe Garibaldi* conquered Sicily and Southern Italy.

5. Vittorio Emanuele II received the title, *king of Italy*, in March 1861.

Essays (200–500 words each)

Instructions to be given to the students: Write in complete sentences. Underline your thesis. Give three supports or examples that explain why you think what you do and that support your thesis.

1. Compare and contrast Napoleon I and Napoleon III. How was Napoleon III like and unlike his uncle?

2. Describe what you think are the good and bad aspects of nationalism, based on the events covered in this chapter.

Chapter Test

Please answer the following in complete sentences.

I. **Short Essay—Answer one of the following:**

1. What aspects of the revolutions in 1848–1849 show that they were inspired not just by Liberal reforms but by nationalism as well?

2. Why did the government of the Second Republic in France become so unpopular? Why did Louis-Napoleon Bonaparte become so popular? Describe the steps he took to become emperor. Why were the French people willing to make him emperor?

II. **Short Answer:**

1. Pope Pius IX established a two-house legislature for the Papal States, but he kept the power to veto any law it made. Why did he do this?

2. What was the name of the list of demands passed by the Hungarian diet in Pressburg and calling for popular representation in the diet, equality for everyone before the law, and absolute religious freedom?

3. List three demands the Viennese revolutionaries asked from the Habsburg government in 1848.

4. Why did Italian Liberals turn against Pope Pius IX?

5. Who was the conqueror of Sicily and Naples in the war for Italian unity in 1861?

6. Please identify:

    a) A vote by which all the people of an entire country or a district express an opinion.

    b) The Italian word for "rebirth"—the name for the movement for a new Liberal order in Italy.

Answer Key to the Chapter Test

Students' answers should approximate the following:

I.

1. We can see the influence of nationalism in the 1848–49 revolutions in that rebels did not fight just for Liberal reforms but for their national groups. In Vienna, for instance, the rebels fought solely for the Germans in Austria and ignored the Slavs. They cheered the Austrian victories against Italian Liberals simply because the victors were Austrian. The Magyars in Hungary insisted on rights for Magyars while denying the same rights to other national groups, such as Slavs and Romanians. The Frankfurt Diet in Germany contemplated replacing the Habsburgs with the Hohenzollerns simply because Austria had too many Slavs. The Liberal reformers of the diet wanted a Germany for Germans only.

2. The government of the Second Republic became increasingly non-democratic, which made it unpopular amongst French people. Louis-Napoleon gained popularity among the French by acting as their champion against the antidemocratic policies of France's National Assembly. In December 1851, Louis-Napoleon, in a *coup d'etat,* overthrew the National Assembly—and the people did not complain. Likewise, when in January 1852, Louis-Napoleon established a new constitution that gave the president the powers of a dictator. The people saw him as their champion against the anti-Democratic forces in society. In December 1852, the French people voted to approve the establishment of another empire, under the Emperor Napoleon III. They did this because they longed for the stability and peace they thought they had enjoyed under Napoleon I.

II.

1. The pope kept the right to veto all laws passed by his legislature because he thought the pope can never be subject to any earthly power.

2. The list of demands was called the *Ten Points.*

3. The Viennese revolutionaries demanded the following reforms from the Habsburg government (possible answers):

    a) one diet for the entire Austrian Empire

    b) an end to all censorship of the press and freedom for university professors and students to express their ideas

    c) religious freedom

    d) little or no government interference in business

    e) the right to bear arms

4. Italian Liberals turned against Pius IX because he refused to bless or join their war against Austria.

5. *Giuseppe Garibaldi* was the conqueror of Sicily and Naples.

6. a) A *plebiscite* is a vote by which all the people of an entire country or a district express an opinion.

    b) *Risorgimento* is the Italian word for "rebirth"—the name for the movement for a new Liberal order in Italy.

CHAPTER 13: An Era of Change and Conflict

Chapter Overview

- In February 1848, Karl Marx and Friedrich Engels published the *Communist Manifesto* in London. Marx, who with Engels wrote the *Manifesto*, was a German Jew whose family had converted to Protestantism. He had been a newspaper editor and had called for resistance to the Prussian government in the 1848 revolution. After moving with his family to London, England, Marx wrote his most famous work, *Das Kapital* ("Capital"), which was published in 1867.

- The Industrial Revolution, which began in Britain in the 18th century, gradually led to great changes in British society. Especially after 1830, city populations increased dramatically. By 1851, the British government could announce that for the first time in English history, more people were living in cities than in rural areas.

- The years after 1830 saw a phenomenal growth in factory production of goods other than textiles in England. New inventions—especially Bessemer's new process of purifying molten pig iron—meant that, increasingly, crafts and trades that had been based in small shops or in the home were being industrialized.

- The first 60 years of the 19th century witnessed revolutions in communications and transportation technology. The telegraph was invented, and telegraph cable was laid across the English Channel and then across the Atlantic, from Great Britain to America. Photography was developed, with the invention of the daguerreotype. The development of steam and steel technologies led to the development of railroad transportation and steamships.

- In the middle of the 19th century, England was by far the most industrialized nation in Europe. British political economists in the Manchester School developed the *laissez-faire* ideas of Adam Smith and influenced thinkers on the continent. But, on the continent, only Belgium had undergone significant industrialization before 1830. By mid-century, France had undergone industrialization, mostly in the north; but most of the French remained farmers and town dwellers. Germany industrialized even later than France; as late as 1870, around 64 percent of Germans lived in the country. Thus, with a few exceptions, as of 1870, Europe remained a mostly agricultural land.

- The Industrial Revolution led to the growth of new social classes alongside the old social classes in Europe. The first of the new classes was the high bourgeoisie or high middle class, which was the class of the capitalists, bankers, managers, and professionals. The next class was the petty bourgeoisie or lower middle class, made up of small shopkeepers and artisans.

The lowest class was the proletariat—the propertyless workers, both skilled and unskilled.

- The problems that arose because of industrialism and *laissez-faire* capitalism inspired various reform movements. Some favored keeping industrialism but reforming how it works. Some socialists thought the best way to reform industrialism was to change the environment in which people are raised and live. Other socialists thought it was necessary for workers to take control of government, but through peaceful, democratic means. Still other socialists thought that socialist change could not be won except by violence. These violent socialists included anarchists, like Mikhail Bakunin, and Communists who followed the thought of Karl Marx.

- Social Catholicism found a great champion in Bishop Wilhelm von Ketteler. Ketteler applied traditional Catholic teachings to the social conditions of his time and presented a program that differed both from socialism and *laissez-faire* as well.

- The mid- to late 19th century witnessed great advances in science. In particular, Louis Pasteur came out with his germ theory, and Charles Darwin with his evolutionary theory. Darwin's theory supported materialist ways of looking at the world.

Chapter Goals

This chapter treats of the social changes that occurred in mid-19th century Europe and the development of ideas to help people understand these changes and to deal with them on a practical level. The social changes were developments of the conditions created by a growing and changing capitalist order. The ideas, too, were a response to the conditions created by the changing condition of society. The teacher should help students to work through what might seem difficult ideas and to see them in the light of the concepts Catholics were developing in this period on the social order.

Period Music

Consult the list of composers in Chapters 11 and 12 of this teacher's manual.

What Students Should Know

1. **Who Karl Marx was and what he wrote**

   February 1848, Karl Marx and Friedrich Engels published the *Communist Manifesto* in London. Marx, who with Engels wrote the *Manifesto*, was a German Jew whose family had converted to Protestantism. He had been the editor of a newspaper in which he defended peasants against the Prussian government. The government shut down the newspaper in 1843. This experience made Marx a socialist and convinced him that the poor could win their rights only by a violent overthrow of the existing government. Marx wrote the Communist *Manifesto* with Friedrich Engels in 1847 and called for resistance to the Prussian government in the 1848 revolution. After moving with his family to London, England, Marx wrote his most famous work, *Das Kapital* ("Capital"), which was published in 1867.

2. **The progress of the Industrial Revolution and its effects on British society**

   The Industrial Revolution, which began in Britain in the 18th century, continued and expanded in the 19th century. During this period, there was a phenomenal growth in factory production of goods other than textiles in England, including pig iron and steel, food products, furniture, and arms and munitions. Such production gradually led to great changes

Key Terms at a Glance

proletarian: someone who belongs to the proletariat (the working class)

pig iron: crude iron that is refined to make steel

electromagnetism: magnetism brought about by a current of electricity

common law: a kind of unwritten law, developed in England, that comes from custom or the decisions of judges

ironmonger: a dealer in metal and hardware

Utopian (or Romantic) socialism: a name given to various ideas that described ideal societies where all people are treated as equals and have an equal access to the goods of the earth. Utopian socialists often wanted to change society radically (by abolishing marriage, for instance), but they generally opposed using violence to bring about change.

naturalist: one who studies *natural history*—the study of the natural world

mutation: change, especially a fundamental change in a thing

natural selection: a theory that says nature "selects" to preserve those individuals in a species that are the "fittest" to survive by giving them traits that make them better able to survive than other individuals that do not have those traits

materialism: the idea that holds that everything can be explained by causes we can detect through our senses and denies the existence of the soul or any nonmaterial, spiritual being

in British society. New inventions—especially Bessemer's process of purifying molten pig iron to make steel—meant that, increasingly, crafts and trades that had been based in small shops or in the home were being replaced by factory production. Especially after 1830, city populations increased dramatically and urban areas grew. By 1851, the British government could announce that for the first time in English history, more people were living in cities than in rural areas.

3. **The changes in communications and transportation technology**

The first 60 years of the 19th century witnessed revolutions in communications and transportation technology. The telegraph was invented, and telegraph cable was laid across the English Channel and then across the Atlantic, from Great Britain to America. Photography was developed, with the invention of the daguerreotype. The development of steam and steel technologies led to the development of railroad transportation and steamships. Railroad mileage increased dramatically by the 1870s. By the middle of the 1870s, England was by far the most industrialized nation in Europe.

4. **What the Manchester School was and what it taught**

British political economists in the Manchester School developed the *laissez-faire* ideas of Adam Smith and influenced thinkers on the continent. The Manchester School said employees should never demand higher wages than their employers could pay them because to do so would be to go against natural law. Such ideas were highly favored by capitalists, industrialists, and members of Parliament.

5. How the industrial revolution spread outside Great Britain

On the European continent, only Belgium had undergone significant industrialization before 1830. By mid-century, France had undergone industrialization, mostly in the north; but most of the French remained farmers and town dwellers. Germany industrialized even later than France; as late as 1870, around 64 percent of Germans lived in the country. Thus, with a few exceptions, as of 1870, Europe remained a mostly agricultural land.

6. What the old social classes of the ancient regime were

The old social classes or estates were the lay nobility and the clergy (which made up the aristocracy) on the one hand, and the commons (peasant farmers, craftsmen, merchants, etc.) on the other. Over all was the king.

7. What the new social classes of industrialized society were

The Industrial Revolution led to the growth of new social classes alongside the old social classes in Europe. The first of the new classes was the high bourgeoisie or high middle class, which was the class of the capitalists, bankers, managers, and professionals. The next class was the petty bourgeoisie or lower middle class, made up of small shopkeepers and artisans. The lowest class was the proletariat—the propertyless workers, both skilled and unskilled.

The high bourgeoisie was the class of privilege. With the old nobility, it controlled access to secondary education and, thus, university education, and the ability to rise in society.

Aristocrats looked down on the high bourgeoisie because they did not come from old families; but the aristocrats often relied on the high bourgeoisie for loans of money. The high bourgeoisie prided themselves on being hardworking and moral (unlike the nobility, they thought); on account of their virtue, they thought, God had blessed them with wealth. The high bourgeoisie valued family life and tried to instill their families with moral ideals. Yet, the business life—with its ruthless and at times underhanded dealings—conflicted with the high middle class's sense of moral superiority. Yet, this was justified by appeal to the "natural laws" of business. Many social reformers, too, came from the high bourgeoisie.

The petty bourgeoisie inhabited a middle place between the high bourgeoisie and the proletariat. Though they had a high rate of literacy, the petty bourgeoisie were not well educated or refined. They worried that not only would they be unable to climb into the ranks of the high bourgeoisie but that they would lose the social position they currently had.

The proletariat in the cities was the largest of these new social classes. They were generally worse off, materially and culturally speaking, than the poorest of the peasants. They worked at low-paying jobs for long hours and in bad and dangerous conditions. Whole families had to work in factories, for the father's wage was not sufficient to support his family. They had no job security and, if injured, could be fired without any compensation or anything to turn to. Their living conditions were exceedingly bad and they died in great numbers on account of diseases.

8. What were the movements that sought to reform the social order of the time

The problems that arose because of industrialism and *laissez-faire* capitalism inspired various reform movements.

Some reform movements favored keeping industrialism but reforming how it works. They said laws should govern business to protect workers' rights and improve the conditions in which they worked and lived. Such laws included those forbidding the employment of women and children in mines and decreasing the hours of the workday. Labor unions were reformist in character.

The unwillingness of government to improve working conditions and the difficulty unions faced in their attempts to be recognized led some to think more radical measures were needed to solve the social question. Such people included the socialists who wanted to use peaceful means to bring about a society of perfect social justice. Among these were the Utopian or Romantic socialists, who thought the best way to reform industrialism was to change the environment in which people are raised and live. They wanted to realize societies where all were equal and had equal access to the goods of the earth. Other socialists thought it was necessary for workers to take control of government, but through peaceful, democratic means. Laws then could be made that would gradually move society toward a socialist order.

Still other socialists thought that socialist change could not be won except by violence. These violent socialists included anarchists, like Mikhail Bakunin, and Communists who followed the thought of Karl Marx. Both Marx and Bakunin belonged to the Communist First International, which published the *Communist Manifesto* in 1847.

9. The Communist doctrine of Karl Marx

Karl Marx did not want to use moral but scientific arguments to defend socialism or Communism. The main points of his doctrine are as follows:

a) Man is a material creature. There is no immortal soul and no God.

b) Each man exists merely to produce goods, for his own and others' good.

c) A man is more productive if he works with others than simply by himself. Thus, men live in society in order to become better producers of goods.

d) Throughout history, all societies were made up of basically the rich oppressor and the poor oppressed classes. The rich invented moral codes and religion to keep the poor obedient.

e) History is a continual class struggle. The last struggle before Marx's time was the overthrow of the feudal society by the bourgeoisie, which established industrialism and the capitalist order.

f) In its own stage of history, the bourgeoisie oppressed the proletariat. The next stage of history would be when the proletariat rise up and violently overthrow the bourgeoisie and establish a Communist society. In a Communist society there would no longer be any classes, no oppressors, and no oppressed.

g) The establishment of a Communist society, however, would not be the last stage in history. For a time government would be necessary (a "dictatorship of the proletariat") in order to put down all reactionaries who oppose the socialist order. But the final age of history would be an age of anarchy where everyone lived in harmony with his neighbor, where each contributed to society "according to his ability" and each received from society "according to his need."

10. **Wilhelm Emmanuel von Ketteler's ideas on how to reform the social order**

    Ketterler was the Catholic bishop of Mainz in German in the mid-19th century. He is remembered for his contributions to the social teaching of the Catholic Church. He drew his ideas from Catholic tradition and theology—in particular, from Thomas Aquinas's teachings on the nature of man, human society, and the state. His basic ideas are as follows:

    a) Only man's sin could explain the evils of the world.

    b) To overcome the evils of the time, one had to embrace charity and recognize the dignity of men of every class.

    c) There is a right to private property, but no one has the right to do with his property just as he wishes. Property serves the good of the one who owns it, but it also exists to help others with their needs. Private property is both a personal possession and the common property of all. One should willingly share his wealth with those who are in need.

    d) Capitalism treats men as no better than machines and so was to be condemned along with Communism.

    e) Spiritual solutions were important for solving the social crisis but were not sufficient. Laborers should join in associations or unions for mutual aid and to achieve higher wages, safer working conditions, and other advantages.

    f) The Church has the right to speak about economic and political affairs because they involve morality; for, the Church is mankind's guide to the moral life.

    g) The state has a role in realizing social justice. Laws should govern working conditions, hours of labor, child labor, and other matters.

    h) A wage should be high enough so that a father could support his family without girls and women having to work.

11. **What advances were made in science**

    The mid- to late 19th century witnessed great advances in science, particularly medical science. In particular, Louis Pasteur came out with his germ theory, which led to a better understanding of the causes of disease and the development of immunizations. Improved surgical techniques were also introduced. These practices, along with better nutrition and improved sanitation, reduced the death rate throughout much of Europe.

12. **Darwin's theory of natural selection**

    The English naturalist, Charles Darwin, developed a theory of the origin and development of species in the animal and plant world. Differences we see within species, he said, are the result of mutations in such things as color, size, length of limbs, etc. Some mutations make it easier for animals and plants to survive; some make it harder. Those animals or plants with more beneficial mutations tend to survive, while those with less beneficial characterics could become extinct. Thus, natural selection.

    By natural selection, Darwin said, nature "selects" to preserve those individuals in a species that are the "fittest" to survive. Natural selection occurs both in species and between species. Over a long period of time, many mutations can create a new species from existing species. More complex species develop from less complex ones through a process called evolution.

13. **The effects of Darwin's theory of natural selection**

Darwin's theory supported materialist ways of looking at the world. Materialism is the conviction that everything can be explained by causes we can detect through our senses. Everything is made up of matter alone. Rationalists used Darwin's theory to say that the notion of creation by God is anti-scientific, and this troubled many Christians, leading some to doubt the truth of their religion. Some welcomed the theory of natural selection because they thought it justified *laissez-faire* business practices. As in the natural world, so in business—there is competition and only the fittest survive. This being so, no government or outside body should interfere in the "natural laws" that govern business.

Questions for Review

1. List three inventions that dramatically changed life in Europe in the 19th century.

Inventions that changed life in Europe include the following:

a) the Bessemer process for making steel

b) railroads

c) steamships

d) telegraph

e) photography (daguerreotype)

2. Why, according to the Manchester School, should employers not be forced to pay higher wages to low-skilled workers?

The Manchester School said employers should not be forced to pay higher wages to low-skilled workers because to do so would violate the natural law. In paying low wages, employers were only following natural law, they said.

3. What countries were highly industrialized by 1850? What countries had some industrialization but were mostly agricul- tural? **What parts of Europe were almost entirely agricultural?**

By 1850, Great Britain and Belgium were highly industrialized. France and Germany had some industrialization but were mostly agricultural. The rest of Europe was almost entirely agricultural.

4. What was the new class of the wealthy capitalists in the 19th century called? What did Europe's traditional aristocracy think of the members of this class? What did members of the capitalist class think of the aristocracy?

The new class of wealthy capitalists was called the high bourgeoisie or the high middle class. Europe's traditional aristocracy despised these bourgeoisie as men of low birth. The high bourgeoisie thought the aristocracy was lazy and immoral.

5. What was the name for the class to which small shopkeepers and artisans belonged? What was the class of the propertyless workers?

The petty bourgeoisie was the class to which small shopkeepers and artisans belonged. Propertyless workers belonged to the proletariat.

6. What is a labor union? What does it mean to go on strike? Why did workers in the mid-19th century think it was necessary to form unions?

Labor unions are associations of workers to fight for better wages and improved working conditions. One method they use is to strike—that is, to refuse to work in order to bring employers around to giving in to their demands. Workers in the 19th century thought unions were necessary because they could not trust the government alone to bring about needed changes. Workers needed to band together, for many together were stronger than anyone alone.

7. **What did Marx and Bakunin agree about? About what did they disagree?**

Both Marx and Bakunin thought violent revolution was necessary for achieving a socialist state. Both Marx and Bakunin were atheists and hated religion. Both thought the perfect society would have no laws and allow for absolute freedom. They both believed in common ownership of property.

Unlike Bakunin, however, Marx wanted to base the ideas of socialism, not on morality, but on science. Bakunin disagreed with Marx's idea of the dictatorship of the proletariat. An anarchist, Bakunin thought all government should be immediately abolished.

8. **According to Bishop Wilhelm von Ketteler, what does Catholic tradition teach about private property?**

Ketteler said there is a right to private property, but no one has the right to do with his property just as he wishes. Property serves the good of the one who owns it, but it also exists to help others with their needs. One should be willing to share his wealth with those who are in need.

9. **Why, according to Bishop Ketteler, does the Church have the right to speak about economic and political affairs?**

According to Ketteler, the Church has the right to speak about economic and political affairs because they involve morality—and the Church is mankind's guide to the moral life.

10. **What is materialism? Was Darwin a materialist?**

Materialism is the idea that holds that everything can be explained by causes we can detect through our senses and denies the existence of

the soul or any nonmaterial, spiritual being. Darwin was a materialist in that, in his theory of natural selection, he gave only material reasons for why species develop.

Ideas in Action

1. **For centuries, if people wanted to go anywhere, they walked or rode horses. The speed of an average human being walking is 3 miles per hour (mph); a horse's walking speed is roughly 4 mph, while its trotting speed is 8 mph. Figure out the distance between your home and school, your home and your parish, your home and the grocery store, and so on. Find out how long it takes you to make any of these trips by automobile, and then figure out how long it would take you to make the same trips if you had to walk or ride a horse. (For instance, if your house is 10 miles from your school, and you can walk only 3 miles in an hour, it would take you 3 hours and 20 minutes to walk to school—that is, if you do not stop along the way.) Are there any trips that you make on a daily basis, or even a weekly basis, that you wouldn't be able to make if you had to walk or ride a horse?**

2. **Try your hand at an ancient means of communication. Instead of calling your friend on the telephone or sending him or her an e-mail message, take pen and paper and write a letter. Encourage your friend to write back (using pen and paper) and see how long you can keep up such a correspondence. Is this a more or less satisfying way of communicating? Why?**

3. **Research what factory labor was like in the middle of the 19th century. Imagine yourself as an unskilled laborer working in a typical 19th-century factory, and write a journal of your daily life.**

4. From the 19th century to our own time, the Catholic Church has spoken out on a number of social and political issues, such as workers' rights, war and peace, medical ethics, abortion, and the death penalty. Research the issues the pope and the bishops speak out about in our own time.

5. Discuss what social classes we have in our own time. Do we still have an aristocracy and a peasantry? Do we have high and low bourgeoisie and a proletariat?

Sample Quiz I (pages 357–368)

Please answer the following in complete sentences.

1. Who was the Communist thinker who wrote both the *Manifesto of the Communist Party* and *Das Kapital.*

2. Give one important change the industrial revolution brought about in Great Britain.

3. Name two important inventions of the mid-19th century.

4. Why, according to the Manchester School, should workers never demand higher wages than their employers want to pay them?

5. Which of the new social classes was made up of capitalists, bankers, managers, and professionals?

   a) petty bourgeoisie

   b) proletariat

   c) high bourgeoisie

6. Which of the new social classes listed in question 5 was made up of small shopkeepers and artisans?

Answers to Sample Quiz I

Students' answers should approximate the following.

1. The author of both the *Manifesto* and *Das Kapital* was *Karl Marx.*

2. *Possible answers:*

   a) More and more, crafts and trades that had been based in small shops or in the home were replaced by factories.

   b) City populations increased and urban areas grew.

3. Important inventions include (possible answers):

   a) the Bessemer process for purifying molten pig iron

   b) telegraph

   c) photography

   d) railroads

   e) steam ships

4. The Manchester School said employees should never demand higher wages than their employers want to pay them because to do so would be to go against natural law.

5. The class of capitalists, bankers, managers, and professionals was the (c) *high bourgeoisie.*

6. The class of small shopkeepers and artisans was (a) the *petty bourgeoisie.*

Sample Quiz II (pages 368–378)

Please answer the following in complete sentences.

1. **What is the name for the socialists who thought the way to solve the social problems of their time was to create radically new societies where all people are equals and have equal access to the goods of the earth?**

2. **Did Karl Marx and Mikhail Bakunin think that a socialist society could be brought about by peaceful, democratic means? Please explain.**

3. **Marx thought all human societies have been made up of basically two classes of people. What are those classes?**

4. **What did Marx call the government of the Communist state that would be created after the proletariat overthrew the bourgeoisie?**

5. **Why, according to Bishop Ketteler, does the Church have the right to speak about economic and political affairs?**

6. **What do we call Charles Darwin's theory that says some natural changes or mutations in species help some individuals (the fittest) to survive while others die off?**

Answers to Sample Quiz II

Students' answers should approximate the following

1. The socialists who wanted to create radically new societies were the *Utopian (or Romantic) socialists.*

2. Marx and Bakunin did not think a socialist society could be brought about by democratic means because they thought such a society could only be won by violence.

3. Marx thought society has been made up of basically the *rich oppressor* and the *poor oppressed* classes.

4. Marx called the government of the Communist state the *dictatorship of the proletariat.*

5. Bishop Ketteler said the Church has the right to speak about economic and political affairs because these have to do with morality and the Church is the guide to morality for all mankind.

6. We call Darwin's theory *natural selection.*

Essays (200–500 words each)

Instructions to be given to the students: Write in complete sentences. Underline your thesis. Give three supports or examples that explain why you think what you do and that support your thesis.

1. Compare and contrast the social classes of the ancient regime and the new social classes that arose in the 19th century. How were they alike? How did they differ?

2. Both Karl Marx and Bishop Ketteler wanted to bring about social justice. How were their ways of doing so alike? How did they differ?

3. Do the "new" social classes of the 19th century—the high bourgeoisie, the petty bourgeoisie, and the proletariat—still exist today? What groups in modern society might fall under these designations?

Chapter Test

Please answer the following in complete sentences.

I. Short Essay—Answer two of the following:

1. Why would Charles Darwin's theory of natural selection lead people to reject religious faith?

2. What countries in Europe were highly industrialized by 1870? Which countries had only some industry but were mostly agrarian? What was the rest of Europe like?

3. What did the economists of the Manchester School say about an employer's duty to pay wages to his workers? Would Bishop Ketteler have agreed with these economists? Please explain.

II. Short Answer:

1. Name three important inventions of the mid-19th century.

2. What kind of work did the proletariat in the cities do and in what kinds of conditions did they work?

3. Why, among the proletariat, did not only fathers, but mothers and children work in factories?

4. Besides the proletariat, what other classes made up the new social classes of the 19th century?

5. What is the purpose of human life, according to Karl Marx?

6. Between what two groups is the struggle of the last stage of history supposed to occur, according to Marx? What is to be the result of this struggle?

7. Who came up with the germ theory in the 19th century?

Answer Key to the Chapter Test

Students' answers should approximate the following:

I.

1. Charles Darwin's theory of natural selection could lead people to reject religious faith because it was a materialist theory that supported materialist ways of looking at the world. Materialism is the conviction that everything can be explained by causes we can detect through our senses. It says that everything is made up of matter alone. Rationalists used Darwin's theory to say that the notion of creation by God is anti-scientific, and this troubled many Christians, leading some to doubt the truth of their religion.

2. By 1870, only two countries in Europe—Great Britain and Belgium—were highly industrialized. By mid-century, France had undergone some industrialization, but mostly in the north; most of the French remained farmers and town dwellers. Germany industrialized even later than France; as late as 1870, around 64 percent of Germans lived in the country. Hence, it was partially industrialized. Thus, as of 1870, the rest of Europe remained a mostly agricultural land.

3. The economists of the Manchester School said that employers only had to pay in wages what they were willing to pay their workers. It would be wrong if workers demanded higher wages than the employer was willing to pay. To do so would be to go against natural law. Bishop Ketteler disagreed with this. For Ketteler, employers had to treat their employees as human beings, not machines. An employer had to pay a worker what he needed to live. For instance, he had to pay a father a salary high enough so that the mother of the family and the children would not have to go to work.

II.

1. Important inventions include (possible answers):

   a) the Bessemer process for purifying molten pig iron into steel

   b) telegraph

   c) photography (daguerreotypes)

   d) railroads

   e) steam ships

2. The proletariat in the cities worked at low-paying jobs for long hours and in bad and dangerous conditions.

3. Mother and children in proletariat families worked in factories because fathers did not make enough money to support their families.

4. Besides the proletariat, the new social classes included the *high bourgeoisie* (or *high middle class*) and the *lower bourgeoisie* (or *lower middle class*).

5. The purpose of human life according to Marx is to produce goods for one's own and others' use.

6. The struggle of the last stage of history is to be between the proletariat (workers) and the bourgeoisie (middle class), according to Marx. This struggle will result in the overthrow of the bourgeois class and the establishment of a Communist society.

7. *Louis Pasteur* came up with the germ theory.

CHAPTER 14

New Powers, Old Battles

Chapter Overview

- From June to early August, 1862, Giuseppe Garibaldi gathered forces for the conquest of Rome. In August, he and his forces crossed over into southern Italy. At Reggio, however, Garibaldi was defeated in a battle with Italian forces. Garibaldi fled but was soon taken prisoner. He was released shortly afterward.

- In encyclical letters, allocutions, and apostolic letters, Pope Pius IX condemned the chief errors of Liberalism. These culminated in the 1864 encyclical, *Quanta Cura* ("Condemning Current Errors"), to which the pope attached a controversial *Syllabus of Errors*—a list of ideas condemned by the Church.

- On September 14, 1864, Emperor Napoleon III signed a treaty with King Vittorio Emanuele of Italy in which France agreed to remove her troops from Rome. To help the pope, Catholic faithful from all over the world sent him donations of money, and Catholic men volunteered to fight in the pope's army.

- On September 29, 1867, Garibaldi, leading 10,000 to 20,000 Redshirts, invaded the Papal States. At first successful, Garibaldi was later defeated by papal forces at the Battle of Mentana on November 2, 1867. The French Legislative Body put pressure on Napoleon III, who sent troops to Rome to defend the pope's temporal power.

- The First Vatican Council opened on December 8, 1869. On April 24, 1870, the council approved the dogmatic *Constitution on the Catholic Faith*, which affirmed the fundamental teachings of the Catholic Church and gave the Church's answer to modern rationalism, materialism, and atheism. On July 18, 1870, the council fathers approved the *Constitution on the Church of Christ*, which included a definition of papal infallibility.

- On July 27, 1870, Pope Pius IX learned that French troops would be withdrawn from Rome because France had declared war on Prussia. Pius thereupon suspended the council.

- Wilhelm I, who became king of Prussia in 1861, appointed Otto von Bismarck as his chancellor in 1862. Bismarck's goals were to unite all of Germany under the Hohenzollern emperor and to make a united Germany the greatest power in Europe. By skillful maneuvering, Bismarck goaded Austria and the German diet into declaring war on Prussia. In the Seven Weeks' War, Prussia defeated Austria. The Treaty of Prague, signed with Austria on August 23, 1866, dissolved the German Confederation and in its place established a northern and southern confederation of German states. Prussia dominated the northern confederation, and Austria was cut off entirely from Germany.

- To bring the southern German states into a union with Prussia and the North German Confederation, Bismarck tricked France into declaring war on Prussia on July 19, 1870. The southern German states, as well as the northern states, joined Prussia in a "patriotic" war against France. Throughout August, the Germans were everywhere victorious over the French. Following the Battle of Sedan, Napoleon III on September 2 surrendered his army to the Prussians. Two days later, republicans in Paris abolished the empire and set up a republican government.

- The new French republic refused to surrender to Bismarck, and on September 19, 1870, the Germans laid siege to Paris. The cruel siege lasted four months. At Versailles, on January 18, 1871, the princes of all the German states gathered and proclaimed the German Empire, with Wilhelm I as emperor or *Kaiser*. Ten days later, Paris surrendered. On March 1, 1871, the French National Assembly formally abolished the empire and instituted the Third Republic. On May 10, the French republic signed the humiliating Treaty of Frankfurt with the German Empire.

- Despite assurances that it would respect the pope's temporal authority, the Kingdom of Italy under King Vittorio Emanuele II ordered an invasion of the Papal States in September 1870. Despite the brave resistance of the papal army and the Papal Zouaves, Rome fell to the Italians on September 20. The next month, Vittorio Emanuele annexed the Patrimony of St. Peter to Italy. Pope Pius IX declared the annexation null and illegal and shut himself up as a "prisoner" in the Vatican.

- The German Empire had a government that was monarchical, federal, and democratic. All the German states were united under the rule of the *kaiser*, along with a two-house legislature in which the upper house represented the states and the lower house represented the people directly. Unlike other constitutional monarchies, however, in Germany the *kaiser* maintained significant powers, including the power to appoint the chancellor and ministry.

- Opposition to Bismarck's moves to further centralize power in the central government came in part from the Center, a party made up mostly of Catholics and representing Catholic interests and ideas. Bismarck thought Catholics were disloyal to the state because of their loyalty to the pope. To combat the "Catholic threat," Bismarck instituted what became known as the *Kulturkampf* ("war for civilization"). The German federal government as well as German state governments (especially Prussia's) began passing laws attacking the independence of the Catholic Church in Germany. The *Kulturkampf* met strong resistance from Catholic laity, priests, and bishops. By 1877 every Prussian bishop, along with hundreds of priests, was either in exile or prison.

- Pope Pius IX died in 1878 and was succeeded by Pope Leo XIII. Leo, who was more diplomatic than Pius IX, opened up friendly relations with the German government—helped by the fact that Bismarck was eager to get Center Party support for some of his measures. Though not all anti-Catholic laws were removed, by 1886, the worst of the *Kulturkampf* was over.

Chapter Goals

This chapter treats of events that set the stage for the world of the 20th century. The triumph of Germany over France in the Franco-Prussian War was the first event in a series of events that led directly to the First World War. It also created the German Empire—the first time in centuries that Germany had been united in the form of a nation rather than in a loose confederation of practically independent states. The empire created a new element in the European balance of power that led directly to the precarious alliances at the end of the 19th and the beginning of the 20th century. The meaning of these events will be revealed in subsequent chapters.

The loss of the Papal States marks the beginning of what is often called the "modern papacy." For the first time in centuries, the pope was only the spiritual head of the Church, not a temporal ruler. This state of things, however, would last only about 60 years, until the Lateran Treaty established the Vatican City state. Nevertheless, the pope never again became a temporal king as he had been until 1870.

Period Music

Czech

- Bedrich Smetana (1824–1884)

  Má Vlast, a nationalist tone poem (1863–1866)

  The Bartered Bride, an opera (1874–1879)

French and Belgian

- César Franck (1822–1890)—*Symphony in D Minor*

- Édouard Lalo (1823–1892)—*Symphonie Espagnole*

- Camille Saint-Saëns (1835–1921)

  Danse Macabre (1874)

  The Carnival of the Animals (1886)

German

- Richard Wagner (1813–1883). *Wagner's operas or "music dramas" are an important turning point in the history of music. His innovations became the basis of the Late Romantic style and influenced the music of the 20th century. His operas are quite long, and so a teacher would do well to find recordings of excerpts. The list of his major works is as follows:*

  Der Fliegende Holländer (The Flying Dutchman) (1841)

  Tannhäuser (1843–1845)

  Lohengrin (1846–1848)

  Der Ring des Nibelungen (The Ring of the Nibelungs)—a cycle of four operas: *Das Rheingold, Die Walküre, Siegfried,* and *Götterdämmerung* (1853–1874)

  Tristan und Isolde (1857–1859)

  Die Meistersinger von Nürnberg (1861–1867)

  Parsifal (1877–1882)

- Anton Bruckner (1824–1896). *An Austrian composer who wrote large scale symphonies and delicate a capella Catholic liturgical works*

- Johannes Brahms (1833–1897). A composer *thought by some to be the successor to Beethoven. Brahms's works offer an alternative Romantic expression to Wagner's.*

Russian

- Modest Mussorgsky (1839–1881)

  Boris Godunov, an opera (1868–1873)

  Pictures at an Exhibition (1874)—a suite, originally for piano, but later orchestrated

Key Terms at a Glance

allocution: a formal speech from someone in authority to encourage people to undertake some task

ecumenical council: a gathering of bishops that represents the entire Church and can declare doctrines that all Christians are bound to accept

dogmatic: having to do with teaching or *dogma*

mobilize: to make an army ready for war duty; noun: *mobilization*

federal: referring to a form of government where power is shared between a central power and a number of territorial or state governments

What Students Should Know

1. How Pope Pius IX changed after his return to Rome

Pope Pius IX's sufferings at the hands of Liberals had caused him to abandon any attempts to institute Liberal reforms in the Papal States. Liberals, he had found, would make no compromises. Though he had never been a Liberal, it was if he had awakened to the evil of Liberalism. In encyclical letters, allocutions, and apostolic letters, Pope Pius IX condemned the chief errors of Liberalism. These culminated in the 1864 encyclical, *Quanta Cura* ("Condemning Current Errors"), to which the pope attached a controversial *Syllabus of Errors*—a list of ideas condemned by the Church. The errors condemned in the *Syllabus* had already been condemned in other papal statements. Some were misunderstood—such as, "The Roman Pontiff can and ought to reconcile himself and come to terms with progress, liberalism, and modern civilization." In this statement, the pope was saying that he could not accept what was commonly understood by "progress" and "modern civilization"—a world separated from Christ and the Church.

2. Pope Pius IX's relations with the kingdom of Italy

Pius IX never recognized the kingdom of Italy as a valid political order. To the pope, the kingdom was founded in injustice because it had violently seized control of the smaller realms of Italy, as well as most of the Papal States. The latter was especially bad to Pius, for he saw it as striking at the freedom and independence of the Catholic Church. Like his predecessors, Pius saw his political power as a guarantee that the papacy would not fall under the control of and become the tool of secular powers. When, in 1864, Emperor Napoleon III signed a treaty with King Vittorio Emanuele of Italy in which France agreed to remove her troops from Rome and Italy agreed to pay for the Papal territories it had seized, the pope refused to acknowledge the treaty. To help the pope, Catholic faithful from all over the world sent him donations of money, and Catholic men volunteered to fight in the pope's army. These volunteers became the basis of the pope's international volunteer force, the Papal Zouaves.

3. The Battle of Mentana and its importance

On September 29, 1867, Giuseppe Garibaldi, leading 10,000 to 20,000 Redshirts, invaded the Papal States with the full knowledge and tacit permission of the Italian government. At first successful, Garibaldi was later defeated by papal forces (including French troops and Papal Zouaves) at the Battle of Mentana on November 2, 1867. Garibaldi then withdrew from papal territory. Following this invasion, The French Legislative Body put pressure on Napoleon III, who sent troops to Rome to defend the pope's temporal power.

4. The First Vatican Council and what it accomplished

In 1868, Pope Pius IX called on bishops and clergy of the world to gather in Rome on December 8, 1869, for the opening of an ecumenical council—the first since the Council of Trent in the 16th century. On April 24, 1870, the council approved the dogmatic *Constitution on the Catholic Faith*, which affirmed the fundamental teachings of the Catholic Church and gave the Church's answer to modern rationalism, materialism, and atheism. On July 18, 1870, the council fathers approved the *Constitution on the Church of Christ*, which included a definition of papal infallibility—the dogma that when the pope makes it clear that he speaks as the successor of St. Peter on matters of faith and morals, he can make no error. The council had more work to do, but it could not continue. In late summer of 1870, France withdrew its troops from Rome because Napoleon III had declared war on Prussia. Pius thereupon suspended the council.

5. Who Otto von Bismarck was and what his goals were

Otto von Bismarck was a Prussian *Junker* (nobleman) whose Pietist Lutheran faith made him religiously devoted to the king and realm of Prussia. In 1847, he began his career as a diplomat of the Prussian court, and in 1851 he was sent as Prussia's envoy to the German Confederation's diet at Frankfurt-am-Main.

When Wilhelm I became Prussia's king in 1861, he faced a Prussian parliament that did not want to give in to his demands to outfit the army better so that it would become invincible. In 1862, Bismarck became Wilhelm's prime minister or chancellor. With an iron will and clever maneuvering, Bismarck was able to accomplish the king's goals. Bismarck's own goals were to unite all of Germany under the Hohenzollern emperor and to make a united Germany the greatest power in Europe.

6. How Bismarck made Prussia predominant in Germany

To make Prussia the chief state of Germany, Bismarck had to neutralize the power of Austria. Austria had long been the chief power in Germany and would tolerate no rival to her power. By skillful maneuvering, Bismarck goaded Austria and the German diet into declaring war on Prussia. In the Seven Weeks' War, Prussia defeated Austria. The Treaty of Prague, signed with Austria on August 23, 1866, dissolved the German Confederation and in its place established a northern and a southern confederation of German states. Prussia dominated the northern confederation, and Austria was cut off entirely from Germany. Prussia was now the most powerful state in Germany.

7. How Bismarck used war both to unite Germany and neutralize a powerful rival—France

To bring the southern German states into a union with Prussia and the North German Confederation, Bismarck tricked Napoleon III of France into declaring war on Prussia on July 19, 1870. The southern German states, as well as the northern states, overcame their differences and joined Prussia in a "patriotic" war against France, while the French united in a "patriotic" war against Prussia. This war is remembered as the Franco-Prussian War. Throughout August, the Germans were everywhere victorious over the French. Following the Battle of Sedan, Napoleon III on September 2 surrendered his army to the Prussians. Two days later, republicans in Paris abolished the empire and set up a republican government.

The new French republic refused to surrender to Bismarck, and on September 19, 1870, the Germans laid siege to Paris. The cruel siege lasted four months. At Versailles, on January 18, 1871, the princes of all the German states gathered and proclaimed the German Empire, with Wilhelm I as emperor or *kaiser*. Ten days later, Paris surrendered. On March 1, 1871, the French National Assembly formally abolished the empire and instituted the Third Republic. On May 10, the French republic signed the humiliating Treaty of Frankfurt with the German Empire. In the treaty, France gave all of Alsace and part of Lorraine to Germany and agreed to pay a large sum of money. German troops were to remain in France until the money was fully paid off.

8. How Rome fell

Despite assurances that it would respect the pope's temporal authority, the kingdom of Italy under King Vittorio Emanuele II ordered an invasion of the Papal States in September 1870. It could do this because Napoleon III had withdrawn French troops from Rome at the beginning of the Franco-Prussian War. Despite the brave resistance of the papal army and the Papal Zouaves, Rome fell to the Italians on September 20. The next month, Vittorio Emanuele annexed the Patrimony of St. Peter to Italy. Pope Pius IX declared the annexation null and illegal and shut himself up as a "prisoner" in the Vatican.

9. The events that led to the *Kulturkampf* in Germany

The German Empire had a government that was monarchical, federal, and democratic. Its monarch or *kaiser* (Caesar) was Wilhelm I of Prussia, and it had a two-house legislature. The government was not as centralized as Bismarck wanted it to be, for the German states and people wanted to maintain strong local governments.

Opposition to Bismarck's moves to centralize power further in the central government came in part from the Center, a party made up mostly of Catholics and representing Catholic interests and ideas. Bismarck thought Catholics were disloyal to the state because of their loyalty to the pope. To combat the "Catholic threat," Bismarck instituted what became known as the *Kulturkampf* ("war for civilization"). Bismarck hoped that by means of this "war" he could bring the Catholic Church in Germany fully under the control of the German imperial government. The German federal government as well as German state governments (especially Prussia's) began passing laws attacking the independence of the Catholic Church in Germany. The *Kulturkampf* met strong resistance from Catholic laity, priests, and bishops. Pope Pius IX condemned it. By 1877 every Prussian bishop, along with hundreds of priests, was either in exile or prison. Catholic faithful refused to attend Masses said by government-approved priests in Prussia but, instead, assisted at clandestine Masses said by priests known to be secret representatives of the exiled bishops.

10. How the *Kulturkampf* eventually ended

Pope Pius IX died in 1878 and was succeeded by Pope Leo XIII. Leo, who was more diplomatic than Pius IX, opened up friendly relations with the German government. These overtures were helped by the fact that Bismarck was eager to get Center Party support for some of his measures. To counter the influence of socialists in

Germany, Bismarck turned aside from favoring *laissez-faire* economic policies to embrace laws directed to bettering the lives of industrial workers in the cities—measures which the Center had been supporting. Though not all anti-Catholic laws in Germany were removed, by 1886, the worst of the *Kulturkampf* was over.

Questions for Review

1. **Why did Pope Pius IX want to keep his temporal power? Why did he think the temporal power was important for the Church?**

   Pope Pius IX did not want temporal power for its own sake, but he thought he needed it to preserve the freedom of the Church. The temporal power, he thought, was a gift of God's providence to the pope and the Church to preserve the Church from undue influence by temporal rulers.

2. **Why did the pope call the Vatican Ecumenical Council? What important doctrine did it define?**

   Pope Pius IX called the Vatican Council so that the Church could give a clear answer to the errors of the modern world—Liberalism, rationalism, and materialism. He wanted the council to look at Church laws and revise them, if necessary. The important doctrine defined by the council was the infallibility of the pope.

3. **What were the Papal Zouaves?**

   The Papal Zouaves were a military force formed by volunteers from all over the world to protect the pope and the Papal States.

4. **What were Otto von Bismarck's goals for Germany? Why did he want to separate Austria from a united Germany?**

   Bismarck wanted to unite all of Germany under the king of Prussia and to make Germany the most powerful nation in Europe. To achieve the first goal, Bismarck thought he had to cut Austria off from Germany. One reason for this is that Austria would not tolerate any other German state as her equal, especially Prussia. Austria, too, had a large population of non-Germans and was the champion of German Catholics. Bismarck saw that conflict would inevitably come between Catholic Austria and Protestant Prussia.

5. **Why did Bismarck favor a "patriotic war" against Germany's "ancient foe," France?**

   Bismarck favored a "patriotic war" against France because he thought such a war could stir up German patriotic feelings in the states of southern Germany, which were estranged from Prussia. Such a war could convince the southern German people to join with Prussia in her war effort. Such a war effort, too, could go far to making Germany the foremost nation in Europe.

6. **How did Bismarck trick both the French and the Germans into going to war?**

   King Wilhelm I sent Bismarck a dispatch from Ems, Germany, describing a meeting he had there with the French ambassador. Bismarck took the dispatch and rewrote it so that it appeared that the French ambassador had been disrespectful to Wilhelm and that Wilhelm had rudely dismissed the ambassador. Bismarck then sent the dispatch to the press. The printed Ems Dispatch stirred up patriotic anger in both France and Germany. The French people demanded war, and the French government declared war on Prussia. The Germans, angry over the insult to the king and the declaration of war against a German state, joined with Prussia in the war against France.

7. **What new governments arose in Europe on account of the Franco-Prussian War?**

Germany received a new government when the German states joined with Prussia to form the German Empire. France overthrew the Second Empire and established the Third Republic.

8. **What was the *Kulturkampf*? Why did Bismarck back it?**

The *Kulturkampf* was the "war for civilization"—Bismarck's policies to bring the Catholic Church in Germany fully under the control of the German imperial government. Bismarck wanted to remove papal influence from the German Catholic Church; he thought of the pope as a foreign ruler who wanted to gain power over the German state.

9. **What was the Center Party? What did it stand for?**

The Center Party was a political party made up of men who wanted to preserve a strong role for the states in the empire and were opposed to too much centralization. The Center stood for improving the material lives and moral welfare of all social classes in Germany. It was opposed to economic Liberalism and supported government protections for German farms and businesses, especially small farms and businesses. The Center Party was made up mostly of Catholics and fought for the equality of Catholics in the political and social of life of Germany.

10. **How did Pope Leo XIII's style of ruling the Church differ from that of Pope Pius IX?**

Pius IX confronted the world by defying the powers of the world, using forceful language and excommunication. Leo XIII, however, was tactful and diplomatic. Instead of defying rulers, he held out the hand of friendship to them.

Ideas in Action

1. **Research the history of the persecution of Polish Catholics under Tsar Aleksandr II. Why did the tsar persecute Polish Catholics? How did they respond to the persecution?**

2. **Research the history of the Papal Zouaves— find out who they were, where they came from, why they were formed.**

3. **Research and draw pictures of the national flags and coats of arms used during the period covered in this chapter: North German Confederation, Austria, German Empire, the Kingdom of Italy, Papal States, the French Empire, and the Third Republic.**

Sample Quiz I (pages 383–396)

Please answer the following in complete sentences.

1. In 1864, Pope Pius IX issued the encyclical, *Quanta Cura*. To this encyclical he attached a list of ideas condemned by the Church, which caused a great deal of controversy. What is this list of ideas called?

2. Why did Pope Pius IX insist on keeping his political power as the head of the Papal States?

3. What was the battle where the Papal troops defeated Garibaldi's Red Shirts and forced them to withdraw from the Papal States?

4. What important dogma was defined at the First Vatican Council?

5. What were Otto von Bismarck's goals for Prussia and Germany?

6. In what war did Prussia defeat Austria, with the result that Austria was cut off from Germany?

Answers to Sample Quiz I

Students' answers should approximate the following.

1. The list of ideas condemned by the Church is called the *Syllabus of Errors*.

2. Pope Pius IX thought the temporal power was necessary to preserve the freedom of the Church from the state.

3. The papal troops defeated Garibaldi at the *Battle of Mentana*.

4. The First Vatican Council defined the *infallibility of the pope*.

5. Bismarck's goals were to unite all of Germany under the king of Prussia and to make a united Germany the most powerful nation in Europe.

6. In the *Seven Weeks' War*, Prussia defeated Austria.

Sample Quiz II (pages 396–412)

Please answer the following in complete sentences.

1. How did the government of France change on account of the Franco-Prussian War?

2. How did the government of Germany change on account of the Franco-Prussian War?

3. In the Treaty of Frankfurt, which ended the Franco-Prussian War, what lands did France agree to give to Germany?

4. How did the Franco-Prussian War lead to the Italian conquest of Rome in 1870?

5. What was the *Kulturkampf*? Why did Bismarck call for it?

6. Who became pope after the death of Pius IX?

Answers to Sample Quiz II

Students' answers should approximate the following

1. Because of the Franco-Prussian War, the French overturned the Second Empire of Napoleon III and established the Third Republic.

2. Because of the Franco-Prussian War, the states of southern Germany agreed to come into union with the North German Confederation and form the German Empire.

3. In the Treaty of Frankfurt, France agreed to give all of Alsace and most of Lorraine to Germany.

4. The Franco-Prussian War caused Emperor Napoleon III of France to withdraw the French troops from Rome. Without the protection of France (especially after the French abolished the Second Empire), King Vittorio Emanuele II of Italy could invade the Papal States with little opposition.

5. The *Kulturkampf* refers to Bismarck's policies to bring the Catholic Church in Germany fully under the control of the German imperial government. Bismarck called for it because he thought Catholics were disloyal to the state because of their loyalty to the pope.

6. Leo XIII became pope after Pius IX.

Essays (200–500 words each)

Instructions to be given to the students: Write in complete sentences. Underline your thesis. Give three supports or examples that explain why you think what you do and that support your thesis.

1. What was life like for German Catholics who lived during the *Kulturkampf*? Describe what sufferings and trials Catholics, priests and laity, had to undergo during this period of German history.

2. Write an account of the life of Empress Eugénie, Napoleon III's wife. What part did she play in government? How did she influence her husband?

Chapter Test

Please answer the following in complete sentences.

I. Short Essay—Answer two of the following:

1. Why did Pope Pius IX call the First Vatican Council? What important doctrine did the council define? What is the meaning of that doctrine?

2. What was the *Kulturkampf*? Why did Bismarck think it was necessary? What happened to bishops and priests who resisted the *Kulturkampf*? Was it finally successful? Why or why not?

3. One of Bismarck's goals was to unite Germany under Prussia. How did the Seven Weeks' War help him accomplish this? How did the Franco-Prussian War also help him achieve this goal?

II. Short Answer:

1. Was Pope Pius IX just greedy for power when he insisted on keeping the Papal States as his independent state? Please explain.

2. Who fought in the Battle of Mentana? What was its result?

3. What was the list of ideas condemned by Pope Pius IX?

4. Who was the first *kaiser* of the German Empire?

5. What kind of government took over in France after the fall of Napoleon III?

6. On what date did Rome fall to King Vittorio Emanuele II of Italy?

Answer Key to the Chapter Test

Students' answers should approximate the following:

I.

1. Pope Pius IX called the Vatican Council so that the Church could give a clear answer to the errors of the modern world—Liberalism, rationalism, and materialism. He wanted the council to look at Church laws and revise them, if necessary. The important doctrine defined by the council was the infallibility of the pope. This doctrine says that when the pope speaks on matters of faith and morals and in a manner in which he makes it clear that he speaks as the successor of the Apostle Peter, he can make no error.

2. The *Kulturkampf* was Bismarck's attempt to bring the Catholic Church in Germany fully under the control of the German imperial government. Bismarck thought Catholics were disloyal to the state because of their loyalty to the pope, and so he called the *Kulturkampf* to combat what he thought was the "Catholic threat." The *Kulturkampf* met strong resistance from Catholic laity, priests, and bishops. By 1877 every Prussian bishop, along with hundreds of priests, was either in exile or prison. Catholic faithful refused to attend Masses said by government-approved priests in Prussia but, instead, assisted at clandestine Masses said by priests known to be secret representatives of the exiled bishops. The *Kulturkampf,* thus, did not achieve the purpose that Bismarck had set for it.

3. To make Prussia the chief state of Germany, Bismarck had to neutralize the power of Austria. Austria had long been the chief power in Germany and would tolerate no rival to her power. In the Seven Weeks' War, Prussia defeated Austria. The treaty ending the war dissolved the German Confederation and cut Austria from Germany, which meant Prussia became the chief German state. France's declaration of war that opened the Franco-Prussian War stirred up the patriotism of people from all over Germany. All the German states joined in the war against France. This allowed the German states to overcome their differences and unite themselves in one empire.

II.

1. Pope Pius IX did not insist on keeping his temporal power out of a greed for power. He thought the temporal power was necessary to keep the Church fully independent of governments that might use their power to force the Church to do as they wanted.

2. In the Battle of Mentana, papal troops fought Giuseppe Garibaldi's Red Shirts. The battle was a victory for the papal troops, who forced Garibaldi to withdraw from the Papal States.

3. The list of ideas condemned by Pope Pius IX was the *Syllabus of Errors*.

4. The first *kaiser* of the German Empire was *Wilhelm I*.

5. France again became a *republic* after the fall of Napoleon III.

6. Rome fell to Vittorio Emanuele II on *September 20, 1870.*

CHAPTER 15: Into a New Century

Chapter Overview

- After the Germans withdrew from Paris in 1871, the Paris Commune proclaimed the independence of Paris from France. Controlled by Jacobins, Marxists, socialists, and anarchists, the Commune carried out executions of Catholic clergy and laity. The Paris government continued for about two months until it was overthrown by forces of the French republic in May 1871.

- Monarchists at first dominated the government of France's Third Republic. The monarchists, however, were divided between Legitimists, Orleanists, and Bonapartists. Under monarchist control, the republic adopted a constitution that—despite the monarchists—was republican, not monarchical. But on account of mistakes made by monarchists, republicans took control of the government in 1879. Under republican leadership, the government passed Liberal reform laws and anticlerical measures.

- Various factors led to a phenomenal growth in industry in the German Empire after 1870. More Germans moved from farming to industrial work, and cities grew dramatically. The cruelties of industrialization led to the growth of the Marxist Social Democratic Workingman's Party. Fearing their growth, Otto von Bismarck pushed anti-socialist laws through the *Reichstag*. When he saw such measures failed to crush the socialists, Bismarck proposed measures to bring aid to workers and the poor and to regulate the workplace.

- After 1871, Bismarck abandoned war and conquest as a way to secure the safety and prosperity of Germany. He turned, instead, to diplomacy. His strategy was to isolate France by maintaining friendship with Great Britain and forging alliances with Russia and Austria.

- The last 30 years of the 19th century witnessed a new wave of colonization on the part of European powers. Following the lead of King Leopold II of Belgium, who formed a quasi-private colony in Africa's Congo, other countries, including Great Britain, France, Portugal, Italy, and the United States scrambled for colonies not only in Africa but also in Asia and the Pacific. By 1900, nearly all of Africa had been divided among the European powers. Though she was at first opposed to foreign colonization, Germany under Bismarck began establishing colonies in Africa and the Pacific in the 1880s.

- When Wilhelm II became *kaiser* of Germany in 1888, he was determined that he and not Bismarck would rule the empire. After several conflicts with the *kaiser*, Bismarck resigned as chancellor in 1890. With Bismarck gone, Wilhelm pursued a diplomatic policy that ended Russia's friendship with Germany. Instead, Russia formed an alliance with Germany's greatest enemy, France. By his policy of extending German influence across the world, Wilhelm II pushed Great Britain into closer relations with France.

- By 1888, Great Britain was not only the greatest nation in Europe, but the world's greatest power. Wealth from British colonies all over the world flooded into Great Britain. British industry was the largest in the world. The British, too, had the world's largest fleet (including its navy and merchant marine).

- Conflicts between the Liberal and Conservative political parties in British government continued under Queen Victoria. The Liberals favored free trade, generally opposed imperialism, supported greater democracy in the government, and pushed for the disestablishment of the Church of England. The Conservatives generally opposed what the Liberals supported; yet, when they held power in the late 1860s, the Conservatives supported extending the suffrage to more people. More reforms were made when the Liberal, William Gladstone, was prime minister in the late 1880s.

- For centuries, the Irish had suffered bitterly under British rule. After 1829, however, they were able to elect representatives to Parliament and formed their own Irish Nationalist party, which fought for "Home Rule"—the right of the Irish to have their own government and parliament under the English monarch, but separate from Parliament in London. The Irish Nationalists did not win Home Rule; nevertheless, acts passed in Parliament between 1887 and 1903 improved conditions of life for Catholics in Ireland.

- Isolation had long been the basis for Great Britain's foreign policy. But, faced with the

threat of Germany's growing economy and military, Great Britain began seeking alliances with other nations in the 1890s. Alliances in the early 20th century eventually led Great Britain into a "Triple Entente" with France and Russia to counter Germany's Triple Alliance with Austria and Italy.

- After Queen Victoria's death in 1901, Great Britain entered a period of great change. A new political party, Labor, backed the Liberals in a challenge to the political power of Britain's aristocracy. In 1911, a coalition of Liberals, Labor party members, and Irish Nationalists were able to get King Edward VII's support for a bill that drastically cut back on the House of Lords' veto power. Thenceforth, the House of Commons was the chief governing body of the British Empire.

- Tsar Aleksandr II had brought changes to Russian government and society. He abolished serfdom and carried out some Liberal reforms in government. But after assassination attempts by *narodniki* (violent Nihilists who tried to influence the people to adopt socialist ideas), Aleksandr turned toward repression. Yet, after a further assassination attempt, the tsar approved an assembly for Russia. But before the tsar's order could go into effect, Aleksandr was assassinated on March 13, 1881.

- Aleksandr III embraced repression and Russification during his reign from 1881 to 1894. Though his approach was milder, Tsar Nikolai II continued his father's repression. Under both Aleksandr III and Nikolai II, Russia was undergoing a rapid industrialization, which intensified the government's desire for a warm-water port. The building of the Trans-Siberian Railway and Russia's occupation of Port Arthur on the Pacific led to a Russian presence in Manchuria. This, in turn, brought about a war with Japan in 1904–1905, in which the Japanese were victorious and Russia humiliated.

- Like Blessed Pius IX, Pope Leo XIII was a vigorous foe of Liberalism. Yet, while Pius IX had stoutly defied the modern world and inspired the Catholics with the spirit of a warrior, Leo XIII was eager to find opportunities to create friendships and reconcile differences. A skilled diplomat, he brought about good relations between the Holy See and many foreign powers. He sought to reconcile French Catholics with the Third Republic. Leo XIII patronized the sciences and took an interest in labor issues. His *Rerum Novarum* was the first of a long line of papal encyclicals dealing with social issues.

Chapter Goals

In this chapter, special attention should be given to the formation of alliances between the European nations, for these alliances were among the causes of the First World War—the beginnings of which we will deal with in the next chapter.

Period Music

Austria

- Gustav Mahler (1860–1911)

Czech

- Antonin Dvořák (1841–1904)
- Leoš Janáček (1854–1928)

England

- Arthur Sullivan (1842–1900)

France

- Jules Massenet (1842–1912)
- Gabriel Fauré (1845–1924)

Italy

- Ruggero Leoncavallo (1858-1919)—*I Pagliacci,* an opera (1892)
- Giacomo Puccini (1858–1924). A major opera composer. His works include:

  La Bohème (1896)

  Tosca (1900)

  Madame Butterfly (1898)

Norway

- Edvard Grieg (1843–1907)

Russia

- Pyotr Ilyich Tchaikovsky (1840–1893)
- Nikolai Rimsky-Korsakov (1844–1908)

What Students Should Know

1. **What the Paris Commune was and what happened to it**

   After the Germans withdrew from Paris in 1871, the Paris Commune proclaimed the independence of Paris from France. Controlled by Jacobins, Marxists, socialists, and anarchists, the Commune carried out executions of Catholic clergy and laity. The Paris government continued for about two months until it was overthrown by forces of the French republic in May 1871.

2. **The struggles between monarchists and republicans in France's Third Republic**

   Monarchists at first dominated the government of France's Third Republic. The monarchists, however, were divided between Legitimists

Key Terms at a Glance

clericalism: the notion that churchmen, or *clerics*, should have an official place in influencing the government and the social life of a nation

social insurance: protection against the hazards (such as loss of wages and sickness) that endanger the well-being of individuals. Social insurance can take the form of payments of money to individuals and free or inexpensive medical care. These are provided either by government action or by laws that require employers or public organizations to contribute to a fund.

protectorate: the government of a nation by a foreign government, acting as a guardian

entente: a kind of informal alliance between two or more nations

disestablishment: removal from legal *establishment*, especially to end official recognition of a church as the state church

isolation: the state of being isolated—being free of alliances with other countries

Slavophile: referring to nationalists in the late 19th century and early 20th century who adhered to *Slavophilism*—the belief that Slavic and, especially, Russian culture is superior to Western European cultures

Russification: a policy of forcing Russian culture and language on a non-Russian people or group

(the supporters of the House of Bourbon), Orleanists (the supporters of Louis Philippe's family), and Bonapartists. Under monarchist control, the republic adopted a constitution that—despite the monarchists—was republican, not monarchical.

Many if not most churchmen were monarchists, for republicans struck at the liberties of the Church when they gained power. Republicans said they opposed clericalism, the notion that churchmen, or *clerics*, should have an official place in influencing the government and the social life of a nation.

Republicans eventually gained control of the French legislature. Republican objections to those who opposed calls of support for Pope Pius IX led President Patrice MacMahon to dissolve the legislature. But new elections brought in a majority of republicans. MacMahon resigned, in 1879.

3. The republican French government and its anticlerical legislation

The republicans were divided between those who favored the interests of the bourgeoisie (who were moderately anticlerical) and those (the strongly anticlerical faction) who favored the interests of the working class and poor.

The republicans backed measures to create a free, compulsory educational system for children (ages 6–13). One of the aims of this legislation was to remove Catholic priests and religious from French schools. The republicans backed other anticlerical measures. The ministry issued a decree abolishing religious orders and expelling their members from France. The legislature in the 1880s passed laws recognizing only civil marriages and permitting divorce.

4. The industrialization of Germany and its results

Various factors, including gaining Alsace and Lorraine along with five billion francs from the French government, led to a phenomenal growth in industry in the German Empire after 1870. More Germans moved from farming to industrial work, and cities grew dramatically. The cruelties of industrialization led to the growth of the Marxist Social Democratic Workingman's Party. Fearing its growth, Otto von Bismarck pushed anti-socialist laws through the *Reichstag*. When he saw such measures failed to crush the socialists, Bismarck proposed measures to bring aid to workers and the poor (such as employer- and employee-funded medical and unemployment insurance—social insurance) and to regulate the workplace. These measures were backed by the Center Party. They failed, however, to arrest the growth of the Social Democratic Party.

5. **Bismarck's European balance of power strategy**

After 1871, Bismarck abandoned war and conquest as a way to secure the safety and prosperity of Germany. He turned, instead, to diplomacy. His strategy was to isolate France by maintaining friendship with Great Britain and forging alliances with Russia and Austria. By 1888, he had achieved his goal. Of all the great powers, Austria and Russia had made treaties with Germany, and Great Britain was friendly. France was isolated.

6. **What the new wave of colonization was**

The last 30 years of the 19th century witnessed a new wave of colonization on the part of European powers. By the mid-19th century, European powers had little interest in holding colonies overseas. Britain was still a major colonial power (which made sense, given that she had the world's largest navy), yet even her colonies were becoming independent states with ties to Britain.

In the late 1870s and into the 1880s, however King Leopold of II of Belgium formed a quasi-private colony in Africa's Congo—the Congo Free State. A private company formed by the king established plantations for rubber and other products, using forced and mistreated African labor. Following Leopold's lead, other countries, including Great Britain, France, Portugal, Italy, and the United States scrambled for colonies not only in Africa but also in Asia and the Pacific. By 1900, nearly all of Africa had been divided among the European powers. Though she was at first opposed to foreign colonization, Germany under Bismarck began establishing colonies in Africa and the Pacific in the 1880s. Bismarck, however, did not want to push colonization too far because he feared it would lead to conflicts with neighboring nations, which he wanted to keep as friends.

7. **Why Europeans and Americans supported—and opposed—colonization**

Perhaps the biggest reason Europeans and Americans wanted colonies was national pride—a great nation, it was thought, should expand its power over "uncivilized" peoples. These nations wanted to benefit from raw materials and other advantages, but many Europeans thought that, in turn, they had the task or mission to civilize the colonized lands. Other Europeans and Americans, however, thought colonization led to acts of injustice and cruelty and so opposed it.

8. **How Kaiser Wilhelm II abandoned Bismarck's policies and the results of this policy change**

When Wilhelm II became *kaiser* of Germany in 1888, he was determined that he and not Bismarck would rule the empire. After several conflicts with the *kaiser*, Bismarck resigned as chancellor in 1890. With Bismarck gone,

Wilhelm abandoned Bismarck's scheme to maintain peace in Europe. Wilhelm pursued a diplomatic policy that ended Russia's friendship with Germany. Instead, Russia formed an alliance with Germany's greatest enemy, France. By his policy of extending German influence across the world (again, ignoring Bismarck's policies), by intervening in South African affairs, and by building up Germany's navy so as to rival Britain's, Wilhelm II pushed Great Britain into closer relations with France. In 1904, Great Britain and France came to a friendly agreement, though not a military alliance, called the *Entente Cordiale.*

10. The character of British government under Queen Victoria

Queen Victoria's long reign witnessed conflicts between the Liberal and Conservative political parties in British government. The Liberals favored free trade, generally opposed imperialism, supported greater democracy in the government, and pushed for the disestablishment of the Church of England. The Conservatives generally opposed what the Liberals supported; yet, when they held power in the late 1860s, the Conservatives supported extending the suffrage to more people. More reforms were made when the Liberal, William Gladstone, was prime minister in the late 1880s. By 1886, the Liberals had won nearly universal manhood suffrage for British subjects in Parliamentary elections and universal manhood suffrage for city elections.

11. How Parliament addressed the "Irish problem"

For centuries, the Irish had suffered bitterly under English rule. Besides not being able to vote for members of Parliament, they could not own land but had to work as tenant farmers on English-owned estates. No limits were placed on how much rent a landlord demanded, nor did a landlord have to reimburse a tenant for improvements the tenant made on the land. The Catholic Irish had to support the Protestant Church of Ireland. After 1829, however, the Irish were able to elect representatives to Parliament and formed their own Irish Nationalist party, which fought for "Home Rule"—the right of the Irish to have their own government and parliament under the English monarch, but separate from Parliament in London. The Irish Nationalists did not win Home Rule; nevertheless, acts passed in Parliament between 1887 and 1903 improved conditions of life for Catholics in Ireland. Such improvements, however, did not satisfy Irish Nationalists, who were determined to win Home Rule.

12. How Great Britain ended its policy of isolation

Isolation had long been the basis for Great Britain's foreign policy. But, faced with the threat of Germany's growing economy and military, Great Britain began seeking alliances with other nations in the 1890s. Alliances in the early 20th century eventually led Great Britain into a "Triple Entente" with France and Russia, to counter Germany's Triple Alliance with Austria and Italy.

13. The political changes in Great Britain in the early 20th century

After Queen Victoria's death in 1901, Great Britain entered a period of great change. A new political party, Labor (made up of socialists and representatives of the trade unions), backed the Liberals in a challenge to the political power of Britain's aristocracy. In 1911, a coalition of Liberals, Labor party members, and Irish Nationalists were able to get King Edward VII's support for a bill that drastically cut back on the House of Lords' veto power. The Lords could veto a bill only three times. If the bill passed the Commons again, it became law. Thenceforth, the House of Commons was the chief governing body of the British Empire.

Great Britain was the strongest and most prosperous country in the world in the mid-19th century because:

a) It had many colonial holdings from which it derived vast amounts of wealth.

b) It was the most industrialized nation in the world and its manufactured goods were sold all over the world.

c) It had the biggest and best trained navy, along with the largest merchant marine, which carried on trade between Great Britain and countries throughout the world.

14. Tsar Aleksandr II's reform measures

Tsar Aleksandr II had brought changes to Russian government and society. He abolished serfdom (for which he became known as "Tsar Liberator") and carried out some Liberal reforms in government. He established elective governments, called *zemstvos*, for rural areas, and *dumas* for cities. He reformed the courts and permitted a freer expression of ideas in Russian society. But after assassination attempts by *narodniki* (violent Nihilists who tried to influence the people to adopt socialist ideas), Aleksandr turned toward repression. Yet, after a further assassination attempt against him, the tsar approved an assembly for Russia. But before his order could go into effect, Aleksandr was assassinated on March 13, 1881.

15. The character of Russia in the late 19th and early 20th centuries

Aleksandr II's son, Tsar Aleksandr III, embraced repression and Russification during his reign from 1881 to 1894. Though his approach was milder, Tsar Nikolai II, who succeeded Aleksandr III in 1894, continued his father's repression. Under both Aleksandr III and Nikolai II, Russia was undergoing a rapid industrialization, which intensified the government's desire for a warm-water port. To achieve this, Russia looked to the Pacific and built the Trans-Siberian Railway between Moscow and Vladivostok on the Pacific coast. Russia occupied Port Arthur on the Yellow Sea.

16. The Russo-Japanese War and its results

Russia's occupation of Port Arthur on the Pacific led to a Russian presence in Manchuria. This worried Japan, which had become an industrial power with a well-disciplined army and navy. Japan wanted to extend her power into Korea and Manchuria. In 1903, therefore, Japan demanded that Russia remove all troops from Manchuria, unless Russia allowed Japan to move into Korea. Russia's hesitance in replying led Japan to launch a surprise attack on Russian warships at Port Arthur on February 8, 1904. This, in turn, brought about a war with Japan in 1904–1905, in which the Japanese were victorious and Russia humiliated.

17. The character of Leo XIII's papacy

Like Blessed Pius IX, Pope Leo XIII was a vigorous foe of Liberalism. Yet, while Pius IX had stoutly defied the modern world and inspired the Catholics with the spirit of a warrior, Leo XIII was eager to find opportunities to create friendships and reconcile differences. A skilled diplomat, he brought about good relations between the Holy See and many foreign powers. He sought to reconcile French Catholics with the Third Republic. He said the Church supports any form of government, as long as it serves the common good of the citizens. A republic is a valid form of government, and in France it had become the established government. French Catholics, then, said Leo, should support it. Yet, despite such overtures, the

French government continued and expanded its anticlerical measures. Leo XIII patronized the sciences.

18. Why we remember Leo XIII as the working-man's pope

Leo XIII took an interest in labor issues. His encyclical, *Rerum Novarum*—the first time the universal Church addressed the social question—was the first in a long line of papal encyclicals dealing with social issues. In *Rerum Novarum*, Leo came out in opposition to socialism; but, he also condemned many of the principles of *laissez-faire* capitalism. Unlike the socialists, Leo asserted the right to private, productive property; but, against the capitalists, he asserted the worker's right to a just wage. Workers, he said, should not be treated like machines or cattle, nor should children be forced to labor like adults or work be placed upon females as if they were male adults. Workers, Leo said, have the right to organize themselves into unions and engage in peaceful strikes. Wealth production, he asserted, has the ultimate purpose of helping men live a virtuous life. Because of the moral dimension of economics, Leo said the Church has to be involved in solving social problems.

19. Identify the following:

Social insurance: protection against the hazards (such as loss of wages and sickness) that endanger the well-being of individuals. Social insurance can take the form of payments of money to individuals and free or inexpensive medical care. These are provided either by government action or by laws that require employers or public organizations to contribute to a fund.

Nihilists: a group of Russian intellectuals who held there is *nothing* (Latin, *nihil*) they should not question or doubt.

Questions for Review

1. **What is clericalism? What does it mean to be anticlerical?**

   Clericalism is the notion that churchmen, or *clerics*, should have an official place in influencing the government and the social life of the nation. To be anticlerical is to deny that churchmen should have any such function in society.

2. **Why did French Catholics tend to support monarchy? Was Pope Leo XIII also a monarchist? Please explain.**

   French Catholics tended to support monarchy because the republican governments of France tended to be anticlerical and to persecute the Church. Pope Leo XIII was not a monarchist in the sense of someone who thinks monarchy is the only valid form of government. Leo XIII did not condemn monarchy, but he said the Church and Catholics can support forms of government other than monarchy.

3. **How did the life of people in Germany change after Franco-Prussian War?**

   After the war, there was a phenomenal growth in industry in the German Empire. More Germans moved from farming to industrial work, and cities grew dramatically. Industrialized society in Germany resulted in the same evils found in other industrialized nations—low wage jobs, dangerous working conditions, unhealthy living conditions, etc.

4. **What is social insurance? Why did Bismarck support social insurance programs in Germany?**

   Social insurance is protection against the hazards (such as loss of wages and sickness) that endanger the well-being of individuals. Social insurance can take the form of payments of money to individuals and free or inexpensive medical care. These are provided either by government action or by laws that require employers or public organizations to contribute to a fund. Bismarck supported social insurance programs because he hoped to attract workers away from socialism and Marxism. If he improved workers' lives, he thought, they would be less willing to adopt revolutionary ideas.

5. **What was Bismarck's grand strategy to keep peace in Europe? Why did it fail?**

Bismarck's strategy was to keep France isolated from the other European powers. He accomplished this by keeping up friendly relations with Great Britain and by entering into an alliance with Russia. His strategy failed because Kaiser Wilhelm II abandoned the alliance with Russia and adopted measures that made Great Britain think Germany a threat. Both these nations, then, moved toward alliances with France.

6. **Why did many Europeans support foreign colonization in the late 19th century?**

Many Europeans supported foreign colonization because they thought a great nation needed to have foreign colonies. Foreign colonies brought glory to a people. The nation, too, could benefit from raw materials and other goods derived from these nations. In return, the European nations could bring civilization to the lands they colonized.

7. **Why was Great Britain the strongest, most prosperous country in the world in the late 19th century?**

Great Britain was the strongest and most prosperous country in the late 19th century because of three factors:

a) It had many colonial holdings from which it derived vast amounts of wealth.

b) It was the most industrialized nation in the world, and its manufactured goods were sold all over the world.

c) It had the biggest and best trained navy, along with the largest merchant marine that carried on trade between Great Britain and countries throughout the world.

8. **What is isolationism? Why, after being isolationist, did Great Britain begin to seek alliances with other nations?**

Isolation is the state where a nation is free of alliances with other nations. Great Britain began seeking alliances because she feared the growing economic and military power of Germany.

9. **What part of the British government became the most powerful after 1911?**

The House of Commons became the most powerful part of British government after 1911.

10. **Why, according to Pope Leo XIII, is socialism wrong? What is wrong with *laissez-faire* capitalism, according to the pope?**

Leo XIII condemned socialism because it denied the right of private property for individuals and families. He condemned *laissez-faire* capitalism because it treated workers as mere machines or beasts of burden and made them depend on the mercy of their employers. Capitalism denied the right to a just wage and humane working conditions.

Ideas in Action

1. **In the late 19th century, French monarchists were divided between Legitimists, Orleanists, and Bonapartists. These groups still exist today, and each supports a man who, they say, is the rightful king of France. Research who is the rightful king of France accord-**

ing to today's Legitimists, Orleanists, and Bonapartists. Where do the claimants live? What do they do for a living?

2. Most of modern-day Africa's independent nations were colonies of one of the great European powers of the 19th century. Choose an African country to research. Write a paper telling what European nation colonized the African country, how and when it gained its independence, what religion or religions its people practice, what language or languages

they speak, and what kind of government it has today.

3. Listen to some of the music by composers of the late 19th century. Such composers include Richard Wagner, Gustav Mahler, Richard Strauss, Johann Strauss Jr., Nikolai Rimsky-Korsakov, Modest Mussorgsky, Giuseppe Verdi, Giacomo Puccini, Georges Bizet, and Camille Saint-Saëns.

Sample Quiz I (pages 417–431)

Please answer the following in complete sentences.

1. What is clericalism? Who opposed clericalism in the government of the Third French Republic?

2. What was the government established in Paris after the Germans withdrew in 1871? It was controlled by Jacobins, Marxists, socialists, and anarchists.

3. What was Bismarck's strategy for keeping France isolated?

4. Who was the first European ruler to establish a colony in Africa in the 1870s and 1880s? What was the name of this colony?

5. Who was the German *kaiser* who abandoned Bismarck's policy for keeping France isolated? As a result, Russia became friends with France.

Answers to Sample Quiz I

Students' answers should approximate the following.

1. Clericalism is the notion that churchmen, or *clerics*, should have an official place in influencing the government and the social life of a nation. The republicans opposed clericalism in the Third French Republic.

2. The government established in Paris after the German withdrawal in 1871 was the *Paris Commune.*

3. Bismarck's strategy to isolate France entailed maintaining friendship with Great Britain and forging alliances with Russia and Austria.

4. The first European ruler to establish an African colony in the 1870s and 1880s was *King Leopold II of Belgium.* The colony was the *Congo Free State.*

5. *Kaiser Wilhelm II* abandoned Bismarck's policy of isolating France.

Sample Quiz II (pages 431–443)

Please answer the following in complete sentences.

1. In the late 1870s, the Irish demanded from Parliament the right to have their own government and parliament under the English monarch, but separate from Parliament in London. What was the name for this right?

2. What was Great Britain's alliance with Russia and France called? What was Germany's alliance with Italy and Austria called?

3. How did the House of Commons become the chief governing body in the British Empire in the early 20th century?

4. Why was Tsar Aleksandr II called Tsar Liberator?

5. With what nation did Russia go to war in 1906? Who won the war?

6. Give two reasons why Great Britain was the strongest and most prosperous country in the world in the mid-19th century.

Answers to Sample Quiz II

Students' answers should approximate the following

1. The right the Irish demanded was called *Home Rule*.

2. Great Britain's alliance with Russia and France was called the *Triple Entente*. Germany's alliance with Italy and Austria was called the *Triple Alliance*.

3. The House of Commons became the chief governing body in the British Empire by limiting the power of the House of Lords. The Commons with the king were able to force a bill through the Lords that allowed the Lords to veto a bill passed by the Commons only three times. The fourth time the Commons passed the bill, it became law.

4. Tsar Aleksandr II was called Tsar Liberator because he freed the serfs.

5. Russia went to war with Japan in 1906. Japan won the war.

6. Great Britain was the strongest and most prosperous country in the world in the mid-19th century because (possible answers):

   a) It had many colonial holdings from which it derived vast amounts of wealth.

   b) It was the most industrialized nation in the world and its manufactured goods were sold all over the world.

   c) It had the biggest and best trained navy, along with the largest merchant marine that carried on trade between Great Britain and countries throughout the world.

Essays (200–500 words each)

Instructions to be given to the students: Write in complete sentences. Underline your thesis. Give three supports or examples that explain why you think what you do and that support your thesis.

1. Why did some Europeans and Americans support colonization in the late 19th century? Why did some oppose it? Who was right and who was wrong? Or were both sides right in some ways and wrong in others?

2. What is anticlericalism? Give examples of governments we have dealt with so far in this book that were anticlerical. What did they do or say that showed that they were anticlerical? Does anticlericalism still exist today?

Chapter Test

Please answer the following in complete sentences.

I. **Short Essay—Answer one of the following:**

1. What is social insurance? Why did Bismarck begin to favor laws that established social insurance systems in Germany?

2. In *Rerum Novarum,* what right did Pope Leo XIII say people had—a right socialists denied? What rights do workers have? What is the purpose of making wealth, according to Pope Leo? Why must the Church be involved in solving social problems, according to the pope?

II. **Short Answer:**

1. The French republicans were divided between moderates and the more extreme factions. Which group of republicans stood for the bourgeoisie? Which stood for the working class and the poor?

2. Name the great reform the Liberals made in the British government in 1886 that was supposed to make Parliament less oligarchical.

3. What groups established the Paris Commune in 1871?

4. What big economic change occurred in Germany after 1870? How did it change society?

5. What nations made up the Triple Entente? What nations made up the Triple Alliance?

6. Does a Catholic have to be a monarchist, according Pope Leo XIII? Please explain.

Answer Key to the Chapter Test

Students' answers should approximate the following:

I.

1. The cruelties of industrialization in Germany led to the growth of the Marxist Social Democratic Workingman's Party. Fearing its growth, Otto von Bismarck pushed anti-social-ist laws through the *Reichstag*. When he saw such measures failed to crush the socialists, Bismarck proposed measures to bring aid to workers and the poor (such as employer and employee-funded medical and unemployment insurance—social insurance) and to regulate the workplace. These measures failed, however, to arrest the growth of the Social Democratic Party.

2. Unlike the socialists, Pope Leo XIII in *Rerum Novarum* said people have the right to private, productive property. Workers, said the pope, have a right to a just wage, a right to be treated humanely (not like machines or cattle), and the right to organize themselves into unions and engage in peaceful strikes. Wealth production, he asserted, has the ultimate purpose of helping men live a virtuous life. Because morality is involved in economics, Leo said the Church has to be involved in solving social problems.

II.

1. The moderate republicans stood for the bourgeoisie. The more extreme republicans stood for the working class and the poor.

2. By 1886, the Liberals had won for British subjects nearly universal manhood suffrage in Parliamentary elections.

3. Jacobins, Marxists, socialists, and anarchists established the Paris Commune.

4. Germany experienced a phenomenal growth of industry after 1870. More Germans moved from farming to industrial work, and cities grew dramatically.

5. Great Britain, France, and Russia made up the Triple Entente. Germany, Austria, and Italy made up the Triple Alliance.

6. A Catholic does not have to be a monarchist, according to Pope Leo XIII. He said the Church supports any form of government, as long as it serves the common good of the citizens.

Chapter Overview

- For many at the beginning of the 20th century, the new century seemed to promise an age of peace, prosperity, and progress after the wars and bitter political struggles of the 19th century. Yet, despite the appearances of prosperity and peace, Europe still suffered from poverty and mutual hatreds between classes and peoples.

- The firing of four workers at the Putilov factory in St. Petersburg, Russia, in December 1904 inspired a massive strike of industrial workers in the city. The killing of workers by tsarist troops on "Bloody Sunday," January 9, 1905, helped ignite revolution throughout Russia. Both Liberals and Marxists supported the revolution. Liberals demanded a constitutional government from Tsar Nikolai II, to which he agreed in the *October Manifesto* of October 17, 1905. Socialists continued the revolution against the government, despite the manifesto. But in December 1905, government forces crushed a socialist uprising in Moscow. The crushing of the socialists weakened the Liberals and allowed the tsar to maintain his autocracy. Nikolai II and his prime minister, Pyotr Arkadyevich Stolypin, however, established reforms to allow peasants to purchase land.

- By 1900, the various nationalities that made up Austria-Hungary were filled with the spirit of nationalism. Besides the Austrian Germans, only the Magyars had achieved their own diet; all others had to send representatives to the imperial *Reichsrat* in Vienna. This *Reichsrat* had obtained full legislative powers and, in 1907, its members were elected by universal suffrage—which meant that the *Reichsrat* became dominated not by Germans, but by Slavs.

- Nationalism was not just an internal problem for Austria-Hungary; it affected the empire's relations with its neighbors. Austria's occupation of Bosnia and Herzegovina brought it into conflict with Serbia, which wanted to bring these provinces as well as parts of Austria and Hungary inhabited by South Slavs into a united Yugoslav kingdom. Austria-Hungary's annexation of Bosnia and Herzegovina increased tensions not only with Serbia but with Russia as well.

- Tensions between Germany and France increased in the early 1900s. The First Moroccan Crisis in 1905 and the second in 1911 showed Germany that the alliance between Great Britain and France was strong. Following these crises, France and Germany, fearing one another, both increased the size of their military. Germany had been building up her navy until it was the second largest in the world, after the British navy. This further alienated the British from Germany and strengthened Britain's alliance with France and Russia in the Triple Entente.

- Unable to win "unredeemed Italy" from Austria or to become the greatest power in the Adriatic, Italy looked for conquests elsewhere. In 1911, Italy went to war with the Ottoman Empire and by 1912 had won Tripoli and Cyrenaica in North Africa, and the Dodecanese Islands in the Aegean Sea. Italy united Tripoli and Cyrenaica into the colony of Libya.

- The Italian victories in North Africa showed the small Balkan states of Greece, Bulgaria, and Serbia that the Ottomans were not as powerful as they seemed. In 1912 these three states, along with the small kingdom of Montenegro, went to war with the Ottoman Empire to win those parts of the Balkans still under Turkish control. After the war ended in May 1913, the Ottoman Empire surrendered all of European Turkey, except for Constantinople and the lands immediately surrounding it, to the four kingdoms. Disagreements between these kingdoms, however, led to another war. Bulgaria attacked Greece and Serbia, which were joined by Montenegro and Romania. Greece, Serbia, Montenegro, and the Ottoman Empire increased their territorial holdings following the end of the war in August 1913, while Bulgaria had to surrender territory. The war, however, did not ease tensions in the Balkans.

- The Balkan wars only increased the ill feeling between Serbia and Austria-Hungary. Serbian nationalists feared the heir to the Habsburg throne, Archduke Franz Ferdinand, because he planned to grant Slavs in the empire equal status with Germans and Magyars. A Serbian terrorist group, called the Black Hand, prepared a plan to assassinate Franz Ferdinand. The plan was carried out on June 28, 1914; a Black Hand operative assassinated Franz Ferdinand and his wife, Sophie, while they were on an official visit to Sarajevo in Bosnia.

- Following the assassination of the archduke and his wife, Emperor Franz Ferdinand allowed his foreign minister, Count Leopold von Berchtold, to send a harsh ultimatum to Serbia. Serbia did not agree to the ultimatum, and Berchtold urged the emperor to declare war. Franz Josef declared war on Serbia on July 28, 1914.

- Despite attempts to forestall a war, the European nations began to form up in their alliances. The day after Austria-Hungary's declaration of war, Tsar Nikolai II of Russia ordered a mobilization of the Russian army. When Kaiser Wilhelm II's attempts to convince Russia to end the mobilization failed, Germany (which had promised to support Austria-Hungary) declared war on August 1, 1914. On August 3, Germany declared war on Russia's ally, France. To knock France out of the war before the Russians could put their army into play, Germany moved into Belgium in order to invade northern France. The violation of Belgium's neutrality caused Great Britain to declare war on Germany on August 4. Soon other nations joined the rival alliances, and nearly all of Europe was at war.

- Eighteen days after invading Belgium, German armies controlled the entire country. They next moved into France and advanced to within 30 miles of Paris. The five-day First Battle of the Marne ended in a stalemate between the German armies and those of the allies, France and Britain. On the Eastern Front, Russian armies pushed far into East Prussia and defeated the Germans in battle. At the Battle of Tannenberg, however, the Germans so decisively defeated the Russians that they were forced to end their invasion.

- On the Western Front, the Germans captured vital positions around Verdun and the important Belgian city of Antwerp and the French city of Lille. Still, the war in the west turned into a war of attrition, with neither side gaining any significant territory.

Chapter Goals

This chapter begins with bitter irony. The hopes of Liberals that at the beginning of the 20th century mankind had entered a new age of peace, prosperity and progress were very soon dashed by the events that culminated in the "Great War"—World War I. Teachers can use this as an object lesson in how little people understand their own time, how hard it is to discern the real "signs of the times."

Period Music

English

- Frederick Delius (1862–1934)
- Ralph Vaughn Willians (1872–1978)

Finnish

- Jean Sibelius (1865-1957)—a nationalist composer

  The Swan of Tuonela (1895)

  Finlandia (1899–1900)

French

- Claude Debussy (1862–1918)—a leading impressionist composer

  Prelude to the Afternoon of a Fawn (1894)

  La Mer (The Sea) (1905–1906)

- Maurice Ravel (1875–1937)

German

- Richard Strauss (1864–1949)—a composer who took the late Romantic style to its limits

  Also Sprach Zarathustra (Thus Spoke Zarathustra) (1896)

- Max Reger (1873–1913)—a composer known for his organ works and violin sonatas

Italian

- Pietro Mascagni (1863–1945)

  Cavalleria Rusticana (1890), an opera

Russian

- Alexander Scriabin (1872–1915)
- Sergei Rachmaninoff (1973–1945)

Spanish

- Isaac Albéniz (1860–1909)
- Manuel de Falla (1876–1946)

What Students Should Know

1. **The basis for early 20th century optimism**

    For many at the beginning of the 20th century, the new century seemed to promise an age of peace, prosperity, and progress after the wars and bitter political struggles of the 19th century. Yet, despite the appearances of prosperity and peace, Europe still suffered from poverty and mutual hatreds between classes and peoples. Some of the grounds of optimism were as follows:

    a) Reason and science, it was thought, were replacing religious "superstition," and Liberalism and republicanism were overcoming "tyrannical" monarchical governments.

    b) Nations were trying to insure peace by drawing up and enforcing international

Key Terms at a Glance

international law: a body of rules that govern the relations between nations

convention: an agreement or contract between states or governments

soviet: from the Russian word meaning "council"

partial mobilization: the mobilization of only a part of a nation's armed forces

Mensheviks: "the minority"—the name given to Social Democrats who opposed Vladimir Ilyich Lenin's methods for carrying out a socialist revolution

Bolsheviks: "the majority"—the name given to Social Democrats who formed around Lenin and adopted his methods of revolution

law—a body of rules that govern the relations between nations.

c) Parliamentary government was spreading all over the world, and democracy was on the rise.

d) Though low wages and poor working conditions still prevailed in industry, labor unions were winning victories for many workers—shorter working days, higher wages, and better safety standards in factories.

e) Governments were beginning to grant social insurance.

f) Literacy was increasing because of compulsory education.

2. **The course of the Russian Revolution of 1905 and the firing of four workers at the Putilov factory in St. Petersburg, Russia, in December**

1904 inspired a massive strike of industrial workers in the city. The killing of workers led by the Orthodox priest, Georgy Gapon, by tsarist troops on "Bloody Sunday," January 9, 1905, helped ignite revolution throughout Russia. Both Liberals and Marxists supported the revolution. Liberals demanded a constitutional government from Tsar Nikolai II,

to which he agreed in the *October Manifesto* of October 17, 1905. Socialists continued the revolution against the government, despite the manifesto. But in December 1905, government forces crushed a socialist uprising in Moscow. The crushing of the socialists weakened the Liberals and allowed the tsar to maintain his autocracy. Nikolai II and his prime minister, Pyotr Arkadyevich Stolypin, however, established reforms to allow peasants to purchase land.

3. **The Russian Marxist socialist parties**

Socialist Revolutionary Party: A Marxist party founded in 1900 that sought to organize peasants in the countryside.

Social Democrats: Led by Georgy Valentinovich Plekhanov, the "father" of Russian Marxism, this group focused on organizing the proletariat in the cities.

Mensheviks: A faction of the Social Democrats that thought Russia was not ready for true socialism and supported working with Liberals to reform laws with a view to a future transformation of Russia into a Marxist state

Bolsheviks: Another faction of the Social Democrats. Led by V.I. Lenin, the Bolsheviks demanded a violent revolution and the over-throw of the tsarist state.

4. **The ideas of Vladimir Ilyich Lenin on how to carry out a successful revolution**

Convinced that the workers by themselves would never carry out a successful Marxist revolution, Lenin thought what was needed was an organization of professional revolutionaries that would, like missionaries, carry the message of revolution to the workers. The members of this organization had to be highly disciplined, absolutely obedient to their leaders on the "Central Committee," and willing to sacrifice themselves and all they loved for the revolution. They must allow nothing—not friendship or love of family—to stand in their way. Lenin said the lives of those who opposed the working-class revolution were of no value whatsoever.

5. **The condition of Austria-Hungary in the early 20th century**

By 1900, the various nationalities that made up Austria-Hungary were filled with the spirit of nationalism. Besides the Austrian Germans, only the Magyars had achieved their own diet; all others had to send representatives to the imperial *Reichsrat* in Vienna. Emperor Franz Josef had given the *Reichsrat* full legislative powers, and Liberals elected to the body passed laws granting freedom of religion and other individual rights and created a fairer court system. By the 1870s, the *Reichsrat* had seemingly turned Austria into a Liberal constitutional monarchy. In 1907, the *Reichstrat's* members were elected by universal suffrage—which meant that the *Reichsrat* was no longer the domain of the wealthier classes nor of the Germans. In fact, it became dominated by Slavs.

6. **Austria-Hungary's relations with the Yugoslavs**

Nationalism was not just an internal problem for Austria-Hungary; it affected the empire's relations with its neighbors. Austria's occupation of Bosnia and Herzegovina in 1876 brought it into conflict with Serbia, which wanted to bring these provinces as well as parts of Austria and Hungary inhabited by South Slavs into a united Yugoslav kingdom. Austria-Hungary's annexation of Bosnia and Herzegovina in 1908 increased tensions not only with Serbia but with Russia as well. Russian nationalists had adopted "Pan-Slavism"—the belief that all Slavic nations should be united in some way to Russia to form one great Slavic and Orthodox empire.

7. **Worsening relations between Germany, on the one hand, and France and Great Britain, on the other**

Tensions between Germany and France increased in the early 1900s. In the First Moroccan Crisis in 1905, after France had ignored Germany in seeking international blessing to interfere in Morocco, Germany pressured France into calling the Algeciras Conference on the future of the sultanate. The conference showed Germany that only Austria-Hungary stood with her and that France and Great Britain's friendship was firm. The same thing was seen in the second Moroccan Crisis in 1911, when Germany demanded and received part of French East Africa from France. Following these crises, France and Germany, fearing one another, both increased the size of their military. Germany had been building up her navy until it was the second largest in the world, after the British navy. This further alienated the British from Germany and strengthened Britain's alliance with France and Russia in the Triple Entente.

8. **Italy's conquests in Africa**

Unable to win "unredeemed Italy" from Austria or to become the greatest power in the Adriatic, Italy looked for conquests elsewhere. In 1911, Italy went to war with the Ottoman Empire and by 1912 had won Tripoli and Cyrenaica in North Africa, and the Dodecanese Islands in the Aegean Sea. Italy united Tripoli and Cyrenaica into the colony of Libya.

9. **The Balkan Wars and their results**

The Italian victories in North Africa showed the small Balkan states of Greece, Bulgaria, and Serbia that the Ottomans were not as powerful as they seemed. Inspired by nationalism, in 1912 these three states, along with the small kingdom of Montenegro, went to war with the Ottoman Empire to win those parts of the Balkans still under Turkish control. After the war ended in May 1913, the Ottoman Empire surrendered all of European Turkey, except for Constantinople and the lands immediately surrounding it, to the four kingdoms. Disagreements between these kingdoms, however, led to another war. Bulgaria attacked Greece and Serbia, which were joined by Montenegro and Romania. Greece, Serbia, Montenegro, and the Ottoman Empire increased their territorial holdings following the end of the war in August 1913, while Bulgaria had to surrender territory. The war, however, did not ease tensions in the Balkans.

10. **The events that led up to the assassination of Archduke Franz Ferdinand**

The Balkan wars only increased the ill feeling between Serbia and Austria-Hungary. Serbian nationalists feared the heir to the Habsburg throne, Archduke Franz Ferdinand, because he planned to grant Slavs in the empire equal status with Germans and Magyars. Just like Magyars, the Slavs would have their own diet under the emperor. The Yugoslav national-ists feared this arrangement would make their people content under Austrian rule. A Serbian terrorist group, called the Black Hand, pre-pared a plan to assassinate Franz Ferdinand. The Serbian government knew of the plan, but did little to stop it. The plan was carried out on June 28, 1914; a Black Hand operative assas-sinated Franz Ferdinand and his wife, Sophie, while they were on an official visit to Sarajevo in Bosnia.

11. **How Austria-Hungary sparked the Great War**

Following the assassination of the archduke and his wife, Emperor Franz Ferdinand allowed his foreign minister, Count Leopold von Berchtold, to send a harsh ultimatum to Serbia. Serbia agreed to all the terms of the ultimatum, except to what would undermine her sovereignty. At the same time, the Serbians ordered a partial mobilization of their army. Austria rejected Serbia's reply and ordered a partial mobilization as well. The situation was tense because Russia was Serbia's ally, and France and Great Britain's. War between Austria-Hungary and Serbia, thus, could include Russia, France, and Great Britain, as well as Austria-Hungary's own ally, Germany. Attempts on both sides to assure peace failed, and Berchtold urged the emperor to declare war. Though he had opposed war, Franz Josef, at Berchtold's urging, declared war on Serbia on July 28, 1914.

12. **How other nations entered the war**

Despite attempts to forestall a war, the European nations began to form up in their alliances. The day after Austria-Hungary's declaration of war, Tsar Nikolai II of Russia ordered a mobilization of the Russian army. When Kaiser Wilhelm II's attempts to convince Russia to end the mobilization failed, Germany (which had promised to support

Austria-Hungary) declared war on August 1, 1914. On August 3, Germany declared war on Russia's ally, France. To knock France out of the war before the Russians could put their army into play, Germany moved into Belgium in order to invade northern France. The violation of Belgium's neutrality caused Great Britain to declare war on Germany on August 4. Soon other nations joined the rival alliances, and nearly all of Europe was at war.

13. The course of the War in 1914

Eighteen days after invading Belgium, German armies controlled the entire country. They next moved into France and advanced to within 30 miles of Paris. The five-day First Battle of the Marne ended in a stalemate between the German armies and those of the allies, France and Britain. On the Eastern Front, Russian armies pushed far into East Prussia and defeated the Germans in battle. At the Battle of Tannenberg, however, the Germans so decisively defeated the Russians that they were forced to end their invasion. On the Western Front, the Germans captured vital positions around Verdun and the important Belgian city of Antwerp and the French city of Lille. Still, the war in the west turned into a war of attrition, with neither side gaining any significant territory.

14. Who were the Central Powers in 1914

In 1914, the Central Powers were Germany and Austria-Hungary.

15. Who were the Allies in 1914

In 1914, the Allies were Great Britain, France, Russia, and Serbia.

Questions for Review

1. **Please give some reasons why people at the beginning of the 20th century were so confident that human society was progressing toward a better world.**

Possible answers:

a) Reason and science, it was thought, were replacing religious "superstition," and Liberalism and republicanism were overcoming "tyrannical" monarchical governments.

b) Nations were trying to insure peace by drawing up and enforcing international law—a body of rules that govern the relations between nations.

c) Parliamentary government was spreading all over the world, and democracy was on the rise.

d) Though low wages and poor working conditions still prevailed in industry, labor unions were winning victories for many workers—shorter working days, higher wages, and better safety standards in factories.

e) Governments were beginning to grant social insurance.

f) Literacy was increasing because of compulsory education.

2. **Why did Russian workers and peasants stage a revolt in 1905?**

The catalyst for the revolt was the firing of four workers at the Putilov factory in St. Petersburg. More fundamentally, the Russian people were unhappy with how the war with Japan was going; Russian workers were discontent with their low pay, poor working conditions, and the government's refusal to let them organize unions.

3. **Who was the leader of the Bolsheviks? How did the Bolsheviks differ from Mensheviks?**

Vladimir Lenin was the leader of the Bolsheviks. While the Mensheviks thought the progress toward a Marxist state had to be gradual, the Bolsheviks wanted a violent revolution to overthrow the tsarist state and establish a Marxist one.

4. **What was the *Ausgleich* of 1867? In what other ways did Emperor Franz Josef change the government of Austria-Hungary?**

The *Ausgleich* was a settlement made between Emperor Franz Josef of Austria and his kingdom of Hungary. Hungary was to have her own diet apart from Austria's, though Franz Josef remained Hungary's king. Austria and Hungary were joined only in matters having to do with war and foreign policy.

5. **Why did Serbia resent Austria-Hungary? What was Pan-Slavism?**

Serbia wanted to unite all South Slavs (Yugoslavs) into one kingdom. Populations of South Slavs, however, lived in Austria-Hungary, and Austria-Hungary occupied and then annexed the South Slav regions of Bosnia and Herzegovina. Pan-Slavism was the belief that all Slavic nations should be united in some way to Russia to form one great Slavic and Orthodox empire.

6. **Why did the Moroccan crises lead to worse relations between Germany and Great Britain?**

Great Britain thought Germany was aggressively seeking to expand her holdings and picking fights. Germany saw how firm Great Britain's friendship was with France, Germany's enemy, and so came to distrust Great Britain further.

7. **Why did the Serbian Black Hand want to assassinate Archduke Franz Ferdinand? On what date was he assassinated?**

The Black Hand wanted to assassinate the archduke because it feared that if he became emperor he would carry out his plan to give the Slavs the same status in the empire enjoyed by Austria and Hungary. This could make the South Slavs so content within the empire that they would not want to join a Yugoslav kingdom. Franz Ferdinand was assassinated on June 28, 1914.

8. **Why did Germany declare war on Russia? Why did Germany invade France?**

Germany declared war on Russia because Russia had mobilized her army against Germany. This was tantamount to a declaration of war. Thus when the tsar ignored the *kaiser's* ultimatum, calling on him to demobilize, Germany declared war. Germany invaded France to knock France out of the war before Russia could finish her mobilization and move against Germany. Germany did not want to fight a two-front war.

9. **What is a war of attrition? Explain how the war on the Western Front became a war of attrition after the First Battle of the Marne.**

A war of attrition is one where both sides wear each other down by constant assaults while not gaining any real advantages or victories. The war on the Western Front became a war of attrition because, after the First Battle of the Marne, neither the French nor the Germans could win any advantage. Both sides settled into trench warfare.

10. **How did European nationalism bring about the Great War?**

Each European nation looked solely to the good of its own national group and wanted advantages for it and it alone, even if it meant injustice and harm to other nations. Nations wanted territories or advantages belonging to other nations. This ignoring of the good of all ended in war.

Ideas in Action

1. At the beginning of the 20th century, Europe had a few independent countries that were very small (and they still exist today). For instance, the independent principality of Liechtenstein, which covers only 61.7 square miles, is five times smaller than New York City, which covers 305 square miles. Other small countries of Europe that existed at the beginning of the 20th century are Andorra, San Marino, and Monaco. Choose one of these countries and research its history, government, religion, language, and culture. Prepare a report based on your research.

2. Discuss whether people of our time believe that the world is getting better and better. Is belief in progress as strong today as it was at the beginning of the 20th century?

3. Read the First World War poetry of Siegfried Sassoon, Wilfred Owen, Herbert Read, John McCrae, Edward Thomas, and others. Discuss what different views of the war these authors convey.

Sample Quiz I (pages 449–463)

Please answer the following in complete sentences.

1. Give two reasons why people were so optimistic about the future in the early 20th century.

2. Who was the priest who led the procession of workers to tsar's palace in St. Petersburg on Bloody Sunday, 1905?

   a) Pyotr Stolypin   c) Georgy Plekhanov

   b) Georgy Gapon   d) Aleksandr Romanov

3. Which of the Russian Marxist parties thought Russia was not ready for a socialist government and so favored a gradual reform of the Russian society toward Marxism?

   a) Mensheviks   c) Socialist Revolutionaries

   b) Bolsheviks   d) Social Democrats

4. Which of the Russian Marxist parties listed above demanded an immediate, violent revolution to overthrow the Russian state and establish a Marxist government?

5. What two Slavic lands did Austria annex in 1908?

   a) Herzegovina   d) Dalmatia

   b) Galicia   e) Bosnia

   c) Montenegro   f) Croatia

6. Why did the annexation of these lands make Serbia upset?

7. What did Germany learn about her own allies and France and Great Britain at the Algeciras Conference?

Answers to Sample Quiz I

Students' answers should approximate the following.

1. People were so optimistic in the early 20th century for the following reasons (possible answers):

   a) Reason and science, it was thought, were replacing religious "superstition," and Liberalism and republicanism were overcoming "tyrannical" monarchical governments.

   b) Nations were trying to insure peace by drawing up and enforcing international law—a body of rules that govern the relations between nations.

   c) Parliamentary government was spreading all over the world, and democracy was on the rise.

   d) Though low wages and poor working conditions still prevailed in industry, labor unions were winning victories for many workers—shorter working days, higher wages, and better safety standards in factories.

   e) Governments were beginning to grant social insurance.

   f) Literacy was increasing because of compulsory education.

2. Georgy Gapon (b) was the priest who led the procession of workers to the tsar's palace in St. Petersburg on Bloody Sunday, 1905.

3. The Russian Marxist party that thought Russia was not ready for socialism was the Mensheviks (a).

4. The Russian Marxist party that favored an immediate revolution in Russia was the Bolsheviks (b).

5. Austria annexed Herzegovina (a) and Bosnia (e) in 1908.

6. The annexation of Bosnia and Herzegovina made Serbia upset because Serbia wanted to gather all South Slavs (Yugoslavs) into one kingdom under the king of Serbia. Bosnia and Herzegovina were Yugoslav regions.

7. At the Algeciras Conference, Germany learned that her only true ally was Austria-Hungary and that France and Great Britain would stand firmly with one another in friendship.

Sample Quiz II (pages 463–476)

Please answer the following in complete sentences.

1. Against whom did Serbia, Greece, Montenegro, Romania, and Bulgaria go to war in 1913?

2. On what date was Archduke Franz Ferdinand assassinated? In what city and region was he assassinated?

3. What was the group that carried out the assassination of Franz Ferdinand? With what government was it associated?

4. Why did Germany declare war on Russia in 1914?

5. Why did Germany invade France in 1914?

6. What nations were the Central Powers in 1914?

   a) Austria-Hungary   d) France

   b) Great Britain   e) Serbia

   c) Russia   f) Germany

7. What nations in the list above were the Allies in 1914?

Answers to Sample Quiz II

Students' answers should approximate the following

1. These Balkan nations went to war against the *Ottoman Empire* in 1913.

2. Archduke Franz Ferdinand was assassinated on *June 28, 1914* in *Sarajavo, Bosnia.*

3. The group that carried out the assassination of Franz Ferdinand was the *Black Hand.* It was associated with the *Serbian government.*

4. Germany declared war on Russia because Russia had mobilized her army against Germany. This was tantamount to a declaration of war. Thus when the tsar ignored the *kaiser*'s ultimatum, calling on him to demobilize, Germany declared war.

5. Germany invaded France to knock France out of the war before Russia could finish her mobilization and move against Germany. Germany did not want to fight a two-front war.

6. Austria-Hungary (a) and Germany (f) were the Central Powers in 1914.

7. Great Britain (b), Russia (c), France (d), and Serbia (e) were the Allies in 1914.

Essays (200–500 words each)

Instructions to be given to the students: Write in complete sentences. Underline your thesis. Give three supports or examples that explain why you think what you do and that support your thesis.

1. Were any of the nations involved in the "Great War" eager to go to war in 1914? Why did they go to war?

2. Were people in the early 20th century correct in feeling optimistic about the future?

Chapter Test

Please answer the following in complete sentences.

I. Short Essay—Answer two of the following:

1. Why were people in the early 20th century so optimistic about the future? Please give four reasons for why they were so.

2. Since he thought workers could not themselves carry out a successful revolution, how could the Marxists best succeed in bringing about a revolution, according to Vladimir Ilyich Lenin?

3. Describe the events that led to Austria-Hungary's declaration of war against Serbia.

II. Short Answer:

1. Please describe the basic difference between the Mensheviks and Bolsheviks.

2. Why can we say the government of Austria was a constitutional monarchy by 1914? Who had the right to vote in the Austrian empire?

3. Why did the Serbian Black Hand want to assassinate Archduke Franz Ferdinand of Austria? On what date was he assassinated?

4. Why did Great Britain declare war on Germany in 1914?

Answer Key to the Chapter Test

Students' answers should approximate the following:

I.

1. People in the early 20th century were so optimistic because (possible answers):

   a) Reason and science, it was thought, were replacing religious "superstition," and Liberalism and republicanism were overcoming "tyrannical" monarchical governments.

   b) Nations were trying to insure peace by drawing up and enforcing international law—a body of rules that govern the relations between nations.

   c) Parliamentary government was spreading all over the world, and democracy was on the rise.

   d) Though low wages and poor working conditions still prevailed in industry, labor unions were winning victories for many workers—shorter working days, higher wages, and better safety standards in factories.

   e) Governments were beginning to grant social insurance.

   f) Literacy was increasing because of compulsory education.

2. Convinced that the workers by themselves would never carry out a successful Marxist revolution, Lenin thought what was needed was an organization of professional revolutionaries that would, like missionaries, carry the message of revolution to the workers. The members of this organization had to be highly disciplined, absolutely obedient to their leaders on the "Central Committee," and willing to sacrifice themselves and all they loved for

the revolution. They must allow nothing—not friendship or love of family—to stand in their way. Lenin said the lives of those who opposed the working-class revolution were of no value whatsoever.

3. Following the assassination of the archduke and his wife, Emperor Franz Ferdinand allowed his foreign minister, Count Leopold von Berchtold, to send a harsh ultimatum to Serbia. Serbia agreed to all the terms of the ultimatum, except to what would undermine her sovereignty. At the same time, the Serbians ordered a partial mobilization of their army. Austria rejected Serbia's reply and ordered a partial mobilization as well. The situation was tense because Russia was Serbia's ally, and France and Great Britain's. War between Austria-Hungary and Serbia, thus, could include Russia, France, and Great Britain, as well as Austria-Hungary's own ally, Germany. Attempts on both sides to assure peace failed, and Berchtold urged the emperor to declare war. Though he had opposed war, Franz Josef, at Berchtold's urging, declared war on Serbia on July 28, 1914.

II.

1. Mensheviks thought Russia was not ready for true socialism and so they supported working with Liberals to reform laws with a view to a future transformation of Russia into a Marxist state. The Bolsheviks, however, rejected any sort of gradualism. They demanded a violent revolution and the overthrow of the tsarist state.

2. We can say the Austrian government was a constitutional monarchy by 1914 because it was governed by the emperor and a diet (called the *Reichsrat*). In 1907, the emperor granted universal manhood suffrage, so all men had the right to vote in Austria.

3. The Black Hand wanted to assassinate the archduke because it feared that if he became emperor he would carry out his plan to give the Slavs the same status enjoyed by Austria and Hungary in the empire. This could make the South Slavs so content within the empire that they would not want to join a Yugoslav kingdom. Franz Ferdinand was assassinated on June 28, 1914.

4. Great Britain declared war on Germany because Germany had invaded Belgium and violated her neutrality.

CHAPTER 17: The "Great War"

Chapter Overview

- Benedict XV, who became pope in September 1914, made it the aim of his papacy "to strive in every possible way that the charity of Jesus Christ should once more rule supreme amongst men." He spoke out against the war, calling on the warring powers to accept peace without victory. Despite his labors for peace, both sides in the war ignored the pope.

- By the beginning of 1915, the war on the Western Front had turned into a war of stalemate. Both sides engaged almost solely in trench warfare.

- In early 1915, the Germans were successful in pushing the Russians into Poland. To make contact with Russia, the Allies attempted to seize the Dardanelles and Gallipoli, but were unsuccessful. The Central Powers, however, were victorious in Galicia and by the end of 1915 had conquered all of Poland as well as parts of Latvia and Lithuania. By February 1916, the armies of the Central Powers had taken not only all of Serbia, but Albania and Montenegro as well.

- The British navy set up a sea blockade around Germany that stopped even food shipments from entering German ports. In response, the Germans laid mines off the coasts of Britain and Ireland and carried on unrestricted U-boat warfare on British merchant shipping. Germany also began using airships (Zeppelins) to drop bombs on British cities. By the end of the war, both sides carried out air-bombing raids on civilian targets.

- The Western Front in 1916 saw major battles around Verdun and on the River Somme. Casualties on both sides were great. On the Italian Front, attempts by the Italian army to break through Austrian lines were unsuccessful. In May 1916, the Austrians were able to push the Italian lines back and inflict heavy casualties. But in June, Russian advances against Galicia forced the Austrians to remove part of their forces from Italy. This allowed the Italians to force the Austrians back from the Isonzo River and capture Gorizia. Russian successes convinced Romania to enter the war on the Allied side. But German forces were able to drive the Romanians out of Transylvania. By January 1917, half of Romania was under German control.

- The year 1916 saw attempts by U.S. President Woodrow Wilson and Kaiser Wilhelm II to bring peace to Europe. Neither attempt was successful.

- When he became emperor of Austria and king of Hungary in November 1916, Karl von Habsburg immediately set himself to three tasks: to relieve his people's misery, reform the government, and make peace. But he had difficulty getting his reforms through the *Reichsrat*, and the allies ignored his offers of peace.

- After the sinking the passenger liner *Lusitania* in 1915, the Germans had discontinued unrestricted U-boat warfare on noncombatant ships. But, suffering under the continuing British blockade, Germany commenced U-boat warfare again in early 1917. The sinking of the British passenger liner *Laconia* and the interception of the Zimmerman telegram from Germany to Mexico convinced the U.S. Congress to declare war on Germany on April 6, 1917.

- The year 1917 witnessed new campaigns along the Western Front, including the Third Battle of Ypres. None of these campaigns significantly changed the situation on the Western Front. The Allies, however, gained a new ally—Greece, in July 1917.

- Russia's failures in the war and sufferings at home, along with the activities of Rasputin, brought Tsar Nikolai II into disgrace with his people. Revolution against the tsar broke out in March 1917, and he was forced to abdicate on March 15. The Liberal constitutional government set up in place of the tsar continued the war with Germany while facing insurrections at home from Mensheviks and Socialist Revolutionaries. In July, Vladimir Lenin and the Bolsheviks attempted an uprising but were crushed. In August, the Russian government faced another insurrection, this time from the military, but was able to stop it in September. In November, however, Lenin and the Bolsheviks were able to seize control of Petrograd and establish a Soviet government there. From Petrograd, the Bolshevik revolution spread to other parts of Russia, and the Soviet government was able to put down a counterrevolution

staged by the military. In January 1918, Lenin dissolved the democratically elected Russian assembly and, from thenceforth, ruled Russia as dictator.

- On August 1, 1917, Pope Benedict XV issued a peace proposal called the Seven Points. The Allies rejected the proposal. Emperor Karl I of Austria-Hungary embraced it, but Germany's response was not satisfactory. The pope's peace plan thus came to nothing, though the Fourteen Points for peace issued by President Wilson in early 1918 were similar in many ways to the pope's Seven Points.

- In a treaty signed at Brest-Litovsk on March 3, 1918, Russia's Soviet government made peace with Germany, thus ending the war on the Eastern Front. On the Western Front, Germany began a great offensive that ended in failure in the Second Battle of the Marne. In Italy, at the Battle of the Piave River, Austria suffered a serious defeat that ended her ability to take the offensive again.

- The Allies opened their offensive against German lines on July 18, 1918. The Allies were everywhere victorious, both along the Western Front and in Italy. In late October, Austria-Hungary and Italy opened armistice talks. On November 8, the Germans and the Allies began to negotiate an armistice. On November 9, the German government announced Kaiser Wilhelm's abdication, while Emperor Karl stepped down from power in Vienna. The Allies and the Germans signed an armistice at last on November 11, 1918, bringing an end to the war.

Chapter Goals

The events in this chapter are of immense importance for the history of the remainder of the 20th century. The First World War is one of the great turning points in history. It effectively ended the ancient regime and struck a deadly blow to the culture of Christendom. A new world arose from the ruin of the "Great War."

Period Music

Consult the list of composers in Chapter 16 of this teacher's manual.

What Students Should Know

1. How the pope responded to the war

Benedict XV, who became pope in September 1914, made it the aim of his papacy "to strive in every possible way that the charity of Jesus Christ should once more rule supreme amongst men." He spoke out against the war, calling on the warring powers to accept peace without victory—meaning both sides should lay down arms without demanding anything (such as payment for damages) from their foes.

Benedict said the war came because "in the ruling of states," governments had abandoned "Christian wisdom" and Christian moral ideals. Men sought for wealth, power, and false glory instead of spiritual goods. The answer for the unrest was to return to Christ and his charity and once again embrace "Christian principles."

Each side criticized Benedict for not condemning its enemy; but the pope responded that he could not be certain of accounts of atrocities but that he would condemn atrocities, no matter what side committed them. The pope, said Benedict, must remain impartial and "embrace all combatants in one sentiment of charity."

Despite his labors for peace, both sides in the war ignored the pope.

2. The situation on the Western Front in 1915

By the beginning of 1915, the war on the Western Front had turned into a war of stalemate. Both sides engaged almost solely in trench warfare. The introduction of chlorine gas by the Germans added a new horror to warfare. Though the Allies condemned the use of poison gas, both sides began to use it. In May 1915, Italy declared war on her former ally, Austria-Hungary, and joined the Entente.

Key Terms at a Glance

nuncio: the highest-ranking papal representative, sent by Rome to foreign countries

contraband: goods that may not be imported, exported, or possessed

indiscriminate warfare: acts of war that make no distinction between military and civilian targets; acts of war that strike noncombatants as well as members of the military

reconnaissance: an exploration of an enemy's territory to gain information

strategic bombing: bombing military, economic, or political targets belonging to an enemy; bombing civilian as well as military targets

commissar: a Communist Party official who leads a military unit, teaches party principles, or preserves party loyalty

3. Events on the Eastern Front in 1915

In early 1915, the Germans were successful in pushing the Russians into Poland. To make contact with Russia by means of the Black Sea, the Allies attempted to seize the narrow Dardanelles and Gallipoli straits, but were unsuccessful. By the end of 1915, the Central Powers had conquered all of Poland as well as parts of Latvia and Lithuania. By February 1916, the Central Powers had taken not only all of Serbia, but Albania and Montenegro as well.

4. The British blockade of Germany, and Germany's U-boat and Zeppelin raids

The British navy set up a sea blockade around Germany that stopped even food shipments from entering German ports. In response, to form their own blockade, the Germans laid mines off the coasts of Britain and Ireland and carried on unrestricted U-boat warfare on British merchant shipping. (Germany ended the U-boat warfare on passenger ships for a time after the sinking on May 7, 1915 of the *Lusitania*, a ship carrying American passengers and American-manufactured munitions. The U.S. Government protested, and Germany agreed not to target passenger liners.) The Germans also began using airships (Zeppelins) to drop bombs on British cities. By the end of the war, both sides carried out air-bombing raids on civilian targets and so perpetrated indiscriminate warfare—acts of war that make no distinction between military and civilian targets; that strike noncombatants as well as members of the military.

5. Events in 1916

The Western Front in 1916 saw major battles on the Western Front. Casualties on both sides were great. On the Italian Front, attempts by the Italian army to break through Austrian lines were unsuccessful. In May 1916, the Austrians were able to push the Italian lines back and inflict heavy casualties. But in June, Russian advances against Galicia forced the Austrians to remove part of their forces from Italy. This allowed the Italians to force the Austrians back from the Isonzo River in northwestern Italy and capture Gorizia. Russian successes convinced Romania to enter the war on the Allied side. But German forces were able to drive the Romanians out of Transylvania. By January 1917, half of Romania was under German control. The year 1916 saw attempts by U.S. President Woodrow Wilson and Kaiser Wilhelm II to bring peace to Europe. Neither attempt was successful.

6. Karl von Habsburg and what he did

When he became emperor of Austria and king of Hungary following the death of Emperor Franz Josef in November 1916, Karl von Habsburg immediately set himself to three tasks: to relieve his people's misery, reform the government, and make peace.

Emperor Karl wanted to turn the Dual Monarchy into a federation of autonomous states under the Habsburg emperor, but he was opposed by the powerful Magyar landowners in Hungary because the measure would diminish Hungary's power and influence and by the German members of the Austrian *Reichsrat*. Even Karl's ministers did not support him.

Karl, who had opposed the war from the beginning, sought to end it by offering peace proposals to the allies. Though he offered concessions, the Allies were not interested in peace proposals, nor was Germany. Thus, they came to nothing. In the conduct of his own armed forces, Karl put strict limits on the use of poison gas and ended strategic bombing—the bombing of military, economic, or political targets belonging to an enemy; bombing civilian as well as military targets.

7. How the United States of America entered the war

With its civilian population suffering under the continuing British blockade, Germany commenced U-boat warfare again in early 1917. The United States had been supporting the Allies with armaments, but President Woodrow Wilson had kept his country out of the war. The news that Germany would recommence unrestricted U-boat warfare caused Wilson to cut off diplomatic relations with Germany. Then came the sinking of the British passenger liner *Laconia* (killing eight Americans on board). The British intercepted the Zimmerman telegram to Mexico in which Germany invited Mexico into an alliance if the U.S. joined the Allied side. The publication of the telegram whipped up public opinion in America against Germany and convinced the U.S. Congress to declare war on Germany on April 6, 1917. President Wilson said America's fight would be a fight for freedom against tyranny, of popular government against monarchy. "The world," he said, "must be made safe for democracy."

8. The course of the Russian revolution in 1917

Russia's failures in the war and sufferings at home, along with the activities of Grigori Rasputin, brought Tsar Nikolai II into disgrace with his people. Revolution against the tsar broke out in March 1917, and he was forced to abdicate on March 15. The Liberal constitutional government set up in place of the tsar continued the war with Germany while facing insurrections at home from Mensheviks and Socialist Revolutionaries. In July, Vladimir Lenin and the Bolsheviks attempted an uprising in Petrograd against the government, but were crushed. In August, the Russian government faced another insurrection, this time from the military, but was able to stop it in September. In November, however, Lenin, Lev Trotsky, and the Bolsheviks were able, without a mass uprising of the people, to seize control of Petrograd and establish a Soviet government there. From Petrograd, the Bolshevik revolution spread to other parts of Russia, and the Soviet government was able to put down a counterrevolution staged by the military. In January 1918, Lenin dissolved the democratically elected Russian assembly and, from thenceforth, ruled Russia as dictator.

9. How Pope Benedict XV tried to bring peace

On August 1, 1917, Pope Benedict XV issued a peace proposal called the Seven Points. The Allies rejected the proposal. Emperor Karl I of Austria-Hungary embraced it, but Germany's response was not satisfactory. The pope's peace plan thus came to nothing. The Fourteen Points for peace issued by President Wilson in early 1918 were similar in many ways to the pope's Seven Points, except that Wilson called for breaking up existing states or forming new states based on national identity. The pope's plan did not call for this.

10. The course of the war in 1918

In a treaty signed at Brest-Litovsk on March 3, 1918, Russia's Soviet government made peace with Germany, thus ending the war on the Eastern Front. On the Western Front, Germany began a great offensive that ended in failure in the Second Battle of the Marne. In Italy, at the Battle of the Piave River, Austria suffered a serious defeat that ended her ability to take the offensive again.

The Allies opened their offensive against German lines on July 18, 1918. The Allies were everywhere victorious, both along the Western Front and in Italy. In late October, Austria-Hungary and Italy opened armistice talks. On November 8, the Germans and the Allies began to negotiate an armistice. On November 9, the German government announced Kaiser

Wilhelm's abdication, while Emperor Karl stepped down from power in Vienna. The Allies and the Germans signed an armistice at last on November 11, 1918, bringing an end to the war.

Questions for Review

1. **According to Pope Benedict XV, why did the European nations go to war?**

   According to Benedict XV, the nations of Europe went to war because they had abandoned Christian wisdom and Christian moral ideals in the running of their states.

2. **What is meant by indiscriminate warfare? Did both the Allies and the Central Powers engage in indiscriminate warfare? Please explain.**

   Indiscriminate warfare is acts of war that make no distinction between combatants and non-combatants or between military and civilian targets. Both the Allies and the Central Powers engaged in indiscriminate warfare by means of strategic bombing and blockades.

3. **Why did both the Central Powers and the Allies at different times refuse to listen to calls to end the war? Why was Emperor Karl of Austria-Hungary so eager to bring peace to Europe?**

   At different times during the war, the Central Powers and Allies thought they had the advantage over their enemy. If it appeared they might triumph, they were not interested in peace overtures. The Allies' secret treaty with Italy made them unwilling to entertain Emperor Karl's peace overtures. Neither side wanted to discuss peace from a position of weakness. Emperor Karl was eager to bring peace to Europe because he had opposed the war from the beginning and was a serious Christian who loved peace and justice.

4. **Was the United States ever truly neutral during World War I? Why did the United States finally declare war on Germany?**

   The United States was never truly neutral in the war because, from the beginning, it had been supplying the Allies with munitions while not doing the same for the Central Powers. The United States finally declared war on Germany on the pretext of Germany's resumption of unrestricted U-boat warfare, the sinking of the *Laconia* (in which eight Americans died), and the interception of the Zimmerman telegram.

5. **Why did Germany decide to resume unrestricted submarine warfare in 1917?**

   The German high command hoped that by unrestricted U-boat warfare, Germany could blockade Great Britain and starve it out, like the British blockade was doing to Germany.

6. **How did President Woodrow Wilson's Fourteen Points differ from Pope Benedict XV's Seven Points?**

   Unlike Wilson's Fourteen Points, the pope's Seven Points did not call for the breaking up of existing states or forming new states based on national identity. More specifically, the pope did not call for the breaking up of the Austro-Hungarian Empire.

7. **Why were the Russian people angry with Tsar Nikolai II in 1917?**

   The Russian people were angry with the tsar because the war was going badly, the people were suffering from food shortages and high prices for staples and coal for heating, and on account of the royal family's connection to Rasputin. All classes suspected treason, and they thought the arch-traitor was the tsarina's confidant, Rasputin.

8. **What changes did Vladimir Lenin want to bring to Russia? Was the Bolshevik Revolution an uprising of the Russian people? Please explain.**

Lenin wanted to turn Russia into a version of Marx's dictatorship of the proletariat. He wanted Russia to become the first socialist nation in the world. He wanted an immediate withdrawal from the war, peace with Germany, and no territorial gains. The Bolshevik Revolution was not a popular revolution. It was carried out by a small number of Bolsheviks who captured key points in the city from which they could seize control of the government.

9. **What changes in Austria-Hungary did Emperor Karl's *People's Manifesto* call for? Why did President Wilson reject the *People's Manifesto*?**

In his *People's Manifesto*, Emperor Karl proclaimed that Austria-Hungary would go from a dual kingdom with two legislatures to become a federal state in which, under the House of Habsburg, each racial group would form its own state. Wilson rejected the manifesto because he wanted each of the nationalities of the Dual Monarchy to form its own independent, democratic state. Wilson wanted the abolition of the Habsburg monarchy.

10. **Why did Emperor Karl and Kaiser Wilhelm II have to step down from power before there could be peace?**

U.S. President Woodrow Wilson would not deal with governments that were led by unelected heads of state.

Ideas in Action

1. **Following in the tradition of Pope Benedict XV, the popes of our time have been great advocates for peace. Collect newspaper or magazine stories of the occasions when both Pope John Paul II and Pope Benedict XVI have called for peace.**

2. **Imagine yourself as a person living in one of the following situations during World War I. Write an account of the events of a day in your life.**

   a) **A German, English, French, or American soldier fighting on the Western Front**

   b) **A Russian worker living in Petrograd during the Bolshevik Revolution**

   c) **A German, English, French, Italian, or American woman whose husband or brother is fighting in Europe**

3. **Both the Allies and Central Powers used propaganda—posters, newspaper articles, and other media—to spread their versions of the war. Research the propaganda used on both sides in the conflict. How did each side portray its enemy?**

Sample Quiz I (pages 481–494)

Please answer the following in complete sentences.

1. Pope Benedict XV called on the warring powers to lay down their arms and accept "peace without victory." What did the pope mean by this?

2. On what front did Germany battle Russia? On what front did Germany battle France and England?

3. Why did Germany begin unrestricted U-boat warfare against Great Britain?

4. What were Emperor Karl's goals when he became emperor?

5. Was the United States ever really neutral in the war?

Sample Quiz II (pages 494–516)

Please answer the following in complete sentences.

1. What two events convinced the United States Congress to declare war on Germany?

2. Who was the Russian monk who brought disgrace on the tsar and his family?

3. What group of Marxists gained control of the Russian revolution and established the Soviet government? Name two leaders of this group.

4. What was Pope Benedict's plan for peace called? What was President Wilson's plan called?

5. On what date was the armistice ending the First World War signed?

Answers to Sample Quiz I

Students' answers should approximate the following.

1. By "peace without victory," Pope Benedict XV meant that both sides should lay down their arms without any demands (such as reparations) from their foe.

2. Germany battled Russia on the *Eastern Front*. Germany battled France and England on the *Western Front*.

3. Germany began unrestricted U-boat warfare against Great Britain because the British navy was blockading Germany. Germany hoped the U-boats could set up a blockade of the British isles.

4. Emperor Karl's goals were to relieve his people's misery, reform the government, and make peace.

5. The United States was never truly neutral because it supplied the Allies with American-manufactured munitions, something not done for the Central Powers.

Answers to Sample Quiz II

Students' answers should approximate the following

1. The sinking by a U-boat of the English passenger liner, *Laconia,* in which eight Americans died, and the interception of the Zimmerman telegram sent by Germany to Mexico convinced the Congress to declare war on Germany.

2. The Russian monk who brought disgrace on the tsar and his family was *Grigori Rasputin.*

3. The *Bolsheviks* seized control of the Russian revolution and established the Soviet government. Leaders of the Bolsheviks include *Vladimir Lenin, Lev Trotsky,* and *Josif Stalin.*

4. Pope Benedict's plan for peace was called the *Seven Points.* Wilson's plan was called the *Fourteen Points.*

5. The armistice ending World War I was signed on *November 11, 1918.*

Essays (200–500 words each)

Instructions to be given to the students: Write in complete sentences. Underline your thesis. Give three supports or examples that explain why you think what you do and that support your thesis.

1. Obtain copies of Pope Benedict XV's Seven Points and President Woodrow Wilson's Fourteen Points. Compare them—how are they alike? How do they differ?

2. Describe the life of one of the major characters in this chapter, or any figure of the First World War not mentioned in the chapter. Was he or she an admirable character?

Chapter Test

Please answer the following in complete sentences.

I. **Short Essay—Answer two of the following:**

1. **What goal did Benedict XVI lay out for himself when he became pope? In speaking out against the war, what did he call on both sides to do? Why did the war begin, according to Benedict—and what did he think the solution to the war was?**

2. **Describe the events of the Russian Revolution of 1917 from the beginning until the establishment of Bolshevik government.**

3. **Why did the United States of America enter the First World War? When did the United States declare war on Germany?**

II. **Short Answer:**

1. **Name one country Germany and Austria-Hungary battled on the Eastern Front. What country or countries did Germany battle on the Western Front?**

2. **What is indiscriminate warfare? Give an example of indiscriminate warfare from World War I.**

3. **What were President Woodrow Wilson's goals when the United States declared war on Germany in 1917?**

4. **How did Pope Benedict's Seven Points differ from President Wilson's Fourteen Points?**

5. **At what battle did the Germans' last great offensive end?**

Answer Key to the Chapter Test

Students' answers should approximate the following:

I.

1. Benedict XV, who became pope in September 1914, made it the aim of his papacy "to strive in every possible way that the charity of Jesus Christ should once more rule supreme amongst men." He spoke out against the war, calling on the warring powers to accept peace without victory—meaning both sides should lay down arms without demanding anything (such as payment for damages) from their foes. Benedict said the war came because "in the ruling of states" governments had abandoned "Christian wisdom" and Christian moral ideals. Men sought for wealth, power, and false glory instead of spiritual goods. The answer for the unrest was to return to Christ and his charity and once again embrace "Christian principles."

2. Revolution against the tsar broke out in March 1917, and he was forced to abdicate on March 15. The Liberal constitutional government set up in place of the tsar continued the war with Germany while facing insurrections at home from Mensheviks and Socialist Revolutionaries. In July, Vladimir Lenin and the Bolsheviks attempted an uprising in Petrograd against the government, but were crushed. In August, the Russian government faced another insurrection, this time from the military, but was able to stop it in September. In November, however, Lenin, Lev Trotsky, and the Bolsheviks were able, without a mass uprising of the people, to seize control of Petrograd and establish a Soviet government there. From Petrograd, the Bolshevik revolution spread to other parts of Russia, and the Soviet government was able to put down a counterrevolution staged by the military. In January 1918, Lenin dissolved the democratically elected Russian assembly and, from thenceforth, ruled Russia as dictator.

3. With its civilian population suffering under the continuing British blockade, Germany com-menced U-boat warfare again in early 1917. The United States had been supporting the Allies with armaments, but President Woodrow Wilson had kept his country out of the war. The news that Germany would recommence unrestricted U-boat warfare caused Wilson to cut off diplomatic relations with Germany. Then came the sinking of the British passenger liner *Laconia* (killing eight Americans on board). The British intercepted the Zimmerman telegram to Mexico in which Germany invited Mexico into an alliance if the U.S. joined the Allied side. The publication of the telegram whipped up public opinion against Germany and convinced the U.S. Congress to declare war on Germany on April 6, 1917.

II.

1. On the Eastern Front, Germany and Austria-Hungary battled *Russia* (or *Romania*) Germany battled *France and Great Britain* on the Western Front.

2. Indiscriminate warfare refers to acts of war that make no distinction between military and civilian targets; that strike noncombatants as well as members of the military. Examples of indiscriminate war in the First World War: the blockade of Germany, the bombing of civilian centers by Zeppelins and airplanes, unrestricted U-boat warfare.

3. President Wilson's goals in entering the war were to carry on the battle of popular government against monarchy. "The world must be made safe for democracy," he said.

4. The Fourteen Points for peace issued by President Wilson in early 1918 were similar in many ways to the pope's Seven Points, except that Wilson called for breaking up existing states and forming new states based on national identity. The pope's plan did not call for this.

5. The Germans' last great offensive ended at the *Second Battle of the Marne*

CHAPTER 18: The Rise of Totalitarian Regimes

Chapter Overview

- On the night of July 16–17, 1918, Russia's Bolsheviks assassinated Tsar Nikolai II and his family at Yekaterinburg in Siberia. Following the end of World War I, the new Bolshevik government was confronted by invading Allied armies that supported the White counterrevolutionaries. Though it at first appeared that the Whites might triumph over the Bolshevik Reds, by 1920 the Reds had destroyed the White armies or driven them from Russia.

- To overcome opposition to their rule in Russia, Vladimir Lenin and the Bolsheviks instituted the Red Terror. All those who opposed the Bolsheviks were labeled bourgeois and counterrevolutionary. By 1921, the Red Terror had killed about 140,000 people in Russia.

- The Treaty of Versailles, signed on June 28, 1919, was very harsh toward Germany. It called on Germany to pay high reparations, severely reduced the size of the German military, and forced the Reich to abandon 25,000 square miles of territory and 6 million of its population. Germany had to abandon all her overseas colonies and was deprived of much of her wealth in coal, iron ore, and other metals used in industry.

- Following the war, the Allies divided Austria-Hungary into the nations of Austria, Czechoslovakia, and Hungary. The newly restored independent nation of Poland took Austrian Galicia, Italy seized Trentino and Austrian territories on the Adriatic, and Bosnia and Herzegovina went to the kingdom of Yugoslavia. Hungary lost Transylvania to Romania.

- The new nation of Austria adopted a republican form of government after Emperor Karl stepped down from power. Austria, though, was unstable, and the Allies opposed her union with Germany. Hungary fell into anarchy at the end of the war. In March 1919, Béla Kun established a short-lived Bolshevik government in Budapest. In November 1919, counterrevolutionary forces under Admiral Miklós Horthy seized control of the government. In March 1920, Horthy was elected regent of Hungary.

- The new nations of Central Europe established after the war were unstable. Though they were formed along national lines, they each contained sizable populations of minority groups or were divided into religious groups. Nationalism posed as much of a problem for these new nations as it had for Austria-Hungary. New nations were formed in northeastern Europe as well—Finland, Lithuania, Latvia, Estonia, and Poland. These nations had more homogenous populations and so did not suffer from fights between national groups. Poland carried on a war of conquest against

Russia and suffered from divisions among political groups. In 1926, it became a kind of military dictatorship. Lithuania, Latvia, and Estonia were small, weak nations that could easily be gobbled up by larger neighbors.

- Russia's great sufferings after the war, coupled with the refusal of Russian peasant farmers to cooperate with the revolution, convinced Lenin in 1921 to adopt a compromise called the New Economic Policy (NEP) that allowed for private ownership of land and of some industry. In gaining back much territory it had lost, the Bolshevik government was more successful.

- In December 1922, Russia, Georgia and Armenia, Ukraine, and Byelorussia were formed into the Union of Soviet Socialist Republics (USSR). The Soviet constitution formed for this union was (at least on paper) democratic and federal. In reality, all levels of government were controlled by the Central Committee of the Communist Party (the Politburo) and its chairman, Vladimir Lenin.

- Lenin and the Communist Party (as the Bolsheviks now were called) used every means to disseminate their ideas and crush all opposition. In particular, they carried on a brutal persecution of religion, especially against the Russian Orthodox Church. Yet, despite the persecution, the Communists could not destroy Orthodoxy in Russia.

- After Lenin's death on January 21, 1924, factions fought for control of the Communist Party. In the end, Josif Stalin, the secretary of the Politburo, and his faction won the power struggle. Though at first he espoused Lenin's NEP, in 1929 Stalin ordered the collectivization of all farms. When wealthy peasant farmers resisted, Stalin ordered them to be liquidated. Stalin intensified the persecution of religion in the Soviet Union.

- Originally a socialist and an opponent of Italy's entrance into the First World War, Benito Mussolini eventually turned against both positions. In 1919 he formed the Fascist Party to combat socialists and Bolsheviks in Italy. Backed by rich businessmen and landowners, the Fascists used violence against socialists and other radicals. By late 1921, Mussolini and the Fascists had gained control of most of Italy. By the end of October 1922, Mussolini had control of the Italian government.

- Mussolini's Fascist government adopted many of the policies and tactics of the Bolsheviks in Russia. Like Communist Russia, Fascist Italy was totalitarian. Yet, Fascism was nationalist and favored a corporative organization of business—unlike Communism, which was internationalist and favored government ownership of business. Fascism was also imperialistic.

- Mussolini's totalitarian policies brought his government into direct conflict with the Catholic Church. Realizing the importance of making peace with the Church, Mussolini initiated talks with Pope Pius XI that ended in the Lateran Treaty of 1929. Central to the treaty was the establishment of an independent city-state, Vatican City, with full sovereign powers under the pope. Italy also agreed to a concordat with the Holy See, granting the Church certain rights and freedoms in Italy. It was not long, though, before Mussolini began to violate the concordat, especially by depriving Catholic youth organizations and Catholic Action of their freedom. In 1931, Pope Pius XI struck out at this violation of the concordat in the encyclical, *Non Abbiamo Bisogno*. Mussolini, in turn, pulled back his attacks on the Church in Italy.

- After the war, Germany suffered from a collapsed economy, worthless money, a weak government (the Weimar Republic), and political factions that staged periodic insurrections.

Unable to pay reparations, Germany obtained a moratorium on reparations payments in 1921. The Allies, however, refused to consider a second moratorium in 1922, and Germany went into default. When Germany again said it could not make its payments, French and Belgian troops occupied the industrial Ruhr district in northwest Germany. Unrest followed until, in August 1924, the Allies established a new payment plan for Germany, including a large loan.

- In 1924, the German economy began to recover until, by 1929, German production was greater than it had been before the war. This recovery, however, did not bring prosperity to many in Germany. After the worldwide economic crash in 1929, Germany's recovery collapsed.

- Germany's sorrows after the war gave rise to extremist political parties. One such party was the National Socialist German Workers (Nazi) Party, under its *Führer*, Adolf Hitler. The Nazis called for justice for workers, a renewal of German glory, and an unrelenting struggle against socialists and Jews. Though Nazi membership was small before 1929, after the economic crash, the party grew dramatically. By 1932, Hitler was strong enough to convince Germany's president, Paul von Hindenburg, to appoint him chancellor of the *Reich*. In April 1933, the German *Reichstag* voted Hitler the powers of a dictator for four years.

- Hitler centralized the government such that the powers held by individual states were transferred to the government in Berlin. With all power in his hands, he struck out at his enemies—Communists, members of opposition parties, and Jews. To solidify his power in Germany, Hitler sought better relations with the Catholic Church and, in July 1933, he signed a concordat with the Holy See. But no sooner had Hitler signed the concordat than he began to violate it. And, even though the Church had signed a concordat with Germany, Pope Pius XI condemned National Socialism in his 1937 encyclical, *Mit Brennender Sorge.*

Chapter Goals

This chapter presents three great "isms" of the first half of the 20th century—Communism, Fascism, and Nazism. The teacher should help students clearly delineate the character of each of these systems and to compare them as to their similarities and differences. It is important that students come to understand the true nature of each of these systems.

Period Music

- Arnold Schoenberg (1874–1951)—the originator of serialism or the atonal system in composition

  Verklärte Nacht (Transfigured Night) (1899)—a string sextet composed in the style of the Late Romantics

  Five Piano Pieces, Op. 23 (early 1920s)—Schoenberg's first atonal composition

- Anton Webern (1883–1945)—a student of Schoenberg

- Alban Berg (1885–1935)—a composer of atonal music, such as the opera *Wozzeck*

- Béla Bartók (1881–1945)—a composer who drew from the folk music of his Hungarian people

- Zoltán Kodály (1882–1967)

- Igor Stravinsky (1882–1971)—a Russian composer who experimented in a variety of styles

Ballets:

The Firebird (1910)

Petrushka (1911)

The Rite of Spring (1913)

Pulcinella (1920)

Operas:

Oedipus Rex (1927)

Le Rossignol (The Nightingale) (1914)

What Students Should Know

1. **What befell Tsar Nikolai II**

On the night of July 16-17, 1918, Russia's Bolsheviks assassinated Tsar Nikolai II and his family at Yekaterinburg in Siberia. The royal family were killed to keep them from falling into the hands of counterrevolutionaries, the Whites.

2. **The White counterrevolution in Russia and its results**

Following the end of World War I, the new Bolshevik government was confronted by anti-Bolshevik counterrevolutionaries called the Whites. Not only monarchists and Liberals, but other socialists and Marxists, including the Socialist Revolutionaries, opposed the Bolsheviks. Allied armies invaded Russia to support the Whites. Though it at first appeared that the Whites might triumph over the Bolshevik Reds, by 1920, the Reds had destroyed the White armies or driven them from Russia. Though most Russians were not Bolsheviks, they saw the Whites as fighting for the landlords and the capitalists who had oppressed them. Trotsky thus could organize large numbers of Russians in his Red Army.

3. **What the Red Terror was**

To overcome their enemies who opposed their rule in Russia, Vladimir Lenin and the Bolsheviks instituted the Red Terror. It was purported to be a means to aid the proletariat against other classes, especially the bourgeoisie. Its means were the Cheka (secret police) and mass murder. All those who opposed the Bolsheviks were labeled bourgeois and counterrevolutionary. By 1921, the Red Terror had killed about 140,000 people in Russia.

Key Terms at a Glance

totalitarian: referring to a government that claims absolute power and authority over all individuals and groups in society

German *Reich*: a name referring to both the imperial German government under the Hohenzollerns and the German republic after the war

collectivize: to organize property (for instance, land, factories, tools, farms) so that they are not owned privately but in common or by the government

general strike: refusal by workers *in all or many industries* to work in order to bring employers around to giving in to their demands

Putsch: a German word for a secretly plotted and sudden attempt to overthrow a government

inflation: a decrease in the value of money, which leads to a rise in prices for goods

moratorium: a waiting period, a delay

default: failure to fulfill an obligation. To be *in default* means to fail to keep an obligation

4. What a totalitarian state is

Bolshevik Russia is an example of a totalitarian state—a government that claims absolute power and authority over all individuals and groups in society.

5. What the Treaty of Versailles was

The Treaty of Versailles, signed on June 28, 1919, was the agreement that officially brought an end to the First World War. The treaty was very harsh toward Germany. It called on Germany to pay high reparations, severely reduced the size of the German military, and forced the *Reich* to abandon 25,000 square miles of territory and 6 million of its population. Germany had to abandon all her overseas colonies and was deprived of much of her wealth in coal, iron ore, and other metals used in industry.

6. What happened to the empire of Austria-Hungary

Following the war, the Allies divided Austria-Hungary into the nations of Austria, Czechoslovakia, and Hungary. Austrian lands went to the newly restored independent nation of Poland, Italy, and to the kingdom of Yugoslavia. Hungary lost Transylvania to Romania. The new nation of Austria adopted a republican form of government after Emperor Karl stepped down from power. Austria, though, was unstable, and the Allies opposed her union with Germany. Hungary fell into anarchy at the end of the war. In March 1919, Béla Kun established a short-lived Bolshevik government in Budapest. In November 1919, counterrevolutionary forces under Admiral Miklós Horthy seized control of the government. In March 1920, Horthy was elected regent of Hungary. In March and October 1921, Emperor Karl (king in Hungary) tried to reestablish his rule in Hungary, but failed.

7. Why the new nations of Czechoslovakia and Yugoslavia were unstable

These new governments were unstable because they contained different races and religions. Nationalism caused rivalries between the racial groups, and the governing authority did not have enough respect among all the races to act as a unifying force. The different races at times wanted to separate themselves from the state; the Germans in Czechoslovakia, for instance, wanted to join Germany.

8. What happened to Central Europe after the war

The new nations of Central Europe established after the war were unstable. Though they were formed along national lines, they each contained sizable populations of minority groups or were divided into religious groups. Nationalism posed as much of a problem for these new nations as it had for Austria-Hungary. New nations were formed in northeastern Europe as well—Finland, Lithuania, Latvia, Estonia, and Poland. These nations had more homogenous populations and so did not suffer from fights between national groups. Poland became a kind of military dictatorship. Lithuania, Latvia, and Estonia were small, weak nations that could easily be gobbled up by larger neighbors.

9. The formation of the Soviet Union and its character

In December 1922, Russia, Georgia and Armenia, Ukraine, and Byelorussia were formed into the Union of Soviet Socialist Republics (USSR). The Soviet constitution formed for this union was (at least on paper) democratic and federal. In reality, all levels of government were controlled by the Central Committee of the Communist Party (the Politburo) and its chairman, Vladimir

Lenin. (The Bolsheviks were now called the Communist Party.)

10. Religious persecution under Lenin

Lenin and the Communist Party used every means to disseminate their ideas and crush all opposition. In particular, they carried on a brutal persecution of religion, especially against the Russian Orthodox Church. Like Marx, who called religion the "opiate of the people," the Communists rejected religion because, they said, by promising a future life after death, religion made people bear injustices in this life instead of rising against them. Lenin denied legal rights to the Church, seized Church bank accounts, made Church marriages illegal, and forbade religious instruction of anyone under 18 years of age. The Red Terror killed large numbers of Orthodox priests, and at least 28 Russian Orthodox bishops were murdered between 1918 and 1920. Yet, despite the persecution, the Communists could not destroy Orthodoxy in Russia. Vast numbers of Russians remained faithful to their religion.

11. How Stalin came to power

After Lenin's death on January 21, 1924, factions fought for control of the Communist Party. In the end, Josif Stalin, the secretary of the Politburo, and his faction won the power struggle. In 1929 Stalin ordered the collectivization of all farms. When wealthy peasant farmers (the *kulaks*) resisted, Stalin ordered them to be liquidated. Tens of thousands died in this purge. Stalin intensified the persecution of religion in the Soviet Union.

12. Mussolini and the formation of the Fascist party in Italy

Originally a socialist and an opponent of Italy's entrance into the First World War, Benito Mussolini eventually turned against both positions. The years following the end of the war were hard ones for Italy. The cost of necessities was high and many returning soldiers did not have jobs. Large numbers of people had lost confidence in Italy's Liberal parties, which ran the government. Bolsheviks and anarchists called for revolution, and a general strike ensued in 1919. The same year, Mussolini formed the Fascist Party to combat socialists and Bolsheviks in Italy. The party did not originally have clear ideas, but it was anti-socialist and nationalistic. Backed by rich businessmen and landowners, the Fascist squads, called Blackshirts, used violence against socialists and other radicals. By late 1921, Mussolini and the Fascists had gained control of most of Italy. By the end of October 1922, Mussolini had control of the Italian government, and King Vittorio Emanuele III named him prime minister of Italy.

13. The differences between Fascism and Communism

Mussolini's Fascist government adopted many of the policies and tactics of the Bolsheviks in Russia. Like Communist Russia, Fascist Italy was totalitarian. It was anti-Liberal. Yet, Fascism was nationalist; for Mussolini, the citizen existed only for the glorification of his nation. Communism, on the other hand, was internationalist, calling for a worldwide union of the proletariat, regardless of class or nation. Fascism was imperialistic, while Communism rejected the domination of one nation by another. Fascism favored a corporative organization of business—the organization of different industries into corporations made up of both employers and employees that saw to it that the former earned profits while the latter made a just wage. Communism, on the other hand, favored government ownership of business.

14. Mussolini's relations with the pope

Since Mussolini was an atheist, he mocked the Christian Faith and persecuted believers. Mussolini's totalitarian policies brought his government into direct conflict with the Catholic Church. Realizing the importance of making peace with the Church (because most Italians were Catholic), Mussolini initiated talks with Pope Pius XI that ended in the Lateran Treaty of 1929. Central to the treaty was the establishment of an independent city-state, Vatican City, with full sovereign powers under the pope. In this way, the pope again became a sovereign temporal ruler. Italy also agreed to a concordat with the Holy See, granting the Church certain rights and freedoms in Italy. The Catholic Church was to be the only state-recognized religion in Italy, and all future laws would be guided by Catholic moral teaching. Marriage, too, was recognized as a sacrament. Religious instruction became compulsory in schools.

15. How Mussolini and Pope Pius XI came into conflict

It was not long before Mussolini began to violate the concordat, especially by depriving Catholic youth organizations and Catholic Action of their freedom. In 1931, Pope Pius XI struck out at this violation of the concordat in the encyclical, *Non Abbiamo Bisogno*, in which he asserted that the Church had rights which no one could justly take away. The state could not justly, said the pope, violate the natural rights of the family. Mussolini, in response to the encyclical, pulled back his attacks on the Church in Italy.

16. The condition of Germany after the war

After the war, Germany suffered from a collapsed economy, worthless money, a weak government (the Weimar Republic), and political factions that staged periodic insurrections. Unable to pay reparations, Germany obtained a moratorium on reparations payments in 1921. The Allies, however, refused to consider a second moratorium in 1922, and Germany went into default. When Germany again said it could not make its payments, French and Belgian troops occupied the industrial Ruhr district in northwest Germany. Unrest followed until, in August 1924, the Allies established a new payment plan for Germany, including a large loan. In 1924, the German economy began to recover until, by 1929, German production was greater than it had been before the war. This recovery, however, did not bring prosperity to many in Germany. After the worldwide economic crash in 1929, Germany's recovery collapsed.

17. The rise of Adolf Hitler and the Nazi (National Socialist) Party

Germany's sorrows after the war gave rise to extremist political parties. One such party was the National Socialist German Workers (Nazi) Party, under its *Führer*, Adolf Hitler. The Nazis called for justice for workers, a renewal of German glory, and an unrelenting struggle against socialists and Jews.

18. What Hitler's racial ideas were

Hitler despised socialism not only because it rejected private property but because it claimed that all working men are equal. As he explained in his book, *Mein Kampf* ("My Struggle"), Hitler thought all mankind was divided into races (*Völker*), but not every race or *Volk* was equal. Hitler thought the Aryan or white European race (*Volk*) was the supreme race. Hitler hated Jews because he thought they belonged to a degraded race and were enemies of the German *Volk*. He did not hate Jews for religious reasons; indeed, though baptized a

Catholic, Hitler rejected the Christian Faith because he thought it too Jewish.

For Hitler, nothing was greater and more sacred than the *Volk*. Any action could be justified if it benefited the *Volk*. The *Volk*, he thought, expressed itself through a *Führer* (leader), who thus had the powers of a dictator. As *Führer*, Hitler thought the German *Volk* expressed itself through him.

19. How the Nazi Party grew in numbers and strength

Though Nazi membership was small before 1929, after the economic crash, the party grew dramatically. By 1932, Hitler was strong enough to convince Germany's president, Paul von Hindenburg, to appoint him chancellor of the *Reich*. In April 1933, the German *Reichstag* voted Hitler the powers of a dictator for four years.

20. How Hitler organized his government

Hitler centralized the government such that the powers held by individual states were transferred to the government in Berlin. All political parties were banned, except the Nazi Party. With all power in his hands, Hitler struck out at his enemies—Communists, members of opposition parties, and Jews. To solidify his power in Germany, Hitler sought better relations with the Catholic Church, and in July 1933 he signed a concordat with the Holy See. But no sooner had Hitler signed the concordat than he began to violate it. In 1937, Pope Pius XI condemned National Socialism (though not by name) in his 1937 encyclical, *Mit Brennender Sorge*. The encyclical condemned Nazism's promotion of a national God and national religion, its belief in racial superiority and the racial inferiority of certain peoples, and its violation of man's freedom to worship God.

Questions for Review

1. **By the end of July 1918, it appeared that the White counterrevolutionaries would be victorious over the Bolsheviks. Why were the Bolshevik Reds finally victorious?**

   The Reds were victorious because many of the Russian people ended up supporting them. Thinking the Whites were merely the tools of the old landlords and capitalists, Russians joined with the Bolsheviks to preserve the gains of the revolution.

2. **Why did Lenin and the Bolsheviks begin the Red Terror? Who were the targets of the terror? About how many were killed in the terror?**

   Lenin and the Bolsheviks began the Red Terror to destroy those who opposed the Bolshevik revolution. By 1921, the Red Terror had killed about 140,000 people throughout Russia.

3. **What is a totalitarian government?**

   A totalitarian government is one that claims absolute power and authority over all individuals and groups in society.

4. **What was the Treaty of Versailles? What did Germany have to agree to in the treaty?**

   The Treaty of Versailles was the peace agreement officially ending the First World War. It said the following in regards to Germany:

   a) Germany had to allow Allied armies to occupy lands between Germany's western border and the River Rhine.

   b) Germany could not keep troops and maintain fortresses anywhere within a strip running 10 miles east of the Rhine.

   c) Germany could not have an army of over 100,000 men.

d) Germany had to abandon large swaths of territory.

e) Germany lost economic control of the Saar basin

f) Germany had to pay a very large amount of money in reparations.

5. **What reason did Emperor Karl give for trying to regain his throne in Hungary?**

Karl thought he had the God-given right and duty to regain his throne.

6. **How are Fascism and Communism alike? How do they differ?**

How they are alike:

a) Both Communism and Fascism are totalitarian.

b) Both are anti-Liberal.

How they differ:

a) Fascism is nationalistic and imperialistic, while Communism claims to fight for the proletarian class, not a particular nation, and is internationalist, rejecting the domination of one nation by another nation.

b) Fascism favors a corporative organization of business. Communism, on the other hand, favors government ownership of business.

7. **Why did Fascism and Nazism have youth movements?**

Both had youth movements because they wanted to train young people to become good members of the party.

8. **Why did Fascism, Nazism, and Communism attack the Church?**

All these movements saw the Church as their chief rival. The Church says man's first loyalty is to God and the truths he reveals. Thus, man must give his first loyalty to the Church, not to a nation or social class, as these movements demanded.

9. **Why did Hitler hate the Jews? Why did he reject the Christian faith?**

Hitler hated the Jews because he thought they belonged to a degraded race and were the enemies of the German *Volk*. Hitler rejected the Christian faith because he thought it too Jewish.

10. **Why did so many Germans come to support the Nazi Party?**

a) The uncertainty of their material welfare following the economic crash of 1929 and Hitler's promises to fight for the common man and worker against rich capitalists and speculators drew some to the Nazi party.

b) The fear that Communists would take control of the government led others to support the Nazis as an opposition party to the Communists.

11. **What was wrong with Nazism, according to Pope Pius XI's encyclical, *Mit Brennender Sorge*?**

The encyclical condemned Nazism because:

a) It promoted the ideas of a national God and a national religion.

b) It exalted one race at the expense of others and divinized it.

c) It violated parents' right to educate their children.

d) It violated the right to worship God.

Ideas in Action

1. By the time the Bolsheviks took power, Russia had had a small Russian Catholic Church—a church that followed the rituals and traditions of the Byzantine East but was in union with the pope in Rome. Research the history of the Russian Catholic Church and how it fared under the Soviet government. Does it still exist today? If so, where? How many members does it have?

2. Among the Christians who suffered under the Soviet Red Terror was Blessed Leonid Ivanovich Feodorov, the bishop of the Russian Catholic Church. Write a report on the life and sufferings of Blessed Leonid.

3. What happened to Empress Zita and Otto von Habsburg, the wife and eldest son of Blessed Karl of Austria, after Karl's death in 1922? How did they carry on the Habsburg family's tradition of service to the common good? Write a report about either one or both of their lives.

Sample Quiz I (pages 521–534)

Please answer the following in complete sentences.

1. Why did so many Russians join with the Bolshevik "Reds" against the counterrevolutionary Whites?

2. Why did Lenin and the Bolsheviks start the Red Terror?

3. What is a totalitarian government?

4. What is the name for the treaty that formally brought an end to World War I?

5. List the three nations into which Austria-Hungary was broken up.

6. What was the name of the new state into which the Communists joined Russia, Georgia, Armenia, Ukraine, and Byelorussia?

7. Who seized control of the Communist Party and the state after Lenin's death in 1924?

Answers to Sample Quiz I

Students' answers should approximate the following.

1. So many Russians joined the Reds because they thought the Whites were fighting for the landlords and capitalists who had oppressed them.

2. Lenin and the Bolsheviks started the Red Terror to rid Russia of the enemies of their government and revolution.

3. A totalitarian government is a government that claims absolute power and authority over all individuals and groups in society.

4. The *Versailles Treaty* formally brought an end to World War I.

5. Austria-Hungary was broken up into *Austria*, *Hungary*, and *Czechoslovakia*.

6. The new state the Communists formed from these regions was the *Union of Soviet Socialist Republics (USSR)*.

7. *Josif Stalin* seized control of the Communist Party and state after Lenin's death.

Sample Quiz II (pages 535–542)

Please answer the following in complete sentences.

1. Name one way Fascism was like Communism. Name one way they differed.

2. What treaty established Vatican City State? In what year was it signed? By whom was it signed?

3. How did Pope Pius XI react to Mussolini's violation of the concordat? How did Mussolini respond?

Answers to Sample Quiz II

Students' answers should approximate the following

1. Fascism was like Communism in that (possible answers):

   a) Both were totalitarian

   b) Both were anti-Liberal.

   Fascism and Communism differed, in that (possible answers):

   a) Fascism was nationalistic, standing for the glorification of the nation, while Communism was internationalist, seeking to unite all proletarians regardless of nationality.

   b) Fascism was imperialistic, while Communism rejected the domination of one nation by another.

   c) Fascism favored a corporatist organization of business (employers and employees organized in corporations in which they worked out their differences according to justice), while Communism wanted state ownership of business.

2. The *Lateran Treaty* established Vatican City State. It was signed *in 1929* between *Benito Mussolini* and the *Holy See* (or *Pope Pius XI*).

3. Pope Pius XI reacted to Mussolini's violation of the concordat by issuing an encyclical in which he condemned Mussolini's actions. Mussolini, in response to the encyclical, pulled back his attacks on the Church in Italy.

Sample Quiz III (pages 542–552)

Please answer the following in complete sentences.

1. What was the name of the German government formed after World War I?

2. What were the aims of the National Socialist (Nazi) Party?

3. Why did Adolf Hitler hate the Jews?

4. In what book did Hitler explain his racial ideas?

5. What event led to a dramatic growth in the Nazi party?

6. What did Pope Pius XI's encyclical, *Mit Brennender Sorge*, condemn in Nazism?

Answers to Sample Quiz III

Students' answers should approximate the following

1. The German government formed after World War I was the *Weimar Republic*.

2. The Nazis called for justice for workers, a renewal of German glory, and an unrelenting struggle against socialists and Jews.

3. Hitler hated Jews because he thought they belonged to a degraded race and were enemies of the German *Volk*.

4. Hitler explained his racial ideas in the book *Mein Kampf* ("My Struggle").

5. The *worldwide economic crash of 1929* led to a dramatic growth in the Nazi party.

6. *Mit Brennender Sorge* condemned Nazism's promotion of a national God and national religion, its belief in racial superiority and the racial inferiority of certain peoples, and its violation of man's freedom to worship God.

Essays (200–500 words each)

Instructions to be given to the students: Write in complete sentences. Underline your thesis. Give three supports or examples that explain why you think what you do and that support your thesis.

1. Sometimes in our day, people give the name *fascist* to "right-wing" or "conservative" political parties and individuals and *communist* or *socialist* to "left-wing" or "liberal" parties. After describing Fascism and Communism, address this question: are any of the modern parties in your country truly Fascist or Communist? Why or why not?

2. Write a short biographical sketch of any of the characters in this chapter or of any character that lived during the time period this chapter covers.

Chapter Test

Please answer the following in complete sentences.

I. **Short Essay—Answer one of the following:**

1. What is a totalitarian state? Why do we call Bolshevik Russia a totalitarian state? Give three examples that it was indeed totalitarian.

2. Compare and contrast Fascism and Communism, how they were alike and how they differed. Was Nazism more like Fascism or Communism?

3. Describe Hitler's views on race (the *Volk*). Which was the supreme race, according to Hitler? Why did he hate Jews? Was it for religious reasons?

II. **Short Answer:**

1. Give two examples that show the harshness of the Versailles Treaty toward Germany.

2. Who established the short-term Bolshevik dictatorship in Hungary?

   a) Béla Bartók   c) Miklós Horthy

   b) Zoltán Kodály   d) Béla Kun

3. Why did Communists reject religion?

4. Did Benito Mussolini have any religious faith? How did he treat Christians during the early years of his rule as prime minister? Why did he decide to make peace with the pope?

5. Why were new nations such as Czechoslovakia and Yugoslavia unstable?

6. Why did Adolf Hitler hate the Christian Faith?

Answer Key to the Chapter Test

Students' answers should approximate the following:

I.

1. A totalitarian state is one whose government claims absolute power and authority over all individuals and groups in society. Russia gives us an example of such a state. The following characteristics reveal the totalitarian character of Bolshevik (Communist) Russia (possible answers):

   a) The Red Terror, the instrument the Bolsheviks used to destroy any opposition to their rule

   b) The absolute control of the Soviet government and all federated governments by the Central Committee of the Communist Party.

   c) The persecution of Christians.

2. Fascism was like Communism in that (possible answers):

   a) Both were totalitarian.

   b) Both were anti-Liberal.

Fascism and Communism differed, in that (possible answers):

   a) Fascism was nationalistic, standing for the glorification of the nation, while Communism was internationalist, seeking to unite all proletarians regardless of nationality.

b) Fascism was imperialistic, while Communism rejected the domination of one nation by another.

c) Fascism favored a corporatist organization of business (employers and employees organized in corporations in which they worked out their differences according to justice), while Communism wanted state ownership of business.

Nazism was more like Fascism than Communism because Nazism was extremely nationalistic and rejected Communism's denial of the right to private property.

3. Hitler thought all mankind was divided into races, but not every race or *Volk* was equal. Hitler thought the Aryan or white European race was the supreme race. Hitler hated Jews because he thought they belonged to a degraded race and were enemies of the German *Volk*. He did not hate Jews for religious reasons. For Hitler, nothing was greater and more sacred than the *Volk*. Any action could be justified if it benefited the *Volk*.

II.

1. Possible answers:

a) Germany had to pay high reparations.

b) The treaty severely reduced the size of the German military.

c) The treaty forced the *Reich* to abandon 25,000 square miles of territory and 6 million of its population.

d) Germany had to abandon all her overseas colonies.

e) Germany was deprived of much of her wealth in coal, iron ore, and other metals used in industry.

2. *Béla Kun* established the short-lived Bolshevik dictatorship in Hungary.

3. Communists rejected religion because, they said, by promising a future life after death, religion made people bear injustices in this life instead of rising against them.

4. Benito Mussolini had no religious faith; he was an atheist. In his first years as prime minister of Italy he persecuted Christians. However, seeing that the best way to please the Italian people, who were Catholic, was to make peace with the Church, he sought better relations with the pope.

5. The new governments were unstable because they contained different races and religions. Nationalism caused rivalries between the racial groups, and the governing authority did not have enough respect among all the races to act as a unifying force. The different races at times wanted to separate themselves from the state; the Germans in Czechoslovakia, for instance, wanted to join Germany.

6. Hitler rejected the Christian faith because he thought it too Jewish.

CHAPTER 19: An Even Greater War

Chapter Overview

- When he became Austria's chancellor in May 1932, Engelbert Dollfuss faced great challenges. On the one hand, socialists threatened to carry out a Marxist revolution; on the other hand, German nationalists wanted to join Austria to the German Reich. Dollfuss's vision for Austria was based on Catholic social teaching and Austria's peasant traditions. A new threat appeared in 1933—the Austrian Nazi Party. To save Austria from being absorbed by Hitler's Germany, Dollfuss abolished Austria's republican government and established an authoritarian government. Dollfuss formed an alliance with Fascist Italy and put down a socialist revolutionary movement. On July 25, 1934, a small group of Nazis staged a *Putsch* in Vienna and assassinated Dollfuss.

- It was Mussolini who prevented Hitler from taking advantage of the *Putsch* in Vienna as an excuse to invade Austria. Yet, despite an alliance of France and Italy, Hitler began violating clauses of the Treaty of Versailles. His announcement that he would rearm Germany at first met stern resistance from France, Italy, and Great Britain—France forming an alliance with the Soviet Union and Czechoslovakia against German aggression. This alliance against Hitler was broken when Great Britain and France backed League of Nations sanc-

tions against Italy for her invasion and conquest of Ethiopia. When Italy became isolated from other nations, Mussolini accepted Hitler's friendship and, in 1936, with him formed the Rome-Berlin Axis.

- Because Italy no longer guaranteed Austria's independence, Hitler led troops into the small country and, on March 13, 1938, proclaimed Austria's *Anschluss* with Germany. A plebiscite following the invasion seemed to indicate that the vast majority of Austrians approved the union of their country with Germany.

- In 1928, Josif Stalin announced his first Five-Year Plan to turn the Soviet Union into a great industrial power. But independent farmers, especially in Ukraine, resisted Stalin's moves to collectivize all farms to increase grain production for sale on the international market. Stalin used violence to force collectivization. By his policies in Ukraine, he created a famine that led, in the winter of 1932–1933, to the death of millions of people in Ukraine and parts of Russia.

- The Soviet Union's industrialization under Stalin's first Five-Year Plan was swift. During the second Five-Year Plan (1933–1937), the Soviet Union became one of the largest industrial nations in the world. But to achieve all this progress, Stalin abandoned some key socialist principles.

- In 1932, Stalin began a virulent persecution of religion in the Soviet Union. It is estimated that, by the late 1930s, about 80,000 Orthodox clergy, monks, and nuns had been killed in the Soviet Union. Throughout Russia, the number of bishops and priests decreased dramatically. Though foreign governments ignored the persecutions, Pope Pius XI condemned them in 1930. In 1937, the pope issued his first formal condemnation of Communism, the encyclical *Divini Redemptoris.*

- To secure his power, Stalin began a great purge of members of his own Communist Party, beginning in 1934. It is said that by the time Stalin died in 1953, his purges had taken the lives of tens of millions of people.

- By the beginning of the 20th century, Spain had undergone several political and social struggles between clericals and Liberals, monarchists and republicans. Spain was primarily an agricultural society, had little industry (compared to France and Germany), and was considered backward. In the 1920s, General Miguel Primo de Rivera was dictator of Spain under the authority of King Alfonso XIII; but after Primo de Rivera resigned in 1930, the king promised to restore Spain's constitution. He did so early in 1930; but under pressure from republicans, he gave up the exercise of royal power and went into exile.

- Socialists and radical republicans, who controlled the majority in Spain's *Cortes* after the 1931 elections, established a secular and anti-Church state, passed laws to help workers, and seized the lands of large landowners. The government's actions inspired a reaction among traditional groups, who in CEDA won a majority of seats in the *Cortes* in 1933. But the Popular Front (a coalition of Communists and other radical groups) won the election of 1936.

- Fear that Spain would become a Communist state sparked a revolt among Spanish generals against the government in 1936. Spain was divided between two governments—the republican government in Madrid and the Nationalist government, under General Francisco Franco. The republicans received aid from volunteers from the United States, Germany, France, England, and other nations. They also received arms from the Soviet Union. The Nationalists received aid from Nazi Germany and Fascist Italy. The civil war lasted until 1939, when the Nationalists overthrew the republican government. Following the war's end, Franco established an authoritarian government over Spain.

- Great Britain's prime minister Neville Chamberlain thought it best to appease Hitler because Hitler claimed that he wanted only to bring all German peoples into union with Germany. In 1938, Great Britain and France both allowed Germany to annex Sudetenland, a German-speaking region of Czechoslovakia. Instead of just seizing Sudetenland, however, Hitler made all of Czechoslovakia a German satellite state. Hitler annexed part of Lithuania and carried on a threatening propaganda campaign against Poland. France and Great Britain also did nothing while Mussolini invaded Albania.

- Hitler's aggression against Poland convinced France and Great Britain that they had to take a stand against German expansion. Hitler, however, ignored the Allies; instead, he signed a pact with Stalin to divide Poland between Germany and Russia. In September 1939, both German and Soviet armies invaded Poland. In accordance with a treaty with Poland, Great Britain and France both declared war on Germany on September 3, 1939.

- Following the invasion of Poland, the Soviets forced the Baltic republics to accept Soviet "protection" and invaded Romania. Stalin then ordered the bombing of Helsinki, Finland. In 1940, Germany invaded Scandinavia, conquering Denmark and Norway. German armies then invaded neutral Belgium and Holland, forcing their surrender after 16 days. The Germans then moved into France, and on June 14, 1940, Paris fell to them. On June 21, 1940, France signed an armistice with Germany. Northern France was occupied by German troops while southern France remained independent, though it had to disband its military and pay the costs of the German military occupation of northern France. The war between Great Britain and Germany also became an air war in 1940, in which both sides bombed each other's cities.

- Mussolini, who had allied himself with Hitler, suffered failures in the Balkans and Africa. Hitler was thus forced to come to his aid. German armies invaded Yugoslavia and Greece, driving out British forces in Greece and conquering Crete.

- In June 1942, Hitler broke his pact with Stalin and German armies invaded Russia. Hitler's ally, Japan, also carried on a war of conquest in the western Pacific. A Japanese airstrike on December 7, 1941, brought the United States into the war on the side of the Allies, against the Axis.

Chapter Goals

The teacher should guide students to understand not only the events that, as causes, led to the Second World War, but how these events were rooted in the settlement reached after the First World War, in the Treaty of Versailles. Some historians have seen the Second World War as a continuation, after a 20-year hiatus, of the First World War. The same nations ended up opposing each other—except for Italy, which, even so, may not have allied with Germany if Mussolini had not gone into Ethiopia or the Allies had not opposed that adventure. The grievances of Germany, stemming from the First World War, were at least the remote causes of the Second World War. Hitler's desire for revenge against France was an important catalyst of the conflict, as was the old scourge—nationalism.

Period Music

Consult the list of composers in Chapter 18 of this teacher's manual.

What Students Should Know

1. **What Engelbert Dolfuss's vision for Austria was**

   Dollfuss's vision for Austria was based on Catholic social teaching and Austria's peasant traditions. He favored a society made up not primarily of large businesses but chiefly of small farmers, craftsmen, shopkeepers, and merchants. Each group would be organized in a guild or corporation that looked out for members and their families, made sure they received a just wage or charged a just price for their goods, and protected their interests. The government's role would be to make sure that all the various groups worked in harmony with one another and that the strong did not take advantage of the weak. Dollfuss was especially concerned with preserving Austria's peasantry. He said, "German customs and the Catholic faith are most thoroughly anchored in the peasantry."

2. **How Dollfuss responded to the challenges he faced**

   When he became Austria's chancellor in May 1932, Engelbert Dollfuss faced great challenges. On the one hand, socialists threatened

Key Terms at a Glance

authoritarian: referring to a form of government where power is held by a leader not elected by or answerable to the people

chancellery: the building where a chancellor has offices

sanction: a measure by one or a group of nations to force a nation to obey international law or to do as they demand

Low Mass: a Mass said without music or incense; a Mass that is not solemnly celebrated

intrinsically wrong: referring to something that is always and everywhere wrong or evil or immoral

clerical: referring to clergy; in politics, one who supports the authority of the Church in society

pronouncement: in Spanish, *pronunciamento*— a declaration of revolution, usually by a military authority

to carry out a Marxist revolution; on the other hand, German nationalists wanted to join Austria to the German *Reich*. A new threat appeared in 1933—the Austrian Nazi Party. To save Austria from being absorbed by Hitler's Germany, Dollfuss abolished Austria's republican government and established an authoritarian government—a form of government where power is held by a leader not elected by or answerable to the people. Dollfuss formed an alliance with Fascist Italy and put down a socialist revolutionary movement. On July 25, 1934, a small group of Nazis staged a *Putsch* in Vienna and assassinated Dollfuss.

3. How Hitler and Mussolini became allies

It was Mussolini who prevented Hitler from taking advantage of the *Putsch* in Vienna as an excuse to invade Austria. Yet, despite an alliance of France and Italy, Hitler began violating clauses of the Treaty of Versailles. His announcement that he would rearm Germany at first met stern resistance from France, Italy, and Great Britain—France forming an alliance with the Soviet Union and Czechoslovakia against German aggression. This alliance

against Hitler was broken when Great Britain and France backed League of Nations sanctions against Italy for her invasion and conquest of Ethiopia. While these powers were occupied with Ethiopia, Hitler again violated the Versailles Treaty by moving troops into the Rhineland. Meanwhile, Italy, which had became isolated from other nations, was receiving military supplies from Germany. Mussolini accepted Hitler's friendship and, in 1936, with him formed the Rome-Berlin Axis.

4. The *Anschluss* (union) of Austria with Germany

Because of her pact with Germany, Italy no longer guaranteed Austria's independence. Faced with evidence that the Austrian Nazis were planning on overthrowing his government, Austrian chancellor Kurt Schluschnigg called a plebiscite on the subject of the *Anschluss* (or union) with Germany. Before the plebiscite could be held, however, Hitler led troops into the small country and, on March 13, 1938, proclaimed Austria's *Anschluss* with Germany. A plebiscite following the invasion seemed to indicate that the vast majority of Austrians approved the union of their country with Germany. But the voting was not done by secret ballot, nor was it free.

5. **What the *Holodomor* was**

In 1928, Josif Stalin announced his first Five-Year Plan to turn the Soviet Union into a great industrial power. But independent farmers, especially in Ukraine, resisted Stalin's moves to collectivize all farms to increase grain production for sale on the international market. Stalin used violence to force collectivization. By his policies in Ukraine, he created a famine that led, in the winter of 1932–1933, to the death of millions of people in Ukraine and parts of Russia. The Ukrainians have called this *Holodomor* ("death by hunger").

6. **Stalin's Five-Year Plans and their results**

The Soviet Union's industrialization under Stalin's first Five-Year Plan was swift. During the second Five-Year Plan (1933–1937), the Soviet Union became one of the largest industrial nations in the world. But to achieve all this progress, Stalin abandoned some key socialist principles. Different rates of pay were established for different classes of workers. Workdays were lengthened, and managers gained greater control over workers. A new class, socialist millionaires, came into existence.

7. **Stalin's Five-Year Plan against religion**

In 1932, Stalin began a virulent persecution of religion in the Soviet Union. His goal was to destroy religion once and for all. Propaganda campaigns against religion arose, churches were closed, and mass arrests of believers occurred. It is estimated that, by the late 1930s, about 80,000 Orthodox clergy, monks, and nuns had been killed in the Soviet Union. Throughout Russia, the number of bishops and priests decreased dramatically. Though foreign governments ignored the persecutions,

Pope Pius XI condemned them in 1930. In 1937, the pope issued his first formal condemnation of Communism, the encyclical *Divini Redemptoris.*

8. **What Pope Pius XI said about Communism**

In *Divini Redemptoris*, Pope Pius XI condemned Communism for stripping "human personality of all its dignity" and removing all moral restraints on human action. "By refusing to human life any sacred or spiritual character," said the pope, "Communism attacks human rights and undermines marriage and the family and directs everything in society to one purpose—the production of material wealth." Workers and the poor, said Pius, were attracted to Communism because of the abuses of "Liberal economics" and by the power of Communist propaganda. Communism, the pope said, is "intrinsically wrong," and Christians may not work with it in any way.

9. **What Stalin's purges were and what their effects were**

To secure his power against those he thought were his enemies among the Communists, Stalin began a great purge of members of his own Communist Party, beginning in 1934. It is said that by the time Stalin died in 1953, his purges had taken the lives of tens of millions of people.

10. **The condition of Spain in the early 20th century**

By the beginning of the 20th century, Spain had undergone several political and social struggles between clericals and Liberals, monarchists and republicans. Spain was primarily an agricultural society, had little industry (compared to France and Germany), and was considered backward. In the 1920s, after a humiliating military defeat in Morocco at the hands of native tribesmen and under the threat posed by socialists, anarchists, and Communists, Spain's military men chose General Miguel Primo de Rivera to be dictator of Spain, under the authority of King Alfonso XIII. Spain generally prospered under Primo de Rivera's rule, though he suppressed freedom of speech and of the press and abolished trial by jury. But after Primo de Rivera resigned in 1930, the king promised to restore Spain's constitution. He did so early in 1930; but under pressure from republicans, he gave up the exercise of royal power and went into exile.

11. What the new government of the Spanish republic did

Socialists and radical republicans, who controlled the majority in Spain's *Cortes* after the 1931 elections, established a secular and anti-Church state, passed laws to help workers, and seized the lands of large landowners (though most of the lands seized belonged to small and medium-sized farmers). Not only did the new constitution drawn up by the *Cortes* separate the Church from the state, it forbade members of religious orders from teaching anything but religion in schools, closed Church schools, seized Church property, and forbade public religious processions. The government made it easy to obtain a divorce. The government's actions inspired a reaction among traditional groups, as well as businessmen and industrialists, who in an organization called CEDA ("Spanish Confederation of Autonomous Right-Wing Parties") won a majority of seats in the *Cortes* in 1933. But the Popular Front (a coalition of Communists and other radical groups) won the election of 1936.

12. The events of the Spanish Civil War

Fear that Spain would become a Communist state sparked a revolt among Spanish generals against the government in 1936. Spain became divided between two governments—the republican (or Loyalist) government in Madrid and the Nationalist government, under General Francisco Franco. Both sides committed atrocities against both each other and the civilian population. The republicans or Reds made no distinction between dangerous political opponents and ordinary citizens; they committed acts of sacrilege and destroyed churches. The Nationalists, though they shed much blood, tended to punish real enemies and fewer innocent people. The republicans received aid from volunteers from the United States, Germany, France, England, and other nations. They also received arms from the Soviet Union. The Nationalists received aid from Nazi Germany and Fascist Italy. The civil war lasted until 1939, when the Nationalists overthrew the republican government.

13. The character of Franco's government after the war

Following the war's end, Franco established an authoritarian government over Spain. His government executed tens of thousands of people who had supported the Loyalist cause, while thousands of others fled into exile. The country was thus divided between those who supported Franco and those who vehemently opposed him.

14. How Hitler extended his power

Great Britain's prime minister Neville Chamberlain thought it best to appease Hitler rather than oppose him because Hitler claimed that his only goal was to bring all German peoples into union with Germany. In 1938, Great Britain and France both allowed Germany to annex Sudetenland, a German-speaking region of Czechoslovakia. Instead of just seizing Sudetenland, however, Hitler took control of all of Czechoslovakia, seizing the Czech region (Bohemia) and creating a German satellite state, Slovakia. Hitler annexed part of

Lithuania and carried on a threatening propaganda campaign against Poland. France and Great Britain also did nothing while Mussolini invaded Albania.

15. How the conquest of Poland sparked World War II

Hitler's aggression against Poland convinced France and Great Britain that they had to take a stand against German expansion. Hitler, however, ignored the Allies; instead, he signed a pact with Stalin to divide Poland between Germany and Russia. In September 1939, both German and Soviet armies invaded Poland. In accordance with a treaty with Poland, Great Britain and France both declared war on Germany on September 3, 1939.

16. German and Russian conquests in 1940

Following the invasion of Poland, the Soviets forced the Baltic republics to accept Soviet "protection" and invaded Romania. Stalin then ordered the bombing of Helsinki, Finland. In 1940, Germany invaded Scandinavia, conquering Denmark and Norway. German armies then invaded neutral Belgium and Holland, forcing their surrender after 16 days. The Germans then moved into France, and on June 14, 1940, Paris fell to them. On June 21, 1940, France signed an armistice with Germany. Northern France was occupied by German troops while southern France remained independent, though it had to disband its military and pay the costs of the German military occupation of northern France. The war between Great Britain and Germany also became an air war in 1940 in which both sides bombed each other's cities. Mussolini, who had allied himself with Hitler, suffered failures in the Balkans and Africa. Hitler was thus forced to come to his aid. German armies invaded Yugoslavia and Greece, driving out British forces in Greece and conquering Crete.

17. How Hitler and Stalin became enemies and the effects of Japan's entrance into the war

In June 1942, Hitler broke his pact with Stalin, and German armies invaded Russia. Hitler's ally, Japan, also carried on a war of conquest in the western Pacific. A Japanese airstrike on December 7, 1941, brought the United States into the war on the side of the Allies, against the Axis.

Questions for Review

1. Why did Engelbert Dollfuss think preserving Austria's peasantry was so important?

Dollfuss thought preserving the peasantry was important because he thought the peasantry most thoroughly preserved German customs and the Catholic Faith.

2. Why at first did Mussolini ally himself with Austria, Great Britain, and France against Germany? Why did he later change his mind, turning against these powers, and ally himself with Hitler?

Mussolini knew that Hitler wanted to annex Austria; he feared that, after doing so, Hitler would also try to take the German-speaking South Tyrol, which Italy had won from Austria in the First World War. Thus, he allied himself with France (and thus Great Britain), which also opposed Hitler's ambition for Austria. Mussolini later turned against France and Great Britain because they had opposed his conquest of Ethiopia and backed sanctions against Italy. Hitler, however, stood with Mussolini and sent him military supplies during the war against Ethiopia. In this way, Mussolini and Hitler drew closer together and became allies.

3. What were the Soviet Five-Year Plans? Were they successful?

The Soviet Five-Year Plans were Stalin's campaigns to industrialize all of Russia quickly. The First Five-Year Plan achieved a great deal, though the quality of Russian manufactured goods was not good. A second Five-Year Plan focused on improving the quality of manufactured goods and making workers more skilled and efficient. It, too, achieved many of its goals. It also focused on improving the material living conditions of the masses.

4. **What was the *Holodomor*? When did it occur? Why did it occur?**

The *Holodomor* was Stalin's forced starvation of the Ukrainians and some Russian populations. It occurred in the winter of 1932–33. Stalin wanted to force all peasant farmers into collectivized farming production, but peasants, especially Ukrainian peasants, resisted. Following a poor grain harvest in 1932, Stalin, blaming the peasants, demanded they give an even greater percentage of their harvest than they normally would to the state. The Ukrainians gave up so much grain that they had little left for food or for seed and thus suffered from famine. Instead of supplying grain for food, Stalin had it exported. He blocked foreign food shipments to the stricken area. Thus, millions of Ukrainians and Russians died of starvation.

5. **Why, according to Communists like Stalin, did people become religious?**

Communists said people become religious only because they are unhappy in this world.

6. **What did Stalin do to destroy religion in the Soviet Union?**

To destroy religion, Stalin instituted a different kind of Five-Year Plan. Propaganda campaigns against religion arose, churches were closed, and mass arrests of believers occurred. Tens of thousands of clergy, monks, and nuns were arrested and killed in the Soviet Union.

7. **What is wrong with Communism, according to Pope Pius XI's encyclical, *Divini Redemptoris*?**

Pope Pius XI condemned Communism for stripping "human personality of all its dignity" and removing all moral restraints on human action. "By refusing to human life any sacred or spiritual character," said the pope, "Communism attacks human rights and undermines marriage and the family and directs everything in society to one purpose—the production of material wealth." Pius said Communism is "intrinsically wrong."

8. **Why did Francisco Franco and other Spanish generals revolt against the Spanish government in 1936?**

Franco and other Spanish generals revolted against the Spanish government because they feared it would form a Communist state in Spain.

9. **Why did Hitler feel confident that he could invade Czechoslovakia?**

Hitler felt confident to invade Czechoslovakia because he knew neither Great Britain nor France would oppose him. Both governments allowed him to annex the Sudetenland.

10. **Why did Great Britain and France declare war on Germany?**

Great Britain and France declared war on Germany because of Hitler's invasion of Poland in 1939. A treaty between Poland and these powers said Great Britain and France would come to Poland's aid if she were invaded.

Ideas in Action

1. Research the history of anti-Nazi groups in Germany. Why did different groups oppose Hitler?

2. Study the life of St. Maximilian Kolbe, a Polish priest who gave his life for a Jewish man in the death camp at Auschwitz. Write a play of the incident and perform it.

3. Before and during the Spanish Civil War, many Catholics gave up their lives for the Faith. Pope John Paul II beatified 500 of these martyrs and Benedict XVI another 498. Various students can research the lives of different martyrs or groups of martyrs and make presentations to the class.

Sample Quiz I (pages 557–569)

Please answer the following in complete sentences.

1. Why did Engelbert Dollfuss want to preserve Austria's peasantry?

2. What kind of government did Dollfuss establish to save Austria from being forced to become a part of Nazi Germany? Describe this form of government.

3. Why did France and Great Britain object when Hitler announced that he was going to rearm Germany?

4. What country did Italy invade in 1936?

5. What do the Ukrainians call Stalin's forced starvation of their people in the winter of 1932–1933?

   a) *Anschluss*   c) *bezbozhnik*

   b) *holodomor*   d) *komintern*

Answers to Sample Quiz I

Students' answers should approximate the following.

1. Dollfuss wanted to preserve Austria's peasantry because he thought it best preserved Austria's German customs and her Catholic Faith.

2. Dollfuss established an *authoritarian government* to keep Austria free of Nazi Germany. An authoritarian government is a form of government where power is held by a leader not elected by or answerable to the people.

3. Great Britain and France objected to Hitler's announcement of rearmament because it violated the Versailles Treaty.

4. Italy invaded *Ethiopia* in 1936.

5. Ukrainians call Stalin's forced starvation of their people *holodomor* (b).

Sample Quiz II (pages 569–584)

Please answer the following in complete sentences.

1. **Why did Spanish generals rebel against Spain's republican government in 1936?**

2. **What was the rebel side in the Spanish Civil War called? Who was its leader? What was the government's side called?**

3. **What foreign power or powers backed the republican government during the Spanish Civil War? Who backed the rebel side?**

4. **Who invaded Poland in 1939?**

5. **Why did France and Great Britain declare war on Germany in 1939?**

6. **When and why did the United States declare war on Japan?**

Answers to Sample Quiz II

Students' answers should approximate the following

1. Spanish generals rebelled against Spain's republican government because they were afraid it would become a Communist state.

2. The rebel side was called the *Nationalists*. Its leader was *General Francisco Franco*. The government side was called *republican* (or *Loyalist* or *Red*).

3. The *Soviet Union* backed the republican government. (Volunteers came from Germany, France, England, and other nations.) *Germany* and *Italy* backed the rebels.

4. *Germany* and *Russia* invaded Poland in 1939.

5. Both France and Great Britain had agreed to come to Poland's aid if she were invaded. Thus, when Germany invaded Poland in 1939, France and Great Britain declared war on her.

6. The United States declared war on Japan on December 8, 1941 because the Japanese had attacked the U.S. Fleet stationed at Pearl Harbor in Hawaii.

Essays (200–500 words each)

Instructions to be given to the students: Write in complete sentences. Underline your thesis. Give three supports or examples that explain why you think what you do and that support your thesis.

1. Hitler, Mussolini, on the one hand, and Dollfuss, on the other, made themselves the absolute rulers of their countries. Were they alike in other ways? Did they differ? If so, how?

2. Write an account of the life and character of one of the historical figures in this chapter or of another figure from the time period covered by this chapter.

Chapter Test

Please answer the following in complete sentences.

I. Short Essay—Answer one of the following:

1. What sort of society did Engelbert Dollfuss favor for Austria? What sort of businesses did he want? How did he want workers and employers organized? What role did he want for the government in the economic system? Why were the peasants particularly important to him?

2. How could Hitler get away with violating the Versailles Treaty again and again? Why didn't France and Great Britain do anything to stop Hitler from doing this? What happened with Italy?

II. Short Answer:

1. Why did Stalin create a famine in Ukraine that led to the death of millions in 1932-1933?

2. To what goal, or for what purpose, does Communism direct everything in human life, according to Pope Pius XI? Why, according to the pope, were workers attracted to Communism?

3. For what reason did Stalin carry out his great purges? Roughly, how many people died in these purges?

4. What did Stalin hope to accomplish in his first Five-Year Plan?

5. Why did British prime minister Neville Chamberlain think that the best way to deal with Hitler was to appease him, not oppose him?

6. What happened to France after the Germans conquered Paris?

7. When and why did the United States declare war on Japan? How did the United States end up fighting a war with Germany and Italy as well?

Answer Key to the Chapter Test

Students' answers should approximate the following:

I.

1. Dollfuss's vision for Austria was based on Catholic social teaching and Austria's peasant traditions. He did not think society should be made up primarily of large businesses but chiefly of small farmers, craftsmen, shopkeepers, and merchants. Each business group would be organized in a guild or corporation that looked out for members and their families, made sure they received a just wage or charged a just price for their goods, and protected their interests. The government's role would be to make sure that all the various groups worked in harmony with one another and that the strong did not take advantage of the weak. Dollfuss was especially concerned with preserving Austria's peasantry because he thought the peasants best preserved German customs and the Catholic Faith.

2. Hitler first violated the Versailles Treaty by announcing that he would rearm Germany. Though France, Italy, and Great Britain at first resisted Hitler's move, the alliance with Italy was broken when Great Britain and France backed League of Nations sanctions against Italy for her invasion and conquest of Ethiopia. Concerned with Italy and Ethiopia, Great Britain and France did nothing to hinder Hitler when he moved troops into the Rhineland, in violation of the treaty. Meanwhile, Hitler had been sending military supplies to Mussolini. Thus, Mussolini accepted Hitler's friendship and formed the Rome-Berlin Axis with him in 1936.

II.

1. Stalin created a famine because the Ukrainian peasants would not go along with his plan to form collective farms.

2. Pope Pius XI said Communism directs everything in human life to one purpose, the production of material wealth. Workers and the poor, said Pius, were attracted to Communism because they had been abused under "Liberal economics" and were drawn by the power of Communist propaganda.

3. Stalin carried out his great purges to rid the Communist Party of those he thought were his enemies. By the time his purges ended, tens of millions of people had been killed.

4. In his first Five-Year Plan, Stalin hoped to accomplish the industrialization of the Soviet Union.

5. Chamberlain thought it was best to appease Hitler because he believed Hitler's claim that he only wanted to unite all German speakers into one, German nation.

6. After the Germans conquered Paris, France signed an armistice with Germany. Northern France was occupied by German troops while southern France remained independent, though it had to disband its military and pay the costs of the German military occupation of northern France.

7. The United States declared war on Japan on December 8, 1941 because the Japanese had attacked the U.S. Fleet stationed at Pearl Harbor in Hawaii. Three days after this declaration of war, Germany and Italy declared war on the United States because they had a treaty of mutual defense with Japan.

CHAPTER 20: The End of a War and the Beginning of a New World

Chapter Overview

- In July 1942, Hitler ordered an assault on Stalingrad. In September and October, the Germans were able to push into the city and it appeared that they would be able to drive the Soviet Red Army forces entirely out of Stalingrad. But in late November, the Red Army was able to surround the German armies in Stalingrad. On January 31, 1943, the Germans surrendered to the Russians.

- In Operation Torch, American and British forces were able to surprise German and Vichy French troops in North Africa and take Morocco. Following a British victory against the Germans in Egypt, Roosevelt and Churchill met in Casablanca in January 1943 to lay out their policies for the war. At their meeting, Roosevelt and Churchill agreed that they would demand unconditional surrender from the Axis powers and approved the Combined Bomber Offensive. By May, Allied forces in Tunisia forced the surrender of the German army under General Erwin Rommel.

- From North Africa, the Allies invaded Sicily. By August 1943, Sicily was in Allied hands. During the invasion of Sicily, King Vittorio Emanuele III dismissed Mussolini as prime minister and appointed a new government. Yet, though Italy formally surrendered to the Allies on September 3, 1943, the Germans held important positions on the peninsula, including Rome. Though the Germans contested the Allied advance, the Allies were finally able to push the Germans from their lines south of Rome. On June 4, 1944, the Allies took Rome.

- Roosevelt, Churchill, and Stalin met at Teheran in Iran from November 28 to December 1, 1943. In return for Stalin's continuing help in the war, Roosevelt and Churchill agreed to allow Stalin to dominate a large portion of Eastern Europe after the war.

- Hitler's treatment of various religious and racial groups, especially Jews, grew more brutal throughout the years of the war. It seems that in June 1941, Hitler decided on what became known as the "Final Solution"—the extermination of the Jewish race or the Holocaust. The number of Jewish victims of the Holocaust is usually given as 6 million dead. Adding other victims, the number reaches perhaps 10 or 11 million dead.

- Throughout the war, Pope Pius XII called for peace and spoke out against the cruelties perpetrated by both sides in the war. He condemned the persecution of people simply on account of their race. Though he did not directly condemn Hitler's policies, Pius worked to save Jewish lives.

- On D-Day, June 6, 1944, the Allies crossed the English Channel and invaded northern France. By June 24, the Allies had driven the Germans from Normandy. In the following months, the Allies liberated Paris and entered Belgium, taking Brussels and Antwerp. Following the Battle of Stalingrad in 1942, the Red Army began pushing the Germans out of the Soviet Union. By the summer of 1944, the Red Army had marched as far as Warsaw and forced the surrender of Romania.

- In the autumn of 1944, the Allies in the west began their invasion of Germany, accompanied by the firebombings of German cities. In January 1945, the Russians began their invasion of Germany from the east. While these invasions were going on, Churchill, Roosevelt, and Stalin met at Yalta, on the Black Sea. At this meeting, the Western leaders gave in to more of Stalin's demands. In April 1945, the German war effort collapsed. On April 30, Hitler committed suicide. On May 8, 1945, the Second World War in Europe formally ended.

- Europe suffered much devastation on account of the war. Tens of millions of people had been killed in the course of the war. Populations were displaced. Western European nations ceased to be the great powers of the world, giving way to the two superpowers, the United States and the Soviet Union.

- The United Nations Organization was formed to assure peace and security to the world. The UN possessed more power to impose its will than the League of Nations did. Yet, the UN was dominated by five powers—the United States, the Soviet Union, Great Britain, France, and China. A single veto from one of these powers could hinder resolutions of the whole assembly.

- Reconstruction of Europe after the war was overseen by the United States, Great Britain, France, and the Soviet Union. Dissension between the Soviets and the other powers, however, led to a lack of cooperation between them. Eventually it led to a splitting of Europe (and the world) between a Communist bloc of nations and what were called the free nations. While the United States, through the Marshall Plan, aided the Western European countries, the Soviets did the same for the countries that were included in the Warsaw Pact.

- On August 6 and 9, 1945, the United States dropped atomic bombs on the Japanese cities of Hiroshima and Nagasaki. In the years after the bombings, the UN discussed various measures to eliminate such a destructive weapon. These attempts met a major setback in April 1949, when the Soviet Union announced that it had tested its first atomic bomb.

- The post–World War II world witnessed greater economic, political, and cultural unification among the various peoples of the world, even while they were split into two factions—Communism and the free nations. Western culture, in particular, spread to all the world, including the Communist bloc countries. To prepare the Church to speak the Gospel of Christ more effectively to this world, Pope John XXIII called the Second Vatican Ecumenical Council. The council met for three years, both under John XXIII and his successor, Paul VI. The council made many changes in the life of the Church but also marked the beginning of a crisis in the Church that has continued to our day.

Chapter Goals

This chapter speaks of the forces that make our world of today. Though some phenomena, such as the Cold War, are no longer with us, we still live in the wake of their effects. The United States remains

Key Terms at a Glance

beachhead: an area along an enemy's shore from which an army can land more troops and supplies

Talmud: the writings that provide the authoritative interpretation of Jewish traditions

tenet: a belief, principle, or doctrine that a person or a group holds to be true

social democracy: a political ideal that seeks to preserve capitalism but attempts to reform it by regulating business activities and providing social programs for workers

Third World: the group of nations that do not have the economic development of the rich nations and are generally poor

a dominant cultural force and is, currently, the only world superpower. The Second Vatican Council has made the Church of our day what she is, and the council's effects, both good and ill, are still with us. Though this chapter deals with events that are not "current events," they are the foundations of the world of our day. To understand them is to understand ourselves.

What Students Should Know

1. **What happened in the Battle of Stalingrad and its importance**

   In July 1942, Hitler ordered an assault on Stalingrad, a city on the River Volga in southern Russia. But in late November, the Red Army was able to surround the German armies in Stalingrad. On January 31, 1943, the Germans surrendered to the Russians. The Battle of Stalingrad was perhaps the most important battle of the war, for it stopped the string of victories that had allowed the German army to push as far as Leningrad and Moscow. It showed Hitler that he was not invincible.

2. **What Operation Torch was and its results**

   Operation Torch was the name given to the Allied invasion of North Africa. In the operation, American and British forces were able to

surprise German and Vichy French troops in North Africa and take Morocco.

3. **What Roosevelt and Churchill decided at their meeting in Casablanca**

   Following a British victory against the Germans in Egypt, Roosevelt and Churchill met in Casablanca in January 1943 to lay out their policies for the war. They agreed that they would demand unconditional surrender from the Axis powers, to "impose punishment and retribution in full" upon Axis leaders. Roosevelt and Churchill also approved the Combined Bomber Offensive, which included the strategic bombing of Axis cities. The Royal Air Force (RAF) would carry out strikes at night, while the United States Army Air Force carried out more precise strikes during the day. The point of the strikes was not just to destroy Germany's military, industrial, and economic system but to terrorize the German people until they were unwilling or unable to continue the war.

4. **What happened in the invasion of Italy**

   After the Germany army in North Africa under General Erwin Rommel surrendered to the Allies in May 1943, the Allies invaded Sicily. By August 1943, Sicily was in Allied hands. During the invasion of Sicily, King Vittorio

Emanuele III dismissed Mussolini as prime minister and appointed a new government. Yet, though Italy formally surrendered to the Allies on September 3, 1943, the Germans held important positions on the peninsula, including Rome. Though the Germans contested the Allied advance, the Allies were finally able to push the Germans from their lines south of Rome. On June 4, 1944, the Allies took Rome.

5. What the Teheran Conference between Roosevelt, Stalin, and Churchill decided

Roosevelt, Churchill, and Stalin met at Teheran in Iran from November 28 to December 1, 1943 to discuss the progress of the war and decide, after victory, how to rebuild Europe. In return for Stalin's continuing help in the war, Roosevelt and Churchill agreed to allow Stalin to dominate a large portion of Eastern Europe after the war. At the end of the war, nearly half of Europe would discover that it had been saved from Nazism only to be sacrificed to Soviet Communism.

6. What the Holocaust was

Hitler's treatment of various religious and racial groups, especially Jews, grew more brutal throughout the years of the war. It seems that in June 1941, Hitler decided on what became known as the "Final Solution"—the extermination of the Jewish race or the Holocaust. The number of Jewish victims of the Holocaust is usually given as 6 million dead. Adding other victims, the number reaches perhaps 10 or 11 million dead. In extermination camps built throughout Poland, Jews were subjected to starvation, cold, hard labor, scientific experimentation, and finally death. To kill large numbers quickly and easily, the Nazis built poison-gas chambers; and to dispose of the corpses, they erected enormous gas-fired crematoria. Besides the extermination camps, the Nazis built thousands of concentration and

slave labor camps not only for Jews, but for socialists, political opponents of the Nazi government, Roma, and Slavs. To create a pure, Aryan race, Hitler's government had set up a euthanasia program to rid Germany of the mentally retarded, the physically disabled, and the emotionally disturbed. Other victims of the Holocaust included Catholic and Orthodox priests and religious, as well as Protestant ministers who had spoken out against national Socialism, aided in the escape of Jews and others wanted by the government, or done other acts of resistance.

7. What Pope Pius XII did during the war

Throughout the war, Pope Pius XII called for peace and spoke out against the cruelties perpetrated by both sides in the war. He condemned the bombing of cities, towns, and villages. He condemned the persecution of people simply on account of their race. Though he did not directly condemn Hitler's policies, Pius worked to save Jewish lives. He urged Europe's Catholic bishops to do whatever they could to save the lives of Jews and other persecuted peoples. The Holy See sent diplomatic protests against anti-Jewish violence to Axis governments. Responding to the pope's call, Catholics clergy, religious, and laity hid Jews and helped them escape. The Holy See harbored Jews and provided them false passports. One estimate says that 860,000 Jews escaped death at the hands of the Nazis because of actions taken or encouraged by Pope Pius XII.

8. The course of the war in 1944

On D-Day, June 6, 1944, the Allies crossed the English Channel and invaded northern France. By June 24, the Allies had driven the Germans from Normandy. In the following months, the Allies liberated Paris and entered Belgium, taking Brussels and Antwerp. Following the Battle of Stalingrad in 1942, the Red Army began pushing the Germans out of the Soviet Union. By the summer of 1944, the Red Army had marched as far as Warsaw and forced the surrender of Romania.

9. How the Second World War ended

In the autumn of 1944, the Allies in the west began their invasion of Germany, accompanied by the firebombings of German cities. In January 1945, the Russians began their invasion of Germany from the east. While these invasions were going on, Churchill, Roosevelt, and Stalin met at Yalta, on the Black Sea. At this meeting, the Western leaders gave in to more of Stalin's demands. They allowed him to form a new government for Poland. The allies agreed to divide Germany into four zones, each controlled by one of the Allied powers—the United States, Great Britain, the Soviet Union, and France. In April 1945, the German war effort collapsed. On April 30, Hitler committed suicide. On May 8, 1945, the Second World War in Europe formally ended.

10. The casualties of the war

It has been estimated that the war killed 50 million to 65 million people in Europe and the Far East combined; in Europe alone, the number of dead may have reached 15 million to as much as 20 million. Millions were displaced from their home countries during the course of the war.

11. What the United Nations Organization is and how it works

The United Nations Organization was formed to assure peace and security to the world. It was to act like a world parliament of nations and assure peace and security to all peoples everywhere. Its charter was approved in San Francisco, California, in October 1945. The UN was and is divided into two bodies: the Security Council and the Assembly. Five powers—the United States, the Soviet Union, Great Britain, France, and China—sit on the Security Council, while the remaining member nations send representatives to the Assembly. Each nation in the Assembly has one vote. Yet, the five nations on the Security Council dominate the UN; a single veto from one of these powers could hinder resolutions of the whole assembly. The UN has the power to approve the use of force (economic sanctions and even war) against nations that oppose its decrees. It can establish its own permanent armed forces.

12. The origins of the Cold War and the Iron Curtain

Reconstruction of Europe after the war was overseen by the United States, Great Britain, France, and the Soviet Union. Dissension between the Soviets and the other powers, however, led to a lack of cooperation between them. Eventually it led to a splitting of Europe (and the world) between a Communist bloc of nations (all of Eastern Europe) and what were called the free nations. Germany was divided between the western sector, dominated by the "free nations," and eastern Germany, dominated by the Soviet Union. While the United States, through the Marshall Plan, aided the Western European countries, the Soviets did the same for the countries that were included in the Warsaw Pact. It looked to the "Western" democratic nations as though the Soviet Union had succeeded Nazi Germany as the new threat to freedom in the world. In March 1947, U.S. President Harry Truman responded to this threat by announcing the "Truman Doctrine"—that the United States would stand with free peoples all over the world against oppression. The U.S. and the U.S.S.R., thus, became the two superpowers in the world. This era became known as the Cold War. The line of division between the free nations and the Communist bloc became know as the Iron Curtain.

13. The origins of the nuclear arms race

On August 6 and 9, 1945, the United States dropped atomic bombs on the Japanese cities of Hiroshima and Nagasaki. In the years after the bombings, the UN discussed various measures to eliminate such a destructive weapon. These attempts met a major setback in April 1949, when the Soviet Union announced that it had tested its first atomic bomb. Thus began what became known as the nuclear arms race.

14. Western Europe's turn toward social democracy

The post–World War II world witnessed greater economic, political, and cultural unification among the various peoples of the world, even while they were split into two factions—Communism and the free nations. The late 1940s and the 1950s were periods of economic prosperity for much of western Europe. During this period, European countries granted independence to most of their overseas colonies. Western European countries followed neither laissez-faire economic practices nor Communism or, even socialism. They adopted, instead, social democracy, a political ideal that seeks to preserve capitalism but attempts to reform it by regulating business activities and providing social programs for workers.

15. The path toward European union

Worried that old rivalries might again create problems in Europe and to insure that all western European countries enjoyed economic prosperity, European nations began to seek a greater unity among themselves. They formed a union to ensure that all members could easily trade with one another and protect their industries from competition from outside of Europe. Another union made sure member countries could not hoard coal or iron. The next step in

European unity came on March 25, 1957, when several European nations formed the European Economic Community (EEC). The Treaty of Rome that formed this union removed tariffs between member countries and set up tariffs to protect the EEC from cheap goods imported from other countries. Then in 1993, the European Union was formed, which today includes 27 European states. The EU provides a kind of federal government for its members. The member states have given over some of their authority to the EU government. The EU is not a national union like the United States, but it is more than just an alliance of independent countries.

16. How the world became Europeanized, and Europe became Americanized

In the decades following the Second World War, Western culture spread to all the world, including the Communist bloc countries. The United States of America had a very prosperous economy. Americans became involved in the Western European economy, and because of this, European culture was being influenced by American culture. European business corporations were organizing themselves along American lines. American products entered the European economy. American motion pictures and music became increasingly popular among Europeans. American styles of dress and even American foods began to change how Europeans dressed and fed themselves. Communists and European traditionalists deplored this development, calling it derisively, Coca-colonization.

17. How Western economic practices influenced the Third World

Western economic practices spread all over the world and often led to the exploitation of those in the Third World—the group of nations that do not have the economic development of the rich nations and are generally poor. In seeking to free themselves from oppression, peoples in Europe, Asia, and Africa as well as Central and South American looked to the Communists for help, for the Communists promised to liberate them from slavery to the capitalist West. The result was the spread of Communist ideas and Communist revolts—and even the establishment of new Communist governments—throughout the world.

18. **How the Church confronted the modern world**

Especially since the First Vatican Council in 1870, the Church had been addressing the problems arising from Liberalism, not just by condemnation, but by weeding out what is true in Liberalism from what is false. Pope Pius XII continued the work of the previous popes. He addressed all the problems posed by the political, economic, and scientific worlds in the light of the Gospel. The challenges facing the pope were truly great. New discoveries and inventions were giving men unimaginable power over nature. The old agrarian societies were being destroyed; millions were moving into the cities and losing touch with ancient traditions of thinking and behaving. More and more people all over the world were abandoning religion and seeking truth and security in science and technology.

19. **What the Second Vatican Council sought to do and its aftermath**

To prepare the Church to speak the Gospel of Christ more effectively to this world, Pope John XXIII called the Second Vatican Ecumenical Council. Pope John said he called the council so that the Church might undergo "timely changes" so that "men, families, and nations [would] really turn their minds to those things that are above." He wanted the Church to undergo an updating that would not change

the essence of the Church but make her better able to spread the Gospel to the world. Under Pope John XXIII and Pope Paul VI, the council explored what the Church is, calling her both the Body of Christ and the People of God. It spoke about how the pope and bishops together rule and guide the Church. It discussed the various ways the Church can speak to and work with the people of the modern world. It called for the preservation of ancient traditions while making the Mass and administration of the Sacraments more comprehensible to modern people. The council met for three years, both under John XXIII and his successor, Paul VI. The council made many changes in the life of the Church but also marked the beginning of a crisis in the Church that has continued to our day.

Questions for Review

1. **Why was General Paulus unable to save the German 4th and 6th armies at Stalingrad?**

Paulus and his army were surrounded by the Russians. His men were cold, sick, and starving and so he could not fight his way out, as Hitler had ordered him to do.

2. **Why can we call Stalingrad the most important battle of World War II?**

It is the most important battle of World War II because it stopped the string of victories that had allowed the Germany army to push as far as Leningrad and Moscow. Stalingrad showed Hitler he was not invincible.

3. **What two policies did Roosevelt and Churchill adopt at their Casablanca conference?**

At Casablanca, Roosevelt and Churchill adopted the policy of unconditional surrender and the Combined Bomber Offensive, which included the strategic bombing of Axis cities.

4. **What did Roosevelt and Churchill agree to allow Stalin to do at the Teheran conference?**

At Teheran, Roosevelt and Churchill allowed Stalin to dominate a large portion of Eastern Europe after the war. He would be allowed to annex the Baltic states of Latvia, Lithuania, and Estonia, as well as eastern Poland, to form a "security belt" for Russia. In private talks, Roosevelt said he would be willing to give German East Prussia to Stalin as well and to draw Germany's eastern border at the Oder River.

5. **What groups did Hitler target in the Holocaust? About how many people were killed in the Holocaust?**

In the Holocaust, Hitler targeted primarily Jews, but also Catholic and Orthodox priests and religious, Protestant ministers, Jehovah's Witnesses, Roma (Gypsies), Slavs, socialists, and political opponents. Counting only the Jews, the Holocaust killed about 6 million people. Counting other groups, that number rises to perhaps 10 or 11 million dead.

6. **Why may Pope Pius XII not have spoken out directly against Hitler and his persecution of the Jews? How did Pius XII help the Jews?**

The reason Pius XII may not have spoken out against Hitler and his persecution of the Jews is that experience had shown that, if he did, it would lead to a worse persecution of the Jews. Though he did not directly condemn Hitler's policies, Pius worked to save Jewish lives. He urged Europe's Catholic bishops to do whatever they could to save the lives of Jews and other persecuted peoples. The Holy See sent diplomatic protests against anti-Jewish violence to Axis governments. Responding to the pope's call, Catholic clergy, religious, and laity hid Jews and helped them escape. The Holy See harbored Jews and provided them false passports. One estimate says that 860,000 Jews escaped death at the hands of the Nazis because of actions taken or encouraged by Pope Pius XII.

7. **What is the United Nations Organization? Why was it founded? What powers does it have?**

The United Nations Organization is a union of the world's nations formed to assure peace and security to the world. It acts like a world parliament of nations. It has the power to approve the use of force (economic sanctions and even war) against nations that oppose its decrees. It can establish its own permanent armed forces.

8. **What was the Cold War? What does the term Iron Curtain refer to?**

The Cold War was a period in history where the two great superpowers, the United States and the Soviet Union, and their allies stood opposed as enemies without fighting an actual "hot war" with each other. The era, however, witnessed several small wars between Communists and pro-Western groups or Western powers. The Iron Curtain refers to the division of Europe and the world between the "free" West and the Communist bloc of countries.

9. **What does Coca-colonization refer to? Why did people oppose Coca-colonization?**

Coca-colonization refers to the growing influence of American mass culture on Europe in the decades after the Second World War. People opposed it because, if they were Communists, they opposed the system of the United States. Others opposed it because they wanted to preserve their national and local cultures.

10. **Why did Pope John XXIII call the Second Vatican Council?**

Pope John XXIII called the council to update the Church so that, while she remained true to her traditions, she could better lead the people of the modern world to Christ and the Church.

Ideas in Action

1. Research how the cities that were bombed out in World War II recovered. Collect before and after pictures of the cities. Such cities include Dresden and Nuremberg (in Germany), Rotterdam (in the Netherlands), Coventry (in England), and Hiroshima and Nagasaki (in Japan).

2. Compare a map of Europe today with a map of Europe as it was in 1955. What differences can you detect?

3. Attend a Mass said according to the rite in use before the Second Vatican Council. (This rite goes by the names "Tridentine," "Extraordinary Rite," and sometimes "Mass of St. Pius V.") Write a paper comparing this rite with the rite of the Mass commonly said in parishes today.

Sample Quiz I (pages 589–604)

Please answer the following in complete sentences.

1. What is perhaps the most important battle of the Second World War? (It is the battle that stopped the string of victories that allowed the German army to push as far as Moscow and Leningrad.)

2. At their conference at Casablanca, Roosevelt and Churchill agreed that they would require unconditional surrender from the Axis powers. What other important policy did they agree on?

3. At the Teheran Conference in 1943, what did Churchill and Roosevelt allow Stalin to do after the war was over?

4. What was Hitler's "Final Solution" in regards to the Jews?

5. Name one thing Pope Pius XII did to save Jewish lives during World War II.

6. What name do we give the era after World War II when the world was divided between two superpowers who opposed each other but did not go to war with each other? Who were the superpowers that opposed one another?

Answers to Sample Quiz I

Students' answers should approximate the following.

1. The *Battle of Stalingrad* was perhaps the most important battle in the war.

2. At Casablanca, Roosevelt and Churchill agreed on unconditional surrender and the *Combined Bomber Offensive.*

3. At the Teheran Conference, Churchill and Roosevelt allowed Stalin to control a large portion of Eastern Europe after the war was over.

4. Hitler's "Final Solution" was to exterminate the Jews.

5. Pope Pius XII worked to save Jewish lives by (possible answers):

   a) urging Europe's Catholic bishops to do whatever they could to save the lives of Jews and other persecuted peoples

   b) sending diplomatic protests against anti-Jewish violence to Axis governments

   c) calling on Catholic clergy, religious, and laity to hide Jews and help them escape

   d) harboring Jews and providing them false passports.

6. The era after World War II is called the *Cold War.* The superpowers who opposed one another were the *Soviet Union* and the *United States of America.*

Sample Quiz II (pages 604–620)

Please answer the following in complete sentences.

1. After World War II, the nations of western Europe developed a system that seeks to preserve capitalism but attempts to reform it by regulating business activities and providing social programs for workers. What do we call this system?

2. Name the federal government that today unites 27 European states, which give some but not all of their authority to this government.

3. How did American (U.S.) culture influence European culture after the war?

4. What is the Third World?

5. Who was the pope who called for and opened the Second Vatican Council? Who was the pope that brought it to its conclusion?

Answers to Sample Quiz II

Students' answers should approximate the following

1. The system developed in western Europe after the war is called *social democracy*.

2. Europe's federal government today is called the *European Union*.

3. European business corporations were organizing themselves along American lines. American products entered the European economy. American motion pictures and music became increasingly popular among Europeans. American styles of dress and even American foods began to change how Europeans dressed and fed themselves.

4. The Third World is the group of nations that do not have the economic development of the rich nations and are generally poor.

5. *Pope John XXIII* called for and opened the Second Vatican Council. *Pope Paul VI* brought it to its conclusion.

Essays (200–500 words each)

Instructions to be given to the students: Write in complete sentences. Underline your thesis. Give three supports or examples that explain why you think what you do and that support your thesis.

1. Research and write a short account of the life of St. Edith Stein (Saint Teresia Benedicta of the Cross), a Jewish convert to the Catholic Faith, a philosopher, and a nun who died in the Auschwitz death camp.

2. Some historians have claimed that World War II was a continuation of World War I. Explain why you think this is or is not true.

Chapter Test

Please answer the following in complete sentences.

I. Short Essay—Answer one of the following:

1. **Describe the United Nations Organization. Why was it founded? What powers does the UN possess? Who forms the Assembly? What can the Assembly do? What nations sit on the Security Council? What power does each of these nations have?**

2. **Describe what the Second Vatican Council tried to do, what it was called to do, and how it affected the life of the Church.**

II. Short Answer:

1. **Why can we consider the Battle of Stalingrad the most important battle in the Second World War?**

2. **What were the two goals of the Combined Bomber Offensive Churchill and Roosevelt agreed to at Casablanca in 1943?**

3. **Name two things Pope Pius XII did to save Jewish lives during the war.**

4. **How did the United States begin the atomic age?**

5. **Why have people in Third World nations been attracted to Communism?**

Answer Key to the Chapter Test

Students' answers should approximate the following:

I.

1. The United Nations Organization was formed to assure peace and security to the world. The UN has the power to approve the use of force (economic sanctions and even war) against nations that oppose its decrees. It can establish its own permanent armed forces. The UN was and is divided into two bodies: the Security Council and the Assembly. The member nations of the UN send representatives to the Assembly. The Assembly can approve resolutions. Five powers—the United States, the Soviet Union (today, Russia), Great Britain, France, and China—sit on the Security Council. These five nations dominate the UN. A single veto from one of these powers can hinder resolutions of the whole assembly.

2. To prepare the Church to speak the Gospel of Christ more effectively to this world, Pope John XXIII called the Second Vatican Ecumenical Council. Pope John said he called the council so that the Church might undergo "timely changes" so that "men, families, and nations really turn their minds to those things that are above." He wanted the Church to undergo an updating that would not change the essence of the Church but better enable her to spread the Gospel to the world. To accomplish this, the council discussed the various ways the Church can speak to and work with the people of the modern world. It called for the preservation of ancient traditions while making the Mass and the administration of the Sacraments more comprehensible to modern people. The council made many changes in the life of the Church but also marked the beginning of a crisis in the Church that has continued to our day.

II.

1. The Battle of Stalingrad is perhaps the most important battle in the war because it stopped the string of victories that had allowed the German army to push as far as Leningrad and Moscow. It showed Hitler that he was not invincible.

2. The two goals of the Combined Bomber Offensive were, first, to destroy Germany's military, industrial, and economic system, and, second, to terrorize the German people until they were unwilling or unable to continue the war.

3. Pope Pius XII worked to save Jewish lives by (possible answers):

    a) urging Europe's Catholic bishops to do whatever they could to save the lives of Jews and other persecuted peoples

    b) sending diplomatic protests against anti-Jewish violence to Axis governments

    c) calling on Catholic clergy, religious, and laity to hide Jews and help them escape

    d) harboring Jews and providing them false passports.

4. The United States began the atomic age by dropping atomic bombs on the Japanese cities of Hiroshima and Nagasaki.

5. People in Third World countries often found that western European countries and the United States exploited and oppressed them. They hoped Communism would free them from exploitation and oppression.

Supplementary Reading List

Introduction

1000 Years of Catholic Scientists—Jane Meyerhofer

Copernicus, Galileo and the Catholic Sponsorship of Science—Jane Meyerhofer

Galileo and the Stargazers (audio CD)—Jim Weiss, storyteller

Along Came Galileo—Jeanne Bendick

Isaac Newton: Inventor, Scientist, and Teacher—John Hudson Tiner

Chapters 1–2

Peter the Great and Tsarist Russia—Miriam Greenblatt

Eyewitness: Russia—Kathleen Burton Murrell

Russian Folk Tales (Oxford Myths & Legends)—James Riordan

The following are picture books, well-written and worth reading to understand the Russian folk heritage:

> *The Sea King's Daughter: A Russian Legend*—Aaron Shephard
>
> *Baba Yaga and Vasilisa the Brave*—Marianna Mayer
>
> *I-Know-Not-What, I-Know-Not-Where: A Russian Tale*—Eric Kimmel
>
> *The Fool of the World and the Flying Ship: A Russian Tale*—Arthur Ransome
>
> *The Tale of Tsar Sultan*—Alexander Pushkin

Frederick the Great, Bismarck, and the Unification of Germany—Tom McGowen

Bach—Greta Cencetti

Introducing Bach (Introducing Composers)—Roland Vernon

Introducing Mozart (Introducing Composers)—Roland Vernon

German Hero-sagas and Folk-tales (Oxford Myths and Legends)—Barbara Picard

Germany: Enchantment of the World—Jean Blashfield

The Three Musketeers—Alexandre Dumas (advanced readers)

The Man in the Iron Mask—Alexandre Dumas (advanced readers)

Chapter 3

Vincent de Paul: Saint of Charity—Margaret Ann Hubbard

St. Louis de Montfort: The Story of Our Lady's Slave—Mary Fabyan Windeatt

Outlaws of Ravenhurst—M. Imelda Wallace

Chapter 4

Paris 1789: A Guide to Paris on the Eve of the Revolution (Sightseers Essential Travel Guides to the Past)—Rachel Wright

The Fall of the Bastille: Revolution in France—Stewart Ross

Life During the French Revolution—Gail Stewart

Marie Antoinette: Princess of Versailles, Austria-France, 1769 (The Royal Diaries series)—Kathryn Lasky

The Fair American—Elizabeth Coatsworth

The Scarlet Pimpernel—Baroness Orczy (advanced readers; consider an audio version)

A Tale of Two Cities—Charles Dickens (advanced readers or audio)

Thunder in Valmy—Geoffey Trease (out of print, check library)

Chapters 5–7

Walks Through Napoleon & Josephine's Paris—Diana Reid Haig

Violet for Bonaparte—Geoffrey Trease (out of print, check library)

Chapters 8–9

Child o' War: The true story of a boy sailor in Nelson's navy—Leon Garfield (out of print, check library)

The Navy That Beat Napoleon—Walter Brownlee (out of print, check library)

The Flying Ensign—Showell Styles

Midshipman Quinn—Showell Styles

Horatio Hornblower series—C.S. Forester

The Battle of Waterloo (Great Battles in History)—David Pietrusza

Chapters 10–11

The Romantics: Artists, Writers, and Composers—Sarah Halliwell

Introducing Beethoven (Introducing Composers)—Roland Vernon

The Curé of Ars: The Priest Who Out-Talked the Devil—Milton Lomask

The Curé of Ars: The Story of Saint John Vianney, Patron Saint of Parish Priests—Mary Fabyan Windeatt

Frankenstein—Mary Shelley (advanced readers)

The Iron Tsar—Geoffrey Trease (out of print, check library)

Chapter 12

St. John Bosco and Saint Dominic Savio—Catherine Beebe

Bernadette: Our Lady's Little Servant—Hertha Pauli

The Story of Florence Nightingale—Margaret Leighton (out of print, check library)

We Were There with Florence Nightingale in the Crimea—Robert Webb (out of print, check library)

Florence Nightingale's Nuns—Emmeline Garnett

Chapter 13

St. Catherine Labouré and the Miraculous Medal—Alma Powers Waters

William Wordsworth (British Library Writers Lives)—Stephen Hebron

Louis Pasteur: Founder of Modern Medicine—John Hudson Tiner

Charles Dickens: The Man Who Had Great Expectations—Diane Stanley

David Copperfield—Charles Dickens (advanced readers)

Oliver Twist—Charles Dickens (advanced readers)

A Christmas Carol—Charles Dickens

Under a Changing Moon—Margot Benary-Isbert

Chapter 14–15

Song for a Tattered Flag—Geoffrey Trease (out of print, check library)

Saint Thérèsè and the Roses—Helen Walker Homan

The Little Flower: The Story of Saint Thérèsè of the Child Jesus—Mary Fabyan Windeatt

Chapter 16

St. Pius X : The Farm Boy Who Became Pope—Walter Diethelm

The Good Master—Kate Seredy

Summer Soldiers—Susan Hart Lindquist

Angel on the Square—Gloria Whelan

The Night Journey—Kathryn Lasky

Broken Song—Kathryn Lasky

Thirty-Nine Steps—John Buchan

Chapter 17

The Children of Fatima and Our Lady's Message to the World—Mary Fabyan Windeatt

Our Lady Came to Fatima—Ruth Fox Home

Blessed Pier Giorgio Frassati: Journey to the Summit (Encounter the Saints)—Ana Maria Vazquez

Saint Pio of Pietrelcina: Rich in Love (Encounter the Saints)—Eileen Dunn Bertanzetti

Friend Within the Gates: The Story of Nurse Edith Cavell—Elizabeth Grey (out of print, check library)

No Hero for the Kaiser—Rudolf Frank (out of print, check library)

Private Peaceful—Michael Morpurgo

The Singing Tree—Kate Seredy

All Quiet on the Western Front—Erich Maria Remarque (mature readers, use discretion)

In Flanders Fields—Leon Wolff (mature readers)

Chapter 18

Stalin: Russia's Man of Steel—Albert Marrin

The Impossible Journey—Gloria Whelan

To Fight In Silence—Eva-Lis Wuorio (out of print, check library)

Chapter 19

Saint Maximilian Kolbe: Mary's Knight (Encounter the Saints)—Patricia E. Jablonski (intermediate readers)

Saint Edith Stein: Blessed by the Cross (Encounter the Saints)—Mary Lea Hill (intermediate readers)

More Than a Knight: The True Story of St. Maximilian Kolbe—Daughters of St. Paul

Maximilian Kolbe: Saint of Auschwitz—Elaine Murray Stone

A Man for Others: Maximilian Kolbe, Saint of Auschwitz, In the Words of Those Who Knew Him—Patricia Treece (advanced readers)

The Shadow of His Wings—Fr. Gereon Goldman (advanced readers)

The Diary of Anne Frank—Anne Frank

Irena Sendler and the Children of the Warsaw Ghetto—Susan Goldman Rubin (intermediate readers, good introduction for older readers)

The Story of the Trapp Family Singers—Maria Augusta Trapp

The Sledge Patrol: A WWII Epic of Escape, Survival, and Victory—David Howarth (advanced readers)

The Secret Armies: Spies, Counterspies, and Saboteurs in World War II—Albert Marrin (advanced readers)

Number the Stars—Lois Lowry

Escape from Warsaw (Original title: *The Silver Sword*)—Ian Serraillier

Twenty and Ten—Claire Huchet Bishop

When Hitler Stole Pink Rabbit—Judith Kerr

Journey to America—Sonia Levitin

Snow Treasure—Maria McSwigan

Tomorrow is a Stranger—Geoffrey Trease

The Borrowed House—Hilda van Stockum

The Winged Watchman—Hilda van Stockum

Enemy Brothers—Constance Savery

The Small War of Sergeant Donkey—Maureen Daly

The Mitchells: Five for Victory—Hilda van Stockum

Canadian Summer—Hilda van Stockum

Carrie's War—Nina Bawden

I am David (also titled *North to Freedom*)—Anne Holme

The Hiding Place—Corrie Ten Boom (mature readers)

Journey to Topaz: A Story Of The Japanese-American Evacuation—Yoshiko Uchida

The House of Sixty Fathers—Meindert Dejong

The following books are out of print, but check your library or used bookseller:

I Go by Sea, I Go by Land—P. L. Travers

When the Sirens Wailed—Noel Streatfeild

The Chestry Oak—Kate Seredy

North of Danger—Dale Fife

In Face of Danger—Mara Kay

Assignment: Spy—Oluf Reed Olsen

When Jays Fly to Barbmo—Margaret Balderson

Venture at Midsummer—Eva Lis Wuorio

In Spite of All Terror—Hester Burton
Niko's Mountains—Maria Gleit
Escape—Sigurd Senje
Silence Over Dunkerque—John R. Tunis
His Enemy, His Friend—John R. Tunis
The Dolphin Crossing—Jill Paton Walsh
The Long Escape—Irving Werstein

Chapter 20

Torches Together The Beginning and Early Years of the Bruderhof Communities—Emmy Arnold (advanced readers)
Hiroshima—John Hersey (mature readers)
Blessed Teresa of Calcutta: Missionary of Charity (Encounter the Saints)—Mary Kathleen Glavich
The Kitchen Madonna—Rumer Godden (intermediate readers)
Lord of the World—Robert Hugh Benson (advanced readers)

The following books are out of print, but check your library or used bookseller:

The Ark—Margot Benary-Isbert
Rowan Farm—Margot Benary-Isbert
Castle on the Border—Margot Benary-Isbert
Dangerous Spring—Margot Benary- Isbert
Toto's Triumph—Claire Huchet Bishop
The Level Land—Dola De Jong
Aleko's Island—Edward Fenton
A Present for Yanya—Peggy Mann
Detour to Danger—Eva Lis Wuorio
Shadow Under the Sea—Geoffrey Trease
Yugoslav Mystery—Arthur Catherall

Timeline

The Sixteenth Century

1517 Beginning of the Protestant Reformation

1543 Death of Nicolaus Copernicus and the date of the publication of his *On the Revolution of Heavenly Spheres*

1582 The promulgation of the Gregorian calendar

The Seventeenth Century

1609 Galileo Galilei constructs a telescope.

1613 Tsar Mikhail I establishes the Romanov dynasty over Russia.

1616 The Holy Office in Rome condemns the Copernican heliocentric theory and commands Galileo to teach it no longer.

1618 Beginning of the Thirty Years' War in Germany

1619 Descartes finds the "light" he was searching for.

1620 Sir Francis Bacon writes his *Novum Organum*.

1621 Johannes Kepler publishes his *Epitome of the Copernican Astronomy*.

1628 Sir William Harvey publishes his *Anatomical Investigation Concerning the Motion of the Heart and Blood in Animals*.

1629 Descartes completes his *Discourse on Method*.

1633 The Holy Office in Rome orders Galileo to recant the heliocentric theory.

1642 Death of Galileo

Birth of Isaac Newton

1648 End of the Thirty Years' War in Germany

1651 Thomas Hobbes publishes *The Leviathan*.

1670 Spinoza begins publishing his *Theological-Political Treatise*.

1682	Ten-year-old Pyotr Alexeivich Romanov proclaimed tsar with sister, Sophia, as regent
1685	King Louis XIV of France revokes the Edict of Nantes.
1686	Newton presents his *Principia Mathematica* to the Royal Society of London.
1688	The "Glorious Revolution" drives King James II from England.
	William III and Mary II become the monarchs of England, Scotland, and Wales.
1689	Tsar Pyotr I takes up his sole rule over Russia.
1690	John Locke publishes his *Two Treatises on Government.*
1696	Pierre Bayle begins publishing *The Historical and Critical Dictionary.*
1697	Tsar Pyotr I sets out on his Great Embassy to the West.
1699	Beginning of the Great Northern War
	The Turks give all of Hungary to the Habsburgs of Austria.

The Eighteenth Century

1700	Pyotr I establishes the Holy Synod over the Russian Orthodox Church.
	Karl XII of Sweden defeats the Russians in the Battle of Narva.
1701	The electorate of Brandenburg becomes the kingdom of Prussia.
1702	Anne becomes queen of England, Scotland, Wales, and Ireland.
1703	Tsar Pyotr I captures the mouth of the Narva River in Swedish–controlled Ingria— the site of the future St. Petersburg.
1711	Karl VI becomes Holy Roman emperor.
1713	Emperor Karl VI issues the Pragmatic Sanction.
1714	George I becomes king of Great Britain.
1715	Death of Louis XIV; Louis XV becomes king of France.
1718	The first of Voltaire's plays performed in Paris
	Death of Karl XII, king of Sweden
1721	End of the Great Northern War
1725	Death of Tsar Pyotr I, the Great
1726	Voltaire goes to England.
1727	Death of Sir Isaac Newton
	George II becomes king of Great Britain.
1728	Jean-Jacques Rousseau becomes Catholic.
1729	Voltaire returns from England to France.
1732	Voltaire publishes his *Philosophical Letters on the English.*

1734	The government of Louis XV condemns Voltaire's *Philosophical Letters*; Voltaire flees Paris for Lorraine.
1738	Emperor Karl VI loses southern Italy and Sicily to Spain.
	Pope Clement XII condemns Freemasonry, forbidding Catholics to have anything to do with Masonic rides and lodges.
1740	Maria Theresia becomes archduchess of Austria and queen of Hungary.
	King Friedrich II of Prussia invades Austrian Silesia; the beginning of the War of the Austrian Succession.
	Benedict XIV becomes pope.
1742	Rousseau visits Paris for the first time.
	The Bavarian elector crowned Emperor Karl VII
1745	Maria Theresia's husband, Franz I, crowned Holy Roman emperor
	Maria Theresia agrees to give Silesia to Friedrich of Prussia; end of the War of the Austrian Succession.
1750	Rousseau publishes *The Discourse on Arts and Sciences*.
1751	Denis Diderot issues the first volume of the *Encyclopedia* (completed in 1772).
1755	Rousseau publishes his *Discourse on the Origins and Foundations of Human Inequality*.
1756	King Friedrich II of Prussia invades Saxony; the beginning of the Seven Years' War.
1757	Friedrich of Prussia's forces defeat the Austrians at Leuthen.
1758	Clement XIII becomes pope.
1758–59	Pombal suppresses the Society of Jesus in Portugal.
1760	The Russians capture Berlin.
	George III becomes king of Great Britain.
1762	Rousseau publishes *The Social Contract*.
	Death of Tsar Pyotr II; Katerina the Great becomes tsarina.
1763	The Treaty of Hubertusburg and the Peace of Paris; end the Seven Years' War.
1764	King Louis XV suppresses the Society of Jesus in France.
1765	Death of Emperor Franz I; Josef II becomes emperor and rules the Habsburg domains with his mother, Maria Theresia.
1768	Beginning of Tsarina Katerina the Great's war with the Turks
1769	Clement XIV becomes pope.
1772	Prussia, Russia, and Austria carry out the First Partition of Poland.
1773	Clement XIV suppresses the Society of Jesus.
1774	End of Katerina the Great's war with the Turks

	Death of Louis XV
1775	Pius VI becomes pope.
	Louis XVI crowned king at Reims
1776	Beginning of the American Revolution
1780	Death of Maria Theresia; Emperor Josef II sole ruler
1782	Pope Pius VI comes to Vienna to protest Emperor Josef II's reforms.
1783	End of the American Revolution
	William Pitt made prime minister of Great Britain
1787	Emperor Josef II grants his subjects complete religious freedom.
1788	Rebellion breaks out in the Austrian Netherlands against Josef II's reforms.
	King Louis XVI announces the convocation of the Estates General.
1789	Opening of the Estates General (May 5)
	The Third Estate forms itself into the National Assembly (June 17).
	The Third Estate takes the Oath of the Tennis Court (June 20).
	King Louis XVI recognizes the National Assembly (June 27).
	The storming of the Bastille (July 14)
	The French National Assembly approves the *Declaration of the Rights of Man and of the Citizen* (August 26).
	Louis XVI forced to return to Paris (October 5)
	The French National Assembly decrees all Church property in France belongs to the state (November 2).
1790	The French National Assembly suppresses all religious houses and monasteries in France (February).
	Seven provinces of the Austrian Netherlands declare independence from Emperor Josef II.
	The French National Assembly approves the *Civil Constitution of the Clergy* (July 12).
	Death of Emperor Josef II; Leopold II becomes emperor.
	Leopold II restores imperial power over the Austrian Netherlands.
1791	Pope Pius VI condemns the *Civil Constitution of the Clergy* (April 13).
	Louis XVI flees Paris for Varennes but is captured and forced to return to Paris (June).
	Emperor Leopold II and King Friedrich Wilhelm II issue the Declaration of Pilnitz (August 27).
	The French National Assembly establishes the Constitution of 1791 (September 3).

1792   Death of Emperor Leopold II

Franz II crowned king of Hungary and Bohemia (March 1)

Louis XVI declares war on Franz II (April 20).

The Duke of Brunswick issues his manifesto (July 25).

The French Legislative Assembly deposes King Louis XVI (August 10).

The September Massacres in Paris

The Battle of Valmy (September 20)

Dumouriez defeats the Austrians at Jemappes (November 6).

King Louis XVI indicted for treason (December 10)

1793   The National Convention condemns Louis XVI to death (January 20).

Execution of Louis XVI (January 21)

France declares war on Great Britain (February 1).

The National Convention establishes the Revolutionary Tribunal (March 10).

The beginning of the revolt in the Vendée (March 10)

Dumouriez flees to the Austrians.

The National Convention establishes the Committee of Public Safety (April 4).

Fontenay falls to the Vendeans (May 25).

Royalists revolt in Lyons.

The National Convention orders the arrest of the Girondins (June 2).

The National Convention approves the Constitution of 1793 (June 23).

Assassination of Marat (July 13)

Robespierre joins the Committee of Public Safety (July 27).

Execution of Marie Antoinette and the Girondins (October)

Beginning of the Terror in the Vendée (October)

The National Convention adopts the Revolutionary Calendar (October 24).

Archbishop Gobel and many of his clergy renounce their priesthood (November 7).

Enthronement of the Goddess of Reason in Notre Dame cathedral (November 10)

The Paris Commune forbids all Catholic worship in the city (November 23).

Toulon falls to the revolutionary army (December 19).

Revolutionary forces destroy the Vendean army (December 23).

1794   Execution of Danton, Desmoulins, and 15 others (April 5)

Festival of the Supreme Being (June 8)

The National Assembly passes the Law of the 22nd Prairial.

The National Assembly condemns Robespierre to death (July 27).

Execution of Robespierre (July 28)

The Committee of Public Safety closes the Jacobin Club (November 12).

1795   Insurrection of the 12th Germinal in Paris (April 1)

Insurrection of the 1st Prairial in Paris (May 20)

The National Convention approves the Constitution of the Year III.

Napoleone Buonaparte saves the Convention with a "whiff of grapeshot" (October 5).

1796   Napoleone Buonaparte begins his invasion of northern Italy (March).

Battle of Mondovi (April 21)

Napoleon's victory at Lodi (May 10)

Napoleon enters Milan (May 15).

Napoleon puts Würmser's Austrians to flight at Bassano (September 8).

Death of Katerina the Great (November 17)

1797   Würmser surrenders to Napoleon at Mantua (February 2).

Pope Pius VI signs the treaty of Tolentino (February 19).

Emperor Franz II signs the preliminary Peace of Leoben (April 18).

1798   General Berthier banishes Pope Pius VI from Rome (February 20).

Napoleon sets out on his invasion of Egypt (May 19).

1799   Napoleon returns to France (August 23).

Death of Pope Pius VI (August 29)

19th Brumaire—Napoleon overthrows the Directory (November 10).

Establishment of the Consulate (Constitution of the Year VIII), the dictatorship of Napoleon Bonaparte (December 15)

The Nineteenth Century

1800   Election of Pope Pius VII (March 14)

Napoleon invades Italy (April).

Napoleon's victory at Marengo (June 14)

Pope Pius VII enters Rome (July 3).

Attempted assassination of Napoleon (December 24)

1801   The Austrians sign an armistice with the French (January 11).

Death of Tsar Pyotr; Aleksandr I becomes tsar (March 24).

Napoleon approves the concordat with Rome (July 16), and Pope Pius VII signs it (August 11).

1802	Napoleon makes peace with Great Britain (March 27).
	The French Senate makes Napoleon First Consul for Life (August 4).
	William Cobbett begins publishing the *Political Register*.
1803	Napoleon proclaims his law code (March 5).
	Napoleon tells his navy to prepare for an invasion of England (March 11).
	Execution of the Duke of Enghien (March 21)
	Great Britain declares war on France (May 16).
1804	The French Senate proclaims Napoleon emperor of France (May 18).
	Pope Pius VII crowns Napoleon emperor (December 2).
1805	Russia and Great Britain (later, Austria) form the Third Coalition against Napoleon.
	Napoleon crowns himself king of Italy (May 26).
	Napoleon turns his army from an invasion of England to fight his enemies in Germany (August).
	Mack surrenders to Napoleon at Ulm (October 20).
	Battle of Trafalgar—Horatio Nelson defeats the French fleet (October 21).
	The Battle of Austerlitz (December 2).
	Emperor Franz II and Napoleon sign the Treaty of Pressburg (December 26).
1806	Formation of the Confederation of the Rhine (July 12)
	Franz II dissolves the Holy Roman Empire (August 6).
	Prussia, Russia, and Great Britain form the the Fourth Coalition (October 6).
	Battles of Jena and Auerstädt (October 14)
	Napoleon issues the Berlin Decrees (November 21).
1807	Battle of Preussisches Eylau (February 7–8)
	Battle of Friedland (June 14)
	Napoleon, Aleksandr I, and Friedrich Wilhelm II sign the Treaty of Tilsit (July 7).
	Junot and French troops occupy Lisbon (December).
1808	Under orders from Napoleon, General Miollis occupies Rome (February 2).
	King Carlos IV forced to abdicate; Fernando VII becomes king of Spain (March).
	Napoleon makes Joseph Bonaparte king of Spain. The Spanish revolt against Bonaparte.
	The English under Wellington defeat the French in Portugal (August).
1809	Saragossa falls to the French (February 20).
	Austria and Great Britain form the Fifth Coalition (April 9).
	Andreas Hofer calls for an uprising against the Bavarians and French.

Napoleon occupies Vienna (May).

Battle of Aspern and Essling (May 21)

Andreas Hofer and the Tyrolese stop the Bavarians at Isel Berg and enter Innsbruck (May 30).

General Miollis published Napoleon's decree abolishing the pope's government (June 10).

Pope Pius VI excommunicates Napoleon.

Battle of Wagram (July 4–6)

Pope Pius VI forced into exile (July 6)

Andreas Hofer establishes himself as governor of the Tyrol in Innsbruck (August).

Napoleon and Emperor Franz I sign the Treaty of Vienna (October 14).

Napoleon divorces Josephine (December).

1810 Andreas Hofer taken prisoner (January)

Andreas Hofer executed in Mantua (February 20)

Napoleon weds Maria Louisa of Austria (April 1–2).

Tsar Aleksandr I violates the Berlin Decrees (December).

1812 Pope Pius VI arrives at Fontainebleau (June 19).

Napoleon begins the invasion of Russia (June 26).

Napoleon defeats the Russians at Smolensk (August 17–18).

Battle of Borodino (September 7)

Napoleon enters Moscow (September 16).

Napoleon retreats from Moscow (October 19).

Napoleon departs for Paris (December).

The remnant of the French army crosses the Niemen (December 14).

Napoleon arrives in Paris, stops an uprising (December 18).

1813 Pope Pius VI signs a new concordat with Napoleon.

Russia, Great Britain, Prussia, and Sweden form the Sixth Coalition (February).

Pius VI repudiates the concordat (March 24).

Napoleon wins a series of victories against the Coalition (May).

Metternich brokers an armistice (June 4).

Austria declares war on Napoleon (August 12).

Napoleon's victory at the Battle of Dresden (August 26-27)

Napoleon defeated at Leipzig (October 16-19)

1814	Joachim Murat, the king of Naples, joins the coalition against Napoleon (January 11).
	Pius VI sent from Fontainebleau (January 23)
	Aleksandr I and the allies "liberate" Paris (April 1).
	The abdication of Napoleon (April 11)
	Napoleon sets out for Elba (April 20).
	Pope Pius VI returns to Rome.
	Louis XVIII enters Paris as king.
	The European powers sign the Treaty of Paris with Louis XVIII (May 30).
	Opening of the Congress of Vienna (November 1)
1815	Napoleon returns to France—the beginning of the Hundred Days (March).
	Napoleon sets out from Paris against the Seventh Coalition (June 12).
	The Congress of Vienna signs its "Final Act" (June 9).
	Napoleon's final defeat at Waterloo (June 18).
	Napoleon passes his throne to his son (June 22).
	Napoleon flees to England.
	Napoleon exiled to St. Helena (August 7)
	Aleksandr I, with Prussia and Austria, form the Holy Alliance (September).
	The Congress of Vienna signs the second Treaty of Paris with Louis XVIII of France; formation of the Quadruple Alliance (November 20).
1819	Rebellion in Spain breaks out against King Fernando VII.
	Peterloo Massacre in England (August)
	Under Metternich's direction, the German diet issues the Karlsbad Decrees (September).
1820	King Fernando VII swears to support the Constitution of 1812.
	The Congress of Tropau issues the Troppau Protocol.
	Death of George III; George IV becomes king of Great Britain.
1821	Beginning of the Greek revolution (April 2)
	Napoleon reconciled to the Church (April 29)
	Death of Napoleon (May 5)
1822	Kolokotrones forces the Turks to retreat from Argos (August 6).
1823	The Quadruple Alliance demands Spain renounce the Constitution of 1812. The Spanish Cortes refuses, and the alliance prepares for war.
	The Quadruple Alliance forces take Madrid (May).
	Death of Pope Pius VI (August 20)

	Leo XII becomes pope (October).
	Revolutionaries in Spain agree to lay down their arms; Fernando VII restored as absolute monarch (October).
1824	Death of Louis XVIII; Charles X becomes king of France.
1825	Ibrahim Pasha takes Pylos from the Greek rebels (April 19).
	Death of Tsar Aleksandr I (December 1); Nikolai I becomes tsar.
	Decembrist uprising quelled in St. Petersburg (December 26)
1827	The Concert of Europe agrees to aid the Greek rebels (July 6).
	Allied victory in the Battle of Navarino (October 20)
1828	Russia declares war on the Ottoman Empire (April 26).
	Nikolai I commences his attacks on the Catholic Church in Russia.
1829	Death of Leo XIII (February 10)
	Pius VIII becomes pope.
	The Catholic Relief Act becomes law in Great Britain (March-April).
	Catholic Irish obtain the right to vote for Parliament and to serve as members of Parliament.
	Russia and the Ottomans sign the Treaty of Adrianople (September 14).
1830	Beginning of the July Revolution in Paris (July 27).
	Abdication of Charles X (July 30)
	Louis-Philippe named "King of the French" (August 7)
	Beginning of the Belgian revolution (August 25)
	Beginning of uprising in Congress Poland (November 29)
	Death of George IV (June 26); William IV becomes king of Great Britain.
	Beginning of Last Laborers' Revolt in England (August)
1831	The *Sejm* declares Poland's independence from Russia (January 25).
	Revolution in Bologna against papal government (February)
	Gregory XVI becomes pope (February 2).
	Polish victory in the Battle of Stoczek (February 14)
	Austrian forces end rebellion in the Papal States (April)
	The Russians take Warsaw; end of the Polish rebellion (September 7)
	Another rebellion breaks out in the Papal States (December).
	Giuseppe Mazzini forms Young Italy.
1832	The Austrians end the second rebellion in the Papal States (January).
	Tsar Nikolai I abolishes Congress Poland (February 26).

Nikolai I forbids the publication of papal bulls in Russia and Russian Poland.

European powers recognize the independence of Greece (May 7).

Earl Grey's reform bill becomes law (June).

Pope Gregory XVI issues *Mirari Vos* (August 15).

1833   Parliament abolishes black slavery in the British Empire.

Death of Fernando VII of Spain; Isabel II becomes queen.

Beginning of the Carlist civil war in Spain.

1837   Death of George IV of Great Britain; Victoria becomes queen.

1840   Death of Friedrich Wilhelm III of Prussia; Friedrich Wilhelm IV becomes king.

1846   Death of Pope Gregory XVI (June 1)

Blessed Pius IX elected pope (June 16)

1847   Pope Pius IX establishes an advisory lay senate for the Papal states (April).

Publication of the *Communist Manifesto*

1848   Rebellion in Sicily against Fernando II (January)

Pius IX institutes government reforms in the Papal Sates (February 10).

Beginning of the revolution in Paris (February 22)

Abdication of Louis Philippe; founding of the Second French Republic (February 24)

Lajos Kossuth's address to the Hungarian diet (March 3)

Riots in Vienna; Metternich resigns (March 13).

Rebellion against Austrian rule breaks out in Milan (March 18).

Proclamation of an independent Venetian Republic (March 22)

King Carlo Alberto of Piedmont-Sardinia invades Lombardy (March 24); the Austrians withdraw from Milan (March 26).

Elections for the Constituent Assembly in France by universal manhood suffrage (March 26)

Revolutionaries take control of the government in Vienna (May 15).

First meeting of the Frankfurt Diet in Germany (May 18)

From Innsbruck, Emperor Ferdinand I calls for resistance to the revolution (May 20).

Insurrection in Prague ends in failure (June 12-18).

Workingmen's rebellion in Paris (June 23-27)

Austrians defeat the Piedmontese at Custoza; Carlo Alberto retreats from Milan (July 24–25).

The Austrian imperial army lays siege to Vienna (October 23).

The Austrian imperial army takes Vienna; end of the Viennese revolution (November 1).

Pope Pius IX flees Rome (November 24).

Abdication of Ferdinand I; Franz Josef becomes Austrian emperor and king of Hungary (December 2).

Lajos Kossuth and the Hungarian Diet refuse to recognize Franz Josef as king of Hungary (December 7).

Louis-Napoleon Bonaparte becomes president of France (December 20).

1849   The Austrians occupy Budapest (January 5).

Proclamation of the Roman Republic (February 9)

Austrians defeat the Piedmontese in the Battle of Novara (March 22–23).

Abdication of Carlo Alberto; Vittorio Emanuele II becomes king of Piedmont-Sardinia (March 23).

The Hungarian Diet proclaims the Republic of Hungary (April 14).

Pope Pius IX calls on Catholic rulers to restore his temporal authority (April 18).

Tsar Nikolai I and Franz Josef form an alliance against Hungary (May).

The Frankfurt Diet disbands (May 21).

French forces breach the walls of Rome (June 29).

The French restore the pope's rule over Rome (July 3).

Austrian and Russian victories over the Hungarians (August)

The Hungarians surrender to the Russians at Világos; end of the Hungarian revolution (August 13).

Venetian revolutionaries surrender to the Austrians (August 27).

1851   President Louis-Napoleon leads a *coup-d'etat* in Paris against the National Assembly (December 2).

1852   Louis-Napoleon announces a new constitution for France (January 14).

Count Cavour becomes prime minister of Piedmont-Sardinia.

Louis-Napoleon becomes Emperor Napoleon III of France (December 2).

1853   Beginning of the Crimean War (October)

France, Great Britain, and Piedmont-Sardinia declare war on Russia (November 30).

1855   Death of Nikolai I; Aleksandr II becomes tsar.

The invention of the Bessemer Process

1856   End of the Crimean War (November 30)

1858   Napoleon III pledges support to Piedmont-Sardinia in a war against the Austrians in Italy.

1859	Austria declares war on Piedmont-Sardinia (April 2).
	The French defeat the Austrians at Montebello (May 20).
	Napoleon III triumphs over Franz Josef at Solferino (June 25).
	Revolutions break out in central Italy.
	France and Austria sign an armistice (July) giving Lombardy to Piedmont-Sardinia.
1860	France and Piedmont-Sardinia sign a treaty at Turin (March).
	Piedmont-Sardinia annexes the central Italian states and papal Romagna.
	Pius IX excommunicates King Vittorio-Emanuele.
	Giuseppe Garibaldi proclaims himself dictator of Sicily (May 12).
	Garibaldi becomes master of Sicily (July 20).
	Garibaldi takes the city of Naples (September 7).
	Vittorio-Emanuele's army attacks and defeats papal forces at Castelfidardo in the Papal States (September 18). Piedmont-Sardinia seizes Umbria and the Marches.
	Vittorio-Emanuele and Cavour enter Naples; Garibaldi surrenders his conquests (November 7).
1861	Proclamation of the kingdom of Italy (March).
	Tsar Aleksandr II abolishes serfdom in Russia (March).
	Death of Friedrich Wilhelm IV; Wilhelm I becomes king of Prussia.
	Emperor Franz Josef issues the October Diploma, establishing the Reichsrat.
1862	Otto von Bismarck named chancellor of Prussia
	The Battle of Reggio; the Italian army keeps Garibaldi from invading the Papal States (August 27).
1864	Napoleon II signs a treaty with Vittorio Emanuele II, promising to withdraw French troops from Rome by 1866 (September 14).
	Pope Pius IX issues *Quanta Cura* and *Syllabus of Errors* (December 8).
1865	Treaty of Gastein (August 14) divides Holstein and Schleswig between Prussia and Austria.
1866	Saying Austria had violated the Treaty of Gastein, Bismarck orders the Prussian army to invade Austrian-held Holstein.
	The German diet orders the mobilization of the federal army against Prussia; the beginning of the Seven Weeks' War (June 14).
	Prussia and Austria sign the Treaty of Prague (August 23); Austria cut off from Germany.
1867	Franz Josef issues the *Ausgleich*, forming the Dual Monarchy.
	Garibaldi begins preparations for the conquest of Rome (April).

Pope Pius IX announces the convocation of the Vatican Ecumenical Council (June 25).

Garibaldi invades the Papal States (September 29).

The British Parliament extends the suffrage.

Battle of Mentana; papal forces stop Garibaldi's invasion (November 3–4).

French Legislative Assembly orders Napoleon III to send more troops to Rome (December 4).

1868   Pius IX convokes the Vatican Ecumenical Council (June 29).

A Liberal revolution in Spain overthrows Queen Isabel II. Amadeo becomes king of Spain.

1869   Under Gladstone, Parliament disestablishes the Church of Ireland.

The Vatican Council opens (December 8).

1870   Bismarck leaks the altered Ems Dispatch to the press.

Under Gladstone, Parliament passes the Land Act for the Irish.

The Vatican Council defines papal infallibility (July 18).

The French government declares war on Prussia (July 19); beginning of the Franco-Prussian War.

The pope learns that France will withdraw its troops from Rome (July 27). The pope suspends the council.

Napoleon III surrenders at Sedan (September 2).

The French Legislative Body deposes Napoleon III and proclaims the Third Republic (September 4).

The Italian army invades the Papal States (September 12).

The Prussians begin the siege of Paris (September 19).

The Italian army lays siege to Rome (September 19).

The papal forces surrender; the fall of the Papal States (September 20).

Vittorio Emanuele II annexes Rome and the Papal States; Pius IX declares the annexation "null and illegal."

1871   Wilhelm II crowned *kaiser* of the German Empire at Versailles (January 18).

Establishment of the French republican National Assembly (March 1)

Establishment of the Paris Commune

The army of the French National Assembly lays siege to Paris (April 2).

The French republic signs the Treaty of Frankfurt with the German Empire (May 10).

French troops enter parts of Paris—beginning of *la semaine sanglante* (May 21).

The Paris Commune executes the archbishop of Paris, the "martyrs of Arcueil," and others (May 24–26).

The fall of the Paris Commune (May 28)

1872   The German *Reichstag* banishes the Jesuits from Germany (July 4); beginning of Bismarck's *Kulturkampf.*

1873   The Prussian *Landtag* approves the first anti-Catholic May Laws.

The Prussian bishops call on Catholics to engage in peaceful resistance to the laws (May 2).

The Prussian bishops announce their non-compliance in the May Laws to Bismarck (May 26).

Germany, Russia, and Austria form the League of Three Emperors.

King Amadeo overthrown; establishment of Spain's First Republic

1874   Overthrow of Spain's First Republic; Alphonso XII becomes king.

1875   Pope Pius IX says Catholics may freely disobey the May Laws (February 5).

The French National Assembly adopts a republican constitution.

1876   Queen Victoria proclaimed Empress of India

Russia agrees to Austria's occupation of Bosnia and Herzegovina.

1878   Death of Vittorio Emanuele II (January); Umberto I becomes king.

Death of Pope Pius IX (February 7)

Election of Pope Leo XIII (February 20)

Bismarck begins his campaign against the German socialists.

King Leopold II of Belgium hires Henry Morton Stanley to found a colony for him along the Congo River in central Africa.

1879   Bismarck begins to relax the *Kulturkampf* (July).

1880   Leo XIII issues the encyclical, *Arcanum Divinae Sapientiae.*

1881   Bismarck begins promoting legislation establishing social insurance in Germany.

Germany, Austria, and Russia enter into a secret treaty promising not to support each others' enemies.

Assassination of Tsar Aleksandr II (March 13); Aleksandr III becomes tsar.

1882   Germany, Austria, and Italy form the Triple Alliance (May).

1885   Several nations recognize the Congo Free State as Leopold II's domain.

Leo XIII issues the encyclical, *Immortale Dei.*

Death of Alfonso XII (November)

1886   Alfonso XIII becomes king of Spain.

Nearly every male in Great Britain gains the right to vote.

1887	Russia pulls out of the alliance with Germany and Austria but enters into a "reinsurance treaty" with Germany.
1888	Death of Kaiser Wilhelm I (March 9); Friedrich II becomes *kaiser*.
	Death of Kaiser Friedrich II; Wilhelm II becomes kaiser.
1890	Wilhelm II dismisses Bismarck (March 18).
	Wilhelm II does not renew the reinsurance treaty with Russia.
1891	France and Russia form an *entente*.
	Last of the May Laws rescinded in Prussia
	Leo XIII issues the encyclical, *Rerum Novarum*.
1893	Leo XIII issues the encyclical, *Providentissimus Deus*.
1894	The Franco-Russian Alliance established
	Death of Tsar Aleksandr III; Nikolai II becomes tsar (November).
1899	National representatives at The Hague work out a convention governing disputes between nations.

The Twentieth Century

1900	Russia moves troops into Manchuria.
	Assassination of Umberto I of Italy; Vittorio Emanuele III becomes king.
1901	Death of Queen Victoria (January 22); Edward VII becomes king.
	France places new restrictions on clergy.
1902	Italy secretly promises France to remain neutral in the event of a war with Germany.
1903	Death of Leo XIII; St. Pius X becomes pope.
	Serbia's King Petar I begins to follow an anti-Austrian, pro-Russian policy.
1904	Beginning of Russo-Japanese War (February 8).
	Great Britain enters into the *Entente Cordiale* with France.
	Japan destroys the Russian fleet (May).
	The Japanese defeat the Russians at Liaoyang.
	The firing of the Putilov factory workers in St. Petersburg
	Italy and Great Britain recognize France's protectorate over Morocco.
1905	Bloody Sunday (January 9) sparks revolution in Russia.
	The French government repudiates the concordat with the Church.
	The Russian army defeated at Mukden (March)
	Kaiser Wilhelm lands at Tangier (March).
	Japan destroys the Russian fleet (May).

	Tsar Nikolai II allows the formation of a *duma* (August).
	End of the Russo-Japanese War (September 5)
	General strike in Russia (October 10–14)
	Mensheviks organize a Soviet of Workers Delegates (October 14).
	Nikolai II issues the *October Manifesto* (October 17).
	Socialist revolution in Moscow crushed; Trotsky arrested (December)
1906	Algeciras Conference recognizes France's right to intervene in Morocco.
	Nikolai II issues the Fundamental Laws (March).
	Formation of the Labor Party in Great Britain
	Stolypin becomes prime minister of Russia (July).
	Austria establishes universal manhood suffrage (December).
1907	Formation of the Anglo-Russian Entente
	The Hague Conference draws up a convention governing warfare.
	Austria annexes Bosnia and Herzegovina.
1909	Under pressure, Serbia says it recognizes the annexation of Bosnia and Herzegovina.
	Revolt of tribes in Morocco (October)
1911	The House of Lords approves the veto bill.
	Moroccan tribes lay siege to Fez (March).
	French troops liberate Fez (May); Germany condemns the French intervention.
	The German imperial warship, *Panther*, anchors at Agadir (July 1).
	Germany makes territorial demands; France ignores them. Great Britain stands with France.
	Italo-Turkish War (September-October); Italy takes Tripoli, Cyrenaica, and the Dodecanese Islands.
	France and Germany sign the Treaty of Berlin (November).
1912	Montenegro declares war on the Ottoman Empire (October 8); beginning of the First Balkan War.
1913	The signing of the Treaty of London, ending the First Balkan War (May 17)
	Bulgaria attacks Greece and Serbia (June 16); beginning of the Second Balkan War.
	The Treaty of Bucharest ends the Second Balkan War (August).
1914	Assassination of Archduke Franz Ferdinand in Sarajevo (June 28)
	Germany agrees to back Austria-Hungary in the event of war (July 6).
	Austria-Hungary sends an ultimatum to Serbia (July 23).
	Serbia agrees to most, but not all, of the ultimatum and begins a partial mobilization of her army.

Emperor Franz Josef declares war on Serbia (July 28).

Tsar Nikolai II orders a mobilization of the Russian army (July 29).

Germany sends ultimatums to Russia (July 30) and France (July 31).

Germany declares war on Russia (August 1).

Germany occupies Luxembourg and invades Belgium (August 2–4).

Great Britain declares war on Germany (August 4).

Montenegro declares war on Austria-Hungary (August 7).

Death of Pope Pius X (August 20)

Benedict XV elected pope (September 3)

Japan declares war on Germany (August 23).

Battle of Tannenberg—the Germans destroy the Russian Second Army (August 26–30).

The First Battle of the Marne (September 6–12)

The Germans cut off the ring of fortresses around Verdun (October 1).

Pope Benedict XV issues his first encyclical, *Ad Beatissimi Apostolorum* (November 1).

1915   Germany announces the opening of unrestricted U-boat warfare (February 4).

The Germans defeat the Russians in the Second Battle of the Masurian Lakes (February 7).

Great Britain and France begin "contraband" blockade of Germany (March 11).

Allied assault on the Dardanelles and Gallipoli fails (March 18).

The Germans first use mustard gas at the Second Battle of Ypres (April 22).

Sinking of the *HMS Lusitania* (May 7)

Italy declares war on Austria-Hungary (May 23).

Beginning of Italian assaults on the Isonzo Front (June 23).

1916   Beginning of the German offensive around Verdun (February 21)

British and French offensive along the River Somme (July 1)

Austria-Hungary opens an offensive from Trentino (May 14).

The Russians open their offensive against the Austrians in Galicia (June 4).

The Italians push the Austro-Hungarians from the Isonzo River and capture Gorizia (August 6–9).

Romanian armies invade Transylvania (August 27).

Germans force the Romanians to retreat from Transylvania (October 4).

The Germans take the Romanian city of Constanza (October 22).

The British call off the offensive on the Somme (November 18).

Death of Emperor Franz Josef; Karl I becomes emperor. (November 21).

The Germans take the Romanian capital, Bucharest (December 6).

Murder of Rasputin in Petrograd (December 29).

1917   Emperor Karl submits his peace proposal to the Entente (January 29).

The German government formally announces that it will resume unrestricted submarine warfare (January 31).

The sinking of the *HMS Laconia* (February 26).

Publication of the Zimmerman note in the American press (March 1).

Beginning of massive strikes in Petrograd (March 8)

Beginning of the Russian revolution (March 11)

Duma delegates in Petrograd set up executive committee to govern the city (March 12), as does the Petrograd Soviet the next day.

Abdication of Tsar Nikolai II (March 15)

The United States declares war on Germany (April 6).

Great Britain rejects Emperor Karl's peace proposal (May 23).

The Bolshevik uprising in Petrograd ends in failure (July 18).

Aleksandr Kerensky becomes prime minister of Russia.

The British open the Third Battle of Ypres (July 31).

Pope Benedict XVI issues his peace proposal (August 1).

Bolsheviks overthrow the Russian government (November 7).

End of the Third Battle of Ypres (November 10).

V.I. Lenin proclaims the victory of the "workers' and peasants' revolution" in Russia (November 19).

The Soviet government opens peace talks with Germany (December 22).

A period of disorder begins in Spain.

1918   The Bolsheviks dissolve the Russian constituent assembly (January 6).

President Wilson issues his "Fourteen Points" for peace (January 8).

The Treaty of Brest-Litovsk signed between Russia and Germany (March 3).

Germany opens her last great offensive on the Western Front (March 21).

The Austro-Hungarians begin their retreat across the Piave (June 22).

The Germans open their *Friedensturm* offensive (July 15), which ends in failure two days later.

Assassination of Tsar Nikolai II and his family (July 17)

The Allies begin their offensive against the Germans (July 18).

V.I. Lenin shot in Moscow (August 30)—the beginning of the Red Terror

Germany sends a note to President Wilson, accepting peace based on the Fourteen Points (October 3).

Emperor Karl issues his "People's Manifesto" (October 10).

Austria-Hungary and Italy agree to a truce (November 2).

German and Allied governments begin armistice talks (November 8).

Kaiser Wilhelm's abdication announced (November 9)

Emperor Karl I steps down from power (November 11).

The armistice signed, ending the war (November 11)

1919   Benito Mussolini establishes the *Fasci di Combattimento* (March).

Béla Kun proclaims the Hungarian Soviet Republic (March 21).

Communists establish a soviet republic in Bavaria (April).

Freikorps overthrow the Bavarian soviet government (May).

Germany signs the Treaty of Versailles, including the "Covenant of the League of Nations" (June 28).

Establishment of Germany's Weimar Republic (July)

Béla Kun forced to flee from Hungary (August 1)

1920   Admiral Miklós Horthy elected regent of Hungary (March 1)

Emperor Karl I returns to Hungary but is unable to resume power (October).

Mussolini and the Fascists commence their campaign of violence and terror.

1921   Famine strikes Russia.

Lenin institutes the New Economic Policy.

Adolf Hitler becomes the *Führer* of the Nazi Party.

1922   Death of Pope Benedict XV (January 22)

Pius XI elected pope (February 6)

Lenin intensifies persecution of Christians.

The tenth All-Russian Congress of Soviets establishes the Union of Soviet Socialist Republics (USSR) (December).

Josif Stalin elected general secretary of the Communist Party

Germany declared in default in her reparations payments (December)

1923   General Miguel Primo de Rivera becomes dictator of Spain under Alfonso XIII (September 13).

Adolf Hitler and Erich Ludendorff lead the Beer Hall Putsch (November 8).

1924   Death of Lenin (January 21)

The Dawes Committee comes up with a payment plan for Germany (August).

Mussolini and the Fascists commence their march on Rome (October).

	King Vittorio Emanuele III makes Mussolini prime minister of Italy (October).
1925	Under Stalin's influence, the Communist Party forces Lev Trotsky to resign as commissar for war.
1928	Stalin expels Trotsky and his supporters from Russia.
	Mussolini abolishes all non-Fascist youth groups.
	Stalin announces his first Five-Year Plan.
1929	Trotsky flees to Turkey (February).
	The Holy See and Mussolini sign the Lateran Treaty establishing the Vatican City State, as well as a concordat (February 11).
	Stalin confirmed as dictator of the USSR (April)
	Stalin orders the collectivization of farms and the liquidation of the kulaks.
	The beginning of the worldwide economic crash
1930	Primo de Rivera resigns (January 28).
	Republican uprising in Spain put down (December)
1931	Mussolini's government violates the concordat with the Holy See.
	Alfonso XIII goes into exile; establishment of the Second Spanish Republic.
	Pope Pius XI issues the encyclical *Non Abbiamo Bisogno*, condemning Mussolini (June 29).
	Pope Pius XI issues the encyclical, *Quadragesimo Anno*.
1932	In elections, the Nazi Party becomes the largest party in the *Reichstag*.
	Engelbert Dollfuss becomes chancellor of Austria (May).
	Beginning of Stalin's forced starvation of the Ukrainians.
	Stalin announces his Five-Year Plan against the Church.
1933	President Hindenburg appoints Adolf Hitler chancellor of Germany (January 30).
	The German government arrests Communist leaders and their followers following the February 27 burning of the *Reichstag* building. The government suspends constitutional guarantees.
	Dollfuss becomes dictator of Austria (March).
	Hitler appointed dictator for four years (April 1)
	Hitler's government arrests Center Party and Bavarian People's Party Members (April-June).
	Germany and the Holy See sign a concordat (July 20).
	Hitler begins violating the concordat (August).
	Austria establishes an authoritarian government under Dollfuss (September).
	Stalin announces his second Five-Year Plan.

1934	Dollfuss crushes the Austrian socialists (February).
	Dollfuss assassinated (July 25)
	Hitler becomes president of Germany (August).
1935	Hitler's government deprives Jews of citizenship.
	Hitler begins to violate the Versailles treaty (March 16).
	Great Britain, France, and Italy pledge to resist Hitler's attempts to rearm (April 14).
	Italy invades Ethiopia (October).
1936	Hitler moves German troops into the Rhineland (March).
	Italian troops capture Addis Ababa (May 5).
	The League of Nations places sanctions on Italy.
	Beginning of the Spanish Civil War (July)
	Stalin begins his great purges (August).
	Francisco Franco named head of the Nationalist government of Spain (October1)
	Hitler and Mussolini sign a treaty of friendship (October).
1937	Pope Pius XI condemns National Socialism in the encyclical, *Mit Brennender Sorge*.
	Pope Pius XI condemns Communism in *Divini Redemptoris*.
1938	German troops invade Austria (March 12).
	Hitler proclaims Austria's *Anschluss* with Germany (March 13).
	France and Great Britain allow Hitler to annex Sudetenland (September).
1939	Death of Pope Pius XI (February 10)
	Pius XII crowned pope (March 12)
	The Loyalist government surrenders to Franco and the Nationalists. End of the Spanish Civil War (March)
	German troops occupy Prague.
	Great Britain and France pledge to protect Poland, Romania, Greece, and Turkey (March 31).
	Italy invades Albania (April).
	Hitler and Stalin sign a non-aggression pact and agree to divide up Poland between them (August 23).
	Germany and the Soviets invade Poland (September).
	Great Britain and France declare war on Germany (September 3); beginning of the Second World War.
	Germany and Japan enter into a mutual defensive alliance.
	Stalin forces Lithuania, Latvia, and Estonia to accept Soviet rule.
	Stalin forces Romania to surrender territories to the Soviet Union.

1940	Stalin orders the bombing of Helsinki; Finland surrenders territory to the Soviets.
	Germany invades Denmark (April) and then advances into Norway.
	Germany invades Belgium and Holland (May).
	Churchill and his cabinet approve strategic bombing raids on German cities (May).
	Italy declares war on France (June 10).
	The Germans capture Paris (June 14).
	France signs an armistice with Germany (June 21).
	German strategic airstrikes hit Britain's coastal towns (August).
	German airstrikes hit London (September).
	Italian forces invade Egypt from Libya (September).
	Italian forces invade Greece (October).
	The British push the Italians back into Libya (December).
1941	The Greeks drive the Italians back into Albania (January).
	The Germans drive the British out of Libya (February).
	The Germans conquer Greece and Crete (April).
	The British drive the Italians from Ethiopia (May).
	Hitler decides on the extermination of the Jewish race (June).
	Hitler breaks the non-aggression pact with Stalin (June 22).
	The German invasion of Russia begins.
	The Japanese attack Pearl Harbor (December 7).
	The United States declares war on Japan (December 8).
	Germany declares war on the United States (December 11).
1942	The Battle of Stalingrad begins (July).
	The Allies invade North Africa in Operation Torch (autumn).
	The British drive the Germans from Egypt (October).
1943	Roosevelt and Churchill meet at Casablanca (January).
	The Germans surrender at Stalingrad (January 31).
	British and Americans take Tunis and Bizerte (May 7).
	Rommel surrenders the German army in North Africa (May 13).
	The Allies invade and conquer Sicily (July-August).
	The Allies bomb Rome (July 9).
	King Vittorio Emanuele III forces Mussolini's resignation (July 25).
	Italy surrenders to the Allies (September 3).
	Roosevelt, Churchill, and Stalin meet at Teheran (November 28–December 1).

1944	The Allies liberate Rome (June 4).
	D-Day (June 6)
	The Soviets take Warsaw (July).
	The Allies liberate Paris (August 25).
	The Battle of the Bulge (December)
1945	The Russians reach the Oder River (January 31).
	Churchill, Roosevelt, and Stalin meet at Yalta (February 4–11).
	The Allies bomb Dresden (February 13).
	Death of Franklin Delano Roosevelt; Henry Truman becomes president of the United States (April 12).
	The Russians encircle Berlin (April 25).
	Hitler commits suicide (April 28).
	Germany and the Allies sign an armistice (May 8).
	The United States drops atomic bombs on Hiroshima and Nagasaki (August 6 and 9).
	The French vote to form a new government (October).
	The charter of the United Nations approved (October 24)
1946	Abdication of King Vittorio Emanuele III (May); he names his son, Umberto II, king.
	Italian voters approve the overthrow of the monarchy and the establishment of a republic.
	France approves a new constitution, forming the Fourth Republic (October).
1947	Western European countries suffer financial collapse.
	Formation of the Warsaw Pact
1948	Communists overthrow the government of Czechoslovakia (February).
	The U.S. Congress approves the Marshall Plan (April 3).
	The Soviets begin the blockade of Berlin (June).
	The Allies form an airlift to Berlin.
1949	Formation of the North Atlantic Treaty Organization (April 4).
	The Soviets lift the Berlin Blockade (May).
	Formation of the Federal Republic of Germany (West Germany)
	The Soviet Union successfully tests its first atomic bomb (August).
	The Soviets form the German Democratic Republic (East Germany) (October).
1955	West Germany becomes a full, sovereign state.
1957	The Treaty of Rome forms the European Economic Community (March 25).

1958	Death of Pope Pius XII (October 9)
	John XXIII elected pope (October 28)
1959	Pope John XXIII announces the convocation of an ecumenical council (January 25).
1961	East Germany begins building the Berlin Wall.
1962	Pope John XXIII opens the Second Vatican Council (October 11).
1963	Death of Pope John XXIII (June 3)
	Paul VI becomes pope.
1965	The close of the Second Vatican Council (December 8)
1969	The Holy See issues the revised Roman Rite of the Mass.
1978	Death of Pope Paul VI (August 6)
	John Paul I elected pope (August 26)
	Death of Pope John Paul I (September 28)
	John Paul II elected pope (October 16)
1989	The Berlin Wall demolished
1990	Reunion of East and West Germany (October 3)
1993	Formation of the European Union
1994	Germany establishes Berlin as its capital.
2000	Pope John Paul II beatifies Pius IX and John XXIII.
2005	Death of Blessed Pope John Paul II (April 2)
	Benedict XVI elected pope (April 16)

Pronunciation Guide

Introduction

Albertus Magnus	ahl-BAYR-toos MAH-nyoos *or* MAHG-noos
Eppur si muove	EH-puhr see MWOH-vay
experimentum	eks-PEHR-ih-MEHN-toom
Galileo Galilei	gah-lih-LAY-oh gah-lih-LAY-ee
Instauratio Magna	IN-stau-RAH-tsee-oh MAH-nyah *or* MAHG-nah
Tycho Brahe	TEE-koh BRAH-ha

Chapter 1

François-Marie Arouet	frahn-SWAH mah-REE AH-rouh-ay
Pierre Bayle	pee-AYR BELL
René Descartes	reh-NAY day-KART
Denis Diderot	DEH-nee DEE-deh-roh
Maine	men
Chevalier de Rohan	sheh-VAH-lee-ay duh RO-ahn

Chapter 2

Albrecht	AHL-brekht
Alexei	ah-lex-AY
*Brunswick-Wolfenbüttel	BROONS-vihk VOHL-fen-BÜT-tehl
Franz	frahnts
Friedrich Wilhelm	FREE-drikh VIHL-helm
Fyodor	FYOH-dor
Hohenzollern	HOH-hehn-TSOHL-lehrn
Ivan	EE-vahn
Jacques Duhan de Jandun	zhahk DOO-ahn duh ZHAN-duhn

Hans Hermann von Katte	hahns HAIR-mahn fohn KAHT-teh
Kaunitz	COW-nihtz
Leopold	LAY-oh-pohld
Maria Teresia	mah-REE-ah teh-RAY-see-ah
Maximilian Josef	mahks-ee-MEE-lee-ahn YOH-sef
Mikhail	mikh-AH-il
Moriamur pro rege nostro	moh-ree-AH-moor proh RAY-gay (or RAY-jay) NOH-stroh
Rheinsberg	RINES-behrg
Madame de Pompadour	mah-DAHM duh POHM-pah-door
Pyotr Alexeievich Romanov	PYUH-tr ah-lex-AY-yeh-vyitch ruh-MAH-nuhf

Chapter 3

abbé	ah-BEH
Antoine Arnauld	ahn-TWAHN ar-NOH
Au Louis d'Argent	oh loo-EE DAHR-jahn
Giovanni Battista	jyoh-VAH-nee bah-TEES-tah
Joachim-Pierre de Bernis	jwoah-KEEM pee-AYR duh BEHR-nee
Loménie de Brienne	loh-mehn-YEE duh bree-EHN
Sebastião de Carvalho e Mello	seh-BAHS-tee-ow cahr-VAHL-yoh eh MEHL-yoh
Clairvaux	KLAIR-voh
Paolo Danei	POW-loh dah-NAY-ee

Janssens	YAHN-sens
José (Portuguese)	joh-SZAY
parlement	PAHR-leh-mahn
père	payr
Polignac	pohl-een-YAK
Pombal	POHM-bahl
Rohan	ROH-ahn
Saint-Sulpice	sahn sool-PEES
Ypres	EE-prah *or* EEP

Chapter 4

Autun	OH-toon
Châlons	SHAH-lohn
Champs de Mars	shahmp duh MAHRS
Coblenz	KOH-blents
Cordeliers	kohr-dehl-YAY
Georges Danton	zhorzh DAHN-tohn
Camille	kah-MEEL
Desmoulins	DEH-mou-lahn
Dumouriez	doo-MOHR-ee-ay
*Johann Wolfgang	YOH-hahn VOHLF-gahng
von Goethe	fohn GÖ-teh
Hôtel de Ville	oh-TEHL duh VIL
Marat	mah-RAH
métayer	MEH-tah-yehr
Reims	rahnz
Sainte-Menehould	sahnt MEH-neh-hol
Emmanuel	eh-MAHN-yoo-ehl
Joseph Sieyès	zhoh-SEF see-YEHS
Charles Maurice	sharl mow-REES
Talleyrand-	duh TAHL-leh-rahn
Périgord	PEHR-ee-gor
Poitou	PWAH-too
Tuileries	TWEE-leh-ree
Varennes	VAH-ren
Vendée	VAHN-day

Chapter 5

Garat	GAH-rah
Joseph-Ignace	zho-SEF ig-NYAS
Guillotin	GEE-oh-tahn
la guillotine	lah GEE-oh-teen

Place de la	PLAHS duh lah
République	REH-pyoob-LEEK
Quel homme!	kehl OHM
Quelle résignation!	kehl reh-see-NAH-tsyohn
Quel courage!	kehl coor-AHJ
Vergniaud	VEHR-nee-oh
Vive la République	veev lah REH-pyoob-LEEK
Quesnay	KEH-nay

Chapter 6

Anjou	AHN-zhoo
Barras	BAH-rah
Billaud-Varennes	BEE-yoh VAH-ren
Blois	BLWAH
Bocage	BOH-kajh
Napoleone	nah-POH-lay-OH-nay
Buonaparte	bwoh-nah-PAR-tay
Lazare Carnot	lah-ZAHR CAHR-noh
Jean-Baptiste	zhahn-bah-TEEST
Carrier	CAH-ree-ay
Cathelineau	cah-tehl-ih-NOH
Chaumette	sho-METT
Collot d'Herbois	coh-LOH dehr-BWAH
Condé	KOHN-dee
Couthon	COO-tohn
Dauphin	DOH-fahn
Fabre d'Eglantine	FAH-breh DEH-glahn-teen
Enragés	AHN-rah-jhay
Fouché	FOO-shay
Fontenay	FAHN-teh-nay
Gigot d'Elbee	zhih-GOH dehl-BAY
Grégoire	GREHG-wah
Languedoc	LAHN-geh-dohk
Louis-Charles	LOO-ee SHARL
Maillard	MAY-yard
Mainz	meynts
Marseilles	MAR-say
Marseillaise	mar-seh-YAYZ
Murat	MOO-rah
Jacques Hébert	zhahk EH-bayr
Maximin Isnard	max-ee-MAHN EES-nahr
Nantes	nahnt
Nivôse	NEE-voh-seh

Provence	PROH-vahns
Hérault de	HER-oh duh
Séchelles	SEH-shell
Antoine de	ahn-TWAHN duh
Saint-Just	SAHN-zhoost
sans-culottes	sahn cyoo-LOHT
Thermidor	TAYR-mee-dohr
Toulon	TOO-lohn
Valenciennes	VAH-lahn-syen
Vendémiare	vahn-dah-mee-AYR
Wattignies	WAH-tee-nyee

Chapter 7

Augereau	OH-jehr-oh
Baden	BAH-den
Barthélemy	bar-TEH-leh-mee
Beauharnais	BOH-ahr-nay
Berthier	BEHR-tyay
Bologna	boh-LOHN-yah
Napoleon	nah-POH-leh-ohn
Bonaparte	BOH-nah-part
Chiaramonti	kee-AHR-ah-MOHN-tee
Ercole Consalvi	ehr-COHL-lay kohn-SAHL-vee
Léonard Duphot	LEH-oh-nard DOO-foh
Enghien	AHN-gyen
l'Ecole Militaire	LEH-cohl MIH-lih-tayr
Fréjus	FRAY-zhoos
San Giorggio	sahn jee-OR-jee-oh
Maggiore	mah-jee-OHR-ay
Hesse	HEHS-seh
Leoben	lay-OH-ben
Lépeaux	LEH-poh
Jean-Siffrein	zhahn sih-FREN
Maury	mohr-EE
Nice	nees
palazzo	pah-LAH-tsoh
Peregrinus	pehr-eh-GREE-noos
apostolicus	ah-poh-STOH-lee-coos
moriens in exilio	MOH-ree-ehns in ex-EE-lee-oh
Reveillière	reh-vehl-lee-EHR
Roger-Ducos	ROH-zhay DOO-cohs
Romagna	roh-MAHN-yah

Vivat imperator	VEE-vaht im-pehr-AH-tohr
in aeternum	in ay-TAYR-noom
*Dagobert	DAH-goh-behrt
Würmser	VÜRM-sehr

Chapter 8

Auerstädt	OW-ehr-shtayt
Bagration	bug-ruht-see-OHN
Borodino	bor-oh-DEE-noh
Cádiz	KAH-dees
Dnieper	NEE-pehr
Donäuwurth	DOH-noy-voort
Grande Armée	grahnd AHR-may
Jena	YAY-nah
Jean-Andoche Junot	zhahn ahn-dohsh ZHOO-noh
Johann	YOH-hahn
Kutuzov	koo-TOO-tsoff
Luise	loo-EES-ah
Metternich	MEH-tehr-nikh
Passeyr	PAHS-sair
Radet	RAH-day
Sandwirth	SAHND-veert
Schönbrunn	SCHÖN-broon
Villeneuve	VIL-nuv
Wagram	VAH-grahm
Wirtshaus	VEERTS-house
*Württemberg	VÜRT-tehm-bayrg

Chapter 9

Angoulême	AHN-goo-LEHM
Blücher	BLÜ-khair
Castlereagh	CA-sel-ray
Jan Dvorák	YAHN d-VOHR-zhahk
Thaddäus Hübl	tahd-DAY-oos HÜ-bl
Leipzig	LIPE-tsikh
Ligny	LIH-nyee
Lützen	LÜTS-ehn
Kotzebue	KOHT-tseh-boo
Joseph de Maistre	zhoh-SEF duh MEHST-reh
Poniatowski	POHN-yah-TOV-skee
Quatre-Bras	CAHT-re brah
Reichstadt	REIKH-shtaht

Tugendbund	TU-gent-boont
Vittorio	vih-TOR-ee-oh
Emanuele	eh-MAHN-oo-EH-lay

Chapter 10

Chlapowski	chlah-POV-skee
Diebitsch	DEE-bitsh
Germanos	gehr-MAH-nohs
*Göttingen	GÖT-teen-gehn
Jena	YAY-nah
Kolokotrones	koh-LOHK-oh-TROH-nays
Missolonghi	mis-soh-LOHN-gee
Des Knaben	dehs KNAH-ben
Wunderhorn	VOON-dehr-horn
Märchen	MARE-khen
Nikolai	NIH-koh-lye
Olszynka	ol-SINK-ah
Grochowska	groh-CHOV-skah
Paskievitch	PAHS-kee-EH-vitch
Sejm	SIME
Friedrich von	FREE-drikh fohn
Schlegel	SHLAY-gehl
Stoczek	STOH-tsek
Szczyt	sh-chit
Ludwig Tieck	LOOD-vig TEEK
Dorothea Veit	DOR-oh-TAY-ah FITE
Wackenroder	WAH-ken-ROH-dehr
Otto von	AH-toh fohn
Wittelsbach	WIT-tels-bakh
Demetrios	de-MEH-tree-ohs
Ypsilanti	IP-sil-AHN-tee

Chapter 11

Artois	AHR-twah
Massimo	MAHS-see-moh
D'Azeglio	dahts-AY-lee-oh
Louis Blanc	LOO-ee BLAHNK
Carlo Felice	CAHR-loh feh-LEE-chay
Guglielmo del	goo-lee-EHL-moh del
Carretto	cahr-RET-toh
Louis Eugène	LOO-ee OO-zhen
Cavaignac	cah-vayn-YAHK
Charles Philippe	SHARL fil-LEEP

Annibale Della	ahn-ee-BAH-lay DEH-lah
Genga	GEHN-gah
Pasquale	pahs-KWAH-lay
Tommaso Gizzi	toh-MAH-soh GEE-tsee
Guizot	gee-ZOH
Henri	AHN-ree
Lamartine	lah-mahr-TEEN
Luigi	loo-EE-jee
Lambruschini	lahm-broo-SKEE-nee
Ledru-Rollin	leh-DROO roh-LAHN
La Giovine Italia	lah JYOH-vee-nay
	ih-TAH-lee-ah
Mastai-Ferretti	mah-STYE fehr-REHT-tee
Giuseppe Mazzini	joo-SEP-pay mah-TSEE-nee
Ciro Menotti	CHIR-oh meh-NOH-tee
Mirari Vos	mih-RAH-ree VOHS
La Muette de	la moo-ETT duh
Portici	POR-tih-tsi
Noirot	nwhah-ROH
Proudhon	PROO-dohn
Rouvroy	roo-VWAH
Saint-Simon	sahn see-MOHN
Saxe-Coburg	SAKHS-eh KOH-boorg
Gotha	GOH-tah
Adolphe Thiers	ah-DOLF TYAIR
Willem	VIL-lem

Chapter 12

Bundestag	BOON-dehs-tahg
canaille	CAH-nye
Eugénie de	oo-jeh-NEE duh
Montijo	MOHN-tee-ho
Görgei	GIR-geh-ih
Ferencz Gyulai	FER-ents GYOO-lah-ee
Haynau	HIGH-now
Lajos Kossuth	LYE-osh KOH-zhoot
Lamoricière	lah-mohr-ih-cee-AYR
Daniele Manin	dah-nee-AY-lay mah-NEEN
Oudinot	oo-deh-NOH
Plombières	PLOHM-byair
Pozsony	poh-ZHON-ee
Re' Bomba	RAY BOHM-bah
Reichsrat	RYEKHS-raht

risorgimento	rih-sorj-ih-MEHN-toh
Szöreg	SZHIR-ehg
Ticino	tih-CHEE-noh
Zu Windischgrätz	tsoo VIN-dish-grayts

Chapter 13

Bakunin	bah-KOO-nihn
Daguerre	dah-GEHR
Klemens August Droste-Vischering	KLEH-mehns ow-GOOST DROH-steh FISH-ehr-eeng
Martin von Dunin	MAHR-teen fohn DOO-neen
Engels	AYN-gehls
Gnesen	GNEH-sen
Das Kapital	dahs KAH-pee-tahl
Rheinische Zeitung	RYE-neesh-eh TSYE-toong

Chapter 14

à Berlin	ah behr-LIHN
Aeterni Patris	ay-TEHR-nee PAH-trees
Bazaine	bah-ZEN
Christian	KRIS-tee-ahn
Civitavecchia	chee-vee-ta-VAYK-ee-ah
Coulmiers	cool-me-AY
Deutsches Reich	DOY-tshehs RYEKH
Gastein	GAH-shtine
*Göttingen	GÖT-tin-gehn
Junker	YOON-kehr
Kanzler	KAHNTZ-lehr
Königrätz	KÖN-ikh-grayts
Kulturkampf	kool-TOOR-kahmpf
Landtag	LAHNT-tag
Patrice Mac-Mahon	pah-TREES mahk-mah-OHN
Meuse	mooz
Helmuth von Moltke	HEL-moot fohn MOLT-keh
Quanta Cura	KWAHN-tah COO-rah
Proficiscere anima Christiana	proh-fih-CHEE-sehr-ay AH-nee-mah KREES-tee-AH-nah
Roma o morte!	ROH-mah oh MOHR-tay
Schleswig	SHLES-vig

Windthorst	VINT-horst
zu Paris	tsoo pah-REES

Chapter 15

Arcueil	AR-cuhl
Au Milieu Des Sollicitudes	oh MIHL-lyoo day soh-lihs-ee-TOOD
Arcanum Divinae Sapientiae	ar-CAH-noom dih-VEE-nay sah-pee-EHN-tsee-ay
Boer	boor *or* bör
Boulanger	boo-lahn-ZHAY
Bourard	boo-RAHRD
Captier	cahp-TYAY
Cathala	cah-tah-LAH
Chatagneret	sha-tah-nyehr-AY
Cheminal	shem-ee-NAHL
Georges Clemenceau	Jorj cleh-mahn-SOH
Cottrault	coht-TROH
Darboy	DAR-bwah
Delhorme	del-ORM
Dintroz	DIN-trohs
Entente Cordiale	AHN-tahnt COHR-dee-ahl
Philippe D'Orléans	fil-LEEP DOR-lay-ahn
Gauquelin	goh-kel-LAHN
Aimé Gros	ay-MEE GROH
Immortale Dei	im-mohr-TAH-lay DAY-ee
Lili'uokalani	LEE-lee-woh-kah-LAH-nee
Marce	Mar-SEH
Montmarte	MOH-mahrt
Petit	peh-TEET
Providentissimus Deus	proh-vee-den-TEE-see-moos DAY-oos
Rerum Novarum	RAYR-oom noh-VAH-room
Secchi	SEHK-ee
semaine sanglante	seh-MEHN SAHN-glahnt
Tirpitz	TIHR-pits
Voland	voh-LAHN

Chapter 16

Alois Lexa von Aehrenthal	AH-loys LEKH-sah fohn AYR-ehn-tahl
Ausgleich	OWS-glyekh
Berchtold	BAYRKH-tolt
Theobald von Bethmann-Hollweg	TAY-oh-balt fohn BEHT-mahn HOLE-vayg
Bernhard von Bülow	BAYRN-hart fohn BÜ-lohv
Nedjelko Čabrinović	nehd-YEL-koh chah-brin-OH-vich
Théophile Delcassé	TAY-oh-fil DEL-cahs-eh
Dragutin Dimitriejević	drah-GOO-tihn dee-MEE-tree-yay-vich
duma	DOO-mah
Foch	FOHSH
Georgy Apollonovich Gapon	gyi-AWR-gee ah-poh-loh-NYOH-vyich GAH-pohn
Giolitti	jee-oh-LEE-tee
Trifko Grabež	TRIF-koh GRAH-bezh
Hötzendorf	HÖT-tsen-dorf
Italia irredenta	ee-TAH-lee-ah ihr-eh-DEHN-tah
Erich von Ludendorff	EH-reekh fohn LOO-den-dorf
Kiderlen-Wächter	KIH-dehr-len VAYKH-tehr
narodniki	NAH-rode-NIH-kee
Österreich Este	ÖS-tehr-ryekh EH-steh
Nikola Pašić	NIH-koh-lah PASH-eetch
Georgy Valentinovich Plekhanov	gyi-AWR-gee vuh-lyin-TEE-nyuh-vyich plyi-KAH-nuf
Raymond Poincaré	RAY-mohnd pohn-CARE-eh
Maurice Rouvier	MAW-rees ROO-vyay
Pyotr Arkadyevich Stolypin	PYUH-tr ar-kahd-YEH-vyitch stuh-LEE-pyin
Istvá Tisza	ISHT-vah TIHS-sah

Chapter 17

Ad Beatissimi	ahd BAY-ah-TEE-see-mee
Arras	AH-ras
Armentìeres	AHR-mehn-tyehr
Baden	BAH-den
Basée	BAH-say-eh
Giacomo Giambattista Della Chiesa	jee-AH-coh-moh jyam-bah-TEES-tah DAY-lah KYAY-sah
Compiègne	COHM-pyen
Dicke Bertha	DIH-keh BAYR-tah
Friedensturm	FREE-den-shtoorm
Hertling	HEHR-tleeng
Messines	MEH-seen-eh
Michaelis	mih-KAY-lihs
Eugenio Pacelli	AY-oo-JAY-nee-oh pah-CHEL-lee
Passhendaele	PAH-shun-dell
Pétain	PEH-tahn
Piave	pee-AH-vay
Vladimir Mitrofanovich Purishkevich	VLAH-dih-meer MEE-truh-FAH-nyuh-vyitch poor-ish-KYAY-vyitch
Rasputin	rahs-POO-teen
Somme	sum
Walter Schwieger	VAHL-tehr SHWEE-gehr
Unterseeboot	OON-tehr-szay-BOHT
Xavier	ZAH-vyay
Ypres	EE-prah *or* EEP
Felix Yusupov	FAY-leeks yoo-SOO-puf
Zeppelin	TSEP-peh-lin
Zürich	ZÜ-reekh

Chapter 18

Arkhangelsk	ahr-KHANG-gelsk
Il Duce	il DOO-chay
Fasci di Combattimento	FASH-ee dee cohm-baht-tee-MEHN-toh
Freikorps	FRYE-korps
Führer	FÜR-ehr
Miklós Horthy	MIHK-lohsh HOR-tee
Joseb Besarionis dze Jugashvili	YO-sef be-SAH-ree-oh-nis YOO-gash-VEE-lee

Károly — KAHR-oh-lwee

Béla Kun — BAY-lah koon

Lüttwitz Putsch — LÜTT-veets POOTSH

Tomáš Masaryk — toh-MASH MAH-sah-rik

Mit Brennender Sorge — miht brehn-NEHN-dehr ZOR-geh

Non Abbiamo Bisogno — nohn ah-bee-AH-moh bee-SOHN-yoh

Pax Christi in regno Christi — pahks KREE-stee in RAY-nyoh KREE-stee

Achille Ratti — ah-KEEL-lay RAHT-tee

Philipp Scheidemann — FIHL-leep SHYE-deh-mahn

Baldur von Schirach — BAHL-door fohn SHEER-akh

Schutzstaffeln — SHOOTS-shtahf-fehln

Sturmarbeilung — shtoorm-ahr-BYE-loong

tigre — TEEG-ruh

Volk — fohlk

Völker — VÖLK-ehr

Weimar — VYE-mahr

Yekaterinburg — yeh-KAH-teh-reen-boorg

Chapter 19

Anschluss — AHN-shloos

Azaña — ah-ZAH-nyah

bezbozhnik — behz-BUHZH-neek

Bukharin — boo-KHAR-een

Caudillo de, España por la Gracia de Dios — cow-DEE-yoh day eh-SPAH-nyah, pohr lah grah-SEE-ah day DEE-ohs

Danzig — DAHN-tsig

Divini Redemptoris — dee-VEE-nee ray-dehmp-TOHR-ees

Engelbert Dollfuss — AYN-gehl-bayrt DOHL-foos

Española de Derechas Autónomas — ehs-pah-NYO-lah day deh-RAY-chas ow-TOH-noh-mahs

Falange Española Tradicionalista — fah-LAHN-hay ehs-pah-NYO-lah trah-DEE-see-oh-nah-LEES-tah

Heimwehr — HYME-vayr

Holodomor — hoh-loh-doh-MOHR

Lev Borisovich Kamenev — lev bohr-ees-OH-vyitch kah-MAY-neff

Sergei Kirov — SAYR-gay KEER-off

Khrushchev — KHROOSH-sheff

Nationalrat — nah-tsee-oh-NAHL-raht

Juan Negrín — hwahn nay-GREEN

Ostmark — OHST-mahrk

Pétain — PEH-tahn

Quadragesimo Anno — kwah-drah-JAY-see-moh AHN-noh

Haile Selassie — HAY-luh SLAH-say

Kurt von Schuschnigg — koort fohn SHOO-shnig

Lebensraum — LAY-behns-rowm

Schutzbund — SHOOTS-boont

Sudetenland — soo-DAY-tehn-LAHNT

Vaterländische Front — fah-tehr-LAYN-dee-sheh FROHNT

Vizcaya — viz-KYE-ah

Genrikh Yagoda — GEHN-reech yah-GOH-dah

Grigory Yevseevich Zinoviev — GREE-gohr-yee yev-SAY-yeh-vyitch zih-NUH-vee-eff

Chapter 20

aggiornamento — ah-jyoor-nah-MEHN-toh

Auschwitz — OW-shvitz

Belzec — BEL-zhets

Chelmno — KHEL-meh-noh

Dignitatis Humanae — dih-nyee-TAH-tees (or dig-nee-TAH-tees) hoo-MAH-nay

Goebbels — GÖB-behls

Luftwaffe — LOOFT-vah-feh

Majdanek — mye-DAH-nik

Sobibor — SOH-beeh-bohr

Treblinka — treh-BLEENK-ah

Untermenschen — OON-tehr-MEHN-shen

Georgy Konstantinovich Zhukov — gyi-AWR-gee kuhn-stuhn-TEE-nyuh-vyitch ZHOO-kuhff

* (*Note: Pronunciation for the ü and ö in German*: The ü and the ö in German have no exact equivalent in English. In pronouncing the ü (or *ue*), the tongue should be so placed as to make a long *e* sound, with the lips rounded as if one were pronouncing a long *u*. In pronouncing ö (or *oe*), the tongue should be so placed as to make a short *i* sound, with the lips rounded as if one were pronouncing a long *o* sound.)